A New Kind of Youth

A New Kind of Youth

Historically Black High Schools and
Southern Student Activism, 1920–1975

. . . .

JON N. HALE

The University of North Carolina Press Chapel Hill

This book was published with the assistance of the John Hope Franklin Fund of the University of North Carolina Press.

Set in Charis by Westchester Publishing Services
Manufactured in the United States of America

Complete Library of Congress Cataloging-in-Publication Data
for this title is available at https://lccn.loc.gov/2022029987.

ISBN 978-1-4696-7138-3 (cloth: alk. paper)
ISBN 978-1-4696-7139-0 (pbk.: alk. paper)
ISBN 978-1-4696-7140-6 (ebook)

Cover illustration: Thomas J. O'Halloran photograph featuring Black youth participating in the March on Washington for Jobs and Freedom (August 28, 1963). Courtesy of the U.S. News & World Report Magazine Photograph Collection, Library of Congress Prints and Photographs Division (LC-DIG-ppmsca-37257).

"To those who seek to answer the traditional Masai greeting, 'And how are the children?'"

Contents

Illustrations

A New Kind of Youth

Introduction

. . . .

"It felt like Sojourner Truth's hands were pushing me down on one shoulder and Harriet Tubman's hands were pushing me down on another shoulder," Claudette Colvin recalled of the day she was arrested in Montgomery, Alabama, for refusing to move from her bus seat.[1] It was March 2, 1955, and Colvin was a fifteen-year-old student at Booker T. Washington High School.

In making her choice to clearly and publicly violate city segregation ordinances, Colvin drew inspiration from freedom fighters like Sojourner Truth and Harriet Tubman, though there were other historical factors that informed her actions. Colvin endured arrest, harassment, and jailing not long after her classmate, Jeremiah Reeves, had been sentenced to death after being convicted of assaulting a local White woman under dubious circumstances. Her exercise in civil disobedience occurred around the time that her English teacher, Miss Geraldine Nesbitt, was teaching the United States Constitution, offering seemingly innocuous lessons in citizenship that nevertheless carried radical implications for racialized, criminalized, and oppressed Black youth. After her arrest, Colvin would receive help with her legal defense from the National Association for the Advancement of Colored People (NAACP), which had already set about organizing local Youth Council chapters in the city. Their goal was to challenge the *de jure* segregation that shackled most African Americans in Montgomery. They hoped to achieve it, in part, by empowering, educating, and inspiring young people.[2]

Popular history tells us that Rosa Parks, who refused to give up her bus seat nearly nine months later on December 1, 1955, inspired the Montgomery bus boycott. The story of the boycott and the way it connected to Dr. Martin Luther King Jr.'s ascent to international prominence is perhaps the most iconic narrative of the southern Black freedom struggle. Yet that story is incomplete without Claudette Colvin and her high school peers across the South. Their cohort's trajectory complicates the common tropes of progress that define United States history.[3]

The story of high school student activism and the dynamic pedagogical and intellectual context that supported it, including a robust network of elder organizers, recasts the history of the southern freedom struggle. Over and over again high school activists proved to be catalysts of the movement, and Black high schools served as critical sites for launching protests. Some examples are better known than others, such as the high school student walkout in Prince Edward County, Virginia, in 1951. After students orchestrated a walkout, they contacted the law firm of Hill, Martin, and Robinson in Richmond, Virginia, and invited the NAACP to visit. Mass meetings followed and local families began a lawsuit, *Davis v. County School Board of Prince Edward County, Virginia*, which was one of the five pivotal court cases that made up the *Brown v. Board of Education* (1954) decision.[4] Lesser-known protests motivated similar engagement at the local level even if they did not come to shape the national movement. Twenty-four Burke High School students in Charleston, South Carolina, organized the first direct action nonviolent protest in the city at the downtown S. H. Kress department store in 1960. The sit-in launched a sustained direct-action protest that lasted over three years.[5] In McComb, Mississippi, an entire high school walked out in protest of the conviction and expulsion of Brenda Travis, a student at Burgland High School who sat-in at a local Woolworth lunch counter in 1961 after Freedom Riders swept through the state. This protest shaped the agenda for the historic Freedom Summer campaign during the summer of 1964, the largest voter registration campaign that catalyzed the organization behind the Voting Rights Act of 1965.[6]

The story of activism at the high school level—including actions orchestrated both inside and outside the actual school building—elucidates a dynamic interplay between youth, high schools, civic leaders, and civil rights organizations since the 1920s. Many crucial high school protests are largely forgotten beyond a local setting, confined to the memories of those who participated or, in some instances, afforded historic markers that document the youthful resistance in sites like Charleston, South Carolina, even as they are dwarfed by memorials commemorating the Confederacy. Nevertheless, high school activists and their supporters shaped the movement in profound ways. Their story broadens our understanding of the complexity of the long southern freedom struggle through the 1970s.

As this book delineates, high school protests stemmed from a subterranean youth movement within the larger freedom struggle, and they figured prominently in the trajectory of the movement from the 1920s through full-scale desegregation in the 1970s. Following youth and youth activism during the freedom struggle illuminates how high school protest developed at the intersection of the Black high school, evolving notions of youth and childhood, and the protest politics of civil rights organizations, most notably the NAACP and the Southern Negro Youth Conference (SNYC). High school student-led protests of the Black freedom struggle were predicated upon a history of institution building and youth organization that extended intellectual arguments of Black liberation and propelled the movement forward from local to national levels, and vice versa. Teachers and civil rights organizations took an active interest in the Black high school since the 1920s. For these key stakeholders, a high school education was one way to undermine what many thought to be an immutable system of segregation. Though small in number due to a public system entrenched in the principles of White supremacy, the foundations of the historically Black southern high school included the politics of protest alongside the politics of respectability, and many educated within this matrix demonstrated an unyielding agency. Black high schools and student activism fomented at times revolutionary politics and intellectual underpinnings that challenged the logic and implementation of Jim Crow policy. It profoundly shaped the perception of agency among adults and youth and inspired a participatory role in the freedom struggle from the Second World War through full-scale desegregation in 1970.[7]

A New Kind of Youth begins with the premise that children and adolescents were central to the long civil rights movement. Even though youth have been active participants in the major events of the classic phase of the civil rights movement, Black high school youth have been traditionally marginalized in the historiography as compared to college students. Colleges were central battlegrounds of the civil rights movement, to be sure. Historians Stefan Bradley, Eddie Cole, Ibram X. Kendi, Joy Ann Williamson Lott, Martha Biondi, and others have elucidated how campuses such as the University of California-Berkeley, Northwestern University, the University of Illinois, Columbia University, and southern campuses such as the University of Mississippi, Tougaloo College, and South Carolina State University, among others, were the sites of some of the most defining moments of the civil rights movement for both Black and White students. Historians Jelani Favors and Ramon Jackson recently documented the role of historically Black colleges and universities (HBCUs) in fostering ideologies and strategies of resistance.[8] These campuses encompassed a wide spectrum of organizations aimed at a variety of issues, including desegregating public spaces, securing voting rights, protecting academic freedom, and reforming curricula throughout the 1960s. Protest often evolved from the radical work of college students in the Student Nonviolent Coordinating Committee

(SNCC), offshoots like the Southern Student Organizing Committee (SSOC), or other groups that attracted the talent and commitment of college-age activists like the Congress of Racial Equality (CORE), and, to a lesser extent by the 1960s, the NAACP.[9] Yet these college-aged youth often define the category of youth. Take, for instance, David Halberstam's narrative assertion while writing from the perspective of student activists at Fisk University in *The Children*: "We are a bunch of children. We're nice children, bright and idealistic, but we are children and we are weak. We have no police force, no judges, no cops, no money."[10] Halberstam's assertion is not unique in how children and youth are often conflated with college-aged students or, in the case of Robert Cohen's *Rebellion in Black & White*, "student activism" is synonymous with *college* student activism.[11] Though organizations for college students and organizations created by them like SNCC had tremendous impact on the youth movement, focusing on the college campus limits the categorization of youth activism to those aged eighteen or older, which does not account for the social and political nuances of activism among Black high school students.

An overemphasis on the college campus also overlooks the close affinity between historically Black colleges and high schools. Historically, many high schools, like Booker T. Washington in Montgomery, where Claudette Colvin attended, began as a high school program located on a college campus. Many historically Black colleges included instruction for children in elementary school. Through various arrangements, institutions such as Tougaloo College in Mississippi, Southern University in Louisiana, and Claflin University in South Carolina offered instruction from elementary school through college.[12] Moreover, many teachers—many of whom were women—also taught how and what they learned while in college, affirming a mutual bond between the two levels. Black teachers in historically Black high schools would have taught in essence the same "second curriculum" evident in Black colleges, or what historian Jelani Favors defines as "a pedagogy of hope grounded in idealism, race consciousness, and cultural nationalism."[13] This curriculum was intentional and direct, strategically incorporated into the classrooms, hallways, and school campus. Such pedagogy, what historian Jarvis Givens defined as a "fugitive pedagogy," was protected from the gaze of White supervisors and incorporated into the daily routine of teaching and instruction.[14] The educative space itself—protected behind the walls of a historically Black institution—was one in which students could debate, refine, and articulate ideals of new antiracist and equitable frontiers.[15]

High schools have in many cases been cast as seemingly apolitical institutions, at least in comparison to college campuses. To focus more on the secondary institutions where many of these collegiate activists were first inspired by the long freedom struggle, this book builds upon the scholarship of Alison Stewart, V. P. Franklin, Daphne Chamberlain, Sharon Pierson, Jay Driskell, Craig Kridel, Alexander Hyres, and others who have documented the rise of Black high schools across the South, including the famous Dunbar High School in Washington, D.C., Lanier High School in Jackson, Mississippi, Booker T. Washington High School in Atlanta, historically Black high schools in Charlottesville, Virginia, as well as Black laboratory and other "progressive" schools across the South.[16] As such, *A New Kind of Youth* contributes to the work of reconstructing how Black high schools across the South emerged as prominent sites of political socialization and intellectual pillars of the movement. This book further illuminates how the contours of high school activism originate with the construct of youth and adolescence and are more sophisticated than mere instances of activism that unfolded in the shadows of the historically Black college or university. As a historical study of southern Black high school activism, this book adds to the historiography of the Black freedom struggle by focusing on high schools as a site of resistance and an incubator of strategic protest in critical instances, arguing that high schools were integral though often overlooked pillars of support during the fledging freedom struggle.

The historically Black high school often stood under the shadows and directions of the Black church. "So far-reaching are these functions of the church," W. E. B. Du Bois noted in his classic study *The Philadelphia Negro*, "that its organization is almost political."[17] Movement sociologist Aldon Morris claimed unequivocally nearly a century later that "the black church functioned as the institutional center of the modern civil rights movement."[18] Yet historically Black high schools were political and functioned as institutional centers, too. *A New Kind of Youth* illustrates that, while the Black high school never rivaled the prominence of the Black church as a movement center, it complemented it and served as a far-reaching institution that supported in its own way a widescale social and political movement. The historically Black high school Claudette Colvin attended, Booker T. Washington High School, served the community alongside Dexter Avenue Baptist Church. The historically Black A. H. Parker High School similarly served the community as did the 16th St. Baptist Church in Birmingham. In repeated social and political arrangements across the South, historically Black high schools served alongside and complemented the Black church in maintaining the freedom struggle. As such, this book builds upon historian Katherine Charron's assertion that "no longer does the black church stand alone as the primary institutional base for the civil rights movement; the schoolhouse—often the *very* same building—becomes an equally important site."[19]

While recognizing the instrumental value of the historically Black high school, this history complicates a dominant narrative of high school and secondary education in the United States. By focusing on activism that either centered upon the southern high school or drew student leaders from the classrooms of historically Black southern high schools, this book provides a different perspective than that established by William Reese, Edward Krug, David Angus, Jeffrey Mirel, David Labaree, and others who focus largely on White and Northern secondary school systems.[20] This book traces the evolution of a regional system of high schools that parallel yet diverge from White northeastern and midwestern systems in important ways. State investment in southern high school development lagged behind that of the Northern states. While they reflected the class and economic based considerations of those in the North, southern institutions became bulwarks of White supremacy while simultaneously harboring the potential for Black empowerment and activism. The racialized underpinnings in the former Confederacy made race and racism more visible, bringing to the fore that which was rendered invisible to the North, both to high school advocates and those who studied the institutions since then.

Placing high school activism at the center of the freedom struggle narrative challenges how some scholars, educators, and activists themselves have understood both youth and the larger civil rights movement. When the role of young people has been examined as a part of the larger movement, one historiographical trend has cast high school student activism in disparaging, paternalistic, or dismissive terms. For NAACP organizer Medgar Evers, the young students he worked with in the NAACP Youth Council prior to his assassination in 1963 were but a mere "stepping stone toward our goal of first class citizenship."[21] "The greatest weakness of student protest is that it is conducted by students," quipped author Gerard DeGroot. "They are, almost by definition, young, reckless and prone to immaturity."[22] Vanessa Siddle Walker reasoned in her analysis of the public schools in Caswell County, North Carolina, students "are the ones around whom the entire story revolves, but they are not the significant players in the story." Students, rather, were the "recipients."[23] Yet a multitude of high school protests, and the networks of professional organizers behind them, suggest that young people were politically conscious and active and that they spearheaded sophisticated protests that had a significant impact on the larger movement.

To situate the prominence of young people during the freedom struggle, *A New Kind of Youth* draws upon a more recent strand within the civil rights historiography that has increasingly focused on youth and childhood. Rebecca de Schweinitz has outlined the construction of youth and childhood in United States history and examined how these social-political constructs underpinned the long movement for freedom through organizations like the NAACP, how conceptions of youth shaped the movement toward *Brown,* and how notions of youth were utilized to appeal to a White consciousness not fully committed to the idea of civil rights. Scholars including Daphne Chamberlain, Shirletta Kinchen, Wilma King, Susan Eckelmann Berghel, Thomas Bynum, and others have examined how children and adolescents participated in and shaped the larger struggle both in the South and across the nation. They have documented the specific role of youth activists on the front lines of the movement across the nation or in less direct but equally assertive means by supporting the campaigns of major civil rights organizations such as the NAACP, SNYC, the Southern Christian Leadership Conference (SCLC), or the Black Panther Party from behind the front lines.[24] These scholars have also demonstrated that youth activism occurred decades before the 1960s and 1970s, when many observers thought high school activism began. As Mark Libarle and Tom Seligson, public high school teachers from New York wrote in *The High School Revolutionaries* in 1970, "For the first time in history, high school students throughout the United States are protesting the situations in which they find themselves." They elaborated, observing (falsely) "Now, for first time, a generation of people between the ages of ten and twenty are voicing concerns about their ineligibility for basic human rights and political freedoms."[25]

High school protest and the politics that propelled it did not begin in 1970, nor did it end there. Historians V. P. Franklin, Wesley Hogan, and Sekou Franklin have examined in detail youth activism and the youth movement "after the rebellion."[26] The work of Franklin, Hogan, and others have examined student activism after the 1970s, including the work of youth organizations like Southerners on New Ground and the Black Student Leadership Network. They have extended the historical through line to the contemporary activism of young people who have taken to the streets to advocate for Freedom Schools, gun control, environment justice, and the

Black Lives Matter movement by drawing upon the same strategies, tactics, and passion of previous generations engaged in the freedom struggle.

A New Kind of Youth begins with and builds upon this historiography and focuses on high school youth—aged fourteen to eighteen—to disentangle this cohort from the broader categories of youth and children. This book builds upon the assertions of historians and scholars who separate teenagers and adolescents from the broader categorization of youth and children, including Dionne Danns, Dara Walker, V. P. Franklin, Aaron Fountain, Johanna Fernandez, Vincent Willis, Kathryn Schumaker, Rufus Burrow Jr., and Gael Graham. These works have examined in more detail the specific role of high school youth in regions and cites outside the South, including Chicago, Detroit, San Francisco, Los Angeles, that also included work with Latinx and Indigenous students. With an emphasis on the 1960s, this scholarship elucidates how the youth movement advanced the struggle for quality education after the *Brown* decision, embraced Black Power ideology and formed unions, pushed forward the antiwar protests during the Vietnam War, and legally asserted the rights of youth in ways that reshaped interpretations of constitutional rights through the prism of age.[27]

Though *A New Kind of Youth* begins by drawing a distinction between adolescence and adulthood, it also recognizes that high school activism necessarily encompasses the work of elders and adults who advocated for adolescents, including teachers and civil rights youth organizers. It expands the network of youth activism to include high schools, teachers, and civil rights organizations, namely SNYC and NAACP Youth Councils. Examining the politics behind and the evolution of high school activism also extends the periodization of youth participation back to the 1920s with the development of the modern high school and the intentional organization of Black youth into a burgeoning civil rights movement. An elongated time frame broadens the spectrum of youth activism to include a political education, community organizing, campaigns to improve the quality of education, and participation in the political process through traditional means such as voter registration. Additionally, by tracing Black high school student activism throughout most of the twentieth century, this book examines how the freedom struggle unfolded across the South while attempting to provide local nuance to how the politics of historically Black high schools and student activism varied across both locales and states within the former Confederacy.

The role of high school student activists is predicated upon the canonical work that delineates the social construction of youth and adolescence

over time in the United States and the fluidity that belies its categorization and mediates our cultural understandings of it.[28] At the same time,
this book examines how categorizations of youth were *racially* constructed through familial and social networks as well as the state. Jennifer Ritterhouse and Leann Reynolds, for instance, document how
southerners were raised to learn, accept, and ultimately normalize social
relations grounded in ideologies of White supremacy, illustrating how
"natural" racial divisions appeared under Jim Crow, though space was
also maintained to challenge its presumed immutability.[29] Historian
Wilma King has analyzed the specific features of enslaved children and
the "stolen childhood" that the institution of enslavement wrought upon
Black youth through modern history.[30] This historiography also illustrates
how the ideals of youth and adolescence were unevenly applied to Black
youth, if at all. As Geoff Ward and Tera Agyepong have illuminated, White
policymakers denied "delinquent" Black children and adolescents the
Progressive ideals of juvenile justice, including rehabilitative measures
and resources to achieve them. This subjugated Black youth and adolescents to racialized criminalization and punitive, disproportionate con-
finement from 1900 through the *Brown* decision and the tumultuous period
of desegregation.[31]

A New Kind of Youth expands on this literature by incorporating the
Black high school as a site that paralleled institutional arrangements of
the Black church, the burgeoning juvenile justice system, and the courts
that increasingly criminalized or attempted to "save" youth. The Black
high school was an integral site that accompanied the social arrangements
within family units that socialized youth to enter and in profound instances challenge a society grounded in White supremacy. The high school
was an institution that complemented the juvenile justice system in that
the state did not equitably fund or build high schools for the genuine benefit of Black youth, effectively denying them the path to citizenship and
the social, political, and economic mobility promised to White adolescents. Where Black high schools did exist, the discriminatory presump-
tions of Black youth influenced how Whites designed high schools to
prepare second-class citizens. Within the schools, Black teachers and
administrators extended values instilled in many Black homes that
sought to protect youth from such social and institutional discrimination
through myriad ways, including the politics of respectability and assimi-
lation but, in significant cases, education to disrupt and challenge racist
and unjust policy.

The concept of youth and adolescence is based on constructed categories that have never been fixed and remain fluid today. As a result, maintaining parameters around a single cohort or a fixed age bracket is a miscalculated endeavor in reconstructing a history of student activism. Anytime during the freedom struggle, adults who worked with youth—from teachers to community organizers—employed varying and sometimes competing age ranges of youth, which may have been limited to anyone in college or younger or anyone not yet in high school. Moreover, those who constructed the boundaries of youth throughout the freedom struggle acted as youth agents or advocates for youth agency as much as youth themselves. Therefore, the high school youth movement and the activism it generated was never a youth-only movement, nor should it be understood through a framework defined solely by young people. The youth movement and high school youth activism included adults and elders who led the movement—including but not limited to teachers, pastors, ad community-based civil rights organizers—and the high schools they supported, as much as the young people who joined the front lines of the movement.[32] Youth activism encompassed a multifaceted network of collective agency that incorporated young students and their elders alike. As much as some scholars, educators, or organizers may want to see youth and high school adolescents as independent change agents or write them into the historiography as their own autonomous entity, the historical record left behind a much more nuanced network to consider.

A New Kind of Youth builds upon this analysis of youth by focusing on adolescent youth in high school in the South and demonstrating how high school activists, the institutions they attended, and the networks that supported them shaped the larger freedom struggle. By providing a lens of high school youth through which to see the freedom struggle since the 1920s, this analysis illuminates the multilayered connections and affinities between high school students, their teachers, administrators, parents, and civil rights organizations that engaged in youth organization. The high school provides a dynamic analysis and depth to our understanding of how the freedom struggle developed across the South and the tensions that defined it. Black high school students and the institutions they attended were a foundational pillar of the Black freedom struggle. Southern high school protests were in notable instances critical incubators of local civil rights struggles in a segregated society. They were sites of unlikely yet resilient demonstrations and progressive discourse that defined the movement at both the local and national level.

The Construction of Youth and the
Rise of the Black High School

Though often overshadowed by the work of Black colleges or Black churches, southern Black high schools were an integral part of the southern freedom struggle alongside these recognized pillars of Black resistance. The Black high school followed modern constructs of youth and childhood during the first decades of the twentieth century. The conceptual origins of Black high school activism can be traced to both the promises and contradictions inherent to social constructs erected around adolescence. In particular, racialized inconsistencies within the categorization of adolescence presaged the evolution of Black high school activism.

The field of education embraced the burgeoning modern concept of youth by institutionalizing the high school as a public space devoted to the unique needs of adolescents during the early twentieth century. Both Black and White high schools were fashioned upon the affirmation of adolescence, a stage of development that was physiologically, biologically, and cognitively distinct from both early childhood and young adulthood.[33] The cultural, social, and intellectual shift to embrace the modern construct of youth, along with professional criteria that distinguished childhood from adolescence, necessitated a brick and mortar stand-alone high school, one architecturally and intellectually distinct from elementary school and college. Secondary "high school" education and the category of adolescence provided the impetus and rationale to educate older children and young adults, or "adolescents," in separate grades if not in distinctly autonomous buildings and institutions altogether. Investment from a multitude of levels—by the state, the middle class, professionals in the field of education, and others—yielded tangible gains and the public high school experienced considerable growth. School boards and state legislatures throughout the 1930s who passed compulsory education laws that raised the minimum age to sixteen facilitated the growth of the high school. Whereas 519,000 students enrolled in a public high school in 1900, over 6 million enrolled 40 years later. The percentage of seventeen-year-olds who graduated from high school grew to just over 50 percent by 1940 as well, marking the first time that one-half of the nation's school age population completed a secondary education.[34]

Despite the significant shift toward protecting and defending youth rather than economically exploiting them, there was no equally shared and widely acknowledged *right* to adolescence. Systemic racism filtered how society conceptualized and applied the modern constructs of adolescence to young people of color. Black "adolescents," in short, never benefited from the categories of youth constructed by White professionals and educational reformers who only crafted them with White adolescents in mind. Though cast in a concrete and essentialized space, race complicated its categorization and the lived realities of youth and adolescents in the South communicated a very different truth that challenged the universality of childhood and the prolongation of it through adolescence.

A racialized conception of youth translated into systemic and racist policy that limited access to secondary schools for Black students. After the *Cumming v. School Board of Richmond County, Georgia* (1899) decision, southern states were not compelled to offer public secondary education to Black pupils. As a result, Black enrollment in high school was statistically diminutive compared to that of White students. By 1940 after the "explosion" in secondary school enrollment and construction, Black students only accounted for less than 15 percent of all high school students in the country. In the South, Black enrollment was estimated to be less than one-third of that of Whites. One study found that 425 counties across the former Confederacy offered no high school at all by 1940.[35]

States failed to fully invest in public secondary education for students of color, committing scarce resources to the basic provisions of even a rudimentary education in a region where none previously existed. They also refused to build a strong secondary system because of an unchecked and virulent racism, which determined education should, at best, prepare Black adolescents for a position of economic subservience. High school was never a privilege or a right but essentially a struggle that only a few managed to overcome.

A lack of access to public school meant that secondary education would be largely acquired through private means as the duty fell upon the shoulders of the Black community to compensate for the deficiencies of the state.[36] It paradoxically fueled, for some, an ideology and pathway of resistance to the subservience that Whites attempted to impose on Black high schools. Black teachers as a distinct set of political actors, as Jarvis Givens argues, practiced a "fugitive pedagogy," a shared practice to engage in humanizing, liberatory praxis in schools shaped by anti-Black polices.[37] In a system privatized out of necessity, some Black administrations and faculty chose to maintain a challenging college preparatory curriculum and a course of study predisposed to critical thinking and raising political consciousness. Black institutions of higher learning across the nation required a type of examination or completion of some form of secondary education and often opened high school departments on a college campus. These programs necessitated a rigorous high school or normal school curriculum or, at least, coursework in the liberal arts tradition. In Baton Rouge, Louisiana, administrators at Southern University, for instance, required that students be at least fourteen years of age and satisfactorily complete examinations in English grammar, geography, history, and arithmetic.[38] For admission into the Classics Department at Claflin College in Orangeburg, South Carolina, students were expected to have a grasp of geometry, Roman history, and Greek grammar and history.[39] The Avery Normal Institute in Charleston, South Carolina, offered sociology, Greek history, and literature for students in a classical liberal arts curriculum.[40] The curriculum affirmed an elite status, following the principles of a liberal education outlined in the "Committee of Ten" report that established a classical curriculum for high schools in 1894.[41]

This course of study was distinct from and therefore challenged the vocational, industrial, and manual education models fashioned in the philosophy of Booker T. Washington, which came to dominate educational discourse at the turn of the century when such training reigned supreme. Though dominant, even Black public high schools supported by the state and those that bear the name of Booker T. Washington—the patron saint of vocational education and a popular name bestowed upon Black high schools during the Progressive Era—included a classical curriculum that implemented college preparatory courses and the "second curriculum" of extracurriculars that sought to actualize the aspirations of a free and democratic society. Booker T. Washington High School in Columbia, South Carolina, typified the breadth of courses offered at public Black high schools. Here students were offered the upper branches of math, science, history, and foreign languages including French, in addition to vocational and shop classes. Students engaged in the National Honor Society, chorus, drama, band, science clubs, Negro History Week, student council, and other extracurriculars.[42] Grounded in a curriculum of higher ideals aimed at professional training, the Black high school developed a curriculum that cultivated critical thinking and analysis, which helped lay the foundation for activism in future decades.

The high school Claudette Colvin attended, Booker T. Washington High School in Montgomery, Alabama, exemplifies Black secondary education in the South. Booker T. Washington High School was founded during Reconstruction as a product of Black civic engagement and private efforts aimed at the public good. Its history and curricular trajectory belie its namesake, illustrating the dynamic affordance of a second curriculum and curricular or "fugitive pedagogy" behind closed doors. In partnership with the Freed-men's Bureau Association, the American Missionary Association founded Swayne College in 1868 as a facility designed to host six teachers to teach four hundred students.[43] *The American Missionary* reported that Swayne College supported a "Higher Department," which reflected common categorization of higher or secondary education at the time and presumably served high school–age students. As such, the school offered courses in basic literacy, advanced reading, arithmetic, and geography.[44] Additionally, the original site of Swayne College held profound symbolic significance as it was erected on a former market used for the sale of enslaved persons.[45] The school enjoyed the support of local civic leaders, most notably Elijah Cook. He was born into slavery and rose to be elected as a representative in the state house of Alabama until 1876 as part of the wave of Black politicians that represented recently freed people. Later achieving economic independence as a mortician, Cook established strong networks as a Mason and a member of the Booker T. Washington Negro Business League, which yielded further support for public education.[46] He helped establish other schools for Black children and young adults in the city. In addition to helping found Swayne and serving on its original board of trustees, Cook helped relocate the Lincoln School of Marion, the predecessor to Alabama State University, to Montgomery in 1887. He also helped support the founding of the Alabama Normal and Theological School, later known as Selma University, in 1878.[47]

By 1914 school attendance at Swayne surpassed the modest structure already in place. The city also began to incorporate some funds for the construction of a larger school. J. A. Lawrence, the principal at Swayne who also served as the treasurer of the Swayne School Improvement Association, successfully petitioned the school board in Montgomery to raise the capital through public funding necessary to complete the building.[48] Once raised, the city commissioners voted to spend another $4,500 on completing the new building, illustrating the infusion of both public and private capital in financing Black schools. Especially as the school board worked with city commissioners to secure amenities such as desks and blackboards, multiple funding sources with different motivations funded Black secondary schools. Swayne also illustrates how Black communities were ultimately responsible for the erection of new high schools and how the principal often served as a critical negotiator in securing funds and support to build secondary institutions for Black scholars. Once the city officially assumed oversight of the school, public commissioners renamed the institution to honor the passing of the renowned

Alabamian educator and famed education advocate, Booker T. Washington, in November 1915.[49] It was a fitting name for Whites who fashioned the school with the intention of promulgating a second-class, vocational citizenship among Black families in Montgomery.

The origins of the Charleston Industrial School, later known as Burke High School, further illustrate the historic complexity and idiosyncrasies of Black secondary education, explicating how schools that served a public need began with private means while concomitantly cultivating aspects of resistance across the community it served. The Charleston Industrial School emerged from the organizational efforts of the Black community to acquire an education after universal public education was written into the state constitution in 1868. Reverend John L. Dart, born a free person of color in Charleston, completed high school in 1872 as the valedictorian of the first class at the Avery Normal Institute, a private school founded in 1865 by the American Missionary Association. Dart later graduated with a bachelor's degree from Atlanta University in 1879. He studied at Newton Seminary in Massachusetts, where he was ordained as a Baptist minister. Rev. Dart spearheaded local efforts with "a number of the leading and progressive colored men of this city . . . undertook the work of establishing a school for colored children."[50] Dart and the Charleston coalition sought to provide a free and public education to the more than five thousand children of color in the city without access to a free public school "to prepare them to go forth and uplift the race."[51] Dart was successful in serving the public good through private means, establishing the Charleston Normal and Industrial Institute in 1894. As the president of the board of trustees for the new school, Dart took it upon himself to establish a national network of fundraisers to raise the necessary capital to offer free public instruction. A growing student population quickly outgrew the modest schoolhouse and construction of separate schools for boys and girls began in 1897.[52]

The Charleston Industrial School also illustrates how Black civic leaders like Rev. Dart embraced a moral and vocational orientation of Black high school education, in part to appeal to White donors. In his original school prospectus, Dart warned of the dangers associated with not educating poor Black children, stating that "the many boys and girls who are now growing up in ignorance, idleness and crime must become, in future, a large criminal and dependent class."[53] As a means "to go forth and uplift the race," the school trained "Christian and Industrial Workers for the Colored Race," an ideology that fit neatly with industrial education models advocated by Booker T. Washington and his vast army of supporters.[54] As the original

Boys Industrial School, Charleston, South Carolina, 1901. Courtesy of the Avery Research Center for African American History and Culture, College of Charleston, Charleston, SC.

prospectus stated, the Charleston Industrial School "taught not only reading and writing, but the lessons of morals, temperance, sewing, cooking, nursing, housework, carpentering, etc."[55] The plea to address the moral condition appealed to benefactors like Jason Scherer of the Lutheran Pastors' Association, who wrote to Rev. Dart that he was "strongly impressed with the gravity of the problem connected with the character of our colored population. [The Lutheran Pastors' Association] believes there is great need of wise work among the Negroes, and that industrial schools . . . are to be especially commended."[56]

Though Rev. Dart accommodated a Christian conviction that many Whites in the South shared (and funded), he also used his platform to combat racial injustices that marred his home state during the nadir of race relations. In 1898 in Lake City, South Carolina, a mob of Whites attacked the home of Postmaster Frazier R. Baker, his wife, and five children. They burned the Baker home, one part of which was used as the post office. Then the mob shot into the home, killing Frazier and his youngest daughter. John

Girls Industrial School, Charleston, South Carolina, 1901. Courtesy of the Avery Research Center for African American History and Culture, College of Charleston, Charleston, SC.

Dart became an impassioned advocate for justice in the aftermath of the murder. In an effort to call attention to the injustice, he published a book-let, *The Famous Trial of the Eight Men Indicted for the Lynching of Frazier R. Baker and His Baby*.[57] He penned an open letter to President McKinley, appealing to him to condemn and prosecute the lynching.[58] Dart also used the Charleston Industrial School to take in and provide refuge to the Baker family, including the surviving children, and instructed them free of charge in an effort to "awaken a deep sympathy and substantial interest in . . . the education of [Baker's] five children."[59] In the aftermath of a tragedy, Dart connected justice with the quest for an education, illustrating the aspirations and outreach of early southern Black education reformers.

Dart also carried forth traditions of Reconstruction-era Republicanism by calling for free and public education and working to improve political opportunities for African Americans in the first decades of segregation. To amplify his progressive views, Dart used the space at the Industrial School to publish *The Southern Reporter*, a Republican publication covering political events of the day. The editor wrote in the issue April 9, 1904, over twenty-five years after "Redemption" politics, "We have ascertained that many of the conditions are very unsatisfactory and that we are, from a political point of view, in a very bad way and going from bad to worse" and "they have ceased to respect the people, the source of their power." In the face of this calamity, Republicans had "remained inactive and allowed machine politicians to do as they pleased."[60] The *Southern Reporter,* the editor noted, has "exhibited a fearless spirit in calling attention to these evils and irregularities" to encourage the implement the idea that "the day has passed when such things can be done by insolvent and reckless leaders without their action being reviewed by the court of last resort—the sovereign people."[61] Dart called for self-reliance, self-determination, and economic empowerment that underpinned calls of the long freedom struggle. "If the intelligent and property owning classes of the colored citizens of South Carolina would concentrate their elements of strength by more generally supporting business enterprises undertaken by men and women of their people immediately about them it would prove the foundation of race forces which would in time greatly affect public sentiment more favorable to them as a factor of power."[62] For Rev. John Dart and many other civic leaders across the South, education was in and of itself a means to active participation in a larger movement to address larger systemic issues that plagued all people of color at the turn of the twentieth century. His calls for racial empowerment may have constituted a lone cry in the early 1900s, but his bold declarations anticipated the fervor of calls for Black Power decades later.

Like many Black high schools across the South, Booker T. Washington High School and Burke High School did not neatly align with the ideologies of their namesakes or the racist policies that undergirded southern high schools. Rather these schools reflected competing ideologies and compromises. Though these schools reflected the desire and strong support for vocational education or the politics of respectability, Black founders, teachers, and advocates constituted a network that endorsed a contemporaneous belief in critical thinking and professional and academic training, which established a baseline for youth activism and offered a stinging rebuke to education policy grounded in White supremacy.

Youth Political Socialization through Teachers and Civil Rights Organizations

Teachers were critical actors in the youth movement. Teachers shaped the incipient high school student movement by inculcating what they saw as acceptable or necessary roles for youth in a violent anti-Black society. An older historiographical trend often framed educators and the schools where they taught as conservative and passive actors in American history. Indeed, activists' frequent chastisement of Black teachers informs the overarching viewpoint that teachers and the institutions they taught in were inherently passive.[63] The fact that a vast majority of educators and administrators never publicly supported the movement affirms this popular observation.

Young activists agreed. In her autobiography, *Coming of Age in Mississippi*, Anne Moody referred to her teachers and principals in disparaging ways. After Mississippi legislators, like other southern lawmakers, elected to build new segregated Black high schools to equalize schools as opposed to desegregating them, Moody's recollection of the new high school is emblematic of an overarching, popular depiction of Black teachers who accepted the new schools and refused to demand desegregation:

> [The new school] was supposed to be the largest new school in the
> state and it caused much bickering among the Uncle Tom principals
> and teachers in the county. Many of the teachers sought positions
> as heads of various classes or departments and the principals
> challenged each other for the position of head principal. Since
> [Mr.] Willis was the biggest Tom among the principals of the merging
> schools, he was the one chosen by the state board for the job . . . As
> most of them, students, teachers, and principals alike, were bragging
> about how good the white folks were to give us such a big beautiful
> school, I was thinking of how dumb we were to accept it.[64]

Moody's generalization speaks to one historic truth of teachers: they, by and large, were not active or visible participants in the freedom struggle.

But at the same time, activists like Moody remember teachers playing integral roles in passing down information about the movement. Moody recalls a conversation with her homeroom teacher, Mrs. Rice, who was "something like a mother" to her. After her own mother forbade her from speaking of the NAACP, Moody approached Rice and inquired about the civil rights organization; Rice first explained the organization for Moody in school, though outside of class. Later, after an invitation to her home for Sunday dinner, Rice taught Moody "a whole new pool of knowledge about Negroes being butchered and slaughtered by whites in the South." Moody went on to recall: "[Mrs. Rice] told me anything I wanted to know. And made me promise that I would keep all this information she was passing on to me to myself. She said she couldn't, rather didn't, want to talk about these things to the other teachers, that they would tell Mr. Willis and she would be fired. At the end of that year she was fired. I never found out why."[65] Moody's memory points toward a coexistent truth that teachers also served as elders in the movement, clandestine mentors who guided youth to the larger struggle. Her memory illustrates how teachers steered youth into the movement from behind the front lines. Rice acted as a mother and shared histories and modes of resistance with a young, impressionable Moody. The contradiction proffered by Moody—that teachers were both passive bystanders and movement spokespeople—underpins the role of Black educators. Both claims are valid and, to be sure, teachers could be both. The minority of teachers who shaped the movement behind the front lines are an integral part of student activism as well.

This book follows the strand of Moody's memory about teachers supporting activism while building upon a historiography that highlights how educators have shaped—in subtle and not so subtle ways—the history of the civil rights movement. As Vanessa Siddle Walker, Valinda Littlefield, Katherine Charron, Jarvis Givens, Derrick Alridge, Tondra Loder-Jackson, Sonya Ramsey, and others have documented, teachers organized professionally and sought to improve their profession since the founding of public schools through a spectrum of activism that ranged from teaching Black history in the classroom to suing school districts for higher pay.[66] Their work constituted a continuum of activism both within and beyond the classroom walls through innumerable tactics but in a shared commitment to equity and resistance that proffered a model for their scholars to emulate.

In critically examining the role of Black teachers, *A New Kind of Youth* incorporates gender as an interpretive lens to examine a teaching profession largely comprised of women. Black women's options were limited after Reconstruction and the founding of southern public schools for students of color in the first decades of the twentieth century. On one hand, teaching provided an outlet for talented, ambitious, and educated women beyond marriage and motherhood, but this professional avenue was limited because they were still under the leadership of Black men who served in precarious positions of leadership in historically Black high schools. Women who taught *and* chose or were forced to marry and have children were expected to dutifully maintain commitment to their families as they taught in schools, a political and logistical feat by any standard. Because of their positionality, Black women who embarked on careers in education saw their work in myriad ways, not only as an outgrowth of their home life and maternal desires or financial incentives in a racially codified economy, but also as the labor of community building, racial uplift, and liberation. In significant ways, some Black women viewed teaching as a mode of activism to challenge *de jure* segregation and legalized disenfranchisement. The host of ambitions and interest in teaching politicized the spaces in which they taught. As historian Katherine Charron argued in her biography of legendary educator Septima P. Clark of South Carolina, Black women "propagated a communal vision of citizenship that emerged alongside freedom itself."[67] Black women, in short, transformed schools, the communities they served, and, ultimately, the trajectory of the long freedom struggle. Black women cultivated community networks, calling upon local Black business owners, pastors, social clubs organized by and for women, parents and parent associations, community leaders to share information about upcoming events, news, or issues that needed to be addressed.[68] Their labor was intensive, connecting to nearly every aspect of life in the South and, more critically, to larger social, economic, and political agendas. As historian Glenda Gilmore noted, "Black women teachers and activists shaped and reshaped strategies to outmaneuver the daily manifestations of racism they encountered on their way to the front."[69]

Their labor consistently spilled over the schoolyard gates. In addition to supporting a new kind of youth in Black high schools, as historian Barbara Ransby has noted, female teachers in the South were critical in "laying the foundation for contemporary black feminists even before the term was invented." Black women who taught were "carving out public identities as leaders, strategists, and public intellectuals—identities that were generally reserved for men."[70] Because of their positionality as women in a highly racialized and oppressive society, and contrary to some popular beliefs, teachers were not impediments to the movement. To the contrary, Black teachers established the professional networks and intellectual framework that tilled the soil for a youth movement. As historian Valinda Littlefield found, "teachers both directly and indirectly motivated students to challenge an oppressive system."[71] Building upon this historiographical work that elucidates the interconnectedness of race, gender, and education, this book illuminates the impact of Black teachers' labor that ultimately shaped the Black high school as a politicized space.[72]

Black teachers shaped the profession and the institution of Black secondary education in part by building professional education associations. Excluded from the White teacher associations, Black educators were left to organize alternative organizations. Educators in Tennessee were the first to organize a teachers' association in 1877. Their counterparts established the North Carolina Teachers Association in 1881, and Alabama soon followed in 1882. Teachers formed the Virginia Teachers Association in 1887. The first attempts to organize teachers in Mississippi can be traced back to 1893, which resulted in the Mississippi Teachers Association. In South Carolina, the formal organization of Black educators, the Palmetto Education Association, dates to 1900.[73] In a similar pattern to the development of Northern and largely White teacher associations, African Americans organized an alternative national association to coordinate statewide efforts and educators across the South founded the National Association of Teachers in Colored Schools (NATCS) in 1907. The early objectives of the teachers' associations included the general promotion of Black education as part of their work to secure the best possible education in a segregated context. As stated in the constitution of the NATCS, the "objects, aims, and purposes [of the association] shall be to assist in raising the standard and promoting the interests of the teaching profession, and in advancing the cause of education."[74]

Professional Black teacher associations formed coalitions with the NAACP across the South to combat racial covenants that mandated only White teachers could be hired to teach in Black schools. Between 1875 and 1919, Black coalitions across the South successfully challenged "whites only" hiring policies and pressured local and state boards to pass legislation to hire Black faculty to oversee and teach in Black schools.[75] Two decades later, teachers worked with the NAACP to procure equal salaries and achieved a major victory when the Supreme Court supported equalization formulas in *Alston v. Norfolk* (1939), which favored Black teachers.[76] In pursuing equalization in the courts and demanding equality before the law, African American teachers provided powerful examples to their students and the communities they served. Teachers demonstrated their potential in enacting substantive reform.

A critical minority of Black high school teachers practiced a form of pedagogical activism, a method of resistance that included implementing the "second curriculum."[77] As a predominantly female teaching force, Black teachers also extended activist notions of "purposeful womanhood" that historian Kabria Baumgartner examined in the antebellum North to motivate young women, and all students, to take the "opportunity to study, to write, and to purse knowledge" in a racist society that all but denied the opportunity to do so. This pedagogy also included faith, activism, and commitment to moral education that actively taught and fought against a racist society.[78] Southern high school teachers relayed iterations of a second curriculum and a purposeful pedagogy. At the high school level, teachers' pedagogical activism included developing a curriculum grounded in a positive and affirming view of Black culture and the slow and patient work of daily instruction for participatory citizenship. Pedagogical activism was more common than direct forms of activity and indirectly influenced student activists. Black teachers in many cases received rigorous academic training from prestigious historically Black colleges and universities as well as Northern White institutions. Limited in professional pursuits, teaching in high school was more open to talented Black professionals than other fields. Many teachers were predisposed to develop a liberal arts curriculum that fostered independent thinking and critical, if not overtly political, consciousness, which they received while attending postsecondary schools. Behind classroom doors, Black educators embraced a pedagogy that facilitated hidden modes of resistance and established an intellectual foundation for a youth movement. Black teachers held integral positions in society to combat what popular author and social critic James Baldwin warned, "that any Negro who is born in this country and undergoes the American educational system runs the risk of becoming schizophrenic. On the one hand he is born in the shadow of the stars and stripes and he is assured it represents a nation which has never lost a war . . . But on the other hand he is also assured by his country and his countrymen that he has never contributed anything to civilization—that his past is nothing more than a record of humiliations gladly endured."[79] Inoculating youth with Black history, confidence, self-worth, and political efficacy through a second curriculum that countered the message of the state prevented social calamities and, as such, constituted an important aspect of pedagogical activism.

Within the larger context of Jim Crow and the strict racial segregation of the American South, the fight for education was itself an act of resistance. Though not as aggressive or direct as the work of the NAACP prior to and during the Second World War, or the more assertive tactics of student-led associations like the Student Nonviolent Coordinating Committee (SNCC) during the early 1960s, Black teachers and the associations they created constituted a bulwark of the larger freedom struggle. By politicizing education and organizing professional networks, a cadre of Black teachers painstakingly established the intellectual basis for a youth movement that came to fruition in the 1950s and 1960s.

Educators' impact on activism was more subtle compared to civil rights associations that directly politicized Black high schools and students. The

NAACP and SNYC connected youth to a larger movement in ways that superseded the efforts of Black high schools. They saw youth as potential change agents in a burgeoning civil rights movement. The NAACP and SNYC organized youth into local chapters as part of their larger campaigns to challenge White supremacy through educational opportunity and registering voters, among other efforts. The NAACP and SNYC engaged youth directly by organizing youth conferences, for instance, that guided young people into the traditional political process. They also designed and implemented citizenship education programs and supported youth as they engaged their local communities. Compared to teachers and community education advocates, the NAACP and SNYC more actively pursued youth organization and ventured further through the explicit organization of youth and instilling an overtly political education outside of high school that was grounded in participatory notions of citizenship. At the same time, they shared with educators an interest in fostering deep understandings of the struggle for equality.

The evolution of Black high school student activism does not lend itself neatly to a linear or celebratory narrative. High school youth activism in the Black freedom struggle was fraught with tension and conflict. The development of the Black high school, particularly in the urban South, and its unique politics of protest illustrate a dynamic relationship between youth and adults, whose conceptualization of the role of students in the movement often stood in stark contrast with one another. Though high school youth sought to act autonomously, especially by the 1950s, there were always adults who supported and at times opposed youth activism. Intergenerational tension—the conflict engendered when youth acted without the blessings of their elders or when movement leaders did not represent the values of youth—was, to be sure, a defining aspect of the movement. The politics of youth activism also elucidates the ongoing tensions between progressive educators who were dependent upon a White power structure for employment and the more aggressive NAACP and SNYC organizers. This book highlights the parallels between competing modes of resistance embedded in strident activism of direct-action protest and the more subtle modes of resistance behind classroom doors. It also explores the promises of youth on the front lines of the struggle while concurrently documenting the haunting perils of activism during Jim Crow.

The history of the Black high school and the development of high school youth protest were beholden to contradictions that defined Black youth and adolescence and defy any singular understanding, particularly along class and gender lines. Black high schools and the students who enrolled in them held a class status distinct from those who could not afford to sit out of the labor market or who did not live in proximity to a high school. When stand-alone high schools were constructed, they were few and far between. Black families would have to live close enough to a school in order to attend it, forcing many families to board children, if they could afford the financial consequences it entailed.[80] Simply attending a high school conferred a class status that was not shared universally across the South.

Additionally, gender and gendered expectations shaped how high school activism unfolded during the freedom struggle. Young Black women and girls have been at the center of an educational justice movement for equity, access, and opportunity throughout the history of the Black freedom strug-gle. As historian Kabria Baumgartner found, young Black girls were cen-trally involved in school equality cases during the nineteenth century in the northeast, noting that "black girls became symbols of educational justice."[81] The theme is also central to historian Rachel Devlin's work in *A Girl Stands at the Door*: she surmised that "the most numerous and consequential con-tributions to the school desegregation movement were made by African American young women and girls."[82] *A New Kind of Youth* expounds upon this premise, illustrating how young women and girls organized, led, and participated in desegregation campaigns but were also critical actors in demonstrations and protests that extended beyond the issue of desegrega-tion into the larger campaigns of the Black freedom struggle. Black girls were also treated in different ways than Black male adolescents. The same progressive reformers that instituted a juvenile justice system and the high school itself, for instance, targeted adolescent girls to curb what they pre-sumed to be sexual promiscuity, which further endangered, criminalized, and policed the bodies of young Black girls. At the same time, girls har-bored visions of attending school to escape domesticity through a higher education, to contribute toward financial security of their families, and to seek respite from racial and sexual violence that plagued young Black women.[83]

High school activists, youth organizers, and teachers continually came up against policies undergirded by White supremacy that continued to evolve as the freedom struggle unfolded. By the 1970s and full-scale deseg-regation, White authorities refused to extend the same privileges and pro-tections promised to White adolescents. White school boards also adopted policies and state lawmakers altered legislation to police desegregated schools, which were often home to protests and well as physical confronta-tions between Black and White students. New legislation criminalized student activism and targeted students of color, establishing the legal framework for a school-to-prison nexus.

To detail the politicization of adolescence and the genesis of high school student activism in the larger southern Black freedom struggle, this book traces the contours of the high school youth movement, delineating its collective and intergenerational agency and exploring its implications for movement politics across the South as it shifted from a movement that was led by adults to one where students challenged movement elders' claims to leadership.

The first chapter depicts the genesis of youth organization at the nexus of the Black teaching profession, the NAACP, and SNYC during the 1920s and 1930s, which developed in reaction to the violent reality of Black youth who were never afforded the same protections as Whites. Civil rights organizers questioned the racial logic behind modern conceptions of youth by illuminating how Black youth remained unprotected. Adults created a space for youth agency by seeking to provide a sheltered childhood that protected young people from the violent realities of segregation. Though the NAACP, SNYC, and their allies in the teaching profession recognized the inherent potential of youth activism, they shared a more passive vision of youth as *future* foot soldiers, which dictated that adults instill an education designed to inspire future activism among youth. Adults were ultimately uncomfortable with young people actively participating and thus maintained a more cautionary view that harnessed the energy of youth and kept them on the sidelines of a larger movement that adults were supposed to direct.[84]

The second chapter begins with the promises of youth organization during the Second World War and the postwar struggle to eradicate *de jure* segregation. The international fight against fascism did not resolve the contradictions that belied the construction of youth for African Americans. In the violent contradiction of living while Black in the American South, historically Black high schools were increasingly viewed as institutional pillars with a real potential to address systemic inequality. Students inspired by the "Double V" campaign–including returning war veterans–provided a catalyst that demonstrated the latent potential of high school activism.[85] At the same time, a small yet significant number of teachers in Black professional associations risked their careers and demanded higher wages, suing local and state districts for providing unequal salaries despite notions of "separate but equal."[86] Community leaders continued to see the high school as a way to protect youth, but through the expansion of educational opportunity at the high school level by providing more space and better schools.

The NAACP and SNYC established parameters for a burgeoning youth movement that shaped succeeding generations of youth activism. They organized youth conferences, most notably the SNYC annual meeting in South Carolina in 1946, which drafted young people into their ranks and implemented citizenship education for local communities. The network that shaped high school activism ultimately operated with the presumption that youth held the potential to be future foot soldiers and consequently fell short of supporting young people as autonomous change agents.

The student movement during the 1950s is the subject of the third chapter. Students built upon the traditions of the high school and the NAACP, but they also blazed new paths by making more radical and autonomous assertions through direct-action protest. The 1950s ushered in a period of heightened conflict and moments of unprecedented militancy driven by high school youth autonomy, as noted during the high school protests in Prince Edward County, Virginia, and Montgomery, Alabama.[87] Militant protests incited a cautionary reaction among NAACP leadership, who stipulated new constitutional regulations on youth autonomy. It also pushed teachers to embrace more subtle forms of pedagogical activism, particularly in the aftermath of the *Brown v. Board of Education* (1954), which generated an intergenerational schism. As young people made new demands independent of adult networks that traditionally defined the role of youth activists, movement leaders and educators struggled to contain demands among youth for autonomy in a changing era.

The fourth chapter explores how autonomous high school protest during the 1960s propelled the movement forward across the South in locales that did not have a Black college, such as Charleston, South Carolina, and McComb, Mississippi. It also examines movement centers such as Birmingham, Alabama, and the most well-known campaign of youth activism, the Children's Crusade during the spring of 1963, which garnered international coverage because of young activists whom Horace Huntley, John McKerley, and Robin Kelley referred to as *the* "foot soldiers for democracy."[88] Protests in towns with historically Black high schools functioned as many Black colleges did across the South and initiated many of the local sit-ins that are typically credited to college students and galvanized local movements where none had previously existed. Parents rallied to support their children who were arrested yet were critical and highly skeptical of the "outside agitators" who led their kids to jail. Many organizers felt high school students were too young to be directly involved since it was more difficult to gain the trust of parents.[89] The politics of protest that underpinned high school activism in Charleston, McComb, and Birmingham illustrates a nascent movement shaped by political differences among movement leadership, youth who viewed themselves as autonomous change agents, and competing notions of youth that increasingly viewed high school activists as integral change agents. Far from a monolithic campaign, youth activists continued to reflect divisions within the movement as they continued to advance the movement in critical, overlooked ways.

The fifth and final chapter looks at the state's reaction to Black high school student protest and White resistance to desegregated high schools. Youth protests had the unintended consequence of pushing the state not only to solidify but to harden its stance against young activists. Elected officials at the state and local level in coordination with law enforcement criminalized student protest and made the practice of civil rights activism in schools illegal, subject to discipline and punishment. The strong-armed reaction of elected and school officials shaped the criminalization of Black youth that continues to the present day. School and law enforcement agents sternly reproached youth who engaged in protest in part by modifying juvenile codes to remove the legal protections typically afforded to them. As southern states began the slow process of desegregation, police increased their presence in public schools as racist school boards governed newly unified school districts. This precipitated a disciplinary logic that disproportionately punished students of color during desegregation, which shaped the contemporary "school to prison" nexus.

The voices of youth and high school activists are prioritized to the greatest extent possible in this analysis to keep youth at the center of this history. Professional discourse has documented the paucity and problematic nature of utilizing such sources, including student newspapers where available and oral histories and autobiographies to expand the sources from high school youth themselves.[90] Some of the sources for this book include minutes, reports, correspondence about SNYC and NAACP conferences held specifically for youth, and oral history collections, including the robust, invaluable collection of oral histories collected by Horace Huntley around the movement Birmingham. Such sources are vital to grounding analysis in the perspective of youth and providing a counternarrative to the dominant narratives that have shaped the historiography. At the same time, they can be limited in capturing the genuine essence of student "voice": student newspapers were still published under the supervision and ultimate approval of teachers or administrators; oral histories and autobiographies are susceptible to the limitations of memory and historical fact collected after the event; and high schoolers who joined the NAACP or SNYC were expected to follow stringent guidelines passed by their elders. Even when civil rights organizations claimed to be working for or with youth, they were typically led by younger adults like Juanita Jackson, who was twenty-two when she assumed control of NAACP Youth Councils in 1936.[91] Youth leaders like Jackson may have been young and spoke with some authority for young people, but they were still not the age of high school youth.

There are inherent limitations to writing a history of high school student activism, to be sure. The larger point is not the scarcity or limitation of such sources, but that youth themselves are only part of the story in the early decades of the twentieth century. Analysis of "youth" must therefore consider their elders, too. Teachers, administrators, psychologists, and other professionals who worked with, taught, or studied "youth" are integral actors to consider because they defined it during the first decades of the twentieth century. How professionals and elders in Black high schools, SNYC, and the NAACP saw, defined, and worked with youth is a crucial part of the politics behind Black high schools and high school youth activism. The voices of adults advocating for youth, therefore, are critical to outline the politics of activism at the level of the historically Black high school, which begins with the professional discourse surrounding the categorization of youth.

There are also epistemological questions stemming from the positionality and relationship to research on student activism and the historically Black high school. I have followed and documented the role of young people in the Black freedom struggle since reconstructing the history of the Freedom Schools, a network of schools that espoused liberatory pedagogy to educate youth activists.[92] The research, evidence, and lessons from activists who shared their stories, sources, and interpretations with me conveyed an overlooked history of youth activists in the movement. Moving to teach at the College of Charleston in South Carolina in 2011, a historic S. H. Kress building sat on the same block as my office. Learning how students from the historically Black Burke High School orchestrated the city's first sit-in there in 1960, and then a larger local movement in the city, reaffirmed that the story of young people on the front lines was of central importance. Despite the clear record of Burke High School in providing a quality education to all students, I learned firsthand how this historically Black high school was under constant threat of closure as it increasingly became the subject of anxious discourse of White parents who gentrified the city. The histories shared with me, a White scholar, by activists such as Joy Cabarrus Speakes, Dave Dennis, Millicent Brown, Minerva King, Hezekiah Watkins, Gwen Patton, Linda Chapman, Joseph Delpit, and many other student activists have not only been illuminating but a reminder that this history speaks—or should speak—to everyone through a shared and collective counternarrative.

Though the story of high school activism has often been marginalized, and it remains to be told imperfectly, the fact remains that youth shaped the movement. Elder organizers regularly looked to young people as foot soldiers on the front lines of the movement, youth who could help lead the movement when their time came. But when youth pushed back, and acted without their consent, new questions emerged about the tenacity of youth and how it could be incorporated into the movement, if at all. The civil rights movement was not just youthful in a general sense. Perennial questions about youth among elder organizers shaped the contours of the movement and generated productive tensions that positioned youth as integral though overlooked actors in the movement. Within this milieu, young activists shaped the movement in profound ways. Their aspirations, visions, and influence on the nation today remain a critical guide to understanding our past as we look toward the future.

1 The Most Momentous Youth Development That the South Has Ever Seen

The Racialization and Politicization of
High School Youth, 1920–1940

. . . .

In the spring of 1925, sixteen-year-old Richard Wright, hands shaking and voice trembling, stood ready to deliver the class commencement speech as valedictorian of Smith-Robinson Junior High School in Jackson, Mississippi. Wright was apprehensive about speaking in front of his peers. In his autobiography, *Black Boy*, Wright recounted how he had gotten cold feet when speaking in front of his classmates and teachers throughout his school years. He practiced incessantly. As he recalled in retrospect, "I memorized my speech so thoroughly that I could have recited it in my sleep."[1] The speech represented a crowning moment for Wright, who had worked assiduously to cover the cost of books and supplies to attend Smith-Robertson. He became a published author while still in high school, writing a three-part series, "The Voodoo of Hell's Half Acre" for the *Southern Register*.[2] It was a defining moment as well for the Black principal, W. H. Lanier, who arranged for the ceremony to be held in a city ballroom typically reserved for White students.[3] The young prodigy and the faculty at Smith Robertson demonstrated the height of Black excellence in the face of adversity during the "nadir of race relations."

Beneath the carefully orchestrated graduation ceremony, however, was a turbulent reality. The harrowing experiences of an adolescent struggling to survive in the South underpinned Wright's speech. For the young author, like so many other Black students who acquired an education beyond elementary school, growing up in the South was an unending struggle. It was also an act of resistance. Titled "The Attributes of Life," Wright composed his address to explain how the education system from which he was graduating deprived him and continued to deny his peers the support they needed.[4] Wright sought to disrupt any pretense of complacency or complicitly implied in the event as envisioned by his principal and their White guests.

As part of his education, Wright was forced to learn what he later called the "ethics of living Jim Crow." Like children across the South, Wright learned the fierce realities of survival and what it meant to be Black in the South, which he catalogued in his autobiography. From his earliest memories, race punctuated his consciousness as he grappled for a worldview to make sense of what he saw. At the age of eight, Wright lived with his Uncle Hoskins, who owned a bar and saloon frequented by the workers of Arkansas sawmills. Threatened by Whites who were envious of his success, Uncle Hoskins always slept with a revolver on his bed stand. When he failed to return home one night, his family knew he was killed. "There was no funeral," Wright recollected. "There was no music. There was no period of mourning. There were no flowers. There were only silence, quiet weeping, whispers, and fear."[5] This violent reality was reinforced through stories of Whites beating Black children and killing Black men. Wright—like millions of Black youth—was brought up with these stories and exposed to the widespread violence that targeted African Americans, particularly the race riots of 1919 that stuck nearby Elaine and West Helena, Arkansas, where he once lived.[6]

Wright in many ways typified what it was like to be Black in the South in the first decades of the twentieth century. Wright was learning through both formal and informal channels of what Jennifer Ritterhouse called "racial etiquette," or the implicit codes of conduct that essentially taught children where they fit in a racist, anti-Black society.[7] The illogical and hateful nature of it confounded nearly everyone while terrorizing those victimized by it. As Wright recalled of the bizarre racist logic that underpinned his childhood, "It filled me with awe, wonder, and fear, and I asked ceaseless questions."[8] Many of those questions went unanswered, or they were answered vaguely, which helped construct a culture of silence that attempted to racially condition southern youth to accept what Whites wanted to be an immutable and permanent system of segregation.[9]

In the process of learning how to fit in an illogically violent, racist society, Wright and millions of other children of color were denied a childhood. Like many children, Wright struggled to learn how to survive the "white-hot face of terror" that defined the childhood of millions across the South. Though Wright was not the direct target of racialized physical violence, there were enough children and adolescent victims to inculcate an awareness that youth would be afforded no protection, that their lives were constantly in danger. When Wright was eight years old, a mob dragged seventeen-year-old Jesse Washington from a courthouse in Waco, Texas, and horrifically executed him in front of thousands in 1916. Just months prior to Wright's graduation, a White mob apprehended Samuel Smith, aged fifteen, from a hospital in Nolensville, Tennessee, where he was recovering from a gunshot wound from a confrontation with a White grocer, and lynched him.[10] As Wright noted, "I had never in my life been abused by whites, but I had already become as conditioned to their existence as though I had been the victim of a thousand lynchings."[11] Such stories had a profound impact on young people coming of age during the era of segregation and racialized terror.

It was clear to many that Black youth were not going to be afforded the luxuries of childhood at the cusp of a modern movement that defined a new stage of "adolescence." Children like Wright and their families intimately understood that race mediated the "pricelessness" of childhood. Many parents felt that it was incumbent upon them to transmit this stark reality to their children, delivering a different kind of education that would inculcate lessons of survival. Such moments of learning constituted a racialized aspect of Black childhood and adolescence, markedly different from Whites who learned how to perpetuate and benefit from supremacy as opposed to learning how to survive and challenge it (and thrive). Children learned much of the harsh realities of Jim Crow and the tools of survival through lessons outside of schools.[12] Stories of children cut down by supremacist violence were passed down to children as warnings and cautionary tales. Reflecting upon her childhood in Birmingham, Alabama, Carrie Delores Hamilton Lock noted, "We were very aware of the two worlds that we lived in—the black world, the white world . . . We knew about lynchings. We were very aware of how black people disappeared, never to be heard of again. How black men would be shot in the back, walking the streets and the police would say, 'They were shot in self-defense because these people were robbing or killing.' We were very aware of the terrible things that were happening in the black community."[13] These very lessons, contrary to the "rites of passage" granted to economically affluent and privileged White youth, were an integral part of raising Black youth in the South.

Black girls raised in the South faced dangers that made them more vulnerable than young boys and men. Black girls were regularly viewed as both sexually promiscuous or deviant while simultaneously threated by sexual violence, assault, and harassment. Indeed, as historian Darlene Clark Hine noted, one of the most significant motivating factors to leave the South included sexual exploitation and from the constant threat of rape by White men. As Hine noted, "The relationship between Black women and the larger society has been, and continues to be, adversarial."[14] The young girls and women who came of age in the South experienced the same discriminatory effect of laws grounded in White supremacy, but gendered norms determined they experienced it differently as young girls and women.

Raising children in the South was thus grounded in a violent reality that demanded Black children learn to be adults to avoid the treatment doled out for transgressing entrenched racial and social mores. It called for parents—and teachers—to raise or educate children in the Jim Crow South by transmitting a modicum of humility, self-control, and deference. Yet this also translated into forms of critical consciousness and new ways of imagining a reconfiguration of what appeared to be an immutable racialized society. Education in general and extending formal schooling to adolescents specifically presented an alternative to merely surviving a racially codified society. The institution of the high school and secondary education presented opportunities for resistance.

Parents, teachers, community leaders, civil rights association organizers, and other adults drew upon modern concepts of childhood and adolescence. In the 1920s youth was a concept that was fluid and malleable, to be applied by adults and professionals as they saw fit. In an effort to defend Black youth and imagine a new future, teachers and community organizers along with the NAACP or SNYC were allies in a larger "child saving" movement, buttressing the work of Black women who sought, for instance, to restore the juvenile justice system for youth and adolescents of color.[15] Robbing youth of the innocence promised by modern constructs of adolescence inspired modes of resistance in Black communities across the South, irrespective of class, gender, or professional divisions. Elders and youth created a politicized space for a spectrum of critical engagement that ranged from direct confrontation to subtle acts of resistance. Youth organizations appeared in the 1930s in various locales led by civil rights advocates, including but not limited to Ella Baker's Young Negro Cooperative League in New York and Juanita Jackson's City-Wide Young People's Forum in Baltimore.[16] Many high school students also joined NAACP Youth Council chapters or SNYC local chapters. In these organizations, high school activists networked through conferences that focused on Black youth. Through these channels, youth protested police brutality, lobbied and advocated for anti-lynching legislation, and demanded higher quality education, which included building upon the momentum of "Negro History Week" and petitioning and organizing for revamped curriculum that eradicated racist history, stereotypes, and other denigrating passages embedded in their school's textbooks.

But youth activism and participatory engagement in the 1920s and 1930s were carried out at the individual level as evinced in Richard Wright's valedictorian speech or, more commonly, through youth organizations. Engagement through conferences and youth organizations was more definitive of the time, and it tellingly developed in the shadow of elders who acted on behalf of youth and made claims to youth as the concept itself was becoming institutionalized through the high school. Black high school teachers and civil rights organizers shaped the politicization of Black youth across the South by defining youth and the protections it afforded—or failed to afford—to Black adolescents specifically. As the construct of youth and specifically adolescence took hold during the Progressive Era and the Great Depression, youth activism—where it existed—differed from later generations when high schools and NAACP Youth Council chapters were more defined, active, and able to challenge elders. These ideological and social origins of high school youth activism begin with historically Black high schools and civil rights organizations, namely the NAACP and SNYC. These institutions and organizations were uniquely situated as defenders of youth and formed the first lines of institutional defense for Black adolescents. In work that complemented parents and kin who raised children and adolescents to be vigilant, Black educators and civil rights organizations exposed racialized conceptions of childhood and adolescence to challenge the hypocrisy behind denying Black youth the same protections promised to Whites. Questioning the racial logic behind modern constructs politicized youth and the institutions like high schools that served them. As crimes against children and adolescents multiplied, an incipient, dynamic youth movement began to take hold, and some Black schools emerged as key sites of this movement to both protect and prepare youth for a violent reality. Teachers utilized their positions in high schools to instill a critical consciousness through a form of pedagogical activism. At the same time, civil rights organizations sought to organize youth for political ends to challenge systemic racism and discrimination in a larger movement.

Most high school students, teachers, and civil rights organizers did not engage in direct action or protest, with some exceptions. The more common form of activism among high school youth consisted of supporting efforts led by youth organizers in the NAACP and SNYC, ranging from protesting police brutality to demanding school resource equalization. Students participated in annual conferences sponsored by these civil rights organizations, too, which were radical in their content, though the top-down, adult-led nature of the conferences minimized the volume of student voices. This continuum of youth engagement throughout the 1920s and 1930s demonstrated the potential and the work that shaped a nascent youth movement and proffered a truth that would define subsequent decades: that youth can and should be agents of change on the front lines of the freedom struggle.

"Progressive" Origins of the Historically Black High School

Richard Wright's valedictorian speech was an act of protest that elucidates the complexities, promises, and limitations of the Black high school in the 1920s and 1930s in challenging White supremacy. For Wright and his generation, as was the case for those who proceeded him, the schoolhouse itself was a potential site to resist and take aim. The education they received and the teachers and principals that instructed them, as bulwarks of the state, were a logical target, or something to fight against for some students like Wright. His valedictorian speech became an avenue of protest.

The principal, William Henry Lanier, typically wrote the speeches for his star pupils to recite, and when Wright presented the text of his own speech to Lanier, he refused it. Instead, the principal handed him a speech that he himself had written. Cognizant that the audience would include Whites who governed the financial support of the school, Lanier informed Wright, "You can't afford to just say anything before those white people that night."[17] When a recalcitrant Wright refused, Lanier snapped back, "You're just a young, hotheaded fool," commanding, "Wake up, boy. Learn the world you're living in."[18] Wright resisted and ultimately delivered the speech on his own terms, which were likely modified from the original draft.[19]

Though Wright chastised the principal of Smith-Robertson, W. H. Lanier was a respected leader in Jackson and across the state. He had established the first schools in the city of Jackson, which was in and of itself an act of resistance. His ascent as a civic leader exemplified the work of formerly enslaved persons in establishing the first schools for Black students during Reconstruction. Formerly enslaved and recently emancipated people built—most often literally—the first schools in the state of Mississippi with a desire to learn and the collective recognition that education would protect their new status of freedom.[20] Lanier was formerly enslaved and after the Civil War he attended Tougaloo College, Fish University, and Oberlin College before graduating with his bachelor's degree from Roger Williams College in Rhode Island. A consummate educator, he served as president of Alcorn College and later as the first head of the Jackson Colored Public Schools.[21]

Lanier organized Black families to pressure city officials to construct the first public school for African Americans in 1894, the Smith Robertson

School. Its namesake was born in 1847 into slavery and became a success-ful business owner and the city's first Black alderman. Smith Robertson, as the first Black school in the city of Jackson, was also known as the "Mother School."[22] Like many historic Black high schools in the city, it was a central part of the Black cultural life and business in Jackson that centered around the main thoroughfare of Farish St.

Given all that he had accomplished to date, 1925 was a pivotal year for Principal W. H. Lanier. After years of galvanizing support to build a Black public system of education in Jackson, a new apex of academic and profes-sional achievement was slated for the fall of 1925: the construction of Lanier High School. Named in his honor and the result of years of carefully build-ing a school system during Jim Crow, the new Lanier High School repre-sented the latest phase of Black academic excellence, encapsulated in a stand-alone high school committed to serving adolescents and replete with a full academic curriculum.[23] Lanier was not willing to let one "hotheaded fool" ruin the pinnacle of his career by upsetting the White benefactors he had been courting.

The new kind of youth negotiated the politics of resistance that centered around the Black high school. It provided adolescents like Wright a poten-tial stage of protest as a buffer against a brutal world. For Black educators like Lanier, the high school presented a way to meet the needs of their communities through carefully negotiated strategies during Jim Crow. The stage in the arena of the Black high school was set for unfolding tension and resistance.

Black high schools of the first decades of twentieth century such as Lanier High School were storied institutions, offering protection to adolescents and cautious preparation for life in a society defined by White supremacy. Black high school advocates, administrators, and educators established a line of defense for adolescents like Richard Wright alongside parents and pastors. By sheltering young people in school and preparing them for the future, high schools promised not only to shield adolescents from vitriolic racism, but to provide the skills needed for gainful employment. Black high schools also held a latent potential to train critical change agents as they established the foundation for heightened political consciousness. Brokered through Black educators dependent upon a White power structure for employ-ment, Black high schools also perpetuated a passivity that shielded youth and trained them to be critical observers, not active agents in directly chal-lenging racist policy and *de jure* segregation. As Vanessa Siddle Walker outlined, one of the "staple beliefs" shared among Black teachers was to "counter the external negativity of segregation by helping children believe in what they could achieve."[24]

The manifest purpose of Black high schools like Lanier High School was to serve and cater to the newly constructed ideas of adolescence and to claim them for Black youth. Educators utilized the distinct space to create a supportive environment for youth and adolescents that addressed the unique needs of adolescence. In effect, they also constructed an environment that the larger society failed to produce for Black youth. Black high school administrators and teachers were faithfully committed to their work and took cues from educational reformers at the time. High schools fully engaged adolescents in progressive ideals, incorporating a "total environment" for the "whole child." Adult educators and education experts of the Progressive Era sought to nurture the social, emotional, and physical well-being of all students—the tenets of which are regarded as "Progressive Education," which reflected, as Paula Fass noted, "the new science of childhood."[25] High school programming was expanded to meet what social scientists and educators identified for the first time as the unique needs of adolescents, providing a multitude of ways to facilitate student growth and development. For instance, high schools provided extracurricular opportunities in music, sports, and academic pursuits outside the classroom. Nationally popular youth organizations such as the YMCA and Boy Scouts opened chapters in high schools, too. By implementing extensive extracurricular activities, which included elements of student government that imbued notions of self-governance, educators, professionals, and administrators carefully constructed an active high school culture that spoke to the totality of every student.

A whole-child approach suited the prevailing notion among White policymakers that Black education should be used for moral development and industrial training. Yet at the same time, considering the context of the Jim Crow South, a whole-child approach also provided opportunities for civic engagement that held the potential to politically engage students. J. Andrew Simmons, a graduate of the Avery Normal Institute in Charleston, South Carolina, implemented a whole-child approach while serving as the principal of Booker T. Washington High School in Columbia. He strengthened the academic curriculum while increasing the number of activities and extracurricular opportunities at school to meet the interests of his students, fostering a new social environment.[26] Such a prescribed education is harmless on the surface, but the context of Jim Crow engendered politicization. The position of Black high schools exposed youth to more direct political education through rare though significant instances when organizations like the NAACP were involved. Youth were also exposed to critically trained teachers who defined progressive education in a political context. Seemingly innocuous to White observers, extracurricular organizations maintained a latent potential to raise the consciousness of youth growing up Black in the Jim Crow South.

In fostering an environment for the "whole child" in a segregated, racist society, African Americans necessarily engaged in a complicated relationship with the state. They could demand a high school education to claim the same access to schooling and protections for adolescent youth, much like the NAACP, for instance. But given the fact that White supremacists ultimately governed Black high schools, these spaces became a complex battleground fraught with tension. The state offered some support for secondary education, but it was mired in racism that continually demanded Black administrators and educators adopt compromised positions.

The Black high school still constituted a modest, clandestine means for Black educators and civic leaders to claim a right to Black adolescence to contest the hegemonic politics of White supremacy. It held the potential to function as a political space. As such, it cemented the Black high school as an important fixture in the politicization of Black youth. The desire for a right to adolescence and, to a lesser extent, calls for overtly political socialization and education, fostered a modicum of resistance. In some cases, Black high schools provided direct links to the overtly political work of the NAACP. The NAACP worked with students, educators, and administrators across the country, including the South, to establish Youth Council chapters for adolescents. They organized chapters at public and private schools, as well as stand-alone high schools and secondary programs that were part of a college campus.[27] Though few in number and serving only a small segment of the few students enrolled in schools, Black high schools were fertile grounds for activism. Political organizations like the NAACP established an important precedent, awareness, and early inroads with Black high schools across the nation.

As education advocates established, or struggled to establish, the parameters of secondary education, Black high school teachers and administrators were ultimate gatekeepers alongside parents, community elders, and pastors. They provided the most direct link between resistance in the Jim Crow South and their adolescent pupils. Black high school educators occupied a critical presence in schools and the communities they served. They were well educated and in significant instances studied at prestigious institutions outside the South. Taking advantage of funding designated to Black students interested in enrolling in graduate school outside the state—funding appropriated by southern legislators to avoid building "separate but equal" graduate programs or desegregation in their home states—a small though influential cadre of educators earned degrees in higher education from premier universities across the nation.[28]

Teacher education programs of the 1920s and 1930s, often referred to as the Progressive Era of Education, facilitated an intellectual climate inspired in part by northern, urban educators, most notably the philosopher and pedagogue John Dewey, but other contemporaries including William Kilpatrick, Harold Rugg, and George Counts. These "progressive" educators and theorists revamped traditional methods of teaching, incorporating social methods of learning and experience geared at the whole child. In addition to a new pedagogy, many viewed teachers as key actors for political and social change and their schools as a democratic space. For one faction of progressive educators, schools were the logical place to facilitate a redistribution of resources to reconstruct a broken society along radically democratic principles. As Counts noted in *Dare the School Build a New Social Order?*, all "resources must be dedicated to the promotion of the welfare of the great masses of the people."[29] Teacher education programs were often rooted in a mode of social critique, critical thinking, and an ardent commitment to democracy that defined education during the Progressive Era.

Some Black educators studied directly under this vanguard of progressive educational thought in the North. Many educators from the South earned degrees in higher education from premier universities across the nation. As historians Scott Baker and Vanessa Siddle Walker have noted, some Black educators enrolled in graduate programs at the University of Chicago, Columbia, Harvard, Cornell, New York University, and other elite, predominantly White institutions of higher learning. They also studied at high-caliber historically Black colleges and universities such as Morehouse College, Fisk University, and Howard University. Majoring in biology, chemistry, mathematics, or physics from high-quality institutions across the country, many Black teachers completed the rigorous requirements of a collegiate education at a time when just over half of all Americans regardless of race attended high schools. As high schools and secondary education developed, teachers constituted a highly educated segment of the Black professional class.[30]

Yet most teachers did not enroll in the programs at Howard, Fisk, the University of Chicago, or Columbia University. Nor did every teacher read radical progressive thinkers in their teacher education programs. Still, all teachers were exposed to progressive discourse in one form or another through ongoing education and professional development. Most Black teachers received the lessons of progressive education through Black colleges and even more examined progressive ideals as they continued their education after they began teaching through summer programs or memberships in professional teaching associations. Additionally, most teachers enrolled in courses during summer sessions held at local colleges, northern universities, or training schools to earn college credit, study and pass licensure examinations, or to increase their pay.[31]

White progressive educator theorists largely dismissed race but Black public intellectuals, scholars, and educators such as W. E. B. Du Bois, Benjamin Mays, Septima Clark, and Mary McLeod Bethune placed race at the center of teacher education and professional discourse.[32] Through ongoing education and publications stemming from the networks cultivated by the Association for the Study of Negro Life and History, Black teachers studied their craft in professional spaces that addressed race directly.[33] Black intellectual and educational thought permeated Black teacher association journals, conferences, and professional meetings at the local, state, and national levels. At an Alabama State Teachers Association meeting in Montgomery, Alabama, in 1930, Dr. John Hope, president of Atlanta University, NAACP member, and civil rights advocate, addressed the educators present. "The need of the Negro is pressing," Hope stated. "If they are going to work out of it at all it will have to be done through their teachers . . . We as teachers must realize that we have the power."[34] Summer school curricula included the work of Carter G. Woodson around Negro History Week during the 1930s and utilized the printed material of the Association for the Study of Negro Life and History, including the *Journal of Negro History*. Teacher journals such as the *Mississippi Education Journal* printed the work, correspondence, and speeches of Carter G. Woodson as well.[35] Critical Black thought and vigorous debate infused the pages of the popular *Journal of Negro Education*. Examined in isolation, messages of democratic education or Negro history that line the pages of teacher journals and meeting minutes appear innocuous. Taken collectively, however, professional discourse percolated with ideas of democracy, race consciousness, and education as a space to actualize ideals of a more just society.

Teacher education programs and professional teacher associations during the era of Jim Crow provided an opportunity to apply progressive principles in a Black and segregated context. Charles J. Cunningham, a Black educator who studied education in the 1930s in Mississippi and Tennessee, was deeply immersed in the tradition of progressive education. As part of his training, Cunningham thoroughly read and took scrupulous notes on William H. Kilpatrick's *Education for a Changing Civilization*.[36] Far from the bastions of liberal thought on the East coast, Cunningham was still part of the progressive ideology that shaped Black educators. "The development of power," he wrote in his college notes, "is the main business of the school, and all the knowledge obtained should be gained and used in such a way as to be toward this growth of power."[37] Howard University, which offered a course in "The Courts and Racial Integration in Education," is indicative of how some Black educators incorporated the insights of progressive education gained in graduate school into their labor. Lois Simms, an English teacher at Burke High School in Charleston, South Carolina, took this course as part of her graduate program in education. She wrote her thesis on the funding discrepancies between Black and White schools in South Carolina.[38] Her research exposed the discriminatory policies that shaped her profession. Critical assessments like this fueled the ideology of young teachers in segregated schools.

Behind the closed doors of their own classrooms, some Black educators seized the opportunity to apply and renegotiate Progressivism by establishing principles of academic excellence with an active sense of citizenship in fashioning the "second curriculum" in an act of subversive or "fugitive pedagogy" at the high school level. Teachers' lesson plans, coursework, and educational philosophies guided critical thinking and instilled attitudes of political efficacy in Black segregated schools.[39] This included incorporating Black history and literature into the curriculum. But sometimes educators went further. Dr. W. A. Walters of Rust College in Mississippi wrote to his fellow educators, imploring that they must "encourage our civic organizations and Social Clubs to have more periodic discussions of Negro activities and problems."[40] Other teachers believed that a right to an education also included receiving the *same* quality education and exposure to texts as their White counterparts. The work of teachers in Charleston, South Carolina, is suggestive of how Black educators applied a progressive education in the segregated South. High school English teacher Mr. Eugene Hunt of Burke High School introduced his students to notions of democratic equality and the avenues to substantive change in American government through the writings and speeches of Thomas Jefferson and Franklin Roosevelt. His colleague, Mrs. Lois Simms, executed lesson plans that enforced the rigorous study of canonical literature including Charles Dickens, Ralph Waldo Emerson, and Mark Twain.[41]

Through acquiring an education and then teaching what they learned in Black schools, African American teachers embraced a set of principles that constituted a collective ideology of progressivism unique to the Black systems they served and the segregated, unequal circumstances that shaped them. Black educators like Cunningham, Simms, Hunt, and others viewed progressivism, broadly defined, beyond a curriculum and teaching methodology; they viewed progressivism as the means to improve the entire institution of secondary education. As educational historian Craig Kridel noted, Black educators viewed progressivism as a way to supplement accreditation and economic parity in education. How Black teachers taught their students and how they improved secondary education through attempts to equalize resources in a segregated society and to achieve accreditation constituted genuine attempts to meet the needs of their students and the communities they served.[42]

Yet many teachers never ascribed to instill a progressive pedagogy and the principles of active resistance in their classroom. High schools, regardless of their position on an activist spectrum, ultimately reinforced a passivity that defined emergent notions of adolescence and childhood at the dawn of the twentieth century and reinforced the understandings perpetuated by the NAACP and other civil rights organizations. Educators thus protected and refined the inherent potential of students as catalysts but fell short of facilitating active resistance to the segregated social order they studied. Yet for the network of leaders that built high schools and the professionals who met the responsibility to instruct students, high schools as community institutions held extraordinary potential to combat systemic discrimination and were willing partners in the larger fight.

The NAACP Youth Councils

Civil rights organizations during the 1920s and 1930s complemented the work of high school teachers and administrators, and they shared the same modern understandings of youth and adolescence. Yet civil rights organizations advanced a more direct politicization of Black youth.[43] The politicization of youth was grounded in claiming a right to childhood and adolescence for Black youth, much like Black high schools, and the process unfolded amid competing views and interpretations of what it entailed. The relationships forged at the nexus of civil rights organizations and Black high schools engendered conflicting notions of Black youth and adolescence that vacillated between preparing young people for the movement and sheltering them from it. Organizations such as the NAACP and SNYC, much like Black educators and administrators, faced a dilemma as they saw young people as catalysts in a larger movement but at the same time hesitated to embrace their full participation as activists. The adults who led the movement nurtured forms of youth activism but, above all else, sought to provide a sheltered childhood that protected the young from the violent realities of segregation.

Civil rights organizations and their allies in the teaching profession shared a more passive vision of youth as *future* foot soldiers with which they instilled a critical education designed to inspire future activism.[44] Adults were ultimately uncomfortable with young people actively participating and thus maintained a more cautionary view that harnessed the energy of youth and kept them on the sidelines of a larger movement that adults were supposed to direct. The affinity forged between Black educators, administrators, NAACP organizers, and SNYC activists established a blueprint for youth activism that suggested young people were to be organized and acted upon. Connecting the work of the NAACP Youth Councils with the Black high school and other civil rights organizations like SNYC enables a further examination of the work of the association, demonstrating how the mobilization and politicization of youth operated during the 1920s and 1930s, which presaged youth activism for the later phases of the civil rights movement.

As a primary actor in the freedom struggle since its organization in 1909, the NAACP sought to protect children from the violent assaults that enforced a racially segregated society. This was most visible in their support and campaign for the Scottsboro Boys—nine Black youth (aged thirteen to twenty-one years old) who were all sentenced to death, except the thirteen-year-old child, who was sentenced to life in prison. Their convictions, which were later overturned, stemmed from false rape allegations.[45] As noted by the director of youth branches during the Scottsboro affairs, Juanita Jackson, the NAACP sought to organize youth to the point "where there won't be any more Scottsboro boys."[46]

The NAACP was also in a prime position to politicize youth through organizing in Black communities. The NAACP organized young people, or intended to organize young people, since its earliest years. Official reference was made to junior chapters as early as 1921. Calling for a national membership among youth and the funds to facilitate it, Robert Bagnall, director of NAACP branches, wrote in 1923, "Our young people need to be taught proper race pride, proper racial consciousness and organization methods."[47] The NAACP organized what was loosely called in the 1920s "student chapters" or "junior chapters" and organized them under the association's Junior Division. The NAACP's interest in the education of Black youth as a battlefront to combat racial discrimination and foster racial pride is evident in their objectives for the junior chapters. The objectives of chapters organized under the Junior Division included studying the lives of "great Negro men and women"; Black history; culture; literature, including children's stories; learning public speaking; and debate, and through this instruction to "gain poise and power." As a bureaucratic arm of the NAACP, junior chapters were also expected to follow protocol that ultimately supported the national association. The NAACP sent out detailed instructions on how to organize a Junior Division that focused upon inculcating young people in the organizational work of the association. Organizers were expected to identify and host a meeting for youth leaders. Twenty-five members constituted a branch, and they were expected to elect officers and form standing committees.[48] Members were expected to canvas in membership drives, serve as ushers in NAACP meetings, and "give entertainments" for the senior and national branches of the NAACP.[49]

Following the broader periodization of adolescence between the ages of 14 and 24, the NAACP targeted high schools as well as Black colleges and universities that served this population. The association established a youth-based foundation within the first few years of the creation of the Junior Division. The association reported in 1925 that junior branches were formed in Detroit; Los Angeles; Sacramento; Charleston, West Virginia; Kansas City; Des Moines; Indianapolis; Denver; and Little Rock. College chapters were well established in Mississippi in four historically Black colleges, including two with high school departments, Tougaloo College and Rust College. There were chapters also established at Selma University and the State Normal School in Cheyney, Pennsylvania.[50]

The NAACP enacted a categorization of youth throughout the 1920s and 1930s that mirrored national discourse. This included a nebulous, sometimes muddled categorization of youth, where college and high school students were lumped together despite burgeoning discourse around the unique stage of adolescent development. In the 1920s the NAACP, like the rest of the country, largely defined "youth" between the ages of fourteen and twenty-one and did not demarcate differences among young people, thereby merging high school and college students into the same category. Moreover, the initial constitution of the Youth Division specified that people between the ages of 18 and 30 could apply for membership.[51] College-aged students were organized alongside high school students. But by 1935 the NAACP adopted more refined categorizations and placed operational boundaries on "youth" itself, which included dividing programs for young people into "College Chapters" for people between the ages of twenty and twenty-four, "Youth Councils" for those aged sixteen to nineteen, and even Junior Youth Councils or "junior auxiliaries" for people as young as twelve to fifteen years old.[52] Youth Councils were thus organized specifically to encompass new conceptions of adolescence. Organizing NAACP Youth Councils cemented a bond between formal schooling and civil rights initiatives. In the organization's first "youth conference" in 1936, students between the ages of twelve and eighteen constituted the largest contingent of conference goers. Organizers reported that 28 percent of attendees were in middle and high school and nearly 50 percent of youth conference participants enrolled in or had completed high school but had not gone on to college.[53]

Though the NAACP altered their age distinctions to demarcate high school adolescents from younger elementary students and older college scholars by 1935, the distinction remained blurred and high school youth were regularly conflated with college-aged youth. Abetted by the fact that high school departments were often located on HBCU campuses, civil rights organizers—like the general public—often saw high school and college youth as one and the same.

By the 1930s the NAACP felt that more could be done with the organization of young people. In the aftermath of the Scottsboro case, Walter White, then executive secretary of the NAACP, issued a report in 1933 that criticized the organization for its lack of direction for young people. As he wrote to the board of directors, "One of the greatest weaknesses of the Association's program is the lack of a definite program for activity by Junior Branches and younger people. Many of our branches are officered by loyal and faithful, but elderly, people who in an uncomfortably large number of instances discourage initiative on the part of young people. In the meantime other activities and movements are occupying the attention of young people and gaining their support."[54] White recognized that young people "have a zeal, a zest and a fighting spirit which some of the older people in the Association do not have."[55] The national office responded and invested anew in the Junior Division and appointed new leadership in 1935. The

NAACP appointed Juanita Jackson, an activist from Baltimore with extensive experience in organizing youth, to become a national youth director.[56] Jackson was intimately familiar with organizing under Jim Crow. Her mother, Lillie Jackson, was active in the Baltimore NAACP and served as branch president for thirty-five years. One of her greatest victories was the equalization of pay for Black teachers in the Baltimore public schools. Jackson earned a degree in education and a master's degree in sociology from the University of Pennsylvania and was a member of the Alpha Kappa Alpha sorority. Having served as the president of the City-Wide Young People's Forum and as vice president of the National Council of Methodist Youth, Juanita Jackson already demonstrated leadership potential, particularly in the capacity of working with youth.[57]

Juanita Jackson provided youthful, energetic, and bold leadership to the organization. She saw the youth organizing campaign as an extension of critical civic engagement, "challenging young people that this is America, this is a democracy."[58] As Jackson elaborated in a memorandum to the NAACP, "It is the aim of the Youth Council of the N.A.A.C.P. to reach Youth, and to stimulate in them an awareness and understanding of the political, social, educational, and economic problems which confront the American Negro. Upon this understanding it hopes to build a strong youth organization, each unit of which will be a center of education and action in the struggle of the Association for the full constitutional rights of twelve million colored Americans."[59] Another objective included developing "militant leadership."[60] Jackson viewed youth work and the organization of young people as explicitly political and, moreover, that education was intricately linked to political activity. At the same time that White middle class values determined that youth should be protected, Black organizers like Jackson viewed young people in explicitly political terms connected to a larger struggle based on race.

The NAACP youth conferences provide a view into how the association deployed modern notions of youth to politicize young people as part of their larger agenda. The conferences also highlight how adult leadership viewed youth and how youth conceptualized their own work. Jackson maintained an ambitious outlook that anticipated and sought genuine activism. "We are making history here tonight," Juanita Jackson informed the young audience of the first Youth Conference, held in her home city of Baltimore in 1936.[61] They opened the conference with the following song:

Should we sit idly by and sigh,
While lynchings rule the land,
And thousands suffer agony
From Jim Crow's cruel hand?
Shall we allow rank prejudice
To thwart our destiny?
NO! With the NAACP
We'll fight for victory![62]

Facilitated through the NAACP, Jackson contextualized young people's ambitions to join a larger movement to eradicate Jim Crow. This grounded the struggle youth prepared for in deeply moral principles and connected it to issues that directly impacted them.

Youth conferences provided a platform for noted activists and movement luminaries to address the young people who attended. New York–based community organizer and activist Ella Baker addressed the 1936 youth assembly in Baltimore on consumer cooperatives, drawing upon examples from Europe and stating that "the future rise . . . of collective action in a collective society . . . will help us accomplish some of the higher ideals which we have in mind to accomplish."[63] Dr. Hyman Shapiro of Johns Hopkins addressed the conference on the fight against fascism, calling young people and the larger movement to work and organize with "people in factories, mines, on water fronts" and the "doubly, triply exploited . . . Negro worker," as well as White organizations, including the American Students Union.[64] Through the calls for antifascist work and interracial and interclass organization, young people who attended the NAACP youth conferences were exposed to progressive forms of organizing that established an important framework for future organizing.

Working within the top-down leadership structure, young people involved in the NAACP engaged in an ambitious agenda that supported an adult-led movement. Juanita Jackson and NAACP leadership encouraged young people to host open discussion meetings, to sponsor an oratorical contest, to work with the Speakers Bureau of the NAACP to train speakers to lecture on local campuses, to mimeograph a local Youth Council paper, and to write dramatic sketches that illustrated various aspects of the "race problem." Leadership encouraged Youth Councils to be centers of "education, cooperation, and action." The NAACP also expected Youth Councils to "select at least one local program within the scope and program of the Association."[65] Since the NAACP prioritized organization to end lynching, it followed that one of the first areas of interest for Youth Councils was supporting the Costigan-Wagner Anti-Lynching Bill. The NAACP called upon youth branches to participate in the National Youth Demonstration Against Lynching in March 1937. Advised by Walter White, the goal of the anti-lynching agenda was to organize 100,000 White and Black youth in activities ranging from mass meetings, visiting elected officials at the state and federal level, participating in parades and marches, and organizing demonstrations.[66] Leadership also encouraged Youth Councils to develop local programs that sought to abolish injustices in the courts, to secure equal educational opportunities, to eradicate segregation and discrimination based on race and color "wherever it exists," to obtain equal economic opportunity with fair wages, to secure the right to vote, and to "end peonage and debt slavery" of sharecroppers and agricultural workers.[67] Secondary to this was a commitment to "develop a knowledge and appreciation of the history achievements, and contributions of the Negro to American culture."[68] The Association also encouraged Youth Councils to use the tools of "the education of public opinion," the ballot, the courts, legislation, and interracial organization to achieve their larger aims.[69] In an effort to supplement the meager support provided to Black youth by New Deal Programs, the NAACP called for an examination of conditions for relief and developing economic cooperatives among Black youth.[70]

Though organizing was largely determined by adult organizers, young people were afforded the opportunity to organize on their own and identify solutions to the problems their elders presented. Students broke into discussion groups at the national youth conferences that focused on employment and economic relief, lynching, educational opportunities, civil liberties, and organization, promotion, and publicity.[71] Each discussion group was asked a series of questions that prompted young people to explore issues in depth and examine the resources the NAACP made available to them. The Educational Opportunities discussion group listed the inequalities students faced in elementary and secondary schools and were asked to explain the difference. They were asked to explore the inequalities in teachers' salaries and appointments. They were also tasked with examining what the NAACP was doing about educational opportunities and what Youth Councils could do to address the larger situation.[72] In "A Pledge for Youth," Youth Councils affirmed a belief in "fundamental social and economic change," and preserving and extending democracy and committed themselves to "fight relentlessly with the ballot, in the courts, with education of public opinion . . . for equal opportunities in all spheres."[73] On one evening, youth organized "the most significant and impressive mass meeting of the week," which boasted over 1500 members in the overflowing local Sharp Street Church.[74] James Robinson concluded the first conference with a stirring challenge: "the world, with its failing capitalistic order, its prejudices, its intolerance for social change . . . will not yield a single inch more than you make it yield. What will you do with what you have done here at this conference?"[75]

The energy youth delegates invested in the Youth Councils was tempered by the bureaucratic objectives of the national office. They had a vested interest as the prospect of organizing young people was particularly appealing to an organization dependent upon new members. As the hardships of the Depression caused membership to plummet, the NAACP invested in a segment of the population that could bolster its ranks. As the upper echelon of leaders viewed the organization of young people: "The NAACP is [en]suring its future through its youth work."[76] The bureaucratic requirements including participation in membership drives and assisting the national office facilitated the use of Youth Councils as a way to attract new members. Two years after its reorganization the NAACP cited 300 Youth Councils and 50 college chapters. By 1942 the scope of the youth program grew to include branches in 32 states and 132 cities.[77]

As the NAACP reinvested in Youth Councils, they maintained a rigid bureaucratic emphasis that anticipated young people's participation as adults as full-fledged members. The first steps for young people to become involved consisted of educating oneself about the NAACP, informing others of the organization, and then hosting a meeting for those interested in joining the association. NAACP leadership instructed young people to form this committee into an organization, which elected a temporary chairperson, secretary, and treasurer. Once membership fees were collected from twenty-five potential members (fifty cents for those under the age of twenty-one and one dollar for those over this age), members elected officers to the positions of president, vice president, secretary, assistant secretary, and treasurer.[78] Youth Council leaders encouraged young people to form multiple committees to delegate the responsibilities associated with organizational work. Committees focused on several tasks including membership recruitment, finance, press and publicity, distribution of *The Crisis*—the organization's flagship publication—and education.[79]

Inculcating young people with political, bureaucratic, and organizational skills was an important form of political socialization and consciousness raising. An emphasis on voting procedures, committee work, community canvassing, and public speaking served as a precursor to organizational strategies utilized in the grassroots movement in the 1950s and 1960s.

NAACP leaders saw youth as the future of the organization, a vantage point that signified the NAACP's passive, top-down understanding of youth organization. Like their counterparts in secondary schools, NAACP organizers believed in the potential of youth to challenge segregation, yet they too fell short in engaging them as autonomous change agents. Youth were directed, led, and acted upon. It was clear youth were expected to follow the orders of the national office. Youth had the potential to act as change agents, but mostly in ways that NAACP leadership envisioned.

The NAACP also incorporated a politics of respectability that placed firm limitations on youth autonomy and agency. The NAACP's politics of respectability embodied middle class virtues that included a strong work ethic, enrolling in school, and self-respect. The NAACP fashioned what middle class respectability looked like among African Americans and often used children to communicate the message to all Black families.[80]

Images of a bourgeois Black middle class that populated the pages of the *Crisis* suggest that, while claiming the right to childhood and adolescence, the NAACP also embraced White middle-class family and professional ideals. Youth and youth activism would be understood through bourgeois values and the politics of respectability. College graduates, civic leaders, accomplished professionals, and athletes graced the pages of *The Crisis*. The NAACP politics of respectability is also evident in the baby contests they organized as fundraisers for their fledging organization. The photographs of contest winners, such as the image displayed here, aptly met the nation's standards for middle class respectability by way of children who adorned clothes fashioned in a White aesthetic and adopted poised, calculated stances.[81] These images were used to counter prevailing racist stereotypes. They also demonstrate a strain of bourgeois professionalism and class that was expected of NAACP membership in the struggle for full inclusion into the social order of the United States.

Civil rights advocates in the early decades of the movement used images like these of children and posited notions of respectability to argue that African Americans *deserved* equal rights, not that they were wrongfully denied rights.[82] Du Bois and the NAACP in the 1920s and 1930s also targeted children and adolescents through the *Brownies' Book*, a publication specifically for youth that included scores of short stories and vignettes of Black youth who overcame the adversity of racism and became exemplars of the race.[83]

MR. PICKENS AND THE THREE PRIZE-WINNERS

THE INTRODUCER

THE PRESIDING OFFICER

group of women of which Mrs. F. E. Miller is chairman is arranging for the affair which will without doubt be a great success. All of the proceeds are to be given to the N. A. A. C. P. to aid it in carrying on its work. The scope of our activities is constantly increasing and the demands upon us call accordingly for a proportionately growing budget.

To all who have helped in meeting Mr. Peabody's offer and to Mr. Peabody himself for his great generosity the National Office of the N. A. A. C. P. extends its sincere thanks.

RESIDENTIAL SEGREGATION AGAIN

WHEN by a unanimous decision of the United States Supreme Court, Mr. Moorfield Storey won in 1917 for the N. A. A. C. P. the famous Louisville Segregation Case, *Buchanan vs. Warley*, 245 *U. S.* 78, which declared that enforced residential segregation by city ordinance was illegal, it was believed that this question had been settled for all time. So far as that particular method of segregation is concerned that belief was true but during recent years there have appeared various attempts to evade prohibition of enforced segregative activi-

Picture of a prize-winning family in the NAACP's *The Crisis*, April 1924. Courtesy of HathiTrust Digital Library.

Though the very pages of *The Crisis* outlined the hard-fought struggles to condemn and outlaw lynching, the portrayal of children very much akin to the White middle class captured a desire to replicate the social and cultural norms defined by Whites. The notions inherent to a class-based politics of respectability not only shaped the social and cultural mores of the larger freedom struggle but also ascribed a normative set of values that shaped what youth participation in the NAACP meant. Class and respectability-based norms continued to define and distinguish the NAACP from other civil rights organizations throughout the freedom struggle.

To be sure, class and regional influences often mitigated the potentially radical activity among students. Most of the students actively involved in the movement hailed from semi-urban or urban areas from families with a middle class or professional background, which was not representative of the African American population in the South. The NAACP and educators occupied a professional standing among the Black community, which afforded some privileges that surpassed those enjoyed by poor people of color, if any. This privileged a Northern and middle-class sensibility that constructed boundaries and limited participation. Urban and northern areas also afforded more opportunity for organization and political activity than others, particularly rural, southern, and poor Black communities. Given the exclusive nature of high school itself, those who attended high school were drawn from an economically mobile and affluent class simply because high schools were mostly placed in urban locations, which excluded the majority of the rural South. Moreover, attending high school translated into an economic loss for families as adolescents were removed from the workforce and placed in a classroom instead. By 1930, as the high school population grew precipitously, just 11 percent of Black teenagers were in high school and almost three hundred counties in fourteen states provided no high schools for Black students. By 1940 as one-half of the nation's adolescents enrolled in high school, only 20 percent of African Americans between the ages of fourteen and seventeen enrolled in high school but did not necessarily graduate.[84] The poor and rural South were not typically represented in the few scholars who attend a Black high school.

The politics of respectability and privileging a middle-class status placed firm boundaries around youth autonomy. As Rebecca de Schweinitz noted in her analysis of youth agency, the regulation of youth through a politics of respectability "turned the exercise of agency into a project of self-regulation, one that honored young people's quest for freedom and authenticity at the same time it channeled their behavior into a predetermined field of acceptable social conduct."[85] Attempts to shape youth behavior and temper autonomy through conformity to particular ideals and expectations fostered tension within the NAACP, which emerged as a point of contention since the first years of the Youth Division.

The organization of NAACP Youth Councils at Lincoln High School in Kansas City, Missouri, reveals how the issue of autonomy prompted deep-seated questions. In the Kansas City chapter, a question of autonomy arose between junior and senior branches when the president of the senior branch suggested the junior branches pay half-price for membership but give all of the proceeds to the senior branches. The executive director of the NAACP, Walter White, determined that the membership dues should not be funneled into the senior branch treasury.[86] To White, there was "no doubt that the junior branch organization should be a replica . . . of the senior branch." Still, he fully believed that the "success of the junior branch lies, to a large extent, in the autonomy of the junior branches as far as possible."[87] Situating the junior branches as a "replica" of elder branches reinforced a top-down governance structure while also acknowledging that, in theory, autonomy was critical to the mobilization of youth. Though the schism in Kansas City was by no means a major or even a national point of contention, it was indicative of an emerging tension in the association that grappled with the extent to which Youth Councils were expected to support the elder or more senior branches of the NAACP. The extent to which the youngest members of the association, adolescents, the same population whose "right to childhood" they sought to defend, were able to determine their own course of action was at stake. Such questions of autonomy would come to be an integral component of the politics of youth organization in the 1950s and 1960s.

The Southern Negro Youth Congress

The NAACP was not the only game in town, nor was it the only civil rights organization concerned with the organization of young people. Emerging from the Communist Party's efforts to organize in the South, SNYC originated in 1937 after the National Negro Congress created a youth division upon its inception in 1936. It began on the birthdate of Frederick Douglass, on February 12 in Richmond, Virginia, and during the Great Depression, which affected an estimated five million young people who were out of work and out of school.[88] SNYC presented an alternative, supplemental means to youth organization through the NAACP. Though different in their organizational ethos, SNYC and the NAACP shared the premise that young people not yet in college were instrumental to advancing the movement to eradicate racist policy.

Edward E. Strong, the son of a Baptist minister who took missionary trips throughout Texas and Arkansas, was critical to the development of SNYC. Strong took an early interest in Black history, culture, and current events. As a high school student, Strong organized the first NAACP Youth Council in Flint, Michigan. Mentored by John P. Davis—the radical lawyer, labor rights activist, and organizer of civil rights coalitions—Strong helped organize the first "International Negro Youth Congress." When the National Negro Congress met in Chicago in 1936, he was elected as the chair of the youth division, which later became SNYC. He became the organization's first executive secretary after helping organize the first SNYC conference.[89] Strong approached the position to improve the conditions faced by Black youth, noting, "life for Negro kids after ten is little else but hard labor, low pay and no chance for education and advancement."[90] As stated in their fourth annual conference, SNYC envisioned themselves as "a movement designed to help young people help themselves."[91]

Devoted specifically to the organization of youth, SNYC maintained more fluid membership parameters than the NAACP. Records from the 1940 SNYC conference in New Orleans reveal that ages of participants ranged from twelve to sixty-six, and the average age range was between seventeen and twenty-six years old.[92] SNYC organized youth members into a teenage club, for members aged fifteen to twenty, and a young adult association, for members aged twenty to thirty.[93] SNYC operationalized youth as a central organizing component, much like the NAACP Youth Councils, but they were less formal in forming age-based categorical distinctions.

SNYC embraced an organizational ethos that focused on coalition building through federations. They functioned with an advisory board and an executive board that met four times a year. There were officers and staff at the top that issued charters. SNYC organized at the local level, too, with a Community Council at each affiliated chapter. They focused on special interests sponsored by local social clubs, athletics, schools, churches, and fraternities.[94] An earlier version of the constitution outlined a base of "youth federations" chartered by the Congress Executive Committee that were open to organizations led by young people. SNYC also sought to work with organizations under adult leadership that were concerned with the welfare of youth. The youth federation structure was composed as a city federation, county federation, or a campus federation located on either a high school or college campus.[95] Though this version was not formerly adopted, the federated structure illustrates the coalition-building philosophy inherent to the organization. SNYC regularly sought to affiliate and coordinate with other organizations, notably the Communist-led Southern Conference for Human Welfare and the League of Young Southerners. This differed from the NAACP, who primarily sought to lead and organize local efforts on their own.

SNYC examined the "real and practical problems" common across the South and focused on "economic betterment and security and the exercise of the right to vote."[96] SNYC's constitution focused on addressing the right to vote, impartial justice in the courts, equal education, and "an awakened consciousness of the place and function of religion as a force in human relations."[97] In 1938 SNYC called for the establishment of "citizenship institutes" to study local conditions, election laws, and the basic constitutional guarantee of the right to vote.[98] SNYC focused on voting campaigns, but its teachers adopted comprehensive reform plans in other fields such as education, including curriculum development, that directly impacted youth and adolescents.

SNYC embraced an explicit commitment to organize adolescents and established programs in various venues to mobilize them. Following the protocol of local grassroots organizing, SNYC engaged high schools, college campuses with high school departments, and churches that served high school youth. SNYC chapters in Birmingham demonstrate the spectrum of venues they sought to host chapters, including Miles College, Rosedale High School, Hooper City High School, Bethel Baptist Church, and St. Luke Baptist Church.[99] When working at the high school level, SNYC focused on educational and recreational quality, health, and job training.[100]

Like the NAACP, SNYC organized annual youth conferences to provide information and the opportunities for engagement. These events provided the space for youth delegates to strategize around program objectives and to address questions of how to implement an expansive agenda that included issues of labor, education, criminalization of Black youth, religion, health, and cooperation with White youth. By 1939 SNYC hosted annual conferences in Richmond, Virginia; Chattanooga, Tennessee; and Birmingham, Alabama, which made it the largest youth organization that specifically targeted the South.[101] Such conferences exposed students to a deep critique of the United States and provided the strong intellectual foundation for a youth movement. For instance, Marxist historian Herbert Aptheker wanted to illustrate for young people at the 1939 conference the "precious political heritage" of Black youth. He outlined a history of Black political alliances with progressive and liberal parties, going back to Reconstruction, Populism, and the presidential candidacy of George Edwin Taylor on the National Liberty ticket, the first African American to run for the office. Aptheker retold this history to conference attendees to make visible the "contradiction with the stereotype that is told that the rulers today want you to believe."[102]

Part of SNYC development in the 1930s included collaboration with the NAACP. Strong wrote that the "activities and achievements of the NAACP Youth Councils have served as a beacon light to distressed Negro youth everywhere." SNYC sought to join with the NAACP and "people of all races and creed in the common struggle for the elementary rights of the American people."[103] SNYC provided reports on the annual youth sessions held at the larger NAACP conferences with favorable reviews, discussing the "highly successful" and "excellent work" of the organization's youth branch.[104] SNYC supported the NAACP's campaign for educational opportunity and the anti-lynching bill.[105] It also extended its "hand of friendship to the Annual Youth Conference of the NAACP" in 1940.[106] The NAACP sought, on occasion, partnership with SNYC. In 1939 Walter White reached out to Edward Strong, asking for his partnership in the formation of a temporary committee to support amendments to congressional legislation relating to federal aid for health. The NAACP also asked for help in supporting efforts to amend social security provisions. The National Committee worked on the Wagner Bill as well, meeting in Washington, D.C., to coordinate a delegation to work for passage of it.[107]

Though part of the same movement, SNYC diverged from the NAACP in significant ways. SNYC focused specifically on the South. They maintained an autonomous organization that was independent from the Youth Division of the National Negro Congress, the same entity that gave rise to SNYC, but remained closely affiliated with the Communist Party.[108] This institutionalized a degree of organizational autonomy that was not actualized in the NAACP. Whereas SNYC prioritized grassroots coalition building, the NAACP sought to lead initiatives they were involved with. Divergence in autonomy shaped how each organization conceptualized and organized youth as well. Whereas the NAACP sought dues-paying members, which in the 1930s translated into economic class distinctions, SNYC sought to work with a wide range of people that transcended typical class divisions. William

Richardson, the national chairman of the SNYC, wrote in 1938 that the organization was formed upon "the necessity of unifying the organizations which are working to better the conditions of our people."[109] According to one version of SNYC history, their association represented the "first attempt to gather together on a widely representative scale, young, southern Negroes from all walks of life—students, farm hands, sharecroppers, factory and mill workers, coal and ore miners, domestic workers, and young people from business and professional pursuits."[110] SNYC also prioritized recruitment among students and teachers at high schools and college students and college professors.[111] This included affiliation at the local level with clubs already established in high schools, civic organizations in local neighborhoods, the YMCA, trade unions, and colleges.[112]

The level of collaboration illustrated an important facet of coalition building that defined the nature of SNYC organization. When compared to the NAACP, SNYC was much more reflective of the Populist Front of the Communist and Socialist intellectual tradition.[113] A more concerted effort to reach a wider spectrum of youth not typically associated with a politics of respectability distinguished their efforts. SNYC was a collaborative organization whose members sought to align themselves with other organizations. SNYC defined itself in the second bulletin issued from Birmingham—the headquarters of the organizations after relocating from Richmond, Virginia—as a "federation of organizations in the South interested in and dealing with the problems of Negro youth," also noting that "federating existing youth-serving agencies are essential to the successful reaching of our goal."[114] As the executive secretary of SNYC, Edward Strong personally shaped this element of the organization. Strong traveled extensively across the American South, working with students, miners, sharecroppers, and farmers, and he adopted this collaborative approach to organizing. Young people in southern chapters formed coalitions with organizations from the YWCA to the NAACP, to high school art clubs to the American Federation of Labor and the Congress of Industrial Organizations.[115]

Attendance records from SNYC conferences suggest that the organization was successful in reaching a wide range of young people who cut across professional and economic class divisions. Students who attended the third annual conference in 1939 came from Tuskegee Institute and Alabama State Teachers College, but conference-goers were also teachers, farmers, students, church members, WPA members, miners, housewives, domestics, and beauticians.[116] Students who applied to SNYC Leadership Training Schools came from a wide range of backgrounds as well. Many were in college, but they also attracted teachers, tailors, carpenters, undertakers, and cashiers. Many belonged to local unions, such as local AFL or CIO chapters. Some were members of school newspapers, the NAACP, or the YWCA.[117]

SNYC coalition politics translated into flexible agendas that sought to meet the needs of local communities, which precluded any singularly definitive agenda, and was determined at the local level. The councils established in New Orleans in the late 1930s are indicative of a SNYC Agenda determined by the community where members organized a "cooperative enterprise" that included the People's Community Theatre, workers' educational classes, and an initiative to collect data on the Black community for potential action items. The SNYC chapter founded in Miami defined itself as an "educational organization having as its great aim the development of greater opportunities for a more useful life among Negro youth."[118] The SNYC chapter in Birmingham, Alabama, encouraged interested organizers to adopt agendas that focused on improving the economic status of members, increasing opportunities to exercise citizenship rights, extending educational opportunities, and building health and recreation programs.

While adopting a localized framework to facilitate grassroots organization, SNYC firmly connected to a transnational platform around issues of colonialism. The SNYC constitution, for instance, included a platform committed to "peaceful settlement of international differences."[119] As Edward Strong noted in his address, "Negro Youth and the Fight for Freedom and Opportunity": "American Negro young people hold deep affinities for youth in colonial and semi-colonial countries. Their problem and ours are inseparable; their exploiters and ours are identical. The surge of passion that flows from their every heart-beat for self-government, and the same true ring as the cry of Negro Youth in the Southland for the right to vote . . . to the youth untouchables everywhere, we extend our steel hand of comradeship."[120] Reflective of the broader Socialist and Communist movement, Strong's leadership of SNYC promised to move the youth association in divergent and sometimes radical ways. With young people centered in SNYC, a new agenda that challenged the very premise of segregation was unfolding.

The Youth Movement's Agenda

The youth agenda developed at the nexus of Black high school advocates, including teachers and local leaders, the NAACP, and SNYC. But it was first and foremost grounded in the critique of a system that denied Black adolescents protection afforded to Whites of the same age. Black youth organized for protection from law enforcement who vowed to protect and to serve, supposedly without racial biases. Throughout the first phases of civil rights youth work in the 1930s, students abused by White police officers often galvanized local communities around the work of civil rights organizations. In May 1936 police beat a seventeen-year-old student, a young woman, who attended Dunbar High School in Washington, D.C. The National Negro Congress (NNC) organized to demand justice and prosecution for the police responsible for the abuse. They worked with local clergy, the Elks, and other community organizations. NNC even organized a mock trial of the officers involved to generate attention around policy brutality.[121] Students in Houston organized to shape local policies by addressing automobile accidents that occurred in the vicinity of local Black public schools. In 1937 Youth Council members placed enough pressure on local officials to place traffic officers near the school, introducing a new level of basic safety. Youth Council members also sought the legal help of W. Jay Johnson, a White attorney affiliated with the NAACP, to defend a recent high school graduate who had been severely beaten by White police and then charged with disorderly conduct. The charges were dropped.[122] Students worked in myriad ways to defend and claim the very rights to childhood and adolescence that the state denied them.

Young people also challenged unjust practices that affected those who fell outside the categorization of adolescence. A SNYC chapter in Miami, Florida organized one of the largest demonstrations against bus driver brutality held prior to the 1950s and 1960s, when it issued a call to protest inhumane treatment by bus drivers. More than one thousand responded and marched in solidarity against the poor treatment of Black citizens, particularly women, at the hands of White drivers.[123] In 1940 the SNYC chapter in Jefferson County, Alabama organized a series of mass meetings after a White police officer shot and killed O'Dee Henderson, a twenty-four-year-old Black steel worker, after he experienced a confrontation with a White employee. Mass meetings called for the Alabama governor to appoint a special prosecutor, to demand federal charges, to financially support the victim's family, and to hold public hearings on numerous incidents of police brutality in the area.[124] By protesting the treatment of people beyond the recognized age of adolescence, young activists understood that the same system discriminated against elders and youth alike. The legal and political system built upon White supremacy recognized no age distinctions.

This critical consciousness informed the praxis of a youth movement that sought to gain the same categorical protection promised to Whites.

The organizational structures of the NAACP and SNYC created a basis for youth action that exposed and addressed the contradictions inherent to being young and Black in America. Despite creating a space for high school youth, civil rights organizations privileged issues facing college students. Having defined citizenship and voting as one of the most pressing issues of the movement, SNYC focused on youth aged twenty-one or older and therefore gravitated toward college students. The SNYC college program focused on improving facilities, academic freedom, and a "world beyond campus," which included combatting stereotypes that distorted the Black experience and examining problems of national and international interests. It called for petitions, demonstrations, and resolutions in the struggle for "Negro freedom."[125] Mobilizing for the 1940 election, SNYC embarked upon one its most ambitious campaigns, seeking to register ten thousand or more young Black voters for the election.[126]

The bold scope of SNYC voter registration campaigns served as an important predecessor to the voter registration drives led by student activists of the 1960s. At the same time, it also stymied the growth of adolescents as autonomous change agents. Since citizenship was largely defined through participation at the ballot box, young people under the age of twenty-one were not viewed as full citizens. They were seen as allies to those of voting age but did not quite measure up to the citizenship ideal held by movement elders. This in many ways precluded a full investment in the development of youth as independent actors in a larger freedom struggle.

Since high school youth were too young to vote, their self-directed efforts were geared toward a more immediate environment. This meant that their schools and the larger field of education were some of the more pressing issues youth delegates addressed. Organizing to address issues in education also inspired a broader coalition with sympathetic teachers, administrators, and other education advocates. To aid in this effort, the Educational Opportunities committee of SNYC adopted a resolution to sponsor Parent-Teacher Associations, to support legislation aimed at equal educational opportunity, and to shape public opinion to support educational equality.[127] In subsequent years, youth in SNYC continued to focus on education. The first item on the agenda at the 1937 National Youth Program, for instance, was "fighting for educational opportunities" during American Education Week, November 9 to 15, 1936. The group sponsored an item, "Cooperation in the observance of the National Negro History Week" in

February 1937. Charles Hamilton Houston, the Dean of Howard University Law School and architect of the NAACP legal campaign to overturn segregation, served as an advisor to the youth planning committee around education.[128] Such mentorship promised that SNYC members were exposed to critical, radical thinking and imbued with the knowledge and skills to become effective change agents.

Young people and the civil rights organizations during the 1930s offered a robust education reform initiative that aligned with efforts in the NAACP that matched the aspirations of many Black parents and students. This included desegregation, but it was only one part of a larger movement for quality public education. SNYC, for instance, sought to support "educational facilities commensurate with the best established American standards."[129] In 1939 SNYC called to extend educational opportunities through securing passage of the Thomas-Barrabee bill for federal education aid. They also supported the equalization of teachers' salaries and more educational facilities on Black school campuses.[130] Resolutions on education continued to demand federal education aid and higher appropriations for Black education specifically. They sought to work with other groups who shared their goals as well.[131] Equalization and increased resource allocation, not integration, was a defining goal during the 1930s.

SNYC also worked with other organizations to draw attention to the educational plight of Black youth in the South. For example, in collaboration with the 6th SNYC conference, Mrs. G. T. Hamilton, executive secretary of the Atlanta Urban League, spoke of the educational inequities in Atlanta. She brought up the fact that only 17 percent of funds were spent on the improvement of Black schools, though Black students made up 37 percent of the total school population. She highlighted concerns that most elementary and junior high school students in the city attended school for only three and one-half hours a day because of double sessions. She called for 350 more teachers and 390 additional classrooms. She also noted there was not a single kindergarten, nor a single gymnasium, and the Black high school accommodated 4,200 students in school facilities that were built to house 1,500.[132] SNYC was developing a collective platform to articulate injustices that united African Americans across the South.

The youth movement addressed the deeper ideological issues that pervaded schools during the Jim Crow era. Acting in concert with the sentiments of the NAACP and SNYC, as well as Herbert Aptheker and other critical academics, youth publicly denounced the racist curriculum underpinned with White supremacy to which they were exposed in school. Young people also engaged in efforts to revise the curriculum.

One of the most notable campaigns of the era was a concerted drive to revise the history curriculum. The NAACP youth chapters surveyed history textbooks used in local schools across the nation in order to identify and eradicate racist statements and assumptions during the late 1930s. In the 1938 annual conference of the NAACP, Dr. Charles Edward Russell, one of the founders of the association and an avid Socialist, blamed overtly biased textbooks on the plight of African Americans in his address "Mistreatment of the Negro in Public School Textbooks." "Why is it you find in the North today the doors of opportunity slammed in your faces; and why do you find prejudice still rampant?" Russell mused. "This happens because year after year in these textbooks in public schools millions of young people imbibe this impression about colored people."[133] Young people responded and launched a national textbook survey during the 1938–1939 school year with the objectives to erase all racist textbooks from the classroom. The convention organized the Committee on Textbooks & Current Literature, and Russell served as the national chair. William Pickens, a southern organizer for the NAACP from South Carolina, served as the vice-chairman and was joined by national NAACP dignitaries, including Charles Hamilton Houston, Arthur Spingarn, and Walter White.[134] The committee examined history textbooks in local schools to examine the misrepresentation of African Americans through "the omission and distortion of facts, particularly during Slavery and Reconstruction."[135] They sought to compile findings and send reports to the local Senior branch, the Board of Education, and the national NAACP office. They circulated and published their findings, called mass meetings with available branches of the NAACP and the community at large, and reached out to offending textbook publishers and the local press, besides speaking at churches, clubs, and the radio, wherever possible.[136] NAACP youth also published their research in *The Crisis*. Some engaged decision-makers at school board meetings. Students in Nashville, Tennessee, for instance, actively evaluated the curriculum and attempted to acquire racially appropriate and accurate texts.[137]

The campaign to revise the curriculum coincided with Black teachers who sought to eradicate the racist underpinnings of popular school textbooks. Southern teacher associations combatted this ignorance directly. The teachers' association in North Carolina formally opposed the use of textbooks written from a pro-Confederacy vantage point.[138] Other Black teacher associations actively sought to incorporate Black history and culture into the curriculum by emulating the work of Carter G. Woodson and incorporating into classrooms the literature published through his organization, the Association for the Study of Negro Life and History.[139] A Findings Committee of National Association of Teachers in Colored Schools released a report in 1925, in which they wrote, "We earnestly recommend the increased study of Negro History in our schools." The teacher's association in North Carolina wrote in 1928 to the state department of education "to call again to your attention the rather general desire among the Negro school people of the state that there shall be courses in Negro Life and History."[140] Other southern states followed a similar pattern. "If the South wishes to avoid amalgamation of the races, to maintain separate races, it can profitably stock the shelves of its public schools with books designed to bring respect to the Negro," the *Mississippi Educational Advance* published in 1940, adding that "the wealth of contributions from individuals makes rich the society which is democratic."[141] W. A. Walters, faculty in the Department of Social Sciences at Rust College in Mississippi, wrote to his peers at the high school and college, "We educators should start a campaign to have . . . a course in Negro History as a partial requirement for graduation."[142]

A common narrative focuses on the legal struggle to desegregate schools, often traced to the 1930s. Though the movement to desegregate graduate and professional schools set an important precedent in the larger NAACP desegregation strategy, it has at times overshadowed the work of youth people and alternative work by the NAACP that sought to equalize opportunities within Black schools during the 1920s and 1930s. For young people in the South, these decisions opened new doors of possibility. As SNYC organizers stated at the third annual youth conference, "What new horizons for winning complete equality in educational opportunities does this decision offer to Southern Negro Youth?"[143] The forms of activism evident in the 1930s put forth notions that schools should be desegregated and segregation should be eradicated on any and all observable fronts. Yet desegregation was but one means to achieve a quality education. The role of NAACP Youth Councils and SNYC as early as the 1930s indicate that involved actors thought that education should include participatory notions of citizenship based on the needs and aspirations of Black youth, not desegregation alone.

Within this larger context and with the implicit support offered through Black high schools, students demonstrated a willingness to challenge structural and ideological discrimination and policy. Such resistance is evident in the student voice at Booker T. Washington High School in Columbia, South Carolina, where students published essays debating the nature of good citizenship. "The minds of all people are corrupt with prejudice," students editorialized in the student newspaper *The Comet*, "If we rid ourselves of prejudice, we will have made a great step toward building a noble character."[144] In the same medium, students recounted in detail the events of Negro History Week. Robbie Peguese, class of 1939, spoke for the student body when he noted that "we know that the Booker Washington pupil is not asleep to [their] race situation we feel that [they] are by no means an exception to the youth of the nation which will not be satisfied with the complacent attitude but must conquer the obstacles of race prejudice in their paths."[145] Likely harmless to a White supervisor who may have glanced at the student newspaper, words of dismantling prejudice, tackling the "race situation," and fighting complacency established the spirit of resistance for future decades. Such reflections demonstrated a degree of political efficacy that also defined the youth movement.

Addressing areas of educational access and quality generated a very visible and quantifiable means to contest the blatant discrepancy between the legally defensible rights of children and adolescence and lived experiences of Black youth. The struggle to improve the immediate conditions of adolescents in schools inspired a heightened consciousness among Black youth and their elders who advocated for quality education. It also generated an education-based coalition that served as a basis for the civil rights–based education reform initiatives of subsequent decades.

· · · · · ·

At the outbreak of the Second World War, high school advocates, SNYC, and the NAACP had established the foundations for a youth movement. Youth participation anticipated developments in the freedom struggles of subsequent decades in the fields of voter registration and education, among others. Young people also provided new energy to the movement, which movement leaders and elders saw as an opportunity to advance the cause of a larger movement for equality and the eradication of *de jure* segregation. Youth organizers established a presence in the South, which proffered a vision for a new kind of youth. In selecting cities to mobilize like Birmingham, which SNYC saw as "the cradle of a revising faith in the Negro people's destiny in the South," youth organizers created the foundation for a movement that continued to grow over the next three decades.[146] Cities like Birmingham would come to define the youth movement and demonstrate the potential of politically active high school youth.

The NAACP and SNYC, which built upon the work of high school teachers, administrators, and local education advocates, laid an important foundation for a youth movement. The NAACP followed more closely the demarcation of adolescence and created distinct junior councils to reach middle and high school students. On the other hand, SNYC reached out to and included high school-aged youth in their organizations, but they were organized alongside and viewed as equal to college students. The inconsistencies marred a clear distinction between high school and college youth, which in effect blur our historical understandings and erroneously shape notions that youth activism was a primarily college student undertaking.

Civil rights organizers and Black teachers also shared the assumption that youth, especially high school students, would fall under the guidance of adults. Following modern conceptions of youth that were defined from the top-down, educators, civic leaders, and movement elders defined any agenda regarding youth and youth organization. An implicit assumption in the NAACP's top-down organizing was the notion that young people were to be guided and led, or, in other words, to be acted upon. The NAACP consistently categorized young people as passive actors and the beneficiaries of adult educators and organizers' work as a form of protection. The objectives of the Junior Divisions, the predecessor to the Youth Councils, stated that young people should primarily learn the work of the NAACP and serve as ushers at meetings and "give entertainments" to the older members. These expectations are demonstrative of the passive position of young people in the earliest phases of youth organization.[147] In the objectives of the organization sent out in 1933, Youth Council members were instructed to "study, discuss, secure the facts" and to "UNDERSTAND BEFORE YOU ACT." The second objective was to "support the national program and the specific issues each year."[148] The constitution eventually adopted for Youth Councils was even more explicit. It stated, "The Youth Council shall be a constituent and subordinate unit of the Association . . . subject to the general authority and jurisdiction of the Board of Directors of the Association."[149] As Juanita Jackson told her young audience during the first youth conference, she was excited about the number of youth in attendance, specifically "their position and their possibilities, and in what they can do for our association."[150] She went on to tell them: "You have much that we need. We need your idealism, your enthusiasm . . . we need your faith in the possibility." She stressed "intense devotion and loyalty to the cause, and where you can find a greater cause than that of the [NAACP]."[151] She also extended "an opportunity to build a national youth movement."[152] Such sentiment demonstrates a remarkable faith in young people yet implicit in it is the notion of youth used for a larger cause.

Though SNYC was more radical in its message and affiliation with a labor movement, it adopted a paternalistic ideology as well. Youth divisions were subject to the review of adult supervision. SNYC was "designed to enlist the cooperation of adults with the efforts of young people to build a better community."[153] Initial ideas of youth federations were subject to the National Executive Committee. An earlier draft of the constitution created an adult advisory board, which was to be "consulted on all questions of policy" and the chairman of such a board would have a full vote on both the Executive Committee and National Council.[154] Moreover, by focusing on voter registration SNYC privileged an older age designation that encompassed college and college-age students. Youth, in other words, were not fully engaged as autonomous or independent change agents if active citizenship was defined chiefly through voting. Categorically denied the right to vote, civil rights organizations and movement elders fell short in seeing adolescents with the same revolutionary potential they saw in youth who were voting age.

Youth mobilization was still decades from the direct-action protest of the classic phase of the movement. Yet the potential of a more direct assault by youth could be discerned, too. Edward Strong, leader of the SNYC, glimpsed this vision. By the close of the 1930s he noted that "the American Youth Movement has gone forward apace." Looking out upon the landscape of the 1930s, Strong saw in existence the American Student Union, the American Youth Congress, the NAACP Youth Councils, Christian Youth Building a New World, and other youth organizations including his own SNYC that helped define the contours of the organizational landscape in the waning years of the 1930s. Strong saw "250,000 Southern youth [who] participated in the most momentous youth development that the South has ever seen." He went on to note that the movement of his time stood "as the embodiment of the hopes of Southern youth." From his vantage point, a youth movement was, indeed, rising before him, ready to usher in the next decade of the struggle.[155]

2 Behold the Land

The Southern High School Youth Movement during and after the Second World War, 1940–1950

· ·

As a high school member of the Southern Negro Youth Congress (SNYC), Leroy Aiken of the small town of Moncks Corner in Berkeley County, South Carolina, was on the front lines of a freedom struggle that intensified during and after the Second World War. After SNYC's annual conference in Columbia, South Carolina, in October of 1946, Aiken helped organize two SNYC chapters in addition to the club he was already a member of in Berkeley County. As a high school student, Aiken was attuned to nuance in local education matters that held serious significance. As the "Double V" campaign unfolded—a crusade spurred to eradicate fascism at home and abroad—and Black war veterans trickled home, Aiken deployed a keen local perspective to identify issues that would, in time, inspire a movement. "For the first time in the history of little Moncks Corner, Negro schoolchildren are riding to school in school buses," he wrote to SNYC organizer and leader Louis Burnham in 1946. "I think it is the only city in the state where Negro children are riding to school in buses."[1] Aiken was prescient in remarking on the significance of the school bus during the era of Jim Crow. Riding a bus to a Black school in South Carolina was indeed historic. Such accommodations for Black students were rare. Just three years later, Rev. Joseph DeLaine would file a lawsuit for students in nearby Clarendon County for a bus for Black students—his case eventually became part of the *Brown v. Board of Education* (1954) decision.[2]

Aiken personified the potential of high school activists during the 1940s. He struck out on his own to participate in civic life, building on the progressive tenets of the curriculum of Black high schools. He attended civil rights conferences organized for youth, which at the time encompassed those from high school age to college age. Aiken helped organize a leadership training institute with SNYC, where students learned about the freedom struggle and how to participate in it. He was also an editor for one of the first Black student newspapers in his area, *The Berkeley Wildcat*, from Berkeley Training High School. Later, when he transferred to Booker T.

Washington High School in Columbia, he was on staff for the *Washingtonian* yearbook and the student newspaper, *The Comet*. He was also a member of the "Progressive Boys," a group committed to "discussions to become well-rounded citizens and leaders of tomorrow."[3]

At the same time, Aiken continued to learn from and follow the examples of movement elders. In addition to the "second curriculum" in which he was immersed, Aiken was introduced to activist networks and coalitions through SNYC. He worked with the local Progressive Club, which organized for the school bus, encouraged the Black vote, and supported local African Americans for the local school board. He worked and corresponded with Modjeska Simkins, a veteran activist in South Carolina, and John McCray, founder of the Progressive Democratic Party in the state. While in high school, he also apprenticed with McCray's paper, *The Lighthouse and Informer*, a progressive publication in South Carolina.[4] Deeply engaged in a Black high school, immersed in local education politics, and learning the dynamics of resistance through the local community, Aiken was involved in the movement and challenged the existence of Jim Crow as a young activist in collaboration with his elders who were part of the same struggle.

Aiken was emblematic of the new high school activist of the 1940s. As one student in an exploding student population that defined the postwar boom, Aiken and his cohort demonstrated how the Black high school held the latent potential to serve as a critical site in a burgeoning freedom movement. As an institution designed to protect and prepare youth, and as more and more students demanded access, the historically Black high school grew in importance as an integral space in the lives of youth during and after the Second World War. In particular, the historically Black high school held the potential for widespread political organizing as parents demanded greater access to school and the protections and benefits it afforded. By 1940, 50.8 percent of the country's seventeen-year-olds were high school graduates, marking the first time in American history that half of the school-age population completed secondary education.[5] But Black high schools remained drastically under-resourced when compared to White high schools. By 1940 just over 20 percent of African Americans between the ages of fourteen and seventeen enrolled in high school. In fact, in Mississippi still only 5 percent of children attended high school by 1940.[6] Yet a growing wartime demand and rising attendance rates across the South led to overcrowded conditions that laid bare the unseemly provisions for secondary education. The Black high school student population rose by 124 percent in Alabama, 123 percent in Mississippi, 113 percent in Georgia,

69 percent in South Carolina, and 58 percent in Virginia from the 1940s to the early 1950s.[7]

Wartime rhetoric politicized small though critical parts on an explosive enrollment in historically Black high schools in the South. An influx of Black families, which included war veterans, placed a growing number of Black families in direct conflict with White powerbrokers at a time when the nation was fully invested in notions of democracy and eradicating tyranny.[8] The "Double V" campaign heightened awareness of the contradiction posed by racial segregation in the land of the free. The Black high school was thus poised to be a dynamic site during and after the Second World War. With a heightened cognizance of the glaring contradictions that defined life in Dixie, the Black high school was in many ways a powder keg due to gross racial disparities, growing demands for school access, and a shifting wartime context when compared to previous generations.

Student protest did indeed lead to explosive results in the postwar period across the South. In Lumberton, North Carolina, in September 1946, African American students in the local NAACP Youth Council organized a boycott of the small town's two public Black schools—Redstone Academy and Thompson Institute—that lasted two weeks. Student strikers and the young adults who led the Youth Council demanded equitable facilities. Their strike in Lumberton gained national attention and even sympathy from the *Raleigh News and Observer* and the leading Black newspaper, the *Pittsburgh Courier*, who investigated the gross educational disparities on display in Lumberton. Given the role of the NAACP Youth Council, Ruby Hurley, the national secretary for the association's youth chapters, visited Lumberton and recommended legal action. The NAACP decided to take up the students' cause, filing suit in state and federal courts, prompting state officials to allocate additional funding for new school facilities.[9]

The following year, James Carr, a plant manager at the Pentagon and father to Marguerite, enrolled his daughter in the overcrowded and segregated Browne Junior High School in Washington, D.C. The school was built to accommodate approximately nine hundred students, yet in the spring of 1947 over seventeen hundred students enrolled. Carr attempted to enroll Marguerite in the more spacious and accommodating Eliot Junior High School. Forthrightly denied, Carr filed suit on behalf of his daughter the following year in 1948, *Carr v. Corning*.[10] In an indication of a rising student voice, Marguerite Carr made the decision herself and only then did her father move forward with the lawsuit.[11] The suit to desegregate—as opposed to equalize schools—garnered grassroots support from across the community.[12]

When the superintendent rejected the application, the case gained momentum and parents and students at Browne decided to strike.[13] The *Carr* case, which was but one of nearly one dozen cases filed in the late 1940s to desegregate historically Black elementary and high schools, started with young girls and grassroots community support.[14] Grabbing headlines and extensive coverage from the leading Black press like the *Pittsburgh Courier*, the *Afro-American*, and the *Chicago Defender*, these cases placed pressure on the NAACP to take up the mantle of desegregating the entire public school system, not just college or graduate school. Students like Marguerite Carr and the grassroots networks that supported them transformed historically Black high schools into politicized sites through which to renegotiate the rights, protections, and citizenship of Black students and their families during the 1940s.

The youth movement of the 1940s illustrates the affinity between high schools, the NAACP, and SNYC during the postwar freedom struggle. War veterans, Black educators, and civil rights organizations politicized Black high schools and youth. They applied wartime rhetoric to the improvement of Black high schools and viewed young people as allies in a burgeoning movement to eradicate the vestiges of White supremacy and fascism at home. This movement inculcated young people with the critical consciousness and the educative tools to lead a movement but fell often short in amplifying that voice. This created a foundation for organizing that generated an infrastructure for a mobilized youth movement defined by its own terms and tensions.

Politicizing the Southern Black High School through Protest and the Courts

The high school emerged as an integral incubator of activism during and immediately after the Second World War. For war veterans, the conflict laid bare the paradox of fighting fascism abroad while their hometowns remained violently segregated. Those who returned became catalysts in galvanizing local movements connected to a larger freedom struggle. War veterans reinvigorated chapters of the NAACP, bolstered the ranks of registered voters, and compelled their neighbors to challenge Jim Crow.[15] Black high schools became sites of political contestation as well, though less well known. In notable instances, political consciousness inspired by the war dramatically transformed Black high schools into active sites of resistance and grassroots mobilization.

John Wrighten, a military veteran of the Second World War, enrolled at the Avery Normal Institute in Charleston, South Carolina, in his early twenties. Like many returning veterans, he wanted to complete high school after his discharge in order to pursue a degree in higher education. Wrighten enrolled in a course offered by Ms. Julia Brogden, entitled "Problems in Democracy," in which she guided her class in examining segregation policies in a local context. After completing courses through Avery, Wrighten led a local chapter of the NAACP Youth Council and encouraged students at the historic school who were interested in pursuing advanced degrees to apply to all-White colleges in 1944. Students preparing to graduate specifically wanted to attend the local and all-White College of Charleston as opposed to moving to Orangeburg, which was over seventy miles away, to study at the all-Black South Carolina State College. They argued that as a publicly supported institution, the College of Charleston should be open to all students. The state offered scholarships to attend South Carolina State College in an act of appeasement, but they refused to desegregate the school. Wrighten maintained connections with the NAACP Youth Council chapter to keep pressure on school officials to desegregate colleges and universities in the Palmetto State. Three years later, he sued the state of South Carolina for admission to its all-White law school at the University of South Carolina. Though the state ultimately rejected his application, Wrighten paved the way for a new law school for African Americans at South Carolina State College and established the groundwork for litigation that dismantled legal barriers to education across the state.[16]

Though they risked their lives to end fascism abroad, Wrighten and other African American soldiers who served were, at home, refused the hard-fought freedom earned during the war. Like many Black war veterans who returned to a segregated South policed by violence and racism, Wrighten committed himself to the freedom struggle. Wrighten enrolled in the Avery Normal Institute to take adult education courses. It was a logical site to contest the existing order. Founded by local Black Charlestonians in 1865 with support from the American Missionary Association, Avery was a premier institution that instilled a critical liberal arts curriculum to prepare its students for college and professional employment. Before Wrighten, it graduated distinguished and influential civil rights organizers, including Septima P. Clark.[17] As schools like Avery existed across the South since Reconstruction, the potential for student and educational activism was not limited to southern cities with a historically Black college.

Two years after John Wrighten's NAACP work in Charleston, another re-turning war veteran, Elport Chess, set out to complete his education by en-rolling at Lanier High School in Jackson, Mississippi. On his way to school in November 1946, Chess refused to give up his seat to a White passenger when prompted by the driver. City police physically assaulted Chess, removed him from the bus, and arrested him. It was yet another incident in a long pat-tern of police brutality. Two other war veterans, Hargo Barbour and Leon-ard Lucas, were also completing high school at Lanier and decided to take action. They and other students consulted Mr. M. J. Lyells, a social studies teacher at Lanier and an NAACP member, who counseled the students. Under his clandestine guidance and in solidarity with Chess, Barbour and Lucas organized a boycott of the bus that took students to Lanier. They gar-nered the support of local Black churches and the Dotty and Deluxe Cab Companies, who offered the use of their cars for the same price as bus fare. News of the boycott, spread by word of mouth, galvanized support. The boy-cott lasted for several weeks until protesters were assured the offending driver would be dismissed and the bus route remained designated for Black patrons.[18]

Returning war veterans who enrolled in high school to complete their degree after the war provided a catalyst that demonstrated the latent po-tential of high school activism. Coming directly from the front lines of a war carried out to annihilate fascism, war veterans like John Wrighten, Elport Chess, Hargo Barbour, and Leonard Lucas challenged Jim Crow by inspiring local movements while they enrolled in high school.[19] By engag-ing in direct-action nonviolent protests, war veterans catapulted these in-stitutions into the front lines of a nascent civil rights movement. Such instances were exceptional since these veterans were well beyond the age of adolescence. But the local movements they inspired never secured a place for Black high schools in movement historiography as a site of resis-tance that complemented the integral work of Black churches in commu-nity organization. Yet these moments of direct-action protest led by war veterans in high school illuminate a foundation of protest at the sec-ondary level. The role of educators was critical in both instances, for in-stance. Ms. Julia Bogden instilled a political consciousness among her students at the Avery Normal Institute in Charleston, South Carolina, that reflected the critical education many Black educators received as postsec-ondary graduates. Mr. M. J. Lyells similarly reflected a critical influence that teachers exerted over their students in Jackson, Mississippi. Mr. Lyells also demonstrates the affiliation some teachers maintained with the

NAACP.[20] Both of the secondary institutions, the Avery Normal Institute and Lanier High School, were highly regarded institutions and commanded the respect—and political support—of the Black community. Moreover, the NAACP was affiliated through either Youth Councils or supporting protests that emerged from these high schools. The war demonstrated that no more than a spark was needed to launch a movement from a Black high school to directly challenge Jim Crow.

A select cadre of teachers and NAACP organizers further politicized the Black high school. Taking up the issue of equal pay for equal work, Black educators were the frontrunners of the movement during the 1940s.[21] Primed by the principles of Progressivism of the previous decades, their foray into politics contextualized the ephemeral direct-action protests of war veterans. Organized into vast, statewide professional associations since the turn of the century, Black southern teachers were positioned to organize for equality, albeit in a less confrontational manner than war veterans. Their work intersected with the NAACP equalization campaign, which provided an opportunity to directly challenge educational inequality. Demanding salary equalization within a southern Black context became a platform of the burgeoning civil rights movement as it pressured southern states to live up to and thereby challenge the premise of *Plessy v. Ferguson*'s (1896) "separate but equal" doctrine. As upstanding professionals and recognized community leaders acting within the larger context of teacher organization and progressive pedagogy, Black educators fueled the momentum of the civil rights movement by visibly and directly confronting economic discrimination. As a result, teachers became important actors of the movement throughout the Second World War until the politics surrounding the *Brown v. Board of Education* (1954) decision stymied their organizational capacity.[22]

Charles H. Thompson, the influential educator and editor of the progressive *Journal of Negro Education*, generated critical awareness of the equalization campaign undertaken in Maryland in the 1930s, where racial discrimination was legally codified in teacher salary policy.[23] The legal campaign to equalize salaries gained regional prominence when Aline Black, a science teacher in Virginia, sued the school board of Norfolk to pay equal salaries to Black and White educators and inspired a regional blueprint for activism. By 1948 cases were filed in every southern state except North Carolina, which enacted voluntary salary equalization.[24] Teachers in Mississippi, the furthest state from dismantling structural discrimination, joined the struggle to equalize salaries in hostile southern spaces. A. L. Johnson, president of the Mississippi Association of Teachers in Colored Schools, wrote in January of 1948 that "now is the time for us to begin immediate aggressive action." They began to challenge structural inequalities including shorter school terms, a lack of transportation and equipment, and poor building facilities.[25] Mississippi educators and other NAACP members met and invited Thurgood Marshall to file an equalization suit. Gladys Noel Bates, a science teacher at Smith Robertson Junior High School and a card-carrying member of the NAACP, stepped forward to initiate the lawsuit that prodded the Mississippi state legislature to address teacher salary discrepancies.[26] Politicized Black teachers who addressed disparaging salary differentials followed the trajectory of a longer history of professional teacher association organization across the South and clearly demonstrated that teachers were willing and able to engage in civil rights struggles.[27]

The movement toward higher salaries was about far more than a higher salary. Black teachers moved beyond a singular commitment in higher wages and connected their demand for equal salaries to systemic issues that plagued Black schools, as well as the larger system of Jim Crow. Black teachers conceptualized their demands for higher salaries and a greater degree of professionalism as part of a larger struggle. It also cemented an affinity between southern Black teacher associations and the NAACP.[28]

Litigation was dangerous work, and educators knew it. In Mississippi, teachers held a clandestine meeting at the Masonic Lodge in the capital city of Jackson to meet with local NAACP members and Thurgood Marshall to discuss the possibility of filing an equalization suit.[29] Marshall informed teachers in Jackson, as he did in every case, that the community had to raise $5000, which they did through a "welfare fund." Gladys Noel Bates later recalled, "when asked by their superintendents what this fund was for, the rehearsed reply was that it was for illness, deaths, and other needs of teachers."[30] Part of the "welfare fund," however, was actually used to assist Bates after school district officials did not renew her contract in response to her participation in the lawsuit. The state also fired her husband, John, in retaliation.[31] Their fate followed the pattern experienced by other Black educators who stepped forward to challenge the unequal distribution of educational resources. It was a repressive precedent established in 1939 when the school district in Norfolk, Virginia, refused to extend the contract of Aline Black.[32] White school officials made the message clear that open and public endorsement of the civil rights movement would not be tolerated.

The U.S. Court of Appeals ultimately ruled in *Alston v. Norfolk* (1940) that Black educators were entitled to equal pay, which laid the legal foundation for equalizing resources across secondary institutions.[33] Yet this significant milestone demonstrated the limitations of teacher activism. School districts fired any Black teacher who stepped forward to challenge discriminatory pay scales. Dismissal and displacement were particularly harrowing experiences for Black educators at a personal level. To be fired from a job for which professionals were trained and fully vested imperiled the essential livelihood of a vibrant professional class. Though Black teachers were on the front lines of a growing movement that sought to eradicate the vestiges of *de jure* segregation in the 1940s, the vast majority of Black teachers who were not supported by welfare funds could not afford to remain on the front lines and instead engaged in more subtle forms of intellectual and pedagogical forms of activism. Their "fugitive pedagogy" continued in myriad ways. The fact that this work in the classroom was less visible contributed to the prevailing though erroneous thesis that Black teachers were not active in the civil rights movement.

As Black teachers across the South organized and collaborated with the NAACP for equal salaries, the commitment of civic leaders and local education advocates to improve investment in secondary education blazed another path that politicized the space of the southern Black high school. To many Black families, the rapid growth of student enrollment during the war demanded greater investment in schools, yet the state often responded with double sessions or other solutions that ultimately detracted from the schooling experiences of Black students.[34] In 1943 Jessie Lola Cade wrote to her father, John Cade, the university dean at Southern University, that two students had been added to her classroom in Minden, Louisiana, bringing the total number to sixty-five students. "A dozen of them are seated around the wall of the rooms in chairs like those metal ones in the music studio," she wrote. "If any more show up I guess they'll have to sit in the windows."[35]

Local community leaders took up the task of pressing White school boards to address rising enrollment during and after the war. While teachers participated in a legal campaign for equal salaries, education advocates in the local community pushed school districts to support the growing student body through new facilities. The case in Prince Edward County, Virginia, is illustrative of how community members demanded greater facilities for their children. Vernon Johns, a pastor and fiery civil rights advocate who utilized confrontational strategies to advocate for full equality, led local delegations to advocate for change. In 1944 Johns protested to the school board about "discarded" and overcrowded school buses. He and the delegation requested the superintendent investigate the situation. The board approved another bus to transport Black students at the next meeting.[36]

After Rev. Johns left to pastor the congregation at Dexter Avenue Baptist Church, just prior to Dr. Martin Luther King Jr., a delegation led by Dr. Miller, Willie Redd, and Fred Reid became a regular fixture of school board meetings to pressure the district to better meet the needs of their children. They approached the board about overcrowded conditions at Moton High School during the war. They asked for updates, suggested plots of land to survey, and shared insights into the type of school they desired. The school board publicly committed to providing vocational training and the necessary facilities in 1945, stating the school should meet the "needs for the colored people, and be guided by it."[37] The delegation intensified its pressure to build the new facilities. But the board in Prince Edward County only committed $50,000, when the cost of a new school would be $400,000. This forced the community to raise the money, which was supported by historical precedent. Southern districts like Prince Edward County long applied for and received funding for vocational education from White philanthropists like Rosenwald, Peabody, and the General Education Board. It was funding they often received, and White school boards often incorporated this into funding allocations and projections. The board stalled in other ways for the next couple of years and delayed substantive action toward building a new school for four years. Instead of a new school, the board followed through on its resolution and built three additional buildings on the current Moton campus.[38]

It was a disappointing resolution for the delegation and the community Moton served. Instead of building a new facility, the board and district opted to construct "tar paper shacks" to house the over 120 students who pushed R. R. Moton High School beyond its capacity. To add further insult to educational injury, the district built a new White high school, which they saw as an "immediate need," and approved the plan without debate at a cost of over $500,000.[39]

Rev. L. F. Griffin, a student of Rev. Vernon Johns, returned to pastor First Baptist Church in 1948. He maintained affiliation with the NAACP and local organizations, including the Black Parent Teacher Association, and took up the cause for school improvement. The delegation continued to petition the board to build a new school. Hat in hand, they went before the board to petition for a new school location, to advocate for new plans for a school that equaled the newly erected White school, and authored applications for loans since the board was unwilling to raise the money. The board stalled again, reminding Rev. Griffin's delegation of the new additions. While they were considering new sites, the board was careful to note that it would take a considerable amount of time until "finances are arranged." The board continued the same tactics of delay for over a year.[40]

Black delegations did not immediately secure their objective of a new school, and they were regularly burdened by the delaying tactics of recalcitrant White school boards. But in the process teachers and civic leaders across the South tilled the soil of a youth movement. By litigating for equal salaries and petitioning boards for better facilities, Black teachers, civic leaders, and returning war veterans transformed historically Black high schools into legitimate political spaces where demands could be made. These demands held the potential to grow into movements that moved beyond the local district. Moreover, the limitations of teacher and local leaders' activism ultimately necessitated a space for high school activism. But before youth joined the front lines of the movement, civil rights organizations reinvigorated their approach to youth organizing during and after the war.

Feigned Militancy: SNYC and NAACP Youth Organization during the War

The role of civil rights organizations further facilitated the emergence of a youth movement. Without the constraints of working for or with White school boards, civil rights organizations were free to facilitate youth activism directly. The war provided a platform to build upon their organization during the previous decade. As teachers and education advocates politicized the profession of teaching and the high school itself, SNYC and the NAACP focused directly on organizing students and youth. The Second World War invigorated their efforts and provided the NAACP and SNYC with a larger stage to reach their goals. Continuing the push for increased membership of previous decades, the NAACP doubled down on efforts to enroll younger members into its ranks. They conducted a massive campaign during the war to increase enrollment, asking for fifteen thousand members. It was during the war that the NAACP reported its single largest chapter in the history of Youth Councils since 1922. Ella Baker organized a chapter of over five hundred members in Savannah, Georgia, in 1942. Howard High School in Chattanooga, Tennessee, boasted a Youth Council of 275 members.[41]

Civil rights organizers were also emboldened by gains and recognition from the political establishment. As President Roosevelt penned Esther Cooper Jackson and SNYC in 1942, African Americans participated in a conflict that at its basis protected "a universal freedom under which a new basis of security and prosperity can be established for all—regardless of station, race or creed. Their fight has been democracy's fight. And democracy's victory must be their victory—to cherish and extend as the men and women of tomorrow."[42] This recognition and other gains such as President Truman's Commission on Civil Rights in 1946 and Executive Order 9981 (1948) led to the desegregation of the military. The war and postwar period were ripe for further youth mobilization.

While civil rights organizers viewed youth as more active than their counterparts in the teaching profession, established adults still treated young people as passive actors or as future change agents to be trained to support their elders in the present movement. Only later and under the auspices of associations like the NAACP, adults reasoned, could youth—once they had attained adult status—lead the movement. The NAACP and SNYC worked for youth and sought to mobilize youth, but these organizations were not youth led, necessarily. This passive notion of youth activism undergirded conceptions of it while it engendered a dynamic movement that furthered national goals, facilitated transnational connections, launched ambitious educational campaigns, inspired pathbreaking conferences, and inculcated tens of thousands of students with the principles of democratic civic engagement. Inhibited while being provided the tools to lead a frontal assault in a domestic war on racial oppression, the paradoxes of the youth movement during the 1940s illustrate the contours and nuances of resistance that defined the movement for generations to come.

To youth organizers, students were potential allies and their desire to participate held potential in strengthening their movement. But working with youth required addressing an urgency that elders rarely discerned, namely that youth were restless and without the means to channel their energy in the war effort. Ruby Hurley, the new Youth Council director for the NAACP, communicated the predicament of youth and its solution in 1943. "A deep sense of frustration exists in those not yet old enough or otherwise prohibited from wearing a uniform or doing a war job," Hurley noted in 1944. "They have a sense of not belonging, of being shunted aside as unimportant. They could do a job now if some direction were given."[43] Hurley and the NAACP aimed to provide this direction.

At the age of thirty-four, Ruby Hurley assumed the position of NAACP Youth Council secretary in 1943. She reiterated the goals of her predecessor, Juanita Jackson, in the wartime context. She oversaw that youth officers pledged a commitment to youth that aligned with the national organization's goals: "I shall work diligently to inform youth of the problems affecting the Negro; to promote the political, economic, educational and social betterment of colored people and their harmonious cooperation with other peoples; to stimulate an appreciation of the Negro's contribution to civilization; to develop an intelligent, militant youth leadership through devising, working out and pursuing local programs and to cooperate with and support the national programs [of the NAACP]."[44] As Hurley outlined the aims of youth organization, she highlighted a contradiction that defined the NAACP's relationship with youth. Hurley envisioned students as potentially militant allies, an evolution from seeing young people as passive actors during the 1930s. Yet in the same statement where she invoked the spirit of militancy, Hurley still stressed a subservient allegiance "to cooperate with and support the national programs."[45] Drawing upon middle class professional notions of agency supported by an overarching politics of respectability, movement elders ultimately maintained oversight and discouraged militancy from developing in practice.[46] It was a proscribed attempt to channel youth into predetermined paths grounded in the values of "reputable" organizations like the NAACP.

Much of the tenor of youth organization through the NAACP is evident in how Association leaders communicated with youth members. The NAACP Youth Council division regularly published the Youth News Letter beginning in 1942 to disseminate information nationally about student activity and to assist in the larger campaign to attract new members.[47] The pages of the Youth News Letter were largely informative, documenting the new chapters and the names of those elected to positions within the organizations. It informed members of events such as socials, dances, and education programs, but also protest. For instance, NAACP called upon youth to "articulate your protest" in 1944 against MGM motion picture company against the production of "Uncle Tom's Cabin," instead demanding "more pictures of Negro life and employing Negro characters."[48] The tenor reflects a top-down, informative approach that signified a publication that was for youth, but it was not led by them. The words and voice of high school youth themselves were strikingly absent from much of the News Letter.

Hurley and NAACP elders discerned the tensions, however, even as they perpetuated the paternalism that relegated students to the sidelines. Hurley drew attention to the burdens placed upon youth, highlighting how society was quick to point out the problems but failed to proffer meaningful solutions. "The adult community cries to high heaven about the 'zoot-suiters,' 'public conduct,' and 'juvenile delinquency,'" Hurley noted. "But what remedies are applied to these sore points, these manifestations of frustration?" She elaborated by drawing attention to a bureaucratic delay in working with youth. "Committees are appointed to investigate, reports are made," Hurley noted, "and too often no action is taken."[49] Hurley articulated the problems encumbering youth organizers, yet the tension remained unresolved during the war. It was a perennial tension that continued to underpin the next two decades of youth organization.

Youth organizers like Hurley hesitated to genuinely embrace youth militancy and with good reason. To start, by the Second World War it was clear that youth did not always express views consistent with those of their elders. Students presented competing visons of the war that did not so neatly align with the expectations of the war effort, for instance. In the buildup to war, youth flexed their voice in conferences organized for and attended largely by youth. In breakout sessions and working groups that included high school youth, young people who attended the large conferences sponsored by the NAACP and SNYC put forth resolutions that endorsed peace and opposed going to war, criticizing Roosevelt and denouncing the use of military force as imperialistic. NAACP Youth Councils joined the World Youth Congress and supported declarations of peace. In 1940 and with the support of elder pacifist James Farmer of the Congress of Racial Equality, the NAACP Youth Councils endorsed the "Peace Proclamation of Negro Youth," a statement that called for "immediate preparation . . . to join in the fight for peace."[50] The SNYC annual conference held in New Orleans focused on the theme "Keep America at Peace" and similarly denounced Roosevelt's actions in the prelude to war as imperialistic.[51] SNYC chapters in New York created a coalition for peace, the Committee for Concerned Peace Efforts, which formed alliances with the YWCA, student council leaders at New York University, the City College of New York, Hunter College, the American Student Union, the Student Christian Association, and others to call for a National Security Week to "create nation-wide interest in promoting international justice and economic cooperation and in building adequate peace machinery."[52] Youth proclamations prior to 1941 left room for full participation, but they illuminated a desire for pacifism and, with the support of James Farmer, formidable ideology that pushed the boundaries of youth and elders alike.[53]

The American South increasingly drew scorn and indignation as White southerners maintained what civil rights organizations saw as a fascist regime. SNYC leaders like Esther Jackson called into question the contradiction inherent to enlisting African Americans to fight abroad while denying them the right to vote at home. SNYC organizers called upon youth to obey the law and register and serve when conscripted. "At the same time," the organization noted, "our organization will continue its fight against involving our country in war, against discrimination in the armed forces and for a greater democracy at home."[54] SNYC leaders adamantly questioned the integrity of conscripting Black youth into the armed forces. "The question of the participation of . . . Negro Youth in the armed forces," the organization noted in the pages of *S.N.Y.C. News*, "is a major challenge to democracy." They noted how high command generally dismissed the demands of Black organizers. Wartime leaders failed to address the social, political, and economic conditions that disenfranchised African Americans across the nation. Youth organizers ultimately sought to challenge "the right of Jim Crow election boards to register Negro youth for the armed forces when these same boards refuse to register qualified Negro citizens as voters."[55] SNYC reasoned that Roosevelt's conscription of "our generation is fascism pure and simple" in light of legal disenfranchisement.[56] The organization elaborated further through the *SNYC Bulletin* in 1943, arguing: "Our country's total defenses are weakened because the people of the Southern are voteless and unable to rid our government of the reactionary friends of Hitler who have stolen high seats of power in Congress." The abolition of the poll tax, they reasoned, "is an essential war measure to insure the safeguarding of democracy at home and to strengthen our democratic national unity for winning the war."[57] It was the basis civil rights organizations used to call for victory at home in addition to victory in Europe and the Pacific.

NAACP and SNYC youth organizers—and by extension the youth they led—ultimately supported the war effort after the United States entered the conflict in 1941, participating in the "Double V" campaign in earnest. Indeed, the burgeoning youth movement dovetailed neatly with national discourse that supported the war. The NAACP drafted a wartime memo to all Youth Council branches, "Fight for Complete Democracy at Home," which reflected the principles of victory abroad and at home that drove the popular "Double-V" campaign. For those too young to fight or join the wartime industry, the NAACP urged young people to commit to the struggle for "FREEDOM—NOW."[58] SNYC encouraged young people in the same way. At the SNYC fifth annual conference in Tuskegee and the sixth conference in Atlanta, organizers highlighted youth's role in winning the war. The conference encouraged youth to support the war in order to establish a front in Europe "so that we can strike at the heart of the enemy and speed the day of victory which can assure universal peace, freedom, and social advancement to all the nations and peoples of the earth." As such they resolved to strengthen the "national unity and the foundations of our democracy."[59] Couched in terms that resonated with the United States' effort to win the war, the NAACP and SNYC reconciled their push for military victory with the larger goals of their associations as they equated victory in war as a victory for their causes.

The unorthodox nature of youth activism precipitated nuanced views of the youth movement among those who led it. SNYC, for instance, developed an expanded notion of youth organizing during the war and the immediate postwar period that centered upon internationalism. Esther Cooper Jackson, who began service as the SNYC executive secretary in 1942, was a graduate of Oberlin College, who later earned a master's degree in social sciences from Fisk University under the tutelage of the famed sociologist and esteemed president of the institution, Dr. Charles S. Johnson. She maintained strong international connections. She helped organize a Hemisphere Youth Conference for Victory that was held in Mexico City in 1943. She was a delegate to the World Youth Conference in London in 1945 and served as the chair of the American subcommittee on Problems of Dependent Peoples, in which over sixty nations were represented. The purpose of the conference was to "discuss the problems and desires of democratic young people from all parts of the world."[60] She also traveled throughout Europe as part of the Soviet Youth Movement, which explored war-torn cities, including Paris, Frankfurt, Berlin, Brussels, Warsaw, Stalingrad, and Moscow. Her husband, James E. Jackson Jr. whom she met while interning with SNYC, led the organization since 1937, including organizing tobacco workers in Virginia. He served SNYC as vice president and as educational director. A war veteran, he also examined issues stemming from colonialism, much like his partner, in the postwar context.[61]

Under their leadership, SNYC during the Second World War and the postwar period defined conceptions of youth in universal terms that were not confined to the American South. It was a distinguishing aspect of their work. The war fostered a transnational perspective that influenced Black youth organizations such as SNYC and a larger notion of activism. The connections fostered across the globe through Esther Jackson established an international platform for coalition building that SNYC developed at the local level since their origination. Youth stated at the conclusion of the war that peace rested with the strengthening of the United Nations and the disarmament of all nations. They adamantly opposed any program of universal military training for young people, particularly for Black youth. Even though they heroically fought against fascism and imperialism, they were "constantly hampered by Jim Crow and discrimination."[62] By the spring of 1946, SNYC pledged organizational efforts to the struggle to maintain international peace based on "unity of peoples all over the world."[63] Through global connections, SNYC fostered an intellectual underpinning that served as a basis for transnational Black liberation ideology in latter decades. An international perspective provided a tool to fight domestic oppression in the 1940s, including the execution of George Stinney—the fourteen-year-old boy executed on a highly implausible conviction in South Carolina—which highlighted the perennial perils of Black youth in the South.[64] SNYC used the *Bulletin*, for instance, to question publicly the execution of Stinney in the context of the war, while drawing upon international parallels. "The Governor of South Carolina must have closed his eyes to the fact that Negro and white youth of his state are giving their lives on the continent of Europe and in the islands of the Pacific . . . to free the conquered people of the world from the German and Japanese tyrannies."[65] They compared Stinney's execution to young children killed in Poland and Russia. "It is a blot against the state of South Carolina," SNYC argued that the governor would "set his seal upon a court order directing the execution of a 14 year old child."[66] SNYC utilized a transnational context to pressure the state to commute his sentence, illustrating how postwar politics of the Cold War were seen as a viable means to enact change.[67]

Though student activism was not widespread during the war, young people demonstrated agency in earnest before, during, and after the war. Civil rights associations created the means for youth to become active not only in the war effort, but in the burgeoning civil rights movement. Young people forged their own path as SNYC and the NAACP shaped the youth agenda, largely through education. Students had access to schools that educators, administrators, and organizers with SNYC and the NAACP did not. As students, they carried an intimate understanding of the pressing issues facing them and their schools. It was an intuition not shared by movement leaders. Much of youth work during the war therefore focused on education, both in the logistics of using the school as a political space and using the process of education as a way to reach the larger aims of the movement. This rendered their work less visible, but it nonetheless established an important foundation of the youth movement.

Youth added moral and political urgency to spaces that their elders lacked access, namely Black high schools. Students at the historic A. H. Parker High School in Birmingham, Alabama, are indicative of the modes of resistance students inspired in schools during the war. Parker students presented a student program in the spring of 1944 entitled "The Peace Aims of the Citizen— A New Bill of Rights." They spoke on the right to work, fair pay, health care, security, free enterprise, and "the Right to Equality Before the Law" and "The Right to Education."[68] Modest compared to direct action protest, educational programs like those at Parker High School resonated throughout the South as a safe way to demand rights that addressed gross injustices. Presented to faculty and the wider community, students on one hand were ideal ambassadors to amplify the messages of civil rights organizations for an audience that was not involved with the NAACP, such as parents, pastors, and the majority of teachers. While programs like this illustrated how students embraced the aims of their elders, young people also provided new direction, demanding new rights in fields such as education, health care, and the law at the local level where civil rights organizations had often not organized.

Though the Black high school was a critical site of political contestation during the 1940s, students were more active outside their schools, a space regulated and led by elders and, more often than not, college-aged "youth" who were still lumped together with high school–aged youth by civil rights organizers. The agenda of a burgeoning youth movement during and after the war reflected this age hierarchy, focusing on issues of conscription and voting, both of which were beyond the age of high school youth, and further demonstrating how the category of youth was often dominated by college students. Concerted voter registration drives constituted one of the most significant youth activities of the 1940s. SNYC made it clear to its members and the general public that "the battle of the ballot, of representative government, is the battle of the Negro people."[69] Led by the SNYC Executive Board in Birmingham, Alabama, youth helped launch a citizenship education campaign with the goal to attain full voting rights in 1940. Working with James Jackson, who directed the voter registration campaigns, youth experienced firsthand the political processes that developed outside the formal school. Jackson organized in the coalition style of SNYC, affiliating with the local chapters of the United Mine Workers, local steel workers, and other student, church, and social clubs. By 1944 SNYC cooperated with a handful of other groups including local and state chapters of civic leagues and the NAACP to register voters. Attempting to register as many as five thousand voters, SNYC reported that they registered hundreds of previously unregistered Black voters. They also reported abuses to the CIO Political Action Committee, which offered their support to SNYC, vowing to register each of its Black union members.[70]

Though seniors in high school could theoretically be drafted into the army, this was more of a concern for college-age youth. High school youth were conscripted into this campaign, but it was not necessarily a campaign by and for high school youth. Moreover, the mobilization of the Black vote trickled down to high school students through civic education.

SNYC leadership invested a significant part of its organizational capacity in ambitious citizenship education programming as part of the larger campaign to register Black voters. SNYC established a Committee on Citizenship and the Franchise to work out a Citizenship Institutes and Clinics program, as well as campaigns to register "unprecedented numbers of youth in the South in the coming year."[71] After the conclusion of the war, SNYC redoubled its efforts around citizenship education, boldly noting, "We are determined to be the first full-fledged voting generation."[72] The Executive Board elaborated upon their rationale in 1947, stating that "Citizenship Education institutes, courses, and classes must be established and carried on in a continuous effort to provide opportunities for more and more people to know the obligations, duties, responsibilities, and privileges of citizens in a democratic social order." Citizenship courses, they argued, should be premised on the notion that citizens demand their constitutional rights and the right to vote and organize to run for office.[73] Toward this end, SNYC in Birmingham published a substantive primer that was shared widely and used in citizenship courses entitled, "Know Your Government: A Manual of Citizenship Education." The primer outlined the constitution and its history, the structure of the government, representatives, and congressmen.[74] SNYC called for each state branch to hold clinics that educated community leaders in order to "enlighten their communities in matters pertaining to registration and voting." They also called for an educational program to be carried out by all branches that encouraged members to work with other progressive groups.[75]

Other education programming sought to cultivate local Black leadership through leadership training schools. The purpose of the program was to train young people for leadership positions in SNYC or other associations in which participants were involved. They acquainted students with the major problems facing Black youth in the South including voting, jobs, peace, and freedom. They taught organizational techniques for building grassroots organizations. For a $25 tuition fee, young people could attend the leadership school, which lasted two weeks. Organizers structured each day into classes, discussion sessions, and workshops. SNYC staffed the classes with faculty across the country who taught a range of classes on voting, civil rights, job programs for youth, world affairs and peace, education for democracy, and the history of African American politics. Workshops were held on movement music and songs as well as mimeographing and drafting press releases. They were introduced to parliamentary law and practiced public speaking.[76]

In contrast to the NAACP, SNYC embraced a form of coalition building that in many ways extended the organization behind the popular front of previous decades. In the postwar era, SNYC resolved "no longer to be the victims of the old Nazi game of divide and rule."[77] SNYC sought to unite with any association that shared common efforts and this translated into wide collaborative fronts at the local level. Continuing their work of the 1930s, SNYC prioritized working with student organizations, veterans, young workers, women and other associations, including clergy and unionized workers and other associations organized in the same local contexts.

Student activists in SNYC and the NAACP formally presented various demands to their elected representatives around the issue of voting as well. SNYC drafted the "Eight Tasks of the Eightieth Congress." Forming a "youth legislature," SNYC members worked to alert the public that 10 million citizens were denied the right to vote through poll tax laws and encouraged voters to support candidates who supported passing a federal anti-poll tax law and stronger enforcement of the *Smith v. Allwright* (1944) decision that barred the all-White primary. They also adopted strategies specific to their needs and called for legislation to lower the voting age to eighteen, questioning if "eighteen-year-old youth are eligible for the draft, so why not for the vote?" Legislative points also included the passage of an anti-lynch law, an anti-poll tax law, a law establishing a permanent Fair Employment Practices Committee, a sixty-five cents minimum wage law, a law restoring price controls, a law establishing National Health Insurance, a law establishing Social Security to workers in domestic, casual, and agricultural employment, and a law providing federal aid to education.

The demand for federal aid to education was unique to youth and the schools they attended. In advocating for such policies, they positioned themselves not just as students but as citizens with a stake in civic life, arguing "that the whole level of education in the South might be raised to a higher level, and the same type of benefits that are our veterans are entitled to for educational purposes might be extended to the general public."[78] Additionally, SNYC called upon its members and southern youth to write to their Senators and representatives to petition their support to pass the legislation they proposed. Black youth also drafted cards and telegraphs to distribute among the community in efforts to include them in their petition to congress.[79] The NAACP Youth Councils adopted a similar program in 1949, which they called "Operation Civil Rights." Representatives from youth and college chapters visited the vice president, Senate and House majority leaders, and their representative senators, among other political leaders. Young people presented a legislative program that covered education, economic security, social welfare, and civil rights.[80]

In all of these ways youth were drawn into the democratic process during the 1940s. The experience inculcated a skill set that would help them advocate for change through established venues and constitutional provisions. It presaged the direct assault on Jim Crow observed during the 1950s and 1960s by establishing the foundational knowledge of systemic oppression and the legal means to address it. It also provided a model that future youth organizers would embrace as they, too, perpetuated a passive view of student activists.

Behold the Land: Tilling the Soil of the Southern Youth Movement

While civil rights organizations pressed for legislative change during and after the war with pressing urgency and inculcated youth with knowledge of the political process, SNYC and the NAACP continued the work of the 1930s through organizing annual and regional conferences. They envisioned a large platform to help enact the legislative reform they drafted, and large conferences provided an urgency and a moral appeal to invigorate youth. Noted speakers of state, national, and international distinction delivered poignant messages and sought to instill the principles of the freedom struggle, demonstrating a grand vision for the youth movement. Though passive in effect, conferences were an effective platform to actively reach large audiences and advance a political agenda not found in schools.

John McCray, Modjeska Simkins, Rev. James Hinton, and Osceola McCaine, an activist and veteran of the First World War who recently returned to the Palmetto State after fleeing the Nazi invasion in Europe, organized the conference for SNYC through the networks they created. By way of a network established through their service and activism, organizers were able to recruit a sizable crowd that would galvanize a postwar movement in the Palmetto state. McCaine assisted with teacher equalization lawsuits in the state in 1943, working with the state's Black teacher association and consulting with Thurgood Marshall and the NAACP. Simkins was involved with expanding health care services, Black business development, and worked as the State Secretary of the NAACP.[81] In the immediate months prior to the conference during the winter of 1946, the case of war veteran Isaac Woodard garnered international attention. White police officers in Batesburg-Leesville brutally assaulted Woodard, a Black veteran returning home after serving in the Pacific, permanently blinding him.[82] This homegrown network paved the way for SNYC to extend their work to South Carolina.

SNYC's seventh annual conference in 1946 in Columbia illustates the ideological underpinnings of the Black youth movement of the 1940s. Young people organized chapters in Columbia, South Carolina, with goals to "reach the entire youth population of Columbia," and sought to "affiliate youth clubs which already exist. Thus, a community social club, an athletic group, a campus fraternity or sorority or other student groups, a young men's civic group, etc. would be persuaded to affiliate."[83] Similar to previous meetings, SNYC organized the conference as a youth legislature, with a mix of high school and college attendees composing a House of Representatives, Senate, Committees, a Presiding Officer, and a Cabinet in order to identify concrete legislative solutions. Organizers sought to use the youth legislature in South Carolina as a way "to secure for ourselves and our people all the rights and opportunities of a full and unfettered citizenship."[84] Esther Cooper greeted the seven hundred delegates who gathered at the Township Auditorium in the capital city with portraits of noted Black politicians of the Reconstruction era prominently displayed behind her, noting: "We have come here to Columbia, in the heart of the deep South, to rearm ourselves with a deeper realization of our condition and our needs; we have come to give voice and strength and organization power to the burning and unsilenceable demand of our generation for the right to live and prosper."[85] Cooper framed the conference in militant terms and to "rearm" youth to voice "burning" demands of their rights. It struck a chord with the conference and each speaker elaborated upon the theme, electrifying those in attendance. With historians, scholars, and authors such as W. E. B. Du Bois, Herbert Aptheker, and Howard Fast presenting to youth, it was also a moment to educate youth and provide a historical corrective to the whitewashing of U.S. history through the callous though popular inclusion of the Lost Cause narrative in textbooks.[86]

The SNYC conference in Columbia drew notable and influential speakers. One of the first was John McCray, founder of the Progressive Democrats and editor of the *Lighthouse and Informer*, a progressive Black state newspaper. He delivered a stirring address on police brutality, a theme SNYC had espoused since the 1930s. McCray recounted for the young people in attendance the instance of Isaac Woodward, who was blinded by police in South Carolina, as well as cases from Batesburg and Florence, South Carolina, where African Americans were unfairly charged, beaten, and assaulted by police. Expanding on the theme of oppression by law enforcement, McCray also called young people to give more attention to "peonage, being held in involuntary servitude."[87] As an organizer of the Progressive Democrats, McCray called to enfranchise voters and cast ballots in order to send "full delegations . . . until the Democratic party itself makes its choice between 15 million honest loyal American citizens and a few southern reactionaries like [Mississippi Senator Theodore] Bilbo and [Mississippi Congressman John] Rankin."[88] Theodore Bilbo, the rabid segregationist who publicly denounced, intimidated, and harassed Black voters, was recently elected to the U.S. Senate, and civil rights activists with returning Black war veterans were rallying to remove him from office.[89]

Building a new society through political means resonated with other luminaries at the conference. Paul Robeson, who staged a rousing performance at the conference, also spoke of his travels to Russia, Norway, and on the urgency to oust Bilbo for the U.S. Senate. He spoke of "a great responsibility upon all of us here. It is our great destiny to be the vanguard in this struggle."[90] New York Congressman Adam Clayton Powell Jr. addressed southern youth: "We have within our hands the strong new power to bring to pass almost in the twinkling of an eye all the material things we have dreamed about, yet, we are unable. This new world must wait for a race of new men. . . . The new world depends upon you—the new south. American will never achieve greatness until the black and white south has emancipated itself from Bilboism."[91] Noted speakers instilled movement principles and the potential for change with passion, inspiration, and wisdom. It was an unparalleled appeal to youth.

Dr. Du Bois delivered a memorable keynote address, distinguished by its stirring and impassioned, if not prophetic, charge to youth. He titled his address "Behold the Land." He opened by articulating the very nature of the youth movement, recognizing that "the future of the American Negro is in the South."[92] Du Bois called upon youth to reach out to the White working class, whom he saw as potential allies, reiterating a connection to labor that SNYC endorsed since its origination. Du Bois depicted with empathy White youth who were frustrated, if not tormented by an apparently irresolvable contradiction located at the nexus of the search for truth and the realization of Black disenfranchisement. It was a contradiction that cut short any search for higher meaning or purpose. He deplored White politicians, whom he warned must "in the long run yield to the forward march of civilization or die." In concluding his address, Du Bois spoke to the young people directly:

> This is the great sacrifice; this is the thing that you are called up
> to do because it is the right thing to do. Because you are embarked
> upon a great and holy crusade, the emancipation of mankind
> black and white; the upbuilding of democracy; the breaking
> down, particularly here in the South, of forces of evil represented
> by race prejudice in South Carolina; by lynching in Georgia; by
> disenfranchisement in Mississippi; by ignorance in Louisiana and
> by all these in the whole South . . . Here is the chance for young
> women and young men of devotion to lift again the banner of
> humanity and to walk toward a civilization which will be free and
> intelligent; which will be healthy and unafraid; and build in the
> world a culture led by black fold and joined by peoples of all colors.[93]

Du Bois's address presented a direct challenge to young people in the South. His tone directly charged youth to engage in the front lines of the movement. Its sentiment is indicative of the revolutionary rhetoric the SNYC sought to instill among young people across the American South.

As part of the conference, SNYC organizers and attendees moved swiftly to action and drafted the "Columbia Pact of Southern Youth." Led by adults, students in high school worked together with college students and young professionals to draft a statement. The statement's authors identified as "students, veterans, young workers and young women," implying that high school youth were part of a collective, not yet their own autonomous voice.[94] Together they drafted a critical framework for action that drew upon the ideas of Du Bois, McCray, and Powell from the conference. It also incorporated the insights of "great southern statesmen," including Frederick Douglass and Hiram Revels.[95] The statement established the premise for which they organized. Youth stood together "united in righteous indignation and protest" against mob violence, lynching, and brutality. They demanded jobs, an unrestricted right to vote, the right to own the land they worked, medical and health care, better education, and protection from policy brutality.[96] They also spoke of how they understood their work:

> We have come to understand that discrimination against Negro
> youth—in all its forms—is but a device used by economic royalists
> and plantations landlords to cheat the young white people and our
> entire generation of Southern youth of the right to life, liberty and
> the pursuit of happiness in a democratic South. We know that only
> when Negro youth achieve the full citizenship promised them in
> the Constitution, and earned by them in their patriotic devotion
> to the cause of democracy, only then can millions of young white
> people go forward and our Southland prosper.[97]

In short, they stood committed to fight for "opportunity, through unity, to build a free, prosperous and happy South, as part of a democratic and peaceful world."[98]

To enact the list of demands of their representatives, SNYC vowed to "bring pressure to bear" through written appeals to those elected to Congress. Though similar to action taken by the NAACP, SNYC positioned themselves more aggressively. They created a committee designed to "militantly marshal" the allegiances of potential Black voters to particular parties that were not in accordance with the progressive and liberal cadence adopted by SNYC. The youth legislature also called African Americans to run for office in earnest and to vigorously support those campaigns.[99]

SNYC's organization in South Carolina after the Columbia conference exhibited the depth and work the association was able to deploy during this era. High school activist Leroy Aiken played a crucial role in helping older adults and other high school students establish a chapter in Moncks Corner, South Carolina, and established two more chapters in Joys and Huger, with over twenty in each club, after the convention in 1946. "Just to inform you," Aiken wrote to SNYC organizer Louis Burnham, "One of the [clubs] have twenty one members, and the other has twenty three. We have in our club here twenty four. We are planning on organizing a few more."[100] They hosted regular club meetings and discussed Black history. They held rallies, sponsored film screenings, and held small educational programs.[101] The club in Moncks Corner also worked closely with the Progressive Club, a civic league that focused on voting, and other community improvement associations. They supplied the transportation for young people to travel to the leadership training at nearby Harbison. The Progressive Club in Moncks Corner, with the support of local SNYC chapters, supported a candidate for the Progressive Democratic Party who was running for the local school board. He did not win, but the campaign provided invaluable experience and connected youth to progressive community organizers. The two clubs also coordinated together and organized a school bus for local African American students, one of the only such arrangements in the state. SNYC organization after the conference in Columbia also inspired a Progressive Club in the local high school, Berkeley Training High School.[102]

Berkeley Training High School in Moncks Corner, South Carolina, provided speakers and hosted a local institute. Organizing at the local high school provided a platform specifically for high school youth like Leroy Aiken who could amplify their voice particularly through the high school newspaper, *The Berkeley*. In the case of the student newspaper from Moncks Corner, scholars wrote extensively of the activities of the SNYC, they discussed social events, and published poems and essays with titles like "What the Negro is Entitled."[103] I. M. McCoy published a piece in *The Berkeley*, titled "Inferiority." It read: "It is also true [mankind] need not and does not remain in this helpless state, because he has within him when he is born with all the potentialities of greatness and success what he becomes is largely due to the speed and thoroughness with which he casts off the bonds of inferiority."[104] *The Berkeley* provides a rare vantage point into the lives of high school youth, and through it issues such as voting were not readily apparent, but issues like quality of education and social life were present. High school student support for SNYC was strong, too, with students devoting much of the space to covering the association's activities in South Carolina, including various fundraising events like youth socials to support the national association.[105]

Berkeley Training High School also played a critical role in supporting SNYC, providing a direct link between a growing movement and a historically Black high school. Berkeley Training High School opened its doors and used its auditorium to carry forth SNYC's educational platform by hosting a "Youth Institute." The principal of the school, R. A. Ready, welcomed attendees with open arms and provided opening remarks. To mark the progressive moment of the institute, sessions began with music and the Negro

National Anthem. Discussion focused on the areas of labor, health, agriculture, voting, and education. Young people at the institute also focused on enrolling other students in school for economic and social reasons, calling upon the community to engage all young people in the process. "If you want to get ready for what's ahead," the organizers noted in the institute bulletin, "go to school."[106]

SNYC organization in South Carolina also shows how the youth movement paralleled, complemented, and intersected with the work of senior organizers. Forming a "Progressive Club" at Berkeley Training High School and aligning with the Progressive Democrats brought youth into the fold of John McCray's fledging political apparatus that sought to empower Black voters to elect Black representatives and remove White supremacists from office. Local SNYC branches worked with Mojeska Simkins and the statewide NAACP, filling out petitions to oust Theodore Bilbo.[107] Connecting with Simkins introduced the youth organization to a wider network of activism. After the SNYC 1946 conference, for instance, Herbert Aptheker undertook a twelve-stop tour of the South. As part of the tour, he collaborated with Simkins and forged plans for broadening networks built upon organized labor and thereby strengthening SNYC's association with labor-based organization and politics.[108] Through the Progressive Club in Moncks Corner, young people continued the work of Esau Jenkins, who organized a Progressive Club in nearby John's Island. Along with Septima Clark, Jenkins organized at his club the first Citizenship School, an adult literacy program that expanded across the South to include nearly nine hundred schools and sixteen hundred volunteer teachers and registered over fifty thousand voters within a decade. Jenkins also ran for the local school board in a locally concentrated move to elect Black leadership to local offices.[109]

By engaging in the politics of youth, SNYC expanded the work of veteran organizers and their elders in South Carolina, bringing the movement to new sites of organization and introducing the networks of resistance to youth. While not as visible as the protest of latter decades, youth were decidedly part of a youth movement that would continue to flourish.

· · · · · ·

Top-down initiatives reinforced a passive conception of youth, where adults and movement veterans viewed youth as potential agents who could lead the movement in the future. In the meantime, their reasoning continued, youth were to be sidelined, following the directives of their elders. Yet registering voters, engaging elected officials, and actively participating in conferences through SNYC and the NAACP provided a political education to young people that predated the work of the citizenship education programs and the freedom schools of later decades. The process itself, which included drafting mock legislation, disseminating integral information needed to vote, and contacting constituents and representatives replicated the democratic process. The process was educational for the youth involved while also constituting its own form of activism, much like the pedagogical activism of teachers. This educative act was a means that the Student Nonviolent Coordinating Committee and the Council of Federation Organizations later employed in the 1960s. Civil rights organizers provided an education to youth, whom they saw as potential and future change agents. They continued the work of the 1930s and expanded it, setting the stage for the direct action protest of the 1950s and 1960s.

3 Why Don't You Do Something about It?

Youth Activism of the 1950s

• •

On a typical school morning in 1950, Barbara Johns, a sixteen-year-old soph-omore at R. R. Moton High School in Farmville, Virginia, was walking her younger siblings to their bus stop. She forgot her lunch and had to go back to the house. By the time she returned, she had missed the bus and was forced to wait for the bus that carried White students to school. Yet when the White bus approached Johns' home, it simply passed her, even though the driver had to pass the all-Black Moton High School to get to the all-White high school. Johns did not stand idly by. She was determined to challenge the racism that underpinned the incident. It was a turning point for Johns, who was commit-ted to voicing her frustrations over the occurrence in addition to the multi-tude of others that plagued her education.[1] "It wasn't fair we had such a poor facility," Johns wrote after the historic walkout, "when our white counter-parts enjoyed science laboratories, a huge facility, separate gym department, etc." She went on to explain: "I felt we were not treated like other students. Their classes were not held in the auditorium. They were not cold. They didn't have to leave one building and transfer to another. Their buses weren't over-crowded."[2] Johns communicated her and others' deep frustrations to one of her favorite teachers, Ms. Inez Davenport, a music teacher, who shared news of workers going on strike across the United States. To Johns' complaint, Dav-enport replied: "Why don't you do something about it?"[3]

R. R. Moton High School represented a classic example of the kind of high school setting that had nurtured the youth movement up to that point. It was a historically Black high school that galvanized the support of the lo-cal community. Its teachers were committed to instilling the principles of the movement in the classroom behind closed doors. Those in the commu-nity were acutely aware of the indignities generated by Jim Crow and they regularly petitioned the board for better facilities to no avail. Yet the 1950s presented a new context for the rising young activists of R. R. Moton.

In the wake of the Second World War, civil rights activism focused on integration and full participation in U.S. society. On a national level the

NAACP was engaged in a campaign for desegregation, while teachers, once at the forefront of the movement for salary equalization, were primarily focused on delivering a civic education that encouraged them to engage with and make demands on society as full citizens. Civil rights organizers, local community leaders, and youth advocates pressed for integration and trained young people to become activists as organizations like the NAACP made bold claims to a more inclusive democracy.

Against this backdrop, high school youth of the 1950s increasingly appeared on the front lines of the movement, acting in ways that their elders could not. As the nation made slow, gradual changes that held out the promise of incremental steps toward freedom, movement elders, Black intellectuals, and teachers increasingly regarded youth as the primary agents of change. To be sure, movement elders continued to regard young people as passive participants rather than active stakeholders but nevertheless incorporated their work into more ambitious campaigns to eradicate segregation.

A wealth of scholarship has painted a vivid portrait of protest and school desegregation in Prince Edward County, Virginia.[4] This work identifies how a rural Virginian community's demand for a new school led to the historic *Brown* decision and all that followed. The student activist Barbara Johns takes her earned place as a youthful agent of change in dismantling Jim Crow. This chapter builds upon this work by extending the networks and circles of influence of Johns to include her peers, her elders who demanded school improvement for decades before her, and the NAACP's use of youth in the case not just for school desegregation but a means to shape an entire movement. Placed in a context that includes historical antecedent and elders who advocated for youth, a much larger network and a politics of high school activism emerge.

Barbara Johns and her cohort of student activists in rural Virginia were not acting in isolation. Examining the politics and discourse surrounding the Farmville walkout illustrate how the protest was not merely about school desegregation but something much deeper. Alongside other protests during the 1950s—including Baton Rouge, Louisiana, and Montgomery, Alabama— this story offers a snapshot into how youth and conceptions of youth organizing would shape and at times limit movement politics during this crucial decade. In particular, while the NAACP benefited from self-organized youth action, leaders nevertheless saw the movement as *theirs*, and youth activists as a force to be harnessed rather than potential partners in a shared struggle. Yet high school youth were already beginning to seek action outside the top-down protocols of the organization, actualizing the warnings of NAACP organizers and leaders like Walter White and Ruby Hurley of previous decades. The autonomous shift becomes visible in these 1950s protests, as high school activists increasingly claimed their place on the front lines of the movement.

High School Activism and the Evolving Politics of the NAACP

After the bus passed her by, Barbara Johns organized a school-wide movement that ultimately held national implications. Johns began by reaching out to her classmates. Her friends and peers at Moton shared with her a deep resentment with the education they received—much like Richard Wright expressed a quarter century before. Edwilda Allen Issac, who was in the eighth grade at the time of the walkout, remembered that "in biology, we had one frog that we had to share and ours were discards from [the all-white] Farmville High School."[5] Joy Speakes, a student at R. R. Moton and confidante of Johns, recalled, "everything that we had in the school was hand-me-downs. We had books, the books were secondhand books and the books had pages torn out, they had derogatory terms written in it. The conditions that we went to school were substandard to the conditions of the white high school. The football players all had to go over to the white school to practice so that they would be able to play ball at night because we didn't have light." She went on to note that "and here we didn't have a cafeteria, we didn't have a gym, no lab. You know, so all of those amenities we didn't have here."[6] Her classmate, Samuel Williams, made similar observations. He spoke about hand-me-down texts, noting "a lot of profanity written in it when they found out—and pages torn out—when they found out they were coming over here [to Moton]."[7] For Williams and the other students who walked out of their school in protest, the conditions at Moton were "no abstract thing, it was a lot of physical things that we could put our hands on and see, having to have books, having to have uniforms and football, and they [White students] all had that . . . right over around the corner here."[8] The materials "that we didn't have" or they did have but were cast aside by Whites, were a serious injustice to the students that they encountered on a day-to-day basis.

Barbara Johns and others decided to plan a protest, which they orchestrated with a small circle of confidants, largely drawn from members of the student council. These students were, in her words, "the crème de la crème of the school because they were smart and thinkers. I knew them and trusted them and I was a part of them."[9] The planning committee from Moton High School made the conscious decision to inform only a select cadre of peers.

Dubbed the "Manhattan Project," the students planned for a school-wide walkout in secret. Adults would not be included. Students planned the strike through clandestine meetings, outside the purview of not only teachers but elders in the community, including those like Rev. L. F. Griffen who earned the trust of the small Farmville community in his leadership of local civil rights initiatives. They kept their plans secret and even hid their plans from other students, including Barbara John's own brothers and sisters, out of fear they would inform their parents of the strike.[10]

Students planned the walkout for the morning of April 23, 1951. It began with a diversion. One of the student organizers, John Watson, remained out of school and reported to the principal, Mr. M. Boyd Jones, that students were in trouble at the Greyhound bus station in town. A stern disciplinarian concerned for his students, Jones left the school premises immediately. With the principal out of the building, Barbara Jones proceeded with the plan and sent notes to all teachers in the school that called for an assembly. Signed "B. J.," which were the initials of both the principal and Barbara Jones, teachers gathered all the students in the school auditorium without suspicion. Yet all were surprised when the young Barbara Johns, not the principal, began addressing the student body. In the schoolwide meeting that followed, many of the teachers left. Following John's lead, Carrie Stokes, president of the student body, and her twin brother, John, the vice president, called for the students to walk out and strike to protest the inferior conditions of their school. As one student striker, Joy Speakes recalled, John stood up and started a chant, "One bits, two bits, three bits, a dollar. All on strike stand up and holler."[11] The student body responded in earnest and walked out of school. Some marched downtown, while others went home.[12]

Student leaders and their supporters marched downtown and called upon the services of the NAACP. "Gentlemen," they wrote to a team of lawyers in Richmond just hours after the walkout, "due to the fact that the facilities and building in the name of Robert R. Moton High School, are inadequate, we understand that your help is available to us. This morning . . . students refused to attend classes under any circumstances. You know that this is a very serious matter because we are out of school . . . we beg you to come down at the first of this week." They mailed the letter to Oliver W. Hill, who attended law school at Howard University under the tutelage of Charles Hamilton Houston, the architect of the legal strategy for educational equality, and graduated second in his class only to Thurgood Marshall in 1933. His firm worked closely with the Virginia branch of the NAACP and decided to visit the student strikers in Prince Edward County.[13]

The strike and the NAACP's impending visit drew impressive crowds for the small town. "Packing every nook and cranny of the First Baptist Church," the *Richmond Afro-American* reported, "1,000 citizens of this community of 3,475 turned out to hear NAACP attorneys."[14] The parents and resultant coalition formally petitioned the school board to discontinue all discriminatory practices and admit Black students to White schools. But when they ultimately filed suit with the NAACP in *Davis v. County School Board of Prince Edward County, Virginia,* one of the five pivotal court cases that composed the *Brown v. Board of Education* (1954) decision, they changed the course of U.S. history.[15] Indeed, Johns herself invoked scripture regarding the incident, quoting Isaiah 11:6, "And a little child shall lead them." Joy Speakes, one of the student protestors, recalled that "I really, and I still feel, I felt then, it's divine intervention. It was a time for that to happen and [Barbara Johns] was the person at that time to carry it out."[16] Remembered by some as a divinely inspired turning point in the movement, the realities of the student strike reveal it to be a very human endeavor, complete with the tensions that defined high school student activism during the 1950s.

The relationship between youth and their elders remained crucial, even for a youth-led initiative like this one. Though Moton High School students acted of their own accord, the young activists were directly influenced by their elders, who regularly petitioned for more or better educational opportunity in Farmville. The delegations of Black civic leaders and parents regularly petitioned the board since the 1930s. By the year of the protest, all they had to show for it was a series of broken promises and three tar paper shacks the board built to accommodate overcrowding. In some instances, elders in Farmville engaged in more assertive civil rights initiatives, all of which presaged the high school walkout. Barbara Johns was the niece of Vernon Johns, the fiery orator and pastor of Triumph Baptist in Darlington Heights, who compelled his congregation to challenge segregation, much to the chagrin of many in the small Farmville community. He also pastored Dexter Avenue Baptist Church in Montgomery, Alabama, preceding a young Dr. Martin Luther King Jr.[17] Joy Speakes, one of the students who walked out, was the granddaughter of George P. Morton. Morton was one of the active members of the delegations in Farmville that regularly petitioned the school board for better opportunity for their children. When Speakes appeared at home at the start of the school day and told her grandparents what had transpired, they were "receptive to it right away."[18] Early in the case, when plaintiffs had to own land to list their name as a plaintiff, Morton pledged his land to those who needed it.[19]

The students who marched out of the school were cognizant of this local and familial history. Some viewed themselves as following in the footsteps of their elders, such as Rev. Griffin, Rev. Johns, Dr. Miller, George Moton, Willie Redd, Fred Reid, and others who for the past decade petitioned for new and better facilities. They were aware of the efforts to petition the board whose decisions made the unequally funded and ill-equipped school they attended all but unbearable. Moton students in 1951 were therefore determined to break the recalcitrance of the school board. "They were trying to get us a new school, a better school," Speakes recalled of previous attempts, "so they would go to the PTA meetings, they would go to the school board and to the superintendent there to try to get bonds and land for us a better school. But each time they went, they couldn't get anywhere with it."[20] Forced by a school board who consistently denied requests for better facilities, students employed unorthodox if not radical means—in the context of the 1950s—to achieve school improvement.

Barbara Johns and the students who walked out sought to address these immediate concerns, demanding better facilities to accommodate the large Black student population, and a recommitment on the part of local and state governments to provide a quality education.[21] In addition to calling for the same demands as community leaders who regularly pressed the school district for better facilities and a new school, students essentially reaffirmed the goals of Aline Black, Gladys Bates, and the teacher salary equalization cases of the previous decade that demanded equality under the law, not necessarily integration. Their strategies were different, to be sure, as was the autonomous nature of their protest, but students pushed for the same demands as their predecessors.

But the Farmville protest presented new opportunities for the NAACP. The student walkout was timely for the Association, which was moving on from the salary equalization cases they successfully argued in southern courts in the 1940s. By 1951 the NAACP stopped litigating for equal teacher salaries and sought to enroll Black students in White schools. The Association was already laying groundwork in Cumberland County and Buckingham County, Virginia, where Black residents working with Oliver Hill filed a petition charging racial discrimination.[22] The case in Farmville met their legal requirements. The students at Moton pointed out the same injustices that were systemic to the county and the state of Virginia. At the time of the protests, there were fifteen Black schools in Prince Edward County. All schools but the high school were of wood construction, had no toilet facilities except for outside privies, and relied on wood, coal, or kerosene for heat.[23] Though students made no explicit claims to larger systemic issues, they laid bare the disparities behind attending school in the Jim Crow South. A case of clear discrimination could be made in proving the violation of the equal protection clause and material inferiority bred by segregation. Moreover, as the NAACP looked for critical test cases, the Association actively sought local grassroots support to move beyond equalization and demand integration. The Farmville protest promised a groundswell of support they needed as the student-led protests inspired invaluable community support. They provided the momentum the NAACP needed to build a historic case.

In order to bring the mobilization in line with their new legal strategy, the NAACP had to reframe the preliminary goals of the students and their parents, which had broadly focused on equal accommodations. The NAACP sought to harness the local energy by moving beyond the school equalization campaign to focus in on a direct attack on *de jure* segregation. Thurgood Marshall worked with Spottswood Robinson, one of the attorneys in Richmond who took up the Farmville case, and concluded that a direct legal assault on segregation was preferable to pursuing more equalization suits.[24] When the NAACP first pitched the idea to Farmville residents, many were hesitant. The proposition also countered the claims of students, who sought new and better facilities, more akin to the teacher salary equalization suits and the demands of their predecessors who petitioned the school board. After listening to the NAACP, Barbara Johns stood up in defiance and declared: "We're not going to let any Uncle Tom or anybody stop us from what we are doing."[25]

By the conclusion of the community meetings, the NAACP successfully persuaded enough of the Farmville community to pursue desegregation, avoiding yet another equalization case. A new delegation resolved to approach the school board once again, carrying forward the work of previous years with a new mission. Their petition demanded the abolition of segregated schools and the right for Black students to attend White schools.[26] The community remained committed despite the resistance they knew they would encounter. Crosses were burned in the yard of Moton High School.[27] Barbara Johns, fearing for her life, left to live with her uncle, Vernon Johns, in Alabama.[28] The message was clear, segregationists would not tolerate the push for integrating White schools.

The ongoing and increasingly precarious position of Black teachers and administrators played a key role in the struggle as well. The Black principal, Mr. M. Boyd Jones, quickly distanced himself from the student protestors. "[The walkout is a] rebellion against existing school facilities and is deep-seated," Principal Jones told the local press, "this thing was thought out by students who planned the whole scheme of the rebellion."[29] Just three years prior, teachers had been on the front lines demanding equalization. Principal Jones's stance represented a marked shift. By opting not to follow student demands, Jones occupied a recalcitrant and conservative position, as did many teachers. Though many teachers practiced forms of pedagogical activism behind closed doors or remained supportive of student activists in various ways, Jones' conservative stance has often been used to define teachers' political positioning during the civil rights movement as the 1950s and 60s proceeded.

The school board reconvened that summer and held a meeting in a courtroom to discuss the contract of the principal for the upcoming school year. Board members heard a petition by a delegation to request the reappointment of the principal. Mr. Jones also pleaded his case, appearing with his family in a show of support. He also attended the meeting with Dr. J. S. Picott, Executive Secretary of the Virginia State Teachers Association, who provided legal counsel to the embattled Jones. The superintendent and the board did not retain Jones and refused to extend his contract.[30] Jones was not the only casualty. Vera Allen, whose daughter was allegedly part of the inner circle of the planning committee behind the boycott, was not rehired for the following year as well.[31] The moment placed intense pressure on the teachers, who were caught between students who demanded their support and White administrators who demanded acquiescence. As much as local Whites were going to terrorize those involved in the walkout, Prince Edward officials were going to remove any teacher or administrator suspected of supporting the "rebellion."

Teachers and administrators were understandably hesitant to support such protests publicly. School district officials did not renew the contracts of educators or principals who publicly demanded an equal salary. The equalization suits sacrificed a finite number of teachers, and in many instances, teacher associations organized support for educators they knew would be terminated. In this way the economic hardships were mitigated. But after the *Brown* decision in 1954, Black teachers faced endemic unemployment. Across the South in 1956, states passed laws targeting the NAACP, requiring educators to declare all political affiliations in their applications to teach. Southern legislatures adopted other repressive measures, including loyalty oaths and state surveillance to vilify and legally extinguish the NAACP. States therefore openly dismissed or suspended teachers for open affiliation with the NAACP or other "subversive" associations.[32] The prospects of full-scale desegregation, moreover, threatened tens of thousands of teachers with unemployment. As school districts were reorganized to meet the demands of desegregation, institutional discrimination threatened Black teachers with massive layoffs, prospects that threatened a significant portion of the professional class of the Black community. Scholars have estimated that thirty-eight thousand teachers lost their jobs in the seventeen Southern and border states during the decade following the *Brown* decision. In North Carolina, for instance, over two hundred Black principals led high schools but only three remained in the leadership position by 1970. In Alabama, the number of principals dropped from 250 to 40.[33]

Septima Clark, a veteran teacher in South Carolina who was dismissed for her affiliation with the NAACP in 1956, illustrates the economic peril Black teachers faced during desegregation and the ongoing movement. Clark paid into a retirement system for forty years with the expectation that the state would match it upon retirement. The state, however, informed her that her investment would not be matched. The financial loss amounted to over $36,000. "Not so much money," Clark recalled, "but a sizable amount to a school teacher who after four decades of teaching at modest salaries was being thrown out of a job."[34]

The demand for desegregation that eventually emerged from the walkout represented a departure from long-standing demands for equalization and became a point of conflict in years to come. Black delegations had long petitioned the board for equal funding, and after the NAACP filed a lawsuit for desegregation, education officials seriously pursued means of improving Black education. It was part of an emerging southern strategy to "equalize" Black schools to that of Whites with the aim to uphold the *Plessy v. Ferguson*'s (1896) "separate but equal" edict. School officials followed an equalization logic premised on the notion that, in the words of long-time educator, superintendent, and consultant for the state board of education Walter Ivy, "Segregation in the schools . . . developed historically before there were any laws on the subject. It was a natural process then and it is a natural process now. We believe that a continuation of segregation . . . irrespective of whether it is maintained by law is not only possible but necessary for the best development of each group."[35]

Across the South, legislators launched efforts to construct a legally defensible facade of racial equality in education and funded Black education at unprecedented levels. In South Carolina, for instance, a legislative plan appropriated $124,329,394 between 1951 and 1956 to fund public education, which provided the capital to construct new buildings, improve transportation statewide or provide it for the first time, and appropriate increased though still not equal resources to Black schools. African Americans made up about 40 percent of South Carolina's school pupils and received two-thirds of that money appropriated under the equalization plan.[36] There was widespread need for the support. A school survey undertaken in Hinds County, Mississippi, in 1953 is indicative of the status of schools in the South. The report found that "due to inadequate financing the colored school buildings are generally small, the furniture and other equipment obsolete and the surroundings unattractive."[37] Of the first twenty-five schools surveyed, only four schools were of "good" equality. Every other school was described with a common phrase, "the building is dilapidated and should be replaced," or "this building is to be abandoned and the children transported."[38] The imminent threat of a desegregation lawsuit yielded strong support for plans previously submitted by Black delegations. School officials in Prince Edward County Board of Education did not consider desegregation but instead continued to draft plans for a new but separate Black school immediately after the strike and submitted a plan to the state board for approval for building a new high school for $750,000, eight months after the strike, and approved them in January 1952. They planned to open the school in 1953.[39]

These efforts brought about swift and visible improvements for Black schools. As noted in one account of the *Brown* decision offered by the Alabama State Teachers Association, "the general trend among school boards after 1954 was to construct a new gymnasium . . . Along with the new gym, the new construction projects after 1954 typically included the building of a new cafeteria, auditorium, additional restrooms, library, teachers' lounges, science labs, and indoor restrooms."[40] In the capital city of Jackson, the state of Mississippi expended significant funding to equalize Black schools. A new Brinkley Elementary-Junior High School was constructed, which included a new auditorium, classrooms, and offices in 1952. Jim Hill Junior-Senior High School received an upgrade in 1952.[41] The state also constructed a new Lanier Junior-Senior High School. The new ten-acre campus included new tennis courses, basketball courts, a new auditorium-gymnasium, cafeteria, library, and new science labs.[42] Students in McComb, Mississippi, moved into Burgland High School, a Black school built in 1957 as part of the state's equalization attempts. The new school sat on a four and one-half acre lot and contained two brick buildings, one of which contained twelve classrooms and an auditorium, the other an annex that contained four classrooms.[43] The Charleston County School District in South Carolina opened East Bay Street Negro Elementary School in February of 1955, less than one year after the *Brown* decision, which was reported to be "nearly identical to Memminger Elementary School," a school serving Charleston's White population, "in construction, equipment, and quality of finish."[44] Two years later, school officials opened the Columbus Street School for African American students. Additionally, the city transferred Courtenay Elementary from White hands to Black control in 1958.[45] Particularly because of the baby boom growth that had gone unaddressed during the 1940s, increased investment and changes in governance were a welcome change across the South.

The *Brown* decision refracted the debate about equalization in complex ways. Some teacher groups passed motions that approved of equalization process. The Black teachers' association in Alabama noted that teachers "succumbed briefly to the new signs of caring" evident in the equalization attempts, passing a resolution that voiced appreciation for state-supported efforts to improve Black schools.[46] A history of the association also recounts that teachers "kept a low profile" and were "relatively quiet" in the years after *Brown*.[47] Robert Moran, a teacher in South Carolina, wrote in 1952 that "A revolution is taking place in the field of education." Moran pointed out the benefits, such as the $23 million appropriated for new school buildings, but he also raised the issue of teacher pay: "What if anything does the state propose to do about the intellectual death of many school teachers? The State must realize that new buildings alone will neither equalize facilities nor satisfy the Negro's desire for education."[48] Teachers like those in the Palmetto State Teachers Association followed the movement to desegregate schools closely and kept its members up to date on news from across the country.[49]

Increasingly out of step with the NAACP's position on desegregation, teachers' already precarious position grew even more perilous. Equalization suits appeared conservative and antithetical by comparison to the NAACP's challenge to the doctrine of segregation. At the very moment that the NAACP radicalized its assault on *de jure* segregation, teachers who once demanded equalization appeared to demonstrate indifference, and the organization came to dismiss teachers as key change agents. Herbert Wright, Youth Secretary of the Youth Councils in the buildup toward *Brown*, publicly denounced the "spineless Negro school principals and state college presidents" in 1953.[50] Students supported this view as well. According to Willie Sheperson, a student striker at Moton, "there are teachers that still live in the community and they will tell you that man they were gung ho with that strike for those kids and they were with it all the way. That's a lie—its not true . . . they were more concerned about their job . . . Some of them supported us, yes they did, but all of them didn't support us."[51] Teachers continued to provide an important foundation for activism that continued to resonate with some young people, as recalled by the Moton strikers. But the NAACP and the dominant view of education cast them aside as a hindrance since they did not vocally support the movement.[52]

The Moton protesters challenged the NAACP and teachers to act. They raised serious questions about the direction of the movement. Yet layered anxieties about the essential role of youth, and how youth viewed themselves, surfaced during the student rebellion. The student walkout in Farmville brought a question of autonomy to the front, an issue the NAACP grappled with since the inception of Youth Councils. The questions forced in Virginia echoed across the country, creating a constitutional crisis of sorts for the NAACP.

In 1951 the New York City Youth Council chapter proposed the NAACP amend its constitution to grant more autonomy to its youngest members. They specifically proposed that the constitution should not hold youth chapters subordinate to the local branch of the NAACP, though they did not challenge being a "constituent and subordinate unit" of the national association. The Youth Council wrote that, if language pertaining to subordination to the local branch were stricken from the constitution, Youth Councils would be constitutionally equal to the adult branch. "The youth of the Association have shown that they have the imagination and the drive to carry out the program the NAACP," they argued, "if only they are not too shackled by their elders."[53]

The growing rift between youth and more senior leaders had become inescapable. Growing dissension over youth autonomy surfaced in a 1942 report released by the Youth Director, Madison Jones. "While the [youth program] should be one of the most important units in our work, at the present time, due to current procedure, supervision and general official attitude, it is not."[54] In her explanation of this "impotence," she cited an inadequacy of directorship from the national office, laxness of senior branches in setting up youth work committees, and, notably, "reluctance of senior branches to give freedom of action to youth."[55] While youth organizers petitioned for more support, young people themselves demanded different strategies within the NAACP. In Chicago in 1947, the senior chapter clashed with younger chapters over whether junior branches could vote with the slightly older Youth Councils. They argued that younger branches should be included in the voting process. Ideological conflict engendered by Cold War politics challenged Youth Councils as well. In Flint, Michigan, the senior branches accused the youth chapters of Communist affiliation after a schism over a local boycott led by NAACP youth. Other Youth Council members in New York and Boston upheld initiatives to ban Communists from the association in justification of their proposed amendment.[56] At stake was not necessarily allegiance to democratic or Communist principles, or the right to hold separate elections among youth chapters, but rather the right of young people to determine their own agenda. By 1953 Gloster Current, director of branches, identified the issue of youth autonomy as "a matter which must be taken care of as soon as possible."[57]

Leadership responded coldly to growing demands for youth autonomy. Robert Wright, the youth director of the NAACP, responded to inquiries about youth autonomy by citing that "the program and policy of the NAACP [as determined at the] Annual Conference cannot be abrogated or changed to fit the particular needs or desires of an individual chapter."[58] NAACP leadership tightened control of the youth organizations instead and suggested even stronger oversight by older members of the NAACP or college faculty. They proposed requiring chapters to submit reports for permission before affiliating with organizations other than the NAACP. In regard to the college chapters of the NAACP, Wright proposed to Current that college chapters must gain permission from the national board for cooperation with any initiatives or associations outside the purview of the NAACP.[59] Wright also recommended changes that affirmed the constitutional provision that articulated Youth Councils were required to submit reports covering all youth activities to the local branch and the national governing body in order to "keep the Secretary of the Branch and the National Youth Secretary informed of all events affecting the interest of youth."[60] Additionally, leadership recommended and adopted changes that specified a senior advisor, who was to be drawn from a local branch, to supervise Youth Councils. For college chapters, he recommended that a faculty advisor should serve on the council as well.[61]

The Constitution Revision Committee of the NAACP in 1954 definitively rejected the changes sought by youth chapter members. Their revised constitution held that Youth Councils would remain subordinate to the local branch and the national association and were expected to submit regular reports to the Executive Committee to keep the secretary of the branch and the national youth secretary informed "of all events affecting the interest of youth." Cooperation with other groups would have to be approved by the NAACP, and they were denied the right to affiliate with other groups—a departure from previous decades and a stark difference from the organizing tradition of SNYC. Moreover, in keeping with the original constitution, the NAACP maintained the right to suspend or revoke the charter of any Youth Council "whenever the Board shall deem it for the best interest of the Association." They also modified their right of supervision to include a provision to declare any office of the Youth Council invalid if officers failed to report any meetings for more than four months.[62] In short, the NAACP increased already strict oversight in the early 1950s as youth activism began to influence the direction of local protest movements and, in the case of the Farmville student demonstration, shape the national movement as well.

For NAACP leadership in the 1950s, youth and young people were to remain passive participants in the struggle. In a telling statement, Medgar Evers, the popular NAACP field director in Mississippi, articulated, "The support of the Youth Councils shall be used as a stepping stone toward our goal of first-class citizenship."[63] The phrase is significant. At the very moment when the NAACP was mounting an unprecedented challenge to southern segregation, leadership and movement elders valued young people's participation only insofar as they could control them. This tension would continue to undergird the youth movement in the years to come.

Youth Participation in Baton Rouge

In some critical cases a Black high school provided the space for civil rights activism to grow, especially if led by a sympathetic Black principal, and the Black high school students who served as foot soldiers for protests. In Prince Edward County, youth led the movement. But in most other places, youth provided unrecognized support that often pushed the movement forward and sustained it. The bus boycott in Baton Rouge, Louisiana, in 1953 demonstrates how not only youth were integral participants in the struggles of the civil rights movement but how the physical space of historically Black high schools became a political site of resistance.

In June 1953 the Reverend Theodore J. Jemison, a minister of Mt. Zion Baptist in Baton Rouge, led the city in a ten-day boycott of the city buses, largely through the United Defense League, a local organization developed in the specific context of the bus boycott. The boycott wrought a limited victory, in which Whites afforded more seats to Black patrons on the bus but failed to fully eliminate segregation. The boycott demonstrated the value in local organizing outside the jurisdiction of the NAACP and established a blueprint for the Montgomery bus boycott.[64]

The influence of education at both a conceptual and practical level is evident throughout the duration of the Baton Rouge bus boycott. Movement leaders in Baton Rouge were cognizant of the importance of education at an abstract level. For leaders like Rev. T. J. Jemison, citizenship education was integral in raising critical awareness for youth of color in the era of segregation. Rev. T. J. Jemison recalled the importance of citizenship education when looking back on one of the key moments that shaped his leadership during the boycott. Rev. Jemison sought to test a new city ordinance that designated seats for Black patrons and allowed all patrons to sit wherever they pleased in the unmarked seats as long as Whites remained in front and in the rows designated for them, achieving a compromise while in effect affirming a color line. When Jemison sat in an all-White section at the front of the bus following the ordinance, the driver called the police. When the officer arrived, Rev. Jemison recited the new ordinance that permitted him to sit there. The officer backed down and Rev. Jemison remained on the bus. "One of the first lessons I learned in civics," he recalled in retrospect, "was that ignorance is no excuse before the law. And the fact that you don't know it doesn't mean it is not a law."[65] Rev. Jemison maintained the adage that knowledge is power, an ideology that fueled the education of African Americans in the South. For Jemison and other movement leaders, not to mention the teachers that the NAACP cast aside, Black schools served as a critical intellectual bulwark in providing the information needed to become participants in the movement.

Black education made a tangible, practical contribution to the local movement in Baton Rouge as well. Much like Prince Edward County walkout, the bus boycott in Baton Rouge drew unprecedented crowds of two thousand people, if not more. It was a strong showing in a southern context and it was beyond the capacity of Rev. Jemison's Mt. Zion Baptist church, or any other church that was sympathetic to the boycott. A larger space was needed and the all-Black McKinley High School provided that space. As Rev. Jemison recalled, the auditorium at McKinley High School was used to hold mass meetings during the evening of the bus boycott. The high school auditoriums, including the space at Capitol High School, were essential to the boycott as mass meetings drew large crowds.[66] The community would gather to strategize, talk, gain collective strength, and raise money to support the elaborate car system in place, which was free to the passengers who selected to stay off the city buses.

The space provided by Black high schools complimented that of the Black church, allowing activists to gather and the community to meet safely. In the decades before the bus boycott, these same spaces were occupied to hold Negro History Week events to educate the public. In more political ways, the auditorium functioned as a site of political organization, much like that at Berkeley County Training Institute in South Carolina that was used to hold SNYC citizenship courses and training institutes after the Second World War. In succeeding years, the Black high school opened its doors as they did outside Montgomery, Alabama, at St. Jude's Education Institute to host marchers and a concert.[67] The provision of a safe, physical space was critical to fostering the movement.

McKinley High School—the first Black public high school in the state of Louisiana to graduate students—was an integral site to support the bus boycott because of its historic origins.[68] McKinley, like other Black high schools across the South, was the manifestation of Black politics and southern progressivism during the age of Jim Crow. Concerned Black civic leaders formed the "Colored Building Committee" and pressured White city officials to build McKinley High School in 1916. The committee was similar to other delegations across the South, and one that built on years of political organizing and leveraging the small but influential number of Black voters in mayoral and other city council elections for support.[69] Dr. Frazier and the Colored Building Committee forged relationships with moderate White civic leaders, successfully appealing to the city council for additional funds to build a new high school. The council acquiesced in 1926 and devoted $175,000 to the erection of a new modern high school, named in honor of former President William McKinley. It was a brick building that contained twenty classrooms with laboratories for chemistry and physics, shops for manual training, and a library. The central heating system and a "moving picture projector of the regular theatrical type" marked it with modern conveniences.[70] The school, with a capacity of eleven hundred students, was equipped with an auditorium accentuated by a baby grand piano in the music room, and the school sat on landscaped grounds.[71]

McKinley was the premier public school for the African American community in Baton Rouge and the state of Louisiana. "McKinley High School was a gem," Baton Rouge resident Huel Perkins recalled of the school. "People from all of the surrounding towns would move to Baton Rouge so that they could go to school there. I think of people who lived in New Roads, moved over here that they could go. I think of people living in Denham Springs, people that lived in Zachary. They would move in with relatives and friends. Because that time, of course, McKinley was central to black education. It really was."[72] Joseph Delpit, a McKinley graduate, recalled,

McKinley High School, Baton Rouge, Louisiana, built in 1927. Courtesy of State Library of Louisiana, Louisiana Collection.

"McKinley attracted students from as far away that I know, Appaloosa, which is about 40 miles from here, New Roads, and other areas within surrounding Baton Rouge that didn't have schools. As the story's told, those young people, many of them had to work in the cotton fields during that season and then they would go to school after that season was over."[73] Black civic leaders, delegations, and education advocates worked tirelessly to secure a secondary education for their children, and they continued to invest in the institution as a vehicle for collective improvement. When local movements such as the bus boycott emerged, Black high schools like McKinley were logical sites to support it.

McKinley sat in the heart of the South Baton Rouge district. It was the Black residential and business district of Baton Rouge. McKinley High School drew much of its power from "Old South" Baton Rouge, the largely African American neighborhood that contained its own central business district, middle class homes, active churches and civic organizations, and social service institutions that served communities of color not otherwise served by White institutions.[74] As Freddie Pitcher, a student at McKinley High School recalled, the district was made from Black "establishments up and down East Boulevard, the Butler Building where Dr. Butler had his physician's office, his medical office. There was a pharmacy there. Barber shops and beauty shops, you know, down that strip. So that was the hub of the business area."[75] There was also the Chicken Shack, a popular hangout in South Baton Rouge. It served generations of local residents. Thomas Delpit, for whom a street in the town is now named, founded the Chicken Shack in 1935 and served comfort food.[76] It was a crucial establishment for the Black community. Joe Delpit recalls of the locally famous restaurant: "At that time there were no lunch programs at McKinley High School and a lot of the kids who went to McKinley High School would come to the Chicken Shack in order to eat. He would charge, I think the maximum ever was a quarter, if you had no money you paid zero, and if you had only 10 cents you paid 10 cents for your hot meal."[77] Charles Ricard remembers cooking in the kitchen at the Chicken Shack during the 1940s and 1950s with fond memories, recalling that Mr. Delpit, or "Tommy" as they referred to him, gave "everybody a job." He also recalled affably, "Tommy would come in [and say], 'Come here boy, I'm going to fatten you up!'"[78]

Neighborhoods like Old South Baton Rouge provided the base for sustaining protest, if not generating it. It also provided protection and opportunities for Black youth. The neighborhood, and valued local institutions such as the Chicken Shack, served as an institution parallel to the high school in this regard. As such, Black neighborhoods that housed Black high schools expanded and reinforced the educational foundations they established.

In many cases the neighborhood provided foot soldiers who were in high school. Their activism was not causally linked to the high school, but their age illustrated that time and again youth participated on the front lines of the movement. Thomas Delpit's son, Joe, remembers providing transportation during the bus boycott. As part of his work in the family business at the Chicken Shack, the young Delpit learned to drive at a very early age to help deliver food to the homes of customers. Though not permitted by the state, he could be more helpful driving. "I was real slow delivering on the bicycle," Delpit recalled. It was the start of several intentional transgressions to support a collective cause for the greater social good. When the boycott started in 1953, Delpit, at the age of thirteen, helped briefly in the boycott. "I was delivering men," Delpit recalled of driving boycotters to and from their destination though legally underaged, "and they wouldn't send me far."[79] But Delpit remembers participating, or at least seeing local men and women waiting on the corner for rides from the network of taxis, cabs, and volunteer drivers Rev. Jemison and the United Defense League developed.[80]

In one sense Delpit's experiences constituted an informal education that shaped the base of the youth movement. In another sense, it exemplifies the critical role youth played as active participants in the movement. When organizers replicated the concept of the bus boycott in Montgomery, the role of Black secondary education and youth in high school played a similarly influential role.

Student Activism and the Montgomery Bus Boycott

Claudette Colvin, a student at Booker T. Washington High School in Montgomery, Alabama, refused to give up her seat to White patrons on the city bus on March 2, 1955, nearly nine months before the incarceration of Rosa Parks. This incident and the events that unfolded after her arrest propelled the Montgomery bus boycott and the pressure to chip away at the segregationist edifice of Dixie.[81] Colvin was the plaintiff in *Browder v. Gayle* (1956), the court case in which the court ruled that segregated buses in Montgomery violated the equal protection clause.[82] At the time of her arrest, Colvin was a fifteen-year-old junior in high school and represented the potential of high school students to act outside the parameters of desegregating White schools at the very moment the NAACP pushed for integration.[83]

Colvin and the young people she inspired were motivated by aims that stretched far beyond the NAACP's goal of achieving school desegregation. Colvin and her classmates remained incensed that their respected friend, Jeremiah Reeves, was on death row. Mabel Ann Crowder claimed Reeves assaulted and raped her only when two neighbors discovered them "in the act." Her accusations stood in conflict with Reeves' account and testimony from the Black community, who suspected it was an ongoing and consensual relationship. Reeves confessed to the crime, but only after police strapped him to an electric chair, stating that they would execute him if he did not concede. He later recanted, and provided testimony about the coerced confession in court, but to no avail.[84] Dr. Martin Luther King Jr. captured the prejudice that Colvin and her classmates knew intimately when he noted that "the death of Jeremiah Reeves is but one incident, yes a tragic incident, in the long and desolate night of our court injustice."[85]

From the vantage point of youth, their participation conjured up similarly profound sentiments as it did for high school activists during the demonstrations of Prince Edward County. Young people in Montgomery, too, helped shape a milestone in American history and they were destined to do so. More than just anomalous demonstrations in random locations, high school youth were critical change agents in a growing movement, and their activism constituted a unique contribution to the larger struggle.

Additionally, the movement itself was an educative space. Similar to the education youth received in NAACP Youth Council meetings or at SNYC conferences, youth involved in the Montgomery bus boycott received a unique education in community organizing. Gwendolyn Patton illustrates how the trenches of Montgomery doubled as educative places for youth in the movement. Patton was born in Detroit in 1943. Her father was from Montgomery but moved to Detroit in 1940 as part of the Great Migration, one of the millions refusing to submit to endemic discrimination in the South. He first worked as a bus driver, then a welder at the Cadillac factory, and was eventually elected as a committeeman to the United Auto Workers.[86] Patton spent her summers with her grandparents in Montgomery. They were registered voters and were well connected to community organizers. Patton participated in the bus boycott, but indirectly. She would survey the neighborhood with her grandmother, asking questions about her grandparents' neighbors' voting status, the number of times they registered to vote, documenting instances of harassment for attempting to register, and, in some cases, urging them to complete an affidavit.[87] For Patton, community canvassing was activism, a definition that carried forth through the 1960s as more youth became engaged in the movement. Additionally, Patton traced her sense of activism to her family, like many young activists. Her father left the South due to political oppression and joined a union in Michigan. As Patton noted, "In the early days, the movement was a family thing. And the family thing was a mindset . . . Mine was like full force involvement."[88] When Patton moved back to Montgomery at the age of sixteen, she was an activist for life. Movement education presaged the activist-oriented education behind the youth protest of the 1960s.

Like other demonstrations across the South where high school youth participated, the Black high school was an incubator of resistance. Similar to R. R. Moton and McKinley High School, Booker T. Washington High School in Montgomery, Alabama, was of central importance. The school originated during Reconstruction. It was founded in 1868 as Swayne College as a partnership between the AMA and the Freedmen's Bureau. Swayne continued the classical liberal arts tradition and functioned as a college preparatory school.[89] As the support of Reconstruction schools waned during the nadir of Jim Crow, civic leaders and education advocates from Montgomery formed delegations much like those in Prince Edward County, Baton Rouge, and elsewhere across the South. They petitioned the district to build a new school to house the students confined to the original building. The district built a new school in 1914 at public expense with private support.[90] By 1949

Booker T. Washington was dedicated as a new high school on its third location. Dr. H. Councill Trenholm, the president at Alabama State College,
whose father had long desired a Black public high school in Montgomery,
presided over the dedication ceremony, as did White members of the school
board and the city council.[91] At the time of the bus boycott, then, Booker T.
Washington High School was established as a site firmly grounded in the
politics of Jim Crow. Maintaining and carrying forth the traditions of Black
secondary education, Booker T. Washington High School was situated to
support if not initiate some critical aspects of a local movement.

Booker T. Washington presented a logical site for channeling the current
of resistance, where educators continued in their long-standing role of shor-
ing up the foundations of youth activism. Teachers during the 1950s continued to inculcate elements of the Black progressive tradition in the
classroom that raised the political consciousness of students. Teachers at
Booker T. Washington were no different. They were indicative of the ongoing work of Black educators in Black high schools across the South. In the
aftermath of the equalization campaigns and move toward desegregation
during the 1950s, teachers provided other forms of support, most often in
the classroom. "We had been studying the Constitution," Colvin recalled of
an English class she was taking, "I knew we had rights."[92] Colvin remembered fondly the influence of an English teacher in setting a professional
standard and cultivating critical thinking, which ultimately facilitated civic
engagement in notable instances: "Miss Geraldine Nesbitt dressed sharp.
She had a master's degree in education from Columbia University. She
came to school early and stayed late. She was tough, but she was out to
make you learn . . . [Miss Nesbitt] taught us the world through literature.
She taught the Constitution. She taught the Magna Carta and the Articles
of Confederation . . . and applied it to our own situations."[93] Ms. Nesbitt's
academic background and teaching in the classroom were typical of educators after the *Brown* decision. Nesbitt was well educated and taught a
critical and liberal curriculum in an era most often defined by vocational
education heralded by the namesake of Colvin's school, Booker T. Washington. It was not the same form of activism observed in the Baton Rouge
boycotts, for instance, but teachers like Ms. Nesbitt taught enough to trig-
ger a larger intellectual engagement with the struggle to dismantle Jim
Crow. Lessons like those taught by Nesbitt were seemingly innocuous in a
White high school, but they held radical implications for racialized, criminalized, and oppressed Black youth. Additionally, the content and pedagogy

of teachers like Nesbitt challenged the rationale behind the NAACP's dismissal of teachers as key actors in the movement.

Extracurricular activities, particularly Black high school student newspapers, demonstrate the raised consciousness of engaged students during the 1950s. This student-led medium served as a conduit for the activist voice among the student population. *The Parvenue*, the student newspaper of Burke High School in Charleston, South Carolina, illustrates how this forum served as a place for students to publish their ideas, and many authors used the pages of the school newspaper to debate issues of education, citizenship, and race. Students took their role in schools very seriously, and they were conscious of the positions of their institutions in the larger society. "Education is the freedom of knowledge to everyone, in every field and in every aspect of life," Dolly Louise Bonneau wrote from Burke in 1952. "Education today . . . means a happier life, higher standards for recognition, and better security."[94] Students also used *The Parvenue* to debate the merits of various initiatives aimed at the quality of education they received. Lewalter Dilligard discussed the advantages of including Black history as early as 1956. Noting the achievements of George Washington Carver, Mary McLoud Bethune, and Paul Lawrence Dunbar, Dilligard suggested the collective benefits of studying history, which the Social Science department at the school provided.[95] Harmless on the surface, such statements belie the deeper resistance embodied in these statements. In an era where White supremacy denied full equality and resources to Black schools, these statements affirm a strong desire for a liberal education despite the prevailing ideologies of cultural deficiency that oftentimes presumed Black students did not want an education beyond vocational training. Students at Burke actively discussed issues connected to the "race problem" in the 1950s as well. As Ernest Thompson wrote in *The Parvenue* just prior to the *Brown v. Board of Education* (1954) decision, "The main causes of our racial problems are our ignorance and misunderstanding. We the patriotic Americans must eliminate these two stumbling blocks on the road to a better America."[96]

By the 1950s, students like Jacquelyn Martin, a student from McComb, Mississippi, who attended Burgland High School, experienced a critical questioning and a new awakening:

Most people had relatives that lived up north somewhere, so you had those conversations back and forth with people, so yes it was an awareness, and it was one of the things like the Montgomery Bus

Boycott and all that. Yeah, we read about all of that, so we knew what was going on in the greater world. And then we had current events in school where you had conversations about that, you know, so when a teacher asks, you know, what's going on, and you would have a kid stand up and talk about that and other kids would ask questions.[97]

As events unfolded like the Montgomery bus boycott, students like Martin were aware and increasingly asked questions in their classrooms. The lessons of survival were the same as previous generations, but the context of the classroom began to change and youth of the 1950s took new routes to register their discontent.

The pedagogical activism inherent to extracurricular activities like the *Parvenue* from Charleston or Mrs. Nesbitt's lessons in Montgomery define a more common form of resistance found in Black high schools. But this is not to suggest that teachers were not directly active in the buildup to and aftermath of the *Brown* decision. To protect their jobs and maintain a commitment to the freedom struggle, Black teachers covertly supported the movement with a "fugitive pedagogy." Therefore, the full legal assault on desegregation did not preclude active participation in the NAACP, though comments from national directors implied it. In not uncommon cases, teachers still maintained their support of the NAACP and their attempts to desegregate schools. Though not an overwhelming majority, a significant minority of teachers still supported the NAACP, often through clandestine means. Millicent Brown, lead plaintiff to desegregate schools in Charleston, South Carolina, and the daughter of J. Arthur Brown, president of the local branch of the NAACP, recalled that many teachers supported the NAACP and, by extension, the movement privately. As Brown noted, "the *Crisis* [the NAACP's publication] would always come in stacks to our house and then people would come and pick them up because no one wanted to be identified because the mail carrier could tell who the [NAACP] members were . . . that was the level of intimidation that people felt . . . They belonged to the NAACP and certainly later on they would help with contributing money for bail when we started the demonstrations."[98] The fact that teachers stayed with the NAACP as the Association distanced themselves from teachers demonstrates that at least some educators continued to show interest in the movement, which precludes a generalization that teachers opposed the movement.

In exceptional instances, some teachers maintained open affiliation with the NAACP, as Septima Clark did in South Carolina. Women like Ineva May-

Pittman, an elementary school teacher in Jackson, Mississippi, joined the NAACP in the 1950s despite southern legislation opposed to the association and managed to keep their jobs. Mrs. May-Pittman was friends and colleagues with Gladys Noel Bates, the woman who pressed for equal pay in 1948 and lost her job because of it. May-Pittman, to be sure, was acquainted with the dangers associated with the NAACP. After joining the NAACP, May-Pittman served as a youth director for local Youth Councils. As she recalled of her involvement, "Of course, all of that was off the record. You couldn't have a written record of many things, you know, because we couldn't even keep our minutes or anything like that in the NAACP office for fear that they would come in and raid, break in the office and get our roles and harass lots of members and even terminate their employment."[99] As May-Pittman recalls, she and the three women who joined the association with her were comfortable enlisting because their husbands were not dependent upon Whites for employment.[100] It carried with it a class distinction, which privileged an independent middle-class position that often defined participation in the movement.

Teachers like May-Pittman were in a position to share news, updates, and information with their colleagues who could not afford to join the NAACP. As May-Pittman recalled, "We didn't talk about [the NAACP or the movement] in an open meeting or anything. We would talk about it during our break hour in the lounge, after school, or in each others' rooms."[101] Teachers who subscribed anonymously to *The Crisis* or who defied southern law and joined the NAACP served as spokespeople for the movement in Black southern schools where they still exercised strong influence, regardless of the politics of Jim Crow or the movement.

As Black women, most remained committed to forms of engagement shaped by gender, which included community-wide networking and forming relationships through a rich tapestry of social networks. As historian Tiyi Morris demonstrated in her analysis of the work of the women's organization, Womanpower Unlimited, women behind the front lines of the movement facilitated an important network of activism that included the work of women who taught in the local schools.[102] Thelma Sanders, former home economics teacher at Lanier High School and partner of I. S. Sanders, was a successful business owner. She opened Sanders Boutique on Farish Street, the thriving Black business district in the capital city, to provide a high-class fashion alternative for women who were excluded from even trying on clothes. She used her business to help raise funds for the United Negro College Fund, the Urban League, and the National Association of Negro Business and Professional Women's Clubs. She also hosted numerous activists and Freedom Riders as they stayed in Jackson.[103] Both Sanders and her husband were well educated, graduating from Tougaloo College. They were, in the words of her brother, Bo Brown, part of the "real echelon" of college graduates.[104] I. S. Sanders, who served as principal of Lanier High School until 1956, helped form the Jackson Urban League and later the Citizens Committee for Human Rights, further strengthening the connection between education and politics in central Mississippi.[105] In both subtle and, in rare instances, more pronounced ways, teachers were integral parts of local movements across the South.

Beyond the individual connection teachers forged with the NAACP or through local networks, segregated Black teacher associations supported the movement through professional organizing as well. The all-Black American Teachers Association (ATA) exemplifies how Black teachers collectively supported the NAACP and the movement toward desegregation. At the ATA conference in 1953, the national organization officially commended the NAACP for "its continuing and aggressive efforts to achieve the elimination of discriminatory racial differentials in education, in transportation, in housing and in citizenship status." Moreover, the ATA officially recommended that members continue to contribute 10 percent of their funds to the NAACP's Legal Defense and Education Fund, moving from ideological to financial support. It was estimated that the ATA contributed as much as $19,000 to the NAACP over a fifteen-year time frame.[106] The ATA facilitated professional discourse around the issue of desegregation as well. In an address given at the National Advisory Committee on the Education of Negroes in February 1954, just months before the historic decision, Dr. Howard Long Hale optimistically pointed to the advantages of desegregation. He noted the economic benefits of eliminating a dual system. He looked toward the desegregation of the United States military as a blueprint to follow. Desegregation marked "the latest episode in the trek of a subculture stemming from a bondman's status." It was "the doorway for integration."[107]

The month after the *Brown* decision was reached, the ATA published another statement, stating "both tribute and gratitude are justly lavished upon NAACP for the epochal achievement" of the *Brown* decision.[108] Endorsing a call to form the "Christian Council of Human Relations," the ATA sought to promote interracial understanding that the "majesty and force of the law may be upheld and good will among men may be advocated."[109] In the light of the recent decision, the ATA reaffirmed its stance against educational discrimination and called for ongoing and increased federal support. "If we wish for intelligence to survive and to govern mankind," the wrote, "we must dedicate ourselves to it with something of the audacity and courage with which we now prepare for war."[110] All-Black teacher associations at the state level issued statements encouraging just implementation of the decision. The Palmetto Education Association in South Carolina, for instance, published a statement in full compliance with the decision, calling for unequivocal support and working with those seeking implementation of the decision.[111] Educators in South Carolina also reprinted their association objectives, which were revised in 1957, seeking "to encourage teachers to assume their rights and privileges as citizens and to work continuously for the improvement of human relations and understandings in our interpersonal relationships."[112] Having learned firsthand the repercussions of the equalization suits of the 1940s, educators were keenly aware of the decision's unprecedented magnitude. They expected an aggressive reaction.

Black teacher associations were forced to defend their professions, often on their own. The ATA established commissions on teacher security, to provide support and assistance for Black teachers who would encounter dismissal, displacement, and/or job discrimination.[113] Associations like the Palmetto Education Association called upon members to file a complaint if they felt they have been discriminated against after the *Brown* decision. They also publicized issues of unjust dismissal. For instance, the *PEA Journal* reprinted a story about Dr. Chester Travelstead, a dean of education at the University of South Carolina, who was fired by the governor, George Timmerman, over a dispute stemming over the *Brown* decision. The same article also referenced a Baptist minister who spoke in favor of integration in the governor's hometown, Anderson, South Carolina, and was summarily removed from the pulpit.[114]

Activism privileged middle- and upper-class sensibilities that shaped ideas about who should participate in and lead the movement. High school students like those in Prince Edward County, Baton Rouge, and Montgomery were strong potential candidates for the movement because of their social and economic position as high school students. If adolescents were not needed to contribute to a family's finances, which was still a serious consideration for many Black southerners, they were free to attend high school. It also implied a relative privilege to live in an area where a high school existed, which was most often urban and situated in a Black neighborhood with middle and upper classes. To be sure, such class or geographical lines were always blurred and contested. For instance, Claudette Colvin's family lived in the working-class Black neighborhood of King Hills in Montgomery. Her mother cleaned and tended to White homes, and her father was a gardener for wealthy Whites. The circumstances in a rural setting may have limited her access to a high school outside the city in rural Alabama. But her family owned a car, which denoted some financial standing in the city. It also provided a tool in the bus boycott, since the car was used to provide transportation alternative to city buses, thus broadening Colvin's opportunities to participate in the movement compared to her rural counterparts.[115]

The NAACP reaffirmed class distinction through carefully cultivated images and a politics of respectability that espoused exclusivity throughout the 1950s and 1960s. The Colvin case illustrates the process of selective exclusion that defined traditional civil rights politics. The NAACP preferred to use men as lead plaintiffs in desegregation cases like this. As Colvin later became pregnant, she was used in the case *Browder v. Gayle* case with trepidation. As a teenaged mother, movement leaders worried that Colvin tarnished the image of the organization, one that carefully cultivated a professional, "respectable" image. Except for Parks, who continued to mentor the young woman in a very trying time, movement leaders used but largely withdrew public support from Colvin in a move that suggests a particular racial heteronormativity and politics of respectability that governed Blackness.[116] The NAACP embraced the same ideology as other faith-based and education institutions and shunned if not scorned young women who did not live up to patriarchal standards, putting forth a clear image of who could lead the Black freedom struggle.

Colvin's case departed starkly from the traditional youth organizing mechanisms the NAACP continued to rely upon during the 1950s. Movement elders still organized youth as it had during previous decades through annual conferences and Youth Councils. The association steered its efforts to larger desegregation attempts, however, in the midst of the *Brown* decision and its argumentation over implementation. From the perspective of national leadership, youth were viewed as a means to support their larger desegregation agenda. Speaking to delegates in Winston-Salem, North Carolina, Herbert Wright urged young people to work with the national organization to "speed the pace of integration and to help prepare the communities for a smoother transition into the integration pattern."[117] Young people at the 1955 National Youth Legislative Conference at American University voted unanimously to urge the Eisenhower administration to take a stronger stand on enforcing desegregation policy across the country. Students debated the merits of desegregating all public K-12 schools and private religious institutions. Young people provided more nuanced calls, too. They supported the integration of White college faculty with qualified Black professors, as well as demanding vocational training programs for local communities.[118] As nonviolent direct action protests such as school walkouts, as observed in Prince Edward County, or widescale boycotts such as those in Baton Rouge and Montgomery expanded the call of desegregation to public spaces beyond the schoolhouse, youth maintained a focus on quality education rather than a singular call to desegregate schools.

The Youth March for Integrated Schools was one of the most visible demonstrations of the youth movement of the 1950s after the *Brown* decision. Over ten thousand young people and allies of integrated schools marched on the nation's capital and over twenty-five thousand marched the next year in 1959. Organizers and noted supporters included Dr. King, A. Philip Randolph, Roy Wilkins, Daisy Bates, and Jackie Robinson.[119] As part of the march, students issued demands for rapid enforcement of desegregation. In the 1958 letter submitted to President Eisenhower, students demanded integration, calling for federal support and "careful and constructive planning of the nation's march toward integration," including "expert counselling, the financial aid, and the legal authority necessary to achieve this end."[120] They cited the over three hundred student governments who called for integration at the 1957 United States National Student Association's tenth national congress, which represented over 1 million students, the 20,000 young people who marched, the 250,000 signatures they gathered, and 75 national student unions present at the International Student Conference in Lima, Peru in 1958.[121] Youth drew attention to the gravity of the moment to integrate schools, noting that, "For us, the youth, the question of school integration is the central moral issue of our time. Not only are the rights of minorities at stake, American democracy itself, and 'the supremacy of our government, the very survival of the Constitution are at issue."[122]

Dr. King addressed the crowd of thousands at the national Sylvan Theater of the Washington Monument. King commented upon the historic significance of the event, noting that "Nothing like it has ever happened in the history of our Nation," pontificating that it demonstrates "young people . . . have somehow discovered the central fact of American life—that the extension of democracy for all Americans depends upon complete integration of Negro Americans."[123] King encouraged the young people in attendance to become more active:

Become a dedicated fighter for civil rights. Make it a central part of your life. It will make you a better doctor, a better lawyer, a better teacher. It will enrich your spirit as nothing else possibly can. It will give you that rare sense of nobility that can only spring from love and selflessly helping your fellow man. Make a career of humanity. Commit yourself to the noble struggle for equal rights. You will make a greater person of yourself, a greater Nation of your country, and a finer world to live in.[124]

Though inspiring calls to arms, King's remarks highlight how movement leaders viewed youth. They regularly saw youth as foot soldiers to carry out the orders of movement elders. Youth action, such as the walkouts of Prince Edward County or the individual acts of resistance carried out by Claudette Colvin that occurred in the 1950s, were often overlooked to support the overarching drive to vote. Moreover, like Evers, King saw youth in mildly dismissive ways. As King noted, youth "somehow" learned that integration was a crucial component of genuine or participatory democracy. The implication that children and youth stumbled upon the truth espoused in the civil rights movement dismisses the concerted efforts of political socialization and organization found in the high schools many of these youth attended, the work of organizations such as NAACP Youth Councils and SNYC, and the autonomous organizing and direct action of high school youth.

The student-led protests of the 1950s disrupted the dismissive notions put forth by movement elders. When the NAACP framed young people as "victims" of segregated education during the *Brown* case, they promulgated notions of inferiority to argue that mandated segregation was inherently unequal and therefore unconstitutional. As Jonna Perillo noted, "The damaged black psyche argument, and the psychological and postwar social science theories that had enabled its development, created a damaging effect of its own."[125] Student protests also challenged the assumptions of movement elders, including Dr. King and Medgar Evers, who were surprised or failed to truly listen to student voices. One of the damaging effects was that the established civil rights organizations overlooked the value of Black high schools that cultivated an alternative way of living in a segregated society by challenging it. Insisting upon inferiority dismissed nearly one hundred years of organizing a separate and promising network of historically Black high schools throughout the South, one in which students were demonstrating a notion of citizenship and education that pressured a democracy to live up to its ideals. This and other paternalistic views of youth evidenced by movement leaders overlooked the inherent potential of young people as autonomous, independent agents of change. It also overlooked the alternative visions for building a new democratic order.

Young activists put forth a highly effective model of informal political education that engaged youth and young voters in the democratic process. Young people also saw beyond the NAACP's insistence on the desegregation of White schools and envisioned equitable, high-quality schools. Though easily dismissed or cast aside by their elders, youth remained a clairvoyant voice in the movement that continued to push forward the movement in unanticipated ways.

· · · · · ·

By the late 1950s movement elders looked to young people as a critical source of momentum for the movement. Young people in high school initiated walkouts, demanded desegregation, engaged in nonviolent direct action protest, and joined the ranks of the growing army of activists in the ever widening assault on Jim Crow. As adults who led the movement viewed youth as steppingstones and future foot soldiers to carry out the agenda and marching orders of established civil rights leadership, young people began to act autonomously in a landscape that was rapidly changing. Unlike previous decades, youth in the 1950s faced new choices. They could desegregate White schools and public spaces as new legislation began to open up these spaces, providing new access that was denied to their predecessors.

Desegregation, perhaps the most daunting choice students faced during the 1950s, placed an incredible burden on children and youth. While desegregation presented a new opportunity for Black families, the choice students faced was difficult, disruptive, and, in many instances, violent. The nation watched in horror as White segregationists blocked access to nine students who tried to enter Little Rock Central High School through the use of local police in early September 1957. Students there were subjected to violent reprisal, humiliating insults, and premeditated terror from supremacists who acted with impunity. It took an army to force the kids into the all-White school.[126] Lesser-known localized incidents communicated the same lessons to children and young people across the South. One week after the events in Little Rock, Rev. Fred Shuttlesworth, civil rights leader of the Alabama Christian Movement for Human Rights, petitioned the Birmingham board of education to desegregate the all-White

Phillips High School. When Rev. Shuttlesworth led four students to desegregate the school, including his daughter Ruby Fredericka, Whites violently assaulted them, badly beating Shuttlesworth, stabbing his wife in the hip, and causing their daughter to break an ankle.[127] Some cases were not physically violent but nonetheless brought upon incalculable trauma and harm to students of color. Whites reacted to the case in Prince Edward County with extreme measures, for instance, closing public schools and denying any education to those who initially demanded better facilities.[128] Already denied the protections of childhood and adolescence promised to White youth, the choices thrust upon Black youth in the 1950s eroded any semblance of childhood innocence, pushing them into the realities of the civil rights movement, which were similarly violent.

By the end of the 1950s young activists made new choices that propelled the movement forward in unprecedented, yet strategic and calculated ways. Not only were students selecting to enter lily White schools, students were breaking with conventional paths to change typically supported by the NAACP. Students were walking out of school and conscientiously breaking the law instead. Students in Prince Edward County symbolically ushered in an untraditional form of protest led by young people, a student walkout, to great effect, which opened the decade of the 1950s. Students and youth closed the decade with similarly provocative protest. NAACP Youth Council members in Wichita and Oklahoma City in 1958 and 1959 staged a series of sit-ins at segregated lunch counters. In Oklahoma, the ages of demonstrators ranged from six to seventeen. It was led by fifteen-year-old Barbara Ann Posey. The protests were successful, which led to other protests at churches and picketing of other segregated businesses, pressuring the owners to desegregate, and prompting the NAACP to contemplate the utility of direct-action protests.[129] At the NAACP's annual convention in 1959, which celebrated the fiftieth anniversary of the civil rights association, leaders paid homage to Youth Council chapters in Wichita and Oklahoma City. Roy Wilkins noted in the closing remarks of the annual convention in 1960:

We are proud of them, our own NAACP youth who pioneered sit-ins in 1958 [We] pledged anew to them and to all the embattled a continuation of the full support of the NAACP. As these young Negro students recover their freedom, they will be recovering America's also, and redeeming its promise of life, liberty or pursuit of happiness for all. We owe them and their white student cooperators a debt for re-arming our spirits and renewing our strength as a nation at a time when we and free men everywhere sorely need this fresh courage, so generously and so humbly offered . . . It is no extravagance to venture that they, in a sense, constitute another beacon in an old North church, another hoof-beat under a Paul Revere.[130]

Arguably an attempt by the NAACP to claim ownership of the sit-in movement takes certain liberties in framing the history of the movement. Yet there is truth in the matter that high school youth and the NAACP Youth Councils were progenitors of the sit-in movement. The NAACP opted to continue their more conventional legal strategy to challenge segregation, but *youth* in Kansas and Oklahoma arguably established the blueprint for the sit-in movement that captivated the consciousness of the nation over a year later. As more youth acted outside established boundaries of protest, new horizons came into view, as did the enduring tensions that continued to both define and propel the civil rights movement into the turbulence of the 1960s.

4 Young People Who Were Not Able to Accept Things as Status Quo

Youth Mobilization and Direct-Action Protest during the 1960s

• •

"You saw the rise of a new kind of black youth in America and the South-land," student leader James Blake said years after a 1960 sit-in he helped orchestrate in downtown Charleston, South Carolina. "We saw young people who were not able to accept things as status quo."[1] Blake had been one of twenty-four Burke High School students who marched to S. H. Kress & Co., a segregated five-and-dime store on King Street. The students, proudly dressed in fine clothes, occupied nearly one-half of the lunch counter seats. White patrons cleared the store and bystanders circulated rumors of a bomb threat. The students maintained their composure as the manager of the store asked them to leave, and as police arrested them, charged them with trespassing, and put them in jail.[2] The Burke High School students followed the example recently set by four North Carolina A&T students who sat in on the Woolworth's lunch counter on February 1, 1960. The Greensboro students had been members of the NAACP Youth Council while in high school. They, too, drew inspiration from their Black teachers while in high school.[3] As the Greensboro protests captured national headlines—even though high school students and the NAACP Youth Council organized a sit-in nearly two years before in Kansas—students in Charleston learned that sit-ins were a way to take part in the nonviolent demonstrations sweeping the South. "We were fascinated, as you can imagine," Harvey Gantt recalled of that moment, and began to ask, "You know, those kids are in college. Why can't we do the same thing to show our dissatisfaction with segregation?"[4]

The students who led the sit-in at Kress in Charleston exemplified both the continuous elements and the evolving dynamics of high school student protest of the 1960s. Like high school and college activists across the South who participated in the sit-in movement, the students from Burke High School did not act alone or without precedent. In particular, NAACP Youth Councils were already in place throughout the South and active across the country. Though the Greensboro sit-ins inspired youth across the nation, sit-ins like those in North Carolina occurred since the late 1950s. Students of the NAACP Youth Council sat-in at lunch counters in Wichita and Oklahoma City just under two years before the Greensboro sit-in. Moreover, students organized to great effect in North Carolina prior to Greensboro. Students associated with the NAACP across the state sat in bus station waiting rooms, parks, hotels, and other locations before the protests of 1960, establishing a bedrock of nonviolent, intentional resistance.[5]

Local chapters of the NAACP and familial connections shaped the development of high school protest as well. In Charleston, the student protesters were members of the NAACP Youth Council. James Blake served as president under the guidance of I. DeQuincy Newman—who founded the local chapter of the NAACP in Orangeburg in 1943 and worked with the Progressive Democratic Party in the state, an organization that included civil rights leaders who organized the SNYC conference in 1946. Newman assisted with and suffered reprisals from supporting the *Briggs* desegregation case and, by 1960, served as the state field director of the NAACP.[6] Some students were intimately involved through their family. One of the sit-in protesters, Minerva Brown, was the daughter of J. Arthur Brown, who was then president of the South Carolina Conference of the NAACP. As a teenager, Brown was initially the lead plaintiff in the NAACP-sponsored court case that ultimately desegregated the public school system in South Carolina in 1963. She graduated with the case still pending, and her younger sister, Millicent, became the lead plaintiff and made history by being part of the first cohort to desegregate K-12 schools in South Carolina. Their home was a safe place for students to meet and discuss the movement.[7]

As elsewhere across the South, historically Black high schools played a critical role in the development of student protest in Charleston. Burke High School, which originated in 1894 through the social and political work Rev. John Dart, came with all the defining characteristics of an institution of secondary education that cultivated a political consciousness among its students. A cadre of Black teachers throughout the 1960s continued to inspire a critical analysis that helped inspire a local movement as well.[8] Mr. Eugene Hunt, an English and speech teacher at Burke High School, defined the potential of Black teachers to develop the political consciousness of their students. Hunt shaped the academic integrity of Burke as a faculty member in the English Department. He introduced his students to ideas of freedom, equality, and participatory democracy in his classroom.[9] Lessons of democracy and equality were aided by a careful pedagogical approach that instructed students on multiple levels. Classroom learning was expanded through various extracurricular activities such as theater and band, which were integral parts of the second curriculum. "My philosophy of all out-of-class activities is based on the conviction that the most meaningful and beneficial experiences for students are those which are most purposeful and direct," Hunt wrote in the late 1950s. He viewed drama and theater as a way to increase skills in dealing effectively with others, money management, and other principles of "self-sufficiency and independence," a philosophy that pointed to his Northern education at the University of Chicago and Northwestern University, institutions that were critical spaces that propagated the ideas and influence of John Dewey and the progressive education canon.[10]

Hunt's second curriculum—or the informal or "hidden" lessons outside the state-mandated curriculum that is etched in the memory of his students and colleagues—tells of a more direct political education. James Blake, a leader of the Kress sit-in, remembered vividly that it was "in 1958, right in E. C. Hunt's class, and J. Michael Grave's class, was the insurrection movement in the City of Charleston, where we started planning and deciding that we were going downtown to Kress."[11] As Harvey Gantt recalled, Hunt "knew who the activists were in the class and he had good advice about what was going on out there in Charleston."[12] Millicent Brown remembered Hunt encouraging students to participate in politics as well.[13] His colleague, Lois Simms, recalled learning the deep impact of Hunt's teaching and presence at Burke High School from student's writing. "From the homeroom students of Eugene C. Hunt," Simms recalled, "I learned how bitter some of them were about the events of slavery."[14] Understanding that that they had the complete support of some of their teachers, students were ready to act.

High school activism played a critical role in cities and towns like Charleston that had no historically Black college or university, particularly when sit-ins occurred during the academic year as college students were organizing on their own campuses. Charleston had two colleges, the College of Charleston and the Citadel, both of which excluded Black students. South Carolina State College, the nearest postsecondary institution open to African Americans, was over seventy miles away.[15] High school students played an integral role in towns with Black colleges, too, such as Greensboro, once college students left for summer and winter breaks. William Thomas, for example, was inspired and supported by teachers at the all-Black Dudley High School in Greensboro, North Carolina—an institution that stood as an intellectual pillar in Black southern communities. After the first wave of sit-ins during the winter and spring of 1960, Thomas maintained local support and momentum for the local movement when the college students from North Carolina A&T returned home for the break.[16] Thomas and his peers were rooted in the local community as older activists sought to mobilize a movement. As a local cohort, they were invaluable to college activists across the South who were much more willing than the traditional leadership of the NAACP to put them on the front lines of the movement.

The Charleston activists also indicate an evolving notion of autonomy during the early 1960s. Unlike previous decades of student protest, high school activists were visibly joining the front lines of their own accord and demanding their own place in the movement. Despite the NAACP's recognition of the sit-ins, there was little national directive issued about the direct action demonstrations. Protests were conducted locally, which meant that Burke students started it by discussing the Greensboro sit-ins among themselves. While they were supported by their parents, who also served as conduits of knowledge about the movement, the students organized the Kress sit-in on their own. As Harvey Gantt remembered, "This was actually an event planned by us. . . . When we talk about the actual tactics and leadership that occurred and the getting ready for the demonstration, there were really no adults close." After informal discussions, the next step included hosting regular meetings where no parents or teachers were present. Gantt recalled not wanting "to take a chance of entering that kind of conversation [with adults] because we thought it would hold us back."[17] Minerva Brown, Harvey Gantt, James Blake, and other students held meetings in the basement of J. Arthur Brown's house, a space they understood as sympathetic to their purpose. They invited civil rights speakers and politicized college students to address their group. Although Charleston prided itself on genteel race relations, Minerva Brown, who was present at many of the meetings, stated that students were cognizant of the dangers facing them and planned accordingly.[18] As James Blake recalled of the planning stages of the sit-in: "We went through a whole regimentation as to how you would act. When you would go to a lunch counter. How you would act if you were arrested. What you would do if the police places his hand on you. We took our folks through a course for about five to six weeks before we actually pulled the whole demonstration on them. So, it really started with high school students right here in the community."[19]

The college students that inspired youth soon grew to include members of the Student Nonviolent Coordinating Committee (SNCC), which formed under the mentorship of Ella Baker during a southern student conference she organized at Shaw University in Raleigh, North Carolina, on April 16 to 18, 1960. SNCC defined the student and youth voice of the 1960s and, indeed, the civil rights movement.[20] SNCC was not the first to organize youth as they in many ways continued the original mission of SNYC of the 1930s, which disbanded under increasing anticommunist surveillance and criticism that led to the dissolution of the National Negro Congress after the Second World War. SNCC picked up the youth arm of the movement in 1960. But unlike their predecessors in SNYC, SNCC organizers strictly organized college-aged youth. SNCC members represented the historically Black colleges and, under the critical tutelage of Ella Baker, asserted their autonomy from the NAACP and Dr. King's Southern Christian Leadership Conference, whereas SNYC sought more collaboration. SNCC leaders like Chuck McDew, who was elected the first chairman of the organization and was enrolled at South Carolina State College, were there to serve as informal advisors to high school students. For instance, McDew organized sit-ins in nearby Orangeburg two weeks prior to the student-led sit-in in Charleston, and McDew and his comrades served as proximate advisors to high school students like those from Burke High School who wished to replicate the nonviolent strategy.[21] SNCC and college-aged activists in the Congress of Racial Equality worked with students, but at times during the 1960s they also worked to keep high school students off the front lines.[22] "Youth" in the early 1960s largely came to be understood as *college*-aged youth, and the nation finally took notice of the army that had mobilized after decades of organizing young people. It was one that actualized the historic call for youth to march that W. E. B. Du Bois, Juanita Jackson, Esther Jackson, and other youth organizers issued since the 1920s.

Student Activism in Mississippi

Hezekiah Watkins attended Rowan Middle School in Jackson, Mississippi. Watkins closely followed in the newspapers and on the radio the "Freedom Riders" who attempted to desegregate buses and bus terminals along the route through the Deep South, from Washington, D.C., to New Orleans during the spring and summer of 1961, a route that took them directly through Mississippi.[23] "In 1961 when the demonstrators in Alabama were being shown on TV, they were being beaten, hosed by water, spit on, dogs chasing them," Watkins recalled. "We received the nightly news and that was always shown and everybody was saying, 'Don't get involved.'"[24] That the Freedom Riders were coming to Jackson generated great excitement among

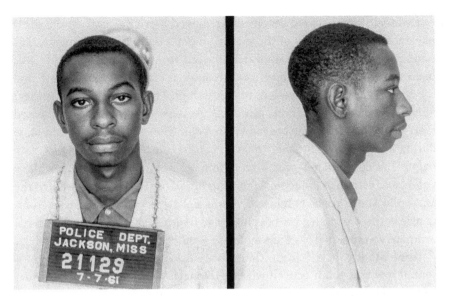

Hezekiah Watkins, photograph upon arrest, July 7, 1961.
Courtesy of Hezekiah Watkins.

Watkins and his peers. Out of curiosity, Watkins and a friend attended a local meeting at the Masonic Temple in Jackson that met prior to their arrival. They then walked to the bus terminal to see the riders. In the excitement of their arrival, Watkins inadvertently stood in the White-only part of the terminal, and Jackson police arrested him along with the Freedom Riders. Though only fourteen, the courts sent Watkins to Parchman Penitentiary, Mississippi's notorious prison. "And believe it or not I did not want to get involved," Watkins recalled. "I was just nosey. I could say being at the wrong place at the wrong time and basically what happened to me was being nosey. Thereafter, after I realized what the cause was all about, I wanted to be a part of it."[25]

Watkins did not attribute his activism to his school, Black colleges or churches in Jackson, or the NAACP Youth Councils. Watkins heard about the Freedom Rides on television and the local meetings by word of mouth. Youth like Watkins eagerly consumed news of the Freedom Riders, which was widely televised on national television and radio. Where traditional modes of entrée into the movement—teachers, college activists, or the NAACP—did not apply, civil rights milestones such as the Freedom Rides paved inroads in areas previously unreached.

Once Wilkins became involved, he played a critical part in the local movement. Unlike many of those who volunteered in the movement, particularly activists who temporarily moved to Mississippi, Watkins was born and raised in the state. He was bound, at least during his youth and the remainder of his education, to Mississippi. The time spent in the local movement after 1961 served him well. As a teenager, Watkins amassed more experience than the typical White volunteers who worked in the state during the Freedom Summer campaign of 1964, the massive civil rights campaign that coordinated over fifteen hundred volunteers to register black voters and establish Freedom Schools to break the back of Jim Crow in the Magnolia State. Yet as batches of volunteers came and went, seasoned organizers, often in college or of college-age themselves, entrusted him to coordinate volunteers from Canton, Mississippi.[26]

Anne Moody of Wilkinson County, Mississippi, similarly played an essential role as a youth activist who was from the state and had likewise developed her political consciousness while in high school. The summer before Moody enrolled in Willis High School, local authorities found the mutilated body of Emmett Till in the Tallahatchie River. As Moody recalled, "Before Emmett Till's murder, I had known the fear of hunger, hell, and the Devil. But now there was a new fear known to me—the fear of being killed just because I was black."[27] Within weeks, Moody also learned about the NAACP and the resistance the organization embodied. The seeds were planted and came to fruition when the freedom struggle reached new heights in Mississippi in the early 1960s, when Moody was a student at Tougaloo College. At Tougaloo, Moody was introduced to the NAACP Youth Council chapter and SNCC, in addition to Medgar Evers. She earned a national reputation for sitting in at the Woolworths in May 1963.[28] She was instrumental in the larger state movement as well. When Dave Dennis, a CORE organizer, introduced her to the local movement in Canton, she served as a critical intergenerational link between youth and elders in the movement.[29] Coming of age in Mississippi and having gone through high school and politically matured as an activist while in college, Moody—and other youth activists born and raised in the state like Hezekiah Watkins—was an ideal organizer.

Youth were critical in extending the movement locally as the face of the movement to recruit students to join. Brenda Travis was a sixteen-year-old student at Burgland High School, a Black school built in 1957 as part of the state's so-called "equalization" attempts, when she first encountered direct-action protests in August 1961.[30] But her foray into the civil rights movement has deeper roots, and her entrée into it illustrates the ways in which college-aged students facilitated direct action nonviolent demonstrations that built upon local leadership, mostly through the established avenues of resistance of the NAACP. C. C. Bryant, a local worker on the Illinois Central Railroad, became the NAACP president of the McComb branch in 1955 and strengthened the infrastructure for local activism.[31] Like local movement leaders across the South, Bryant served in many professional capacities and reached a wide audience in myriad ways. He was a preacher at nearby Society Hill Baptist Church, where he introduced many local people to the ideology of organizing. As Brenda Travis later recalled, "[C. C. Bryant] prompting people every Sunday was my motivating force."[32] Bryant sought and invited younger radical activists to organize in McComb. He invited Bob Moses, a twenty-five-year-old Harvard philosophy major and Harlem math educator who sought to organize voters in Mississippi, to McComb after reading about his work in *Jet* magazine.[33]

It was a fortuitous connection that sparked the political consciousness of high school youth like Brenda Travis. Travis met Moses through C. C. Bryant and was thereby introduced to the movement during the voter registration drive they conducted. As Travis recalled, the voter registration classes reached out to those interested in voting, but the focus of the classes eventually shifted toward organizing for civil disobedience, which included learning how to protect oneself from segregationists during nonviolent demonstrations.[34] Her first form of civil rights education was learning the art of resistance from the established leaders in the area. But this was supplemented with direct action protest when Hollis Watkins and Curtis Hayes, two local eighteen- and nineteen-year-old activists who were following the work of SNCC and the Freedom Rides, accelerated the organizing efforts in McComb when they sat-in at the local Woolworth's in August 1961, the first direct action nonviolent protests in the area. Local police arrested the protestors for disturbing the peace and they spent thirty-six days in jail.[35] In the aftermath that followed, Brenda Travis organized a small sit-in with two other Burgland High School students at the local Greyhound bus terminal. Local police promptly arrested the young activists, and a judge sentenced them to thirty days in jail.[36]

After Travis served her thirty-day jail sentence, the local school board refused to admit her back into school, and the principal subsequently expelled her.[37] This incensed her classmates at Burgland High School. The community was already outraged by the recent murder of Herbert Lee, a local farmer and member of the NAACP, who was gunned down by E. H. Hurst of Hattiesburg, a representative in the Mississippi state legislature. Upon word of Travis's expulsion, Burgland students organized a walkout, triggered by her friend Joe Lewis, who inquired at a schoolwide assembly as to why Travis was expelled. Over one hundred students walked out of the school in protest, carried signs, and sang "We Shall Overcome," much to the dismay of local Whites.[38] Burgland High School students marched to the local Masonic Temple, demanded action, and the crowd that soon gathered in support of the young activists began a march to City Hall.

It was an exhilarating experience for Travis, who felt vindicated by her classmates' support. "I felt exhilarated, triumphant, here I had people behind me and it was just a good feeling, it was feeling like someone was embracing me and believing the way I felt, that things needed to change," Travis recalled.[39] Jacqueline Martin experienced a similar awakening in the midst of demonstrations. "On one hand you were told, 'Get a good education and you can be anything you want to be,'" she recalled, "and on the other hand, what reality is showing you is that that's not what you can do unless things can change."[40] For Martin, Travis, and the Burgland students who stood up for change, they were going to have to be the catalysts for the change they wanted to see.

As inspiring as it was for Travis, who was already exposed to the travails of incarceration, students who entered the movement for the first time through the walkout experienced something different, particularly as local White segregationists mounted a violent response to the protest. Eloise Carter, a Burgland High School student who walked out of school, experienced this moment of protest as a "nightmare" as she was confronted by "policemen with big chains around their wrists, their weapons drawn, batons and German Shepherd dogs."[41] A group that included SNNC organizer Bob Zellner was brutally and savagely beaten by the White mob.[42]

Youth activism in McComb, Mississippi, demonstrates the categorical error of lumping middle and high school students and college-age activists within a generic category of "youth." As high school students, Brenda Travis and her fellow students were younger than Hollis Watkins and Curtis Hayes, who were indeed young at the time of the arrests, just nineteen years old. Activists and the parents that welcomed them into the community were well aware of the difference. "We were the old guys," Bob Zellner recalled about a meeting held at the Masonic Hall in McComb before marching to City Hall, "I was all of twenty-one, and maybe [Charles] McDew and [Bob]

Moses, a little older."[43] Moreover, the movement in McComb illustrates how the organization of young people had serious implications for the larger movement. White violence experienced at protests forced a critical, often divisive question upon local organizers about whether, or to what extent, to work with children and adolescents. College-aged organizers felt compelled to intervene and stop the student marches. High schoolers were too young, many reasoned, and it was more difficult to gain the trust of parents and cautious adults in McComb when young people were arrested, especially for those unfamiliar with the work of the organizations like SNCC or CORE. As Dave Dennis, a CORE field organizer in Mississippi and Louisiana, recalled, "Many times it was our job to keep kids *off* the front lines."[44] Chuck McDew, the SNCC chairperson at the time, elaborated: "We did not want to have the parents alienated. We didn't want the parents to feel that we were using their kids."[45] At the same time, however, students in McComb became the energetic force that pushed the movement forward. As McDew recalled, "It was only after we started working with the kids that we got the large groups of people to go down and attempt to register."[46] The McComb protests solidified commitment to the movement and generated fundamental support for further civil rights activity.

As historian Wesley Hogan noted, "SNCC had to rely on young people, especially teens who did not yet have families dependent on them for support. Youths knew the community, could take risks, and showed up for long hours to do the arduous and repetitive task of canvassing for new recruits and financial support."[47] It was not just SNCC, however, that relied on young people. The lessons of McComb would be applied consistently throughout the movement. The very essence of the freedom struggle by the 1960s depended on high school youth, and even those younger in elementary and middle school, as a critical, reliable cohort of engaged activists if the movement was going to grow. And no city exposed the politics behind and impact of youth involvement more than Birmingham, Alabama.

The Birmingham Children's Crusade

The Children's Crusade in Birmingham, Alabama, in May 1963, was arguably the single largest demonstration of youth protest during the southern freedom movement. It grew from a locally concerted effort that began in 1956 under the direction and leadership of Rev. Fred. L. Shuttlesworth.[48] The Southern Christian Leadership Conference (SCLC), led by Dr. King, selected to join Rev. Shuttlesworth in Birmingham to take a stand. Dubbed "Project

Confrontation," or "Project C" by SCLC executive director Wyatt Tee Walker, the SCLC began organizing a nonviolent campaign to fill the jails of Birmingham to illustrate the brutality of Jim Crow to the nation. Joining the Young Communist League in high school and later becoming an outspoken pastor in Petersburg, Virginia, Walker was one to understand the importance of youth in galvanizing a movement.[49] The plan called for massive demonstrations and an epic showdown with the ugly face of White supremacy, but the first results in April 1963 were lackluster at best. Dozens were in jail, far from the thousands that organizers envisioned. Even after Dr. King was arrested and released the famous "Letter from Birmingham Jail," the jails remained empty and overt support for King and his movement waned.[50]

For the first time in the movement, organizers eyed students as the means to replenish and mobilize an entire city through direct action protest. "We needed more troops," Wyatt Tee Walker noted. "We had run out of troops. We had scraped the bottom of the barrel of adults who could go [to jail.]"[51] Rev. James Bevel, a dynamic, charismatic organizer and leader with SCLC, and Isaac "Ike" Reynolds—proposed to use children and high school activists in the Birmingham campaign to compensate for the lack of adults in the movement. They proposed that young people would be the necessary catalyst to propel the local movement forward.[52] Like Walker, Bevel saw that working children into the movement was a logical progression from where they stood with little support from adults. He was already holding direct action nonviolent workshops for young people, establishing a trustful rapport. Bevel challenged their thinking and taught them the skills of the movement. He appealed to young people and enjoyed wide popularity. Those who knew Bevel were ready to follow him into action. As student activist Miriam McClendon noted, "I just became totally absorbed and fell absolutely in love with Rev. James Bevel."[53] The utilization of activists in high school, or even in lower grades, and at such a large scale, pushed Birmingham to be one of the most explosive fronts of the civil rights movement.

It was ultimately children and high school students—not the college students or college-age youth of SNCC—that tipped the momentum of the Birmingham campaign. The decision did not come easy and, as the movement already revealed in other locations, a resolution to use children in a movement exacted an emotional toll and elicited fierce criticism. King initially rejected the idea, as did established leaders of the local movement in Birmingham, such as the billionaire A. G. Gaston. Having just served time in a Birmingham jail, King knew and shared that prison was no place for children. Others strongly opposed lowering the age of accepted protestors below college age, arguing—quite accurately—that their livelihood could be threatened by assault, beatings, and other abuses while in prison.[54] Their ambitions and future plans could be devastated. The school board, in fact, announced plans under the orders of Bull Connor to expel or suspend students who were arrested during the campaign.[55] Yet Bevel's argument prevailed. Not only were adults not turning up in the ways anticipated by organizers, but young people experienced a profound camaraderie that could be used to mobilize large numbers—if one were arrested, others were compelled to action, much like the solidarity demonstrated in McComb, Mississippi, after authorities arrested and expelled Brenda Travis, or in Prince Edward County, Virginia, where students and their families joined the movement to desegregate schools. Not unlike the most ardent adult activists, children had no financial dependency upon the White power structure.[56] Bevel also levied an unequivocal moral argument. If children were old enough to belong to church as a member, they were old enough to march and serve in jail, if necessary, as part of a movement that embraced and taught nonviolence and Christian doctrine. Finally, Bevel stood on strategic high ground. Students who attended meetings with him began to surpass the number of adults in the regular mass meetings and they were ready to serve.[57]

Youth were part of a force to be reckoned with, and Birmingham organizers sought to capture that energy in what Bevel labeled "D-Day," which was scheduled for Thursday, May 2, 1963. It was planned as an unprecedented assault on the bastion of segregation in Birmingham. As Bevel prophesized, "It will be our town that day."[58] Once the decision was made to use children, King did not actively support the initiative, but he did not stop the active recruitment of youth either, and organizers moved swiftly. Bevel, Reynolds, and other organizers who connected with youth such as Dorothy Cotton and Andrew Young of the SCLC alliance with Alabama Christian Movement for Human Rights (ACMHR), targeted nearby A. H. Parker High School and Ullman High School. As historically Black high schools in the city, these schools held the potential to put forth the activists needed for the campaign. Parker High School stood out as the oldest school in the area. Parker High School originated as one of the first schools for Black pupils in the state of Alabama, known as the Slater School and founded in 1888. Under the careful leadership of A. H. Parker, the school grew to claim the reputation as the largest Black high school in the country and offered both a vocational and critical liberal arts education.[59] It was the school that youth organizers envisioned to furnish the foot soldiers for the campaign.

Youth organizers circulated hundreds of leaflets and flyers in the days leading up to D-Day, calling youth to meet at the Sixteenth Street Baptist Church before the demonstration. Elder organizers in the ACMHR also sought to enlist those students who held influence in the schools, those who were well connected and liked by their peers—the "elite," or popular students, so to speak.[60] Danella Jones Bryant was already involved in the movement as a senior at Parker High School. She volunteered to enlist her peers. "I would go to my school," Bryant recalled, "and I would try and recruit kids, especially in my classroom or in the club that I was involved in, the cheerleaders. Just any of the kids and try to explain to them what was going on and that they needed to join us."[61] As a student who was socially involved at school and active in the local movement, she was exactly the recruiter that Bevel and others had in mind. Anne Thompson, a student at Ullman High School in Birmingham, was responsible for recruiting students there. "My job was to talk to as many students in that area and work with them and invite them and prepare them for D-Day, telling them what we were going to do, what our goals were and be prepared so when we decided to select the date they would be ready."[62] Popular disc jockey Paul Dudley "Tall Paul" White summoned children to Kelly Ingram Park for the "big party" on Thursday as well, and "Shelley the Playboy" broadcast coded marching orders the day of the first demonstration: "Kids, there's gonna be a party at the park. Bring your toothbrushes because lunch will be served." Both in and outside of school and across the city, high schoolers were heavily recruited and compelled to join the movement.[63]

Given the moral weight of using children and the political complications it entailed, young activists had to first be trained to participate in the assault on segregation. A crucial part of the organization was the mass meetings at local Black churches, where youth meetings were held separately from those held for adults. Mass meetings were on a rotating circuit between staple movement churches such as the 16th Street Baptist Church, Thirgood Christian Methodist Episcopal Baptist Church, and New Pilgrim Baptist Church. Often led by James Bevel, the youth meetings discussed the same issues as in the adult meetings and instructed students in the principles of nonviolence. As youth protestor Miriam McClendon recalled, "They discussed the critical issues . . . that were being discussed in the larger mass meeting with the adults, but they tailored it to fit the temperament of the student."[64] Meetings were in many ways like rallies, filled with singing and preaching. This included the songs of the movement that defined the mass meetings of the 1960s. "A typical mas meeting was something that I always looked forward to," Gwendolyn Sanders Gamble remembered. "It included hearing, shouting, singing, having a hallelujah good time, meeting, greeting, loving, caring, and sharing with young people."[65]

Organizers at the meetings trained youth in not only the principles of the movement but the strategies and application of it through nonviolent direct-action protest. They expected to be arrested. One of the first measures taken was to register and sign up in the likely case of incarceration. "Before they went out to demonstrate they had to go in the church to write down their name and address so in case something happened we would know who they had in jail," recalled Notie B. Andrews. She noted that the young people would write how long they were willing to stay in jail, whether it was five or ten days. Movement leaders would organize marches according to their responses.[66] Students were trained to be nonviolent. They learned to not fight back and to take the blows of attackers if necessary.[67] Training led to a transformational education experience tantamount to a "freedom school" experience. "They [organizers] were talking directly to us," James W. Stewart, a student activist from Ullman High School, recalled, "and they were telling us it's our responsibility, it is up to us to draw a line in the sand and say we need to do something to address the racial problem."[68] Students were made aware of the importance of the movement and they were prepared to enter it. As Mary E. Streeter Perry recalled, students who volunteered were told to

> sign up and go to Sixteenth Street Baptist Church to learn how to demonstrate and to learn what to do and what not to do. The do's and don'ts: how it was risky and how we were to be nonviolent . . . It was very educational . . . We were taught to be nonviolent if someone would attempt to be violent to us. We had to group in and protect each other and not to say anything, to just demonstrate; just carry our signs in a nonviolent manner and to walk and talk in a nonviolent manner; just to protect ourselves.[69]

When D-Day arrived, movement leaders did not just wait at the church, student organizers actively recruited students in the schools that morning to get them to Sixteenth Street Baptist Church. Though Margaret Askew, an adult organizer with ACMHR, was blocked from entering the school, she and other organizers began to sing "We Shall Overcome" outside the school, and students who had been attending mass meetings walked out and joined her.[70] Student organizers continued their work the morning of the march, too. Anne Thompson from Ullman High School recalled that "my responsibility was if it happened while I was in class I was supposed to organize my class then go and from room to room and encourage others to come out."[71] "They were walking up and down the hallways beckoning," Miriam McClendon looked back on D-Day at Wenonah High School, and "I looked out there and I saw them and I said, 'Okay, Now is the Time.'"[72] Carl Grace recalled at Fairfield High School that "we began to hear someone down the hall saying, 'Let's go.' Then all of a sudden, it sounded like horses. You could hear the footsteps coming down the hall and voices' saying, 'Let's go.'"[73] Students at A. H. Parker High School walked out as well and walked out despite the best wishes of the principal. Their science teacher, Carlotta Harris, remembered thinking, "A child shall lead them."[74] Willie Eatman, a student at Parker who helped tailor the principal's clothes, asked for his explicit permission, and the principal denied permission.[75] Students marched anyway. Eatman remembered the moment as "something like a D-Day . . . the next thing I know, everybody started coming all out of the windows."[76]

Students who committed to the demonstrations placed their teachers and administrators in a predicament as their involvement was forbidden by "law." Principals received their orders from Superintendent Theo Wright, who instructed them to share with their students and families the message that any students who left school would be disciplined.[77] They, along with their administrative staff, blocked, or attempted to block, recruiters from entering schools, and local organizers were routinely denied access.[78] As Edward Thompson, an advisor at West End High School, noted, "Now when the fellows would come in . . . and ran through, I mean the people who were 'recruiting,' they would come in and disrupt the school. Well, no, no, we stopped them at the door."[79] The principals of the major Black high schools complied and tried to prevent students from leaving through dramatic and even frenzied acts. As Annetta Streeter Gary remembered of the principal at Ullman High School, "Mr. Bell was running around like a chicken with his head cut off. Mr. Bell did not want us to leave that school."[80] Perhaps the biggest obstacle was Parker High School Principal R. C. Johnson, who was known as "Big Red" among students (when he was not present, of course). Carolyn Maull McKintsry recalled Mr. Johnson looking "big and mean." Dannetta Owens, the valedictorian of Parker in 1955, recalled that "Big Red" was a stern disciplinarian. "Just his mere presence would make the students jump back in line," she recalled. On the day of the first march with youth, it was said that Johnson attempted to physically keep students in and the recruiters out, locking the gates to the schoolyard.[81] "It did not stop us," Gary recalled.[82] Or, as Carolyn Maull McKinstry remembered, "Most of us just squeezed through the gate."[83] To walk out in spite of these paragons of discipline was truly taking a stand. Students joined the movement with or without support of their principals and teachers.

Recalcitrant educators did not fully define the narrative of teachers during the Birmingham campaign and the movement in general. Many resisted the push to block students from participating. Though easy to cast teachers as impediments to the march, historian Tondra Loder-Jackson found that many teachers were sympathetic to the march, finding that "Birmingham educators played a mostly supportive role." As Gwendolyn Sanders Gamble, a student activist who marched, recalled, "I know a few teachers who actually turned their heads and looked out the window [as if to say], 'If you want out, I didn't give you permission, I didn't see, so go while my head is turned.'"[84] It was a common type of support teachers provided to retain employment while supporting the aspirations of their students, as well as their own desire for change. As Annetta Streeter Gary, recalled, there were teachers like "Miss [Odessa] Woolfolk, turned like she did not see. Mrs. [Cleopatra] Goree was another teacher that acted as if she did not see."[85] But these teachers were more instrumental than simply turning their backs and implicitly supporting the movement. Goree was a card-carrying member of the NAACP. As the students' "confidant lady," she used her classroom as a space for students to discuss and unpack their participation in the movement.[86] Woolfolk supported her students based on her understanding of democracy and connected her students' work to the struggle to actualize these ideals. "I was teaching American Government, what the Constitution guarantees, what democracy should be about," she recalled. "Sitting in a segregated school system and going to the back door of restaurants—it made sense for students to take a stand."[87] As James W. Stewart recalled, Woolfolk, "challenged us to apply civics to everyday life . . . There were times when we would look at current events. We would give our opinions on current events. No one up until that time had asked us what our opinion was."[88] Deloris Givner Norman noted that some Parker teachers at the time of the walkout forbade participation. Still, others "were behind closed doors and said, 'I'm with you, go on and do it, but we're not a part of it. We can't be a part of it. I wish I could go and do it, but we can't. But we are with y'all all the way.'"[89]

Much to the dismay of Principal R. C. Johnson, it was estimated that more than one-quarter and up to 40 percent of all students left school by the end of the week of protests. Of all the high schools, the *Birmingham*

News—the main White paper in the city—reported that less than 900 of 7,300 high school students attended class the week after D-Day. Only 10,000 of an estimated 23,000 elementary school children reported to school the following week. Overall, the paper reported that only 13,000 of 34,000 students reported to homeroom on the Tuesday after D-Day.[90] As Andrew Young, who had been in Birmingham for about a month before the protests with Wyatt T. Walker, wrote of the event, "Instead of going to school . . . youth decided to come to church."[91]

The excitement was contagious after the first day. "Unable to wait for the next day," historian Taylor Branch wrote of the mass meeting the night after marches, "they walked up and down the aisles as the church thundered in song."[92] Uncertain about using children at first, even staying in his hotel room on D-Day, King stood firmly behind youth after the first day. At a press conference, King and Shuttlesworth declared they were willing to speak with city leaders, but they would "negotiate from strength." They assured the press there was no lack of volunteers willing to continue to fill the jails.[93] Bevel, ecstatic at what the use of children demonstrated to the world, boasted that Thursday evening, "There ain't going to be no meeting Monday night because every Negro is going to be in jail by Sunday night."[94] King stood unfazed by the criticism the day after D-Day, not to mention the rumors and fears of mistreatment and inhumane conditions in the jails. "Young daughters and sons are in jail," King said in a speech about the children—whom he referred to as "political prisoners." He reassured their parents and the community, "Don't worry about them . . . they are suffering for what they believe and they are suffering to make this nation a better nation."[95]

Initially hesitant, King directly advocated for the use of children, linking the use of children to a spiritual reckoning. After the first few days of protest, King addressed the large crowd on the evening of May 5:

> There are those who write history. There are those who make
> history. I don't know how many historians we have in Birmingham
> tonight. I don't know how many of you would be able to write a
> history book. But you are certainly making history, and you are
> experiencing history. And you will make it possible for the historians
> of the future to write a marvelous chapter. Never in the history
> of this nation have so many people been arrested for the cause of
> freedom and human dignity . . . Don't worry about your children.
> Don't hold them back if they want to go to jail. For they are doing a
> job for only themselves but for all of America and for all mankind.[96]

King alluded to the biblical passage of Jesus questioning his father's business at the age of twelve. For King, these young people were about their fathers' business, which was "carving a tunnel of hope through the great mountain of despair."[97] The mass meetings continued, so much so that other movement churches like St. James Baptist, Thirgood Christian Methodist Episcopal, and St. Luke's AME were used to accommodate the overflowing crowds.

Violence defined the second day of the march and demonstrations when Bull Connor ordered firehoses and dogs to be used against the protestors. With reporters on hand, the decision led to the most canonical images of the movement that included the use of German shepherds to break up the marches and disperse the protestors. The dogs were used once before when the movement lacked support and participation. Bull Connor used the dogs mercilessly. Police sicced a dog on Walter Gadsden, a fifteen-year-old student from Ullman High School. One dog bit Milton Payne in the foot and leg. Two German shepherds tore into the leg of Henry Lee Shambry. One dog chased down a seven-year-old, Jennifer Fancher, and knocked her down.[98] It was all captured on film. Once used after children energized the local movement, they captured national headlines, appearing on the front page of *The New York Times* on May 4, 1963.[99]

The images captured by the press and the memories from protestors were seared into American consciousness. The iconic moment is now memorialized in Kelly Ingram Park.[100]

Firehoses also dramatized the campaign in Birmingham. Used as a visible deterrent the first day, police unleashed the firehoses on protestors the second day of protest. In what Taylor Branch described as a "moment of baptism for the civil rights movement," firemen used tactical monitor guns that channeled water through two hoses through a single massive nozzle that was mounted on a tripod. Touted as specialized, high-power hoses to effectively combat the most intense blazes, monitor guns had the capability to strip bark from trees from over a hundred feet away. They could knock brick loose from buildings at a force of one hundred pounds per square inch. Police doused a group of sixty protestors with the hoses, but ten demonstrators remained behind. This group, caught on film, was pummeled directly with the hoses at close range.[101] "I witnessed these firehoses, they were so powerful and when they turned them up into the trees those firehoses would just cut limbs like an invisible hand," Aldridge Willis recalled. "We were cut down. My body was picked up I guess, again, I can only imagine like an invisible hand because the force of the water my legs were knocked out from

Walter Gadsden, a student at Parker High School, after being attacked by police dogs during a civil rights demonstration in downtown Birmingham, Alabama, 1963. Courtesy of Alabama Department of Archives and History, donated by Alabama Media Group.

underneath me."[102] Annetta Streeter Gary vividly portrayed the experience, "I can remember us balling up, hugging together, and the water just washing us down the street . . . Forceful. It was like pins maybe, sticking you in your arms and legs and things. [The] water was very, very forceful."[103] Deborah Hill, a senior at Western Olin High School recalled of the firehoses, "The power was so powerful from the hose the force was just so overpowering it tore my dress. We had to jump into a car and I remember the force was so powerful that the car was just rocking from side to side. We honestly felt that we were going to die. I had never encountered a force so strong in my life."[104] Carolyn McKinstry, a student at Parker High School, recalled that "I was hit with the water hose . . . I had a sweater, a navy blue sweater on. I will never forget, it tore a big hole in my sweater and sort of just swiped part of my hair off . . . I just remember the sting and the pain on my face. It was very painful and you couldn't escape."[105]

Youth filled the jails and local police were overwhelmed since the first day of the campaign. Calling on county deputies for support and running out of the standard paddy wagons and police cars to ferry children to jail, police utilized school buses to transport an estimated seven hundred protesters to "Bull Connor's chapel"—the city jail.[106] Packed like sardines, city jails were quickly filled to standing capacity. Some were temporarily put in jail and then sent home. Some spent the night, others several days.[107] After three days of mass arrest, jails were overflowing and local police held students outside juvenile hall in the courtyard. The police roped off the area, dividing the yard based on gender. As in Mississippi, police ran out of space so they incarcerated young people in the city fairgrounds. Bull Connor selected the state fairgrounds, herding children into cattle pens or corralling students into the yards for livestock. Students who stayed in the fairgrounds yard were forced to sleep outside. There was no water, food, nor a place to sleep. Parents threw food and blankets over the fences. Reporters were denied access, prohibited from documenting the makeshift jail cell.[108]

No matter where they stayed, serving time in jail was a dismal, dehumanizing experience. Danella Jones Bryant recalled what it was like to serve time as a young person still in school. "I remember this big old matronly lady that was screaming and hollering at us and telling us that if we don't get in the bed and shut up what she was going to do to us. It wasn't a very nice experience, but I didn't mind it at the time. I didn't mind it because it was for a good cause." She also recalled that "it was overcrowded. The food was terrible and I knew that I never wanted to go there if I didn't have to. But I always stayed."[109]

"It was an experience that just can't be explained," Annetta Streeter Gary recalled of spending time in the county jail while in high school. "[The matrons] were tough. The food, [you] could not eat the food, period. There was no way to eat the food. They had us scrubbing, gave us rags to scrub along the front of the cells."[110] As Mary Streeter Perry recalled, "We ate out of tin plates, one tin cup and one tin spoon. We had something that looked like grits. Something that looked like soup. We couldn't tell."[111] Others described little hard biscuits, fried fat back, and watery soup. As Floretta Scruggs Tyson recalled, "It was terrifying because we were in a real jail where they had real criminals and my girlfriend and I were so devastated about being there, we slept together because we just didn't want anybody to say anything to us. And there was no privacy there. It was just horrible."[112] James W. Stewart relayed, "When we got inside the jail, they did things to us that I didn't imagine they would do. And I think the most shocking part for me is that these were men in authority . . . when we went into jail, they pushed us around. They put us in a holding facility that should have held maybe thirty people . . . They put [between] three and four hundred boys in the same room. . . . The toilet facilities were deplorable. At the end of this room there were five toilet seats, and that's how you went to the bathroom."[113] Carl Grace experienced the same. "In jail," he recalled, "there were so many [that] we were in there like sardines in a can."[114] Spaces built for eight held seventy-five prisoners. One dayroom had only sixty-two beds, but held two hundred jailed protestors, mostly youth.[115] Miriam McClendon, incarcerated at the fairgrounds at Fair Park Arena, recalled a traumatic episode being put into a "sweat box" for misbehaving. The "sweat box" in her words was a "little small room, closet size and you had to step down into it. Just a few inches, not far and they had water at the bottom of it. It was like a big steel coffin."[116]

The experiences of high school girls in Birmingham such as Annetta Streeter Gary, Danella Jones Bryant, Miriam McClendon, and hundreds of others demonstrated the dangers faced by young girls on the front lines. Out of 319 children booked through one of the juvenile detention centers in Birmingham, for instance, 240 were girls, many of whom remained incarcerated for a longer period of time.[117] The law showed no remorse for young Black girls as they incarcerated hundreds of young girls who chose to protest. Black girls were subjected to at least the same but often harsher disciplinary treatment as men throughout the course of United States history, and Black women and girls, as Nishaun T. Battle noted, were historically "disregarded objects, subject to treatment beyond the law due to the social order of southern society."[118] The intersection of race, sex, and gender illuminates how young girls and women experienced disproportionate incarceration rates. Once in prison, girls and women were vulnerable and susceptible to sexual violence, assault, and rape.[119] As young girls and adolescents occupied much of the front lines, they experienced some of the most horrific aspects of youth incarceration.

Children's age or maturity at times prevented a nuanced understanding of the movement or precluded deeper self-rationalization for joining. Eloise Staples, a freshman at Parker High School, recalled, "I didn't know the implications of what I was doing. I just knew that I wanted to be a part of something that was different and I didn't understand the impact. I knew it was important because there were other children in it." As she went on the explain, "By some way I got caught up in the emotions and the message."[120] Staple's classmate, Willie Eatman, articulated a basic rationale for voting but connected his participation to questions of citizenship and a notion of rights. "It didn't take much," he noted as he explained his rationale for participating in the protests.

The only thing I understood about it because I was young was that the blacks need their rights. Caucasians had a lot of rights. We needed some rights. We didn't have no kind of rights. We couldn't walk the street, we couldn't talk, we couldn't really do anything. I felt like we were just stuck. When they started talking about demonstrating, they started talking about Dr. Martin Luther King, and I said, and it hit my mind, I said, "well this is something I think I'm very interested in." I said "I think I'm going to down to Sixteenth Street Church and see what I need to do."[121]

Yet youth activists made their own choice to engage in protest and the movement itself provided the space to answer questions about their rights in a democracy, and the opportunity to explore them further.

Though youth were integral parts of the movement and earned spots on the front lines of the movement, youth were at times pawns in a larger game. As Wyatt Tee Walker noted, organizers had "run out of troops," and youth merely replenished their supplies.[122] In addition to filling the jails, youth held the potential to inspire their parents, jolt them from what looked like antipathy or what movement leaders understood to be mental shackles hardened over years in a harsh and oppressive system. Andrew Young noted in recollection that children inspired or triggered parental participation in the movement. "This was often the case," he noted, "parents became activists in support of their children after warning them to 'stay out of that mess in the streets.'"[123] He recalled a story when working with an adult who struggled to answer questions posed by her son about her discouragement of non-violent participation. The dissonance that resulted from her inability to answer her son led to a telling moment when "the cobwebs commenced a-movin' from my brain."[124] From this perspective, young people served a function that older adults could not. Yet unlike the narrative that emerged from Prince Edward County, Virginia, children did not lead the adults. They followed orders in Birmingham and filled the ranks. In the process, they saved a floundering campaign and spared the SCLC from receiving another defeat on the heels of the "loss" in Albany, Georgia. Carolyn Maull McKinstry used the term "bearable commodities" to describe the use of children in the movement.

I have to say, in terms of my participation, I felt very much a part of what was going on. I felt that I was needed . . . I agreed spiritually with what they were trying to do . . . So I think most of the children felt that it was a worthy cause. This was something that we needed to do, that we wanted to be a part of . . . I think most of us probably didn't have the real sense of how valuable we were. We felt good that we could make a contribution in this small way. They needed numbers, and we helped them with the numbers.[125]

McKinstry implies that students were aware of their need to the campaign, suggesting a deeper agency than that of mere pawns. They may have been used and "helped them with the numbers," but they voluntarily showed up to join the movement and were willing to accept the consequences.

Birmingham vividly displayed the dilemma of youth protest in the mid-1960s, still unresolved decades after the first attempts to organize youth by the NAACP and SNYC. The decision to recruit thousands of young people in elementary, middle, and high school marred the movement in controversy from the start. Following the first demonstration of students, movement leaders were met with reproach from all levels. Juvenile Court Judge Talbot Ellis in Birmingham was furious, claiming "the youngest, I understand was 8 . . . that's what makes my blood boil."[126] Mayor Albert Boutwell rebuked the Birmingham civil rights leaders as "irresponsible and unthinking agitators." He explained, "When people who are not residents of this city, and who will not have to live with fearful consequences, come to the point of using innocent children as their tools . . . then the time has come for every responsible white and colored parent in this city to demand a halt."[127] The Attorney General, Robert Kennedy, similarly reprimanded the move, noting "school children participating in street demonstrations is a dangerous business. An injured, maimed or dead child is a price that none of us can afford to pay."[128] Malcolm X joined the chorus of criticism. He derided King for the decision to use young people as foot soldiers through a lens of problematic masculinity. "Real men," he noted to a New York Times reporter days after the demonstration, "don't put their children on the firing line."[129] The *Congressional Record* reprinted an editorial shared by Representative William M. Tuck of Virginia, which captured the angst over the "sacrifice" of children:

We are haunted by the eyes of little children . . . These are the helpless pawns of the political and sociological prejudices of their parents and the so-called "white men of good will" who are using them for fodder in their racial war. We are haunted by the wide, dumb, fearful eyes of these little human weapons wielded by men and women of both races with complete disregard of the aftermath . . . Not since the Crusades have little children been so sacrificed upon the altar of their parents' misguided aims. The world still censures the parents of that time for the unmentionable miseries which befell the children's army.[130]

Regardless of the political leanings of those who commented on student activism, the nation took notice of an army that mobilized after decades of organizing youth.

King, initially ambivalent with the use of children, was forced to defend the decision without knowing the results of it. Yet he was comfortable doing so after the resounding numbers and unprecedented momentum generated by youth on the front lines. "I have been inspired and moved today," King told a Birmingham congregation the first night of youth demonstrations, where nearly one thousand signed up to be arrested. "I have never seen anything like it."[131] Beyond the strategic value children brought to the local movement, King and others were dismissive of the chorus of dissent and their expressed concerns for reasons learned in struggle. As King noted in hindsight, "It is clear that the introduction of Birmingham's children into the campaign was one of the wisest moves we made. It brought a new impact to the crusade, and the impetus that we needed to win the struggle."[132] The sudden concern of Whites for children was disingenuous at best and reflected defensive posturing to beat back the civil rights offensive. White leaders who protested the use of children rarely if ever spoke up for the treatment of Black youth when gunned down, lynched, murdered, and assaulted. They did not hesitate to sic dogs or hose down children in the park. They ignored the degrading and harmful conditions imposed by segregation on a daily basis. Nor did they seem to care enough to call for a moratorium on jailing students and exposing them to the very inhumane and dangerous conditions they apparently deplored. As King cynically pondered: "Where had these writers been, we wondered, during the centuries when our segregated social system had been misusing and abusing Negro children?"[133]

Movement organizers were able to leverage the unprecedented success of the children's campaign to negotiate for the basic demands they articulated throughout the demonstrations. These demands focused on the desegregation of all stores, the promotion of Black workers and nondiscriminatory hiring policies, and a biracial committee to examine the desegregation of schools, parks, theaters, and other public places and business. The negotiated plan was a milestone when contrasted with the launch of Project C earlier in the year, when the jail cells remained empty. The truce included the desegregation of lunch counters, restrooms, fitting rooms and drinking fountains within ninety days of the truce, the promotion and hiring of African Americans on a nondiscriminatory basis within sixty days, a biracial committee to oversee desegregation, and the release of incarcerated protestors on bond or personal recognizance. King, aware of the well-being of the children, was adamant to release them from jail. For King, the fate of the nearly two thousand imprisoned youth became the largest point of contention during the negotiation process. King demanded immediate release with all charges dropped and by the announcement of the truce, King promised that movement prisoners were "either out of jail or on the way out of jail." Paying for their release was made possible through a complicated arrangement made through private conversations with the Kennedy Administration who, along with King, agreed to raise $250,000 to cover the bail of jailed children.[134]

Children were crucial to the success of the movement not only because of their numbers. Their position as students in the public school system proved to be strategic as well. As Fred Shuttlesworth predicted after the first day of demonstrations, "It's going to be a bad time for the Board of Education to put those children out of school." He was right. Nearly one-third of all students and only one in seven students showed up at the high school level, laying an unanticipated economic blow to the school system that cost the system an estimated $13,000 to $20,000 each day.[135] Though movement leaders recognized students' invaluable input and bailed them out of jail, the initial Birmingham truce did not provide extended support for students once the dust settled. It called for desegregation and the release of children from jail, but not protection from a retaliatory board. This left students exposed to retribution from the school board, which they exacted with fury as they followed up on their promises to suspend or expel any and all students involved in the demonstrations. Working in conjunction with the Birmingham Police Department, the board of education identified and expelled 1,081 students.[136] James W. Stewart recalled the feeling of being expelled from Ullman High School after being arrested: "When we got back to school, I remember my homeroom teacher came in crying. Her name was Mrs. Evans. She came in crying, and she called our names, and she said, 'You have all been expelled.' Now, I am working on a 3.9 average in my senior year, and I am told I am expelled along with the rest of us. We were just shocked."[137]

Expulsion was a demoralizing blow to youth. It took them out of the very schools established to protect and provide an opportunity for success. Ann

Niles was one such student. Before the demonstrations in May, Niles was active in the Future Teachers of America club and wanted to become a teacher. But she was expelled from the organization and denied a scholarship from local Miles College.[138] This had devastating consequences for a community that highly valued education. Even if students pursued alternative diplomas, the board insisted that expulsion and suspension was recorded on their permanent files, thereby tarnishing their records as they sought employment or admission to colleges and universities. The school board also targeted those who organized students in the schools. They instructed their lawyer to investigate and file suit against "any persons which his investigation indicates are influencing or coercing negro students from attending the public school of this City, for the purpose of coercing such interference with said students."[139] The school board began a concerted effort to hold teachers responsible for large student walkouts, docking pay of teachers if students did not show up to attend class.[140]

While showing calculated restraint, the ACMHR and SCLC proceeded with legal action to meet their responsibility to ensure that 1,192 students remained in school, 202 of whom were under the age of 13. Attorneys Arthur Shores and Constance Baker Motley represented the students but sued on behalf of Linda Cal Woods, the daughter of the ACMHR board member Rev. Calvin Woods, and filed a complaint to enjoin the school board from expelling or suspending any students.[141] The board reluctantly readmitted all students, allowing them to apply for admission into summer school to make up the time lost during the demonstrations but also requesting that the disciplinary action remain on their permanent record.[142]

The Birmingham demonstrations established a strategic stronghold in the city. Students in the movement remained committed afterward, strengthening and extending the frontal assault on Jim Crow after the initial negotiations to desegregate public spaces in downtown Birmingham. In the milieu of mass expulsion, students organized under Rev. Bevel and Andrew Young and successfully petitioned for a seat at the table with movement organizers. After meeting with Dr. King, the students requested a formal liaison between the students and the committee. The committee agreed and at the next meeting, four student representatives were present and added to the board.[143] They earned a literal seat at Dr. King's table. No longer pawns in an elder's game, students guaranteed their voices would be heard.

Young people remained involved in other ways in Birmingham. As high school youth had in previous decades with SNYC, they played a critical role in the voter registration in the months after D-Day.[144] Voter registration began in earnest in early June, at which point school had already let out for the summer break. The Birmingham organizers, which included about twenty students, sought to "mobilize the high school students for the purpose of working in voter-registration." Organizers estimated that approximately three thousand students participated in the drive, which they organized into seventeen districts across the city. They organized committees that focused on transportation, speaking engagements at local churches, child care, and public relations. Seventy-five student leaders also participated in SCLC's training center in Dorchester Center in Georgia, which focused on registering voters. Students also worked and participated in the Citizenship Schools that were part of the larger "clinics" that elder organizers established. By the end of the summer, organizers cited that over forty-five hundred were registered to vote.[145]

The Birmingham Blueprint for Youth Mobilization

Birmingham had an electrifying effect in the state of Alabama and across the South. In the 10 weeks following the Birmingham demonstrations, activists organized approximately 750 demonstrations in over 180 cities where law enforcement incarcerated nearly 15,000 protestors.[146] It prompted anxious national discourse. Associated Press journalist Relman Morin wrote in the summer of 1963 that "Birmingham appears to have dramatized the Negro struggle more than any other incident . . . Almost overnight in Birmingham. Negro Demonstrations erupted in the North. Violence flared in New York, Philadelphia, Chicago, and other northern cities." The article, included in the *Congressional Record*, also quoted a Tennessean editor who commented that "Birmingham engineered the revolution that began in the spring of 1963."[147] High schoolers and students even younger triggered a "revolution" in the streets of the United States, but it also ushered in a new way of thinking about youth and youth organizing. Birmingham put forth a new blueprint for movement strategy where children and high school youth could be used and even followed in expanding the movement's base and placing pressure to achieve its larger aims.

By the mid-1960s, there was a perceptible ideological shift of youth and the role they could play in the movement. Fred Shuttlesworth, who was on the front lines in Birmingham, signified a shift in viewpoints of young people in the 1960s. Preaching to his congregation in Cincinnati, Ohio, Shuttlesworth spoke of "changing philosophies," where "young people are to be seen only—though of seldom and heard never." But he challenged his congregation and organizers to reconsider their role as a church and as parents. This new role was built upon an objective to "seek by every means to make young people conscious of their talents" and to "point out always [the] needs of a better world." He concluded by highlighting a need to "use them in today's program."[148] Bob Moses, the mathematician and teacher from New York who was organizing in the South since 1960, also detected a shift. By 1963 Moses was working in Mississippi in a brutal voter registration and nonviolent campaign, inspiring violence but falling short of the results produced in Birmingham. Moses reflected on working in Mississippi after the Alabama campaign unfolded in 1963: "The Negro community at that time-before Birmingham-was not ready to demonstrate *en masse*. The thinking was that adults should be going down, and not children. And so we didn't have sustained marches of people. Now, after Birmingham, it may be possible to launch this kind of thing."[149] As waves of protest engulfed the South after the spring of 1963, youth were noticeably taking a more active role.

The impact of the Children's Crusade was felt immediately in Alabama. In early June 1963 organizers began working in Gadsden, Alabama, one month after the Birmingham campaign. It was a town that actively resisted Jim Crow but benefited from the mobilization of Birmingham. Around forty activists and organizers mobilized in Gadsden. Some were student organizers, such as James Hood, the class president at George Washington Carver High School who gained experience in Birmingham, and Catherine Patterson, also a student at Carver, who was "moved to action" after the assault of her classmate, Fred Shuttlesworth Jr., when he tried to desegregate schools. "He was a child," she recalled, "just like I was."[150] Hood, Patterson, and other youth activists traveled to Gadsden to help register voters and continue the march for William Moore, a White postmaster killed near town while marching from Chattanooga, Tennessee, to Jackson, Mississippi, to deliver a letter in person to Governor Ross Barnett, asking him to "be gracious and give more than is immediately demanded of you."[151] The Gadsden Freedom Movement even petitioned President Kennedy for support in "breaking down the barriers of this unjust, impractical system of segregation and discrimination." Over fifteen hundred, including most of the delegation from Birmingham, were arrested.[152] As in Birmingham, young people were integral actors. Eddie James Sanders Jr. was seventeen years old when he became involved in Gadsden. As a teenager he experienced the harsh punishment of the law. In his affidavit, the young man elaborated how he was physically abused by law enforcement. State troopers and city police broke up a group he was leading that was attempting to register to vote on June 25. The very next day, leading another group to register, Sanders was literally run out of town. He was beaten and placed on the tracks leading out of town and forced to run several miles until he was well outside of town on the way to nearby Attalla.[153] Iam Sturdivant and Mrs. Annie Pearl Avery, both from Birmingham but organizing in Gadsden, described being struck with an electric prodder—the instrument of torture preferred by Al Lingo, the "tough, pot-bellied, bug-eyed archetype of southern law enforcement." Ned Simmon, acting chief of police, "kept sticking me for about five minutes," Avery recounted, "The electricity from the shocker stunned me so that I could not think for a while."[154] James Foster Smith, aged sixteen, was participating in a "stand-in" in the restaurant in the basement of the Etowah County Court House. He was assaulted and Deputy Sheriff Tony Reynolds threatened to kill the young man the next time he saw him.[155] The numbers of protestors and the exacting, meticulous brutality of Lingo contained the elements of a coordinated assault on segregation enveloping the state of Alabama.

Young people pressed to enforce the desegregation of public spaces in Birmingham promised by city leaders, particularly in July after the city council repealed its segregation ordinances. Movement leaders organized teams, often in pairs to sit at lunch counters and theaters. Annetta Streeter Gary, a student at Ullman High School who was arrested as part of the May demonstrations, volunteered to test the arrangement at two theaters. For the first time in her life, they walked through the front door. They avoided the balcony and sat in seats in the front of the theater. She and her friends also ordered food at a restaurant. Having been through D-Day and prison, Gary recalled, "I was not scared."[156] While students were served or permitted to enter these spaces that were once all-White, they experienced the microaggressions, like mockery or poor service, that defined the experiences of desegregating White schools. There were no physically violent incidents, per se, but the attitude or deeper resentment remained unchanged. Youth participated in other ways as well. As part of the armed self-defense groups that kept watch against White terrorists, John K. Wright recalled maintaining patrol of his home at night. With a shotgun in hand, he helped watch for strangers as tensions escalated during the summer of 1963.[157]

As a result of the Birmingham demonstrations, youth and civil rights leaders attempted to desegregate the schools, the first time since Shuttlesworth led an attempt to desegregate the all-White Philips High School in

September 1957. Attorney Len Holt asked the ACMHR to file a mass petition to desegregate schools in September of 1963, which the committee endorsed.[158] The courts ordered the desegregation of public schools in Alabama in Tuskegee, Mobile, Huntsville, and Birmingham. After Governor George Wallace was defeated in attempting to thwart the desegregation of the University of Alabama in June, he once again ordered state troopers to prevent desegregation and closed the schools.[159] James Armstrong, a local civil rights activist involved from the 1950s, was the lead plaintiff of the case in Birmingham, where a district judge ordered the desegregation of Graymont Elementary and two high schools, Ramsay and West End. Armstrong lived less than two blocks from Graymont Elementary. After years of organizing, he was able to enroll his two children, Dwight and Floyd, but when school began on September 4, state troopers closed the school after Whites touting Confederate flags turned violent.[160] That same day, White supremacists bombed the house of attorney Arthur Shores, who was handling the case, the second bombing he experienced in two weeks.[161] President Kennedy ultimately federalized the guard, which allowed for desegregation plans in Alabama to proceed.[162]

Those in high school made the choice to desegregate schools of their own accord, often as an extension of their activist work in the movement. As Rachel Devlin examined in her analysis of school desegregation, Black adolescent girls often picked up the mantle of becoming the first to enter all-White schools. Carrie Delores Hamilton Lock, a youth activist introduced to the movement through her parents and active in the D-Day demonstrations, was one of twenty-two students who signed up to desegregate West End High School, an all-White school, during the 1964–1965 school year. Though over twenty students registered, she was the only one to show up the first day of school. She desegregated the school and suffered from a traumatic experience. She even fought a White girl who dumped her brand new books in a sink of water. Yet she graduated from the school. "I grew up fast," Lock recalled. "I matured probably faster than the kids around me. It made me very strong. It made me very bitter, but it made me very proud and I knew that I had been set aside. I knew that, for whatever reason, whatever would come in my life, that I would be able to handle it. That, if I had gone through that, that I could handle anything."[163] Shirley Smith Miller learned of the movement by attending mass meetings at New Pilgrim Baptist Church and was involved in the D-Day demonstrations. She enrolled at West End High School two years after it was first desegregated. She was one of three Black students out of a student population of about 1,500. She noted that Delores "ended up having a lot more traumatic things," yet her experience was not easy. She described regular "little things" or microaggressions such as White students who moved over to the other side of the hallway when they passed, social isolation in class and the cafeteria, teachers calling on Black students last, if at all, and regular rejection or exclusion from extracurriculars that culminated in an overarching feeling that "they didn't want us there, and we obviously didn't want to be there."[164]

The movement spread in Mississippi that same summer. In May 1963 over five hundred high school students walked out of their schools to protest legal segregation and to join the local efforts connected to organized protests in downtown Jackson.[165] In a coordinated effort, nearly all of the students attending the three Black high schools in Jackson—Brinkley, Jim Hill, and Lanier—coordinated a walkout. Hezekiah Watkins, politicized at an early age after his experience at Parchman, remembered the walkout in historic terms: "We were able to organize the three high schools and at noon we were going to walk out and we did this within less than a week and the word just traveled just like a wildfire. I'm told that we had 90 percent of the student body walk out of the school and we walked down the highway. Some of us were arrested and some of us weren't. Each school did not know what the other school was going to do . . . But it happened and we made history that day."[166] The police force was not strong enough to handle the large walkout. City police arrested and placed the young protesters in the livestock pens at the state fairgrounds because the jails were overcrowded, and the mayor hesitated to incarcerate youth in the notorious Parchman Penitentiary. The experience was dehumanizing for the young protesters. "I remember walking out of Brinkley High School and we were put in a garbage truck and were taken to the fairgrounds down there until our parents came and got us," Hymethia Thompson, a student at Lanier High School, recalled of a student protest. "Mississippi police wanted our parents to force us to sign a statement saying we would never participate in any more demonstrations."[167] It was not uncommon for Jackson police to arrest demonstrators of any age during the city's largest demonstrations, such as those connected with the Freedom Rides, the school walkout, and marches with Dr. Martin Luther King Jr.[168]

The historically Black Lanier High School in Jackson was at the center of the school walkout. Like other southern high schools, Lanier's roots as a historically Black high school held the potential to lend support for a freedom struggle. It was politicized from its origins, firmly grounded at the nexus of liberation and education. William Henry Lanier helped found the school in 1925. A former slave, Lanier served as a president of Alcorn College and the first head of the Jackson Colored Public Schools. He also served as the principal of Smith Robertson School from 1912 to 1929, the oldest school for people of color in Jackson and similarly founded by a former slave. Lanier attended Tougaloo College, Fisk University, and Oberlin College before graduating with his bachelor's degree from Roger Williams College in Rhode Island. Achieving the promises held by higher education, Lanier oversaw the opening of the school in 1925 as a junior-senior high school and by 1936, the institution served exclusively the ninth through the twelfth grades. The school was, as historian Daphne Chamberlain noted, "the symbol of black academic excellence and tradition in Jackson and in the state of Mississippi."[169] Given the traditions passed down by educators with politicized agendas such as Glady Noel Bates, Ineva May-Pittman, I. S. Sanders, and the bus boycott staged from Lanier after the Second World War, Lanier High School in Jackson—like those across the South—were primed for civil rights activism.

As evident in Mississippi, the idea of using youth activists catapulted the movement to new heights after Birmingham. Bob Moses speculated in early June of 1963 that "Birmingham is directly responsible for what's going on in Jackson now."[170] The protests in Jackson helped stir from slumber the idea of working with youth on a massive scale. Local organizers in Mississippi, bolstered by youth demonstrations and then incensed with the assassination of Medgar Evers, negotiated with Mayor Allen Thompson for a handful of African Americans to be hired and promoted in city departments. President Kennedy was involved in negotiations as well.[171] The world was watching, and organizers pressed forward. After a successful "Freedom Vote" campaign during the fall of 1963, plans were hatched for a larger voter registration project that became the "Freedom Summer" campaign of 1964. It was the largest concerted effort to register voters in the southern movement to date that also mobilized a grassroots political party, the Mississippi Freedom Democratic Party (MFDP).[172]

Jailing high school youth, and those younger, was common during the summer of 1963. Law enforcement filled jails to capacity with high school students and youth even younger in Birmingham and across the South. As the movement spread, smaller, more rural areas were impacted. High school youth brought new life to areas across the South. In southwestern interior Georgia, students resuscitated a stalled movement. High school activists in Americus mobilized the area after SNCC's campaign stalled in nearby Albany. The small town of Americus sat forty miles north of Albany, where

SNCC and other civil rights leaders left in recognized defeat in the fall of 1962. But young people after Birmingham carried forth the momentum in towns that even SNCC had been unable to penetrate. In August of 1963 hundreds of young people marched after dozens of high school-aged students were arrested for attempting to integrate a movie theatre.[173] Police arrested thirty-three young girls, most of whom were of high school age, who engaged in the Americus protests. They were placed in the county stockade in Leesburg, Georgia, and jailed for over a month.[174] SNCC and other community organizers essentially forgot about them until photographer Danny Lyon visited the stockade, spoke with the incarcerated activists, and captured photographs of the deplorable conditions in which they lived. Henrietta Fuller, who was thirteen at the time, captured the harrowing conditions in a sworn affidavit. As Fuller recalled of the room she shared with thirty-two other girls: "There were no beds, no mattresses, no blankets, pillows, no sheets. The floor was cold . . . The smell of the waste was bad . . . I urinated where the water from the shower drains down. Some of the girls used a piece of cardboard that came from the boxes, the cardboard boxes, that the hamburgers were brought in . . . There was a shower but it wasn't clean enough for you to bathe in. Cardboard with waste material had been put there and it needed cleaning and scrubbing."[175] Lyon shared his photographs of the "stolen girls" with SNCC and submitted pictures to the Black and mainstream press across the country and sympathetic congressmen, who published them in the *Congressional Record*.[176] The girls were soon after released, but the images and narratives of incarcerated girls provided a stark reminder that young girls and women were oppressed in different ways and carried a different burden than young men in the movement.

After Birmingham, civil rights organizers in SNCC were more intentional in bringing youth into the movement and training students from elementary through high school to be part of it. In planning for Freedom Summer, Charlie Cobb, a SNCC field organizer, proposed a Freedom School program to be part of Freedom Summer. Organizers of the Freedom Summer campaign wanted to mobilize across the state of Mississippi but they also wanted to utilize young activists—those not yet in college. Replete with an academic curriculum grounded in general education courses but underpinned by the history, philosophy, and analysis of the civil rights movement, the Freedom Schools provided a transformative education grounded in the Black experience rarely taught in traditional public schools, North or South. The Freedom Schools also explicitly incorporated a political curriculum, where students were taught the more tangible aspects of the movement, much like the mass meetings before the Birmingham demonstrations where students learned the nonviolent strategies of the movement. Children—many not even in high school—were provided an opportunity to apply the skills in canvassing the neighborhood or registering people to vote in the alternative elections of the MFDP. Taught by hundreds of volunteers who mobilized in the state of Mississippi, students learned an expanded version of what was taught at the "freedom schools" and "nonviolent high" that evolved from jail cell education lessons led by SNCC workers in McComb in the early 1960s. Students studied Black history, read Black authors and playwrights, and debated the Constitution. They also received a political education, which not only taught the basics of citizenship in regard to the voting process, but also registering voters, canvassing neighbors, and organizing voter registration drives.[177]

Students formed a statewide Mississippi Student Union at the conclusion of the summer voter registration campaign in August 1964 in Hattiesburg, Mississippi.[178] College activists and SNCC organizers convened the conference, which was in the same vein of the original SNYC student conferences. Under the auspices of SNCC student-centered philosophy, the Freedom School convention was led by the Freedom School students. At the conclusion of the convention, students penned a declaration, stating in part: "We . . . the Negroes of Mississippi assembled, appeal to the government of the state, that no man is free until all men are free. We do hereby declare independence from the unjust laws of Mississippi which conflict with the United States Constitution."[179]

The provocative declaration stood in stark contrast to the student-led declaration that SNYC passed in 1946. In 1964, after an unprecedented mobilization of high school youth in the movement, student organizers claimed full citizenship and declared unjust the laws that prohibited immediate freedom and intimated more radical steps in the tradition of the nation's founding Declaration of Independence, writing, "It has become necessary for the Negro people to break away from the customs which have made it very difficult for the Negro to get his God-given rights."[180] The "Columbia Pact of Southern Youth" that SNYC adopted in 1946 similarly referenced the nation's ideals enshrined in the Constitution and sought "common action to make our dream for a better South and a better American come true."[181] But those gathered at the youth conference in Mississippi demonstrated an evolving notion of youth activism that left "common action," unity, and common ground behind. High school youth by 1964 intended to "break away" and asserted their autonomy in doing so. Roscoe Jones, a high school student from Meridian who was elected as president of the student union in Mississippi, elaborated on the agency he and his peers felt. "We young people had a plan. We were going to integrate everything that was open to the public that we had to go through the back door. We were going through the front door in movie houses, everything. We had plans for it all. And it was not adults telling us this. It was student led."[182]

Building upon the sentiment of the student's declaration of independence, students directly participated in and shaped local movements across Mississippi. Student union members and the students trained in the Freedom Schools tried the Civil Rights Act of 1964 in Mississippi and tested the new law in theaters, public parks, libraries, barber shops, and pools. They launched school boycotts to protest discriminatory treatment and racist curricula. Quite significantly, members of the union wore SNCC "One Man, One Vote" pins to wear to school in support of the movement. Forty-five students in Philadelphia demanded the right to free speech and to protest on their own terms when they fashioned SNCC "One Man, One Vote" buttons. Parents of the students who were suspended in Philadelphia for wearing the pins filed suit against the school board. Plaintiffs argued that administrators violated their right to free speech granted when they suspended or expelled them for wearing political pins.[183] Shortly thereafter in Sharkey and Issaquena Counties, over two hundred students wore pins to promote participation in the civil right movement and, when confronted by principal O. E. Jordan, they refused to take off the pins. The principal, like other administrators across the South who were under increasing pressure to curb civil rights activity, followed the instructions of an all-White school board and suspended them. The community decided to boycott and over thirteen hundred students and their families withdrew from the school for nearly a month and over three hundred students remained out of school for the entire year.[184]

The protest students brought into the schools in support of voter registration carried momentous implications for student rights that were being renegotiated over the course of the 1960s and 1970s. The "button cases," as historian Kathryn Schumaker noted in her analysis of lawsuits pertaining to student rights, "laid the groundwork for future cases involving public school students and the Constitution."[185] In the cases of *Burnside v. Byars* (1966) and *Blackwell v. Issaquena* (1966) the court determined that students had the right to wear the buttons as an expression of free speech that was protected by the Constitution. These cases became the legal precedent that the Supreme Court cited in *Tinker v. Des Moines* (1969), which stated that young people in Iowa had a First Amendment right to wear a black armband to school protesting the Vietnam War.[186] The Court did not extend protections to Black students and students of color specifically nor did they recognize the racial nuance that students in Mississippi were bringing to the court and, as Schumaker notes, the cases protected speech that followed the protocol of the politics of respectability that did not lead to "disruption," a construct used to penalize student protest.[187] Yet the case illustrates the wide reach of student-led protest and, once introduced into the courts, crystallized the schools as spaces to demand rights for students that were denied or not considered previously.

The Selma to Montgomery March in the spring of 1965, just under two years after the Children's Crusade, illustrates that the impact of Birmingham continued to reverberate through the state of Alabama after the Freedom Summer campaign in Mississippi. The march revealed how the movement resonated with educators who were pulled into the movement and took stands that they may not have taken during the spring of 1963 at the height of the Children's Crusade. Largely consumed with defending their right to teach in the professional fallout of the *Brown* decision—scholars have estimated that thirty-eight thousand Black teachers lost their positions within the first decade after the decision—teachers remained committed to the movement in myriad ways.[188] Additionally, the march for voting rights in 1965 also demonstrated that historically Black high schools continued to complement the Black church as integral grounds for advancing the movement. In the case of Herman Harris, who during the spring of 1965 was the principal of George Washington Carver Elementary School, the movement and American history marched directly in front of his schoolhouse door.

SNCC and SCLC focused on Selma and the blackbelt counties in Alabama that were majority Black yet only had a handful of registered Black voters. In Selma, for instance, only 156 of approximately 15,000 voters were registered, and in Lowndes County, though 80 percent of the county was Black, there were no African Americans registered to vote in 1965.[189] In January of 1965 organizers including Andrew Young, who gained invaluable experience organizing in Birmingham, utilized young people to escalate the assault on voter discrimination. Organizing mass protests and campaigns to fill the jails, five hundred schoolchildren were arrested in Selma and Marion in late January, another three hundred were arrested the first week of February, and still another four hundred high school students were arrested by the end of the month. Youth pushed the number of those incarcerated to twenty-six hundred. Students launched boycotts of their schools in response to arrests made after activists entered an all-White section of a restaurant. In Marion, which had a population of under four thousand, such numbers and the scope of the campaign were staggering.[190] One student was Charles Mauldin, a seventeen-year-old student at the all-Black Selma Hudson High School. He was recruited by Bernard Lafayette of SCLC and headed up the Dallas County Student Union. Like the high school organizers in Birmingham, Mauldin was responsible for recruiting his peers to the front lines.[191] This established the groundwork for the fifty-mile march between Selma and Montgomery that inspired passage of the Voting Rights Act.

Teachers and administrators like Herman Harris were placed once again on the front lines, whether they liked it or not. Protestors marched the last miles of the historic fifty-four miles to Montgomery to the cheers of children as they marched directly in front of their schools. In another instance of Black institutions providing space to the movement, marchers camped on the night of March 24, 1965, on the campus of St. Jude's Educational Institute, a private Black Catholic school outside the city. "It's kind of hard to turn away 3,000 people who needed a place to stay," Douglas Watson, a fourth-grade student at the time, remembered of the marchers who stayed on the school grounds the final night of the march.[192] The school was critical in providing shelter and a baseball field, which organizers transformed into a massive celebration and demonstration. The Justice Department estimated that thirty thousand people packed into the field where a stage was constructed on wooden boxes, a searchlight illuminated the way for noted celebrities Harry Belafonte, Odetta, Nina Simone, Pete Seeger, and Sammy Davis Jr. Students climbed trees for a birds-eye view of an unprecedented celebrity gathering in Montgomery.[193]

The march was a sight to behold, mesmerizing to the young people. Deborah Webb, a seventh-grade student at Booker T. Washington Junior High School, remembers the disruption prompted by marchers, who were shouting from the streets for youth to join as they were "going downtown and were going to stand." "It was glamorous," Webb recalled of the atmosphere of seeing so many march through the streets. "My friend Janice jumped through the window," she relayed. Students were admonished by the principal over the intercom, who forbade students from participating. "They were admonishing us to keep our eyes on the board and don't look out the window," William Ford recalled when looking back at his time at St. Jude. Many students, including Webb, stayed.[194] Marchers also trekked past George Washington Carver Elementary School nearby, where Herman Harris was principal. As principal, Harris allowed his students to observe the historic march that unfolded before them.[195]

By 1965 educators across the South were compelled to take some stand as the movement literally passed them by. Since SCLC organized the black-belt after Birmingham, teachers, like students, were an important part of the campaign. In January, over one hundred teachers demonstrated outside the Dallas County courthouse at a voter registration drive. Over three hundred students cheered them on. *The New York Times* reported it "was the first time so large a number of public school teachers had been known to participate on an organized basis in the civil rights movement."[196] In his dispatches and letters from a Selma jail, King wrote to Andrew Young to "stretch every point to get teachers to march."[197] Teachers received the call and they responded.

Herman Harris epitomized the changing nature of teachers' role in the movement by 1965. Born on July 1, 1927, in Burkeville, Lowndes County, and graduating valedictorian of Loveless High School in 1944, Harris knew all too well the realities of Jim Crow and the promises of education. Having served in the Army from 1945 to 1946, Harris was one of thousands of veterans who returned home committed to radically change the South.[198] He earned a BS and MEd degree at Alabama State University, taught, and served as a principal for ten years in Montgomery County and City.[199] Harris was also elected as the vice president and president of the Alabama State Teachers Association after serving as president for the local chapters in Butler and Montgomery.[200]

Clearly understanding the role of students in Birmingham, White administrators took pains to curb student participation in student boycotts after 1963. The Alabama State Board of Education in 1965 passed a resolution that withheld state funds from teachers and principals when student attendance dropped below 63 percent. This applied to partial absenteeism if students only missed part of a day as well. In a concurrent session, the state legislature passed a 10 percent increase for all teachers across the state yet stipulated that teachers who encouraged or supported student walkouts, and teachers who themselves participated in demonstrations, would not remain eligible to receive the raise.[201] Southern states took legislative and judicial action before, such as passing laws that targeted young people, as in Mississippi in the buildup prior to the Freedom Summer campaign. But the legislature in Alabama specifically held teachers accountable for Black students and attempted to discipline them through fines for student demonstrations.

As principal at Carver Elementary School in Montgomery with an acute understanding of the nuances of standing up for civil rights in Alabama, Herman Harris took a firm stand on the issue of student demonstrations. In a seething editorial published in the *Montgomery Advertiser*, Harris clearly opposed the legislative move. "I could never feel right showing my face in public again if I didn't speak my thoughts concerning the blackjack legislation," he wrote. "How much longer do you think you can 'keep the Negroes in line' with threats and coercion?" he asked. He went on if further detail: "I shall not relinquish my responsibilities as a principal to become a full-time truant officer so long as I'm still expected to fulfill my duties as a full-time principal. Nor shall I ever place my body in the schoolhouse door to block traffic in either direction."

He went on to write, "I am not a rabble rouser, but neither am I a puppet." Fully aware of the repercussions of his actions, he wrote sternly: "If this [letter] means the axe for me, then let the axe come. . . . I simply cannot do the strenuous task that is mine to do with a club of some kind forever hanging over my head. Either let the club fall or remove it."[202]

Harris's move is noteworthy for the profession. Harris was quick to note that enforcing truancy laws was beyond his and other educators' professional responsibilities and that this was impossible given the magnitude and scope of their other obligations to the profession. This argument extended the professional responsibilities of organized teachers, both Black and White, traditionally relied upon in defending their profession. But at the same time Harris argued that a long history of subjugation to the "axe" shaped the experiences of Black educators—a balancing act felt across the South as teachers negotiated positions in a newly desegregated system as supporters of the ongoing movement.[203] By calling attention to this history, the recent legislation was the most recent manifestation of a long history of attempting to coerce teachers to performing the will of the state that contradicted the will of the Black community. Harris envisioned that his role did not include standing in the doorway, a reference to the infamous southern recalcitrance of blocking the schoolhouse door for those seeking to integrate White institutions. Embracing a more objective position, Harris would not "block traffic in either direction." Like many teachers in Birmingham, Harris did not encourage protest directly, but he did not block it either.

Though moderate to some—Harris stopped short of calling for a walkout— the move marked a significant departure from the public stance of teachers during the 1950s. Unlike principal M. B. Jones in Prince Edward County in the 1950s or Principal R. C. Johnson of Birmingham, Harris took a public stand contrary to that of the school board. Harris expected to be fired. But the result was, surprisingly, one of support. The Montgomery County Teachers Association issued a statement of support soon after Harris's editorial was published. Richard Kennan, Executive Secretary of the National Education Association reached out and offered assistance.[204] As local leader Mrs. Idessa Williams noted in her telegram of congratulations to Harris, she was "proud that one negro educator . . . had guts enough to stand" and let the board know "you are a man."[205] The letter also allowed other educators to express their support. As Mr. and Mrs. L. R. Williams wrote to Harris, "Your frank appraisal of our situation as negro teachers and principals should stir the soul of each teacher in our profession. Cowardness and pseudo security have prevented the rest of us from coming forward to express our feelings and thoughts in a matter so nobly done by you."[206] As the dean of Miles College in Birmingham wrote to Harris, "I hope other 'Negro leaders' will take note and learn that we will never change despicable, oppressive patterns by timidly adjusting to them."[207]

By the end of the 1960s student activism appeared to be a national phenomenon, if not a mainstay in the culture of secondary education. By the late 1960s particularly after the assassination of Dr. King in the spring of 1968, Black students organized of their own accord in the high schools they attended—and far outside the South.[208] Much of their organization focused on curricular reform and improving the quality of their education following the principles of the movement. The League of Revolutionary Workers in Detroit inspired the formation of the Black Student United Front, who organized of their own accord a revolutionary political curriculum to inculcate students in the politics of activism.[209] The Black Student Federation in Boston reflected the strategies and values of the Black Power movement, launching a boycott and demanding the hiring of Black faculty, a racially and culturally relevant curriculum, Black student unions, and a right to wear African-style clothing in school.[210] In the Bay Area of California, the Black Student Union at Berkeley High School successfully pressured administrators to hire more Black faculty, institute a Black studies program, and recognize the birth of Malcolm X as a holiday.[211] An estimated twenty-seven to thirty-five thousand boycotted schools in Chicago in the fall of 1968 and demanded educational reform.[212] In Philadelphia, students in 1967 protested the use of racist curriculum. When police assaulted and arrested the youth activists, it triggered widespread protest in the city.[213] In Los Angeles, high school students and organizers orchestrated large walkouts or "blowouts" in 1968, in which over ten thousand students protested district schools for more Latinx faculty, fairer tracking practices, a culturally relevant curriculum and other demands that reflected the student movement of the late 1960s.[214]

Birmingham represented a turning point. The demonstrations in Alabama and the threat of what historian Taylor Branch called "a nightmarish string of Birminghams" inspired President Kennedy to act. In the months following the demonstrations, Kennedy addressed the nation specifically about civil rights, proposed comprehensive civil rights legislation, and invited national civil rights leaders, about fifteen hundred over the course of the summer after Birmingham, including private audiences with Roy Wilkins, the influential executive secretary of the NAACP, and Dr. King. Fred Shuttlesworth, himself part of the movement's representatives to meet President Kennedy, paraphrased what he heard Kennedy say in the midst of the largest gathering of civil rights leaders at the White House to discuss civil rights legislation: "But for Birmingham, we would not be here today."[215] For many, it was a time to celebrate. "You spoke passionately to the moral issues," King telegrammed to Kennedy after his national address in June. "It was one of the most eloquent profound and unequiv[oc]al pleas for Justice and Freedom of all men ever made by any President."[216]

The culminating event after the summer campaign in Birmingham, the March on Washington, celebrated the success of the inroads made since May. Drawing a crowd of 250,000, the massive march bespoke the hopes and aspirations of a burgeoning movement and a national leader mythologized after the historic event.[217] James Stewart was one of the Birmingham student protestors who attended the march. It was surreal for Stewart to be standing near the Reflecting Pool on the Washington Mall listening to Dr. King deliver his now-famous "I Have a Dream" speech. "That's the guy who spoke to us in the churches and the meetings," Stewart recalled of King working with youth during the Birmingham campaign. "And now he's on the national stage."[218] Looking back on the use of youth in Alabama and the national repercussions it had in moving the needle, the March on Washington may have proved wrong the critics of using young people in the movement.

Any celebration, however, was cut tragically short.

· · · · · ·

Black residents in the city of Birmingham were subject to ongoing terrorist bombings throughout the freedom struggle. Bombing became so common and threatening—approximately fifty bombings between 1947 and 1965— the city earned the epithet "Bombingham."[219] After escalated bombings following the Children's Crusade in May, the ACMHR formally petitioned and requested city police for protection of churches and the homes.[220] Violence and terror were normalized and even encouraged publicly by those who governed, including Governor Wallace, who violently noted, "What this country needs is a few first-class funerals, and some political funerals too."[221] Despite the regularity of bombing and the entrenched violence of the city, few outside of the Klan could have imagined the horrors that were about to befall Birmingham.

On the morning of September 15, 1963, Robert Chambliss, a staunch Klan member and confidant of Bull Connor known as "Dynamite Bob," laid delayed-fused sticks of dynamite that ripped through the basement of the Sixteenth Street Baptist Church. The explosion left a seven-by-seven gaping hole in the side of the church and a crater over two feet deep and five feet wide. It was "Youth Day" at the church and young people were gathered in the church basement for Sunday School. The Reverend John Cross, whose daughter participated in the May demonstrations, held the inaugural Youth Day to grow youth participation in church. Dressed all in white, young people were going to lead the choir at the eleven o'clock service. Mamie H. Grier, the superintendent of the Sunday School remembered the young boys and girls discussing the topic, "The Love That Forgives." The bomb took the lives of "four little girls": Addie Mae Collins, age fourteen; Carol Denise McNair, age eleven; Carole Robinson, age fourteen; and Cynthia Wesley, age fourteen. They and their families, many of whose parents were schoolteachers, paid the ultimate price.[222]

In the immediate aftermath that followed, two more Black youth were killed. Two White Eagle Scouts returning home from a segregationist rally hosted by the West End parents for Private Schools and the National States Rights Party's headquarters, where they purchased a Confederate flag, fired at two Black youth, hitting twice and killing Virgil Ware, a thirteen-year-old riding a bicycle. That same afternoon police officers shot in the back of the head and killed Johnnie Robinson, a Black sixteen-year-old, as he fled a scene where a skirmish broke out in the city and he allegedly threw rocks at a car with a message that said, "Negro, go back to Africa."[223]

The bombing affected the whole of Birmingham. As Deboarh Sanders Avery recalled, "That was a day that I think the whole world mourned."[224] Eloise Staples, a freshman at Parker High School during the May demonstrations of which she was a part, illustrates the close-knit community of the city, where everyone was in some way connected to the bombing. Chris McNair, the father of Denise McNair, one of the four victims of the church bombing, was her homeroom teacher. The sister of Ady Collins, one of the four girls, Jodi, was in her sister's classroom. She was in band with Carol Robinson. "It was really traumatic for us."[225] "It was very sad," Denise Wrushen recalled,

> My teacher lost a child. Ms. McNair was my teacher. A classmate I lost. Carol, a close friend, her sister, you know. And I knew everyone that was killed in the bombing . . . And the thing that was impressed on my mind was I could have easily been there, too. As I can recall that was a youth day and during that time you would go and participate with different churches if you were a youth, you were invited to that youth day, you know because I can remember that the church I was attending they would have visiting youth from other churches, you know and those girls I knew them all.[226]

Carolyn McKinstry was at the church of the day of the bombing. She answered the phone when the bombers called and said, "Two minutes." Her two young brothers were in the basement of the church; they survived. After the bombing she recalled, "I decided that I was probably going, sooner or later I was going to be killed with one of those bombs . . . There was no way to stop what they were doing. There was no way to protect yourself."[227] For Andrew Young, one of the youth organizers in May, "None of us ever imagined it would happen the way it did. It could not have happened except that the frustrations and desire for dignity were already present in the hearts of each of these kids."[228] "I will never forget," student activist James Stewart recalled of the bombing, "they hated us so much that they decided the way to win is to now kill their children . . . It raised the stakes and it made me angrier, but it made me more determined."[229]

Youth accurately perceived the truth of the matter that they were strategically targeted by White supremacists in a violent effort to maintain their position of power. The church was an obvious target—the primary meeting place for children who participated in the demonstrations just four months prior. Young people were the calculated target as well. It was youth, after all, who spurred a lagging movement and won the first steps toward desegregation from lunch counters to schools that the city had ever seen. In the ongoing campaign in Birmingham, Chambliss' bombing constituted a calculated, strategic, and violent defense of White supremacy, and Black youth were targeted in that defense as they had been throughout the past century. As much as youth activism evolved since the 1920s, the violent defense of White supremacy remained constant. The violent assault on Black youth in Birmingham would escalate into a national offensive and Black students, teachers, and high schools were the primary targets.

In Charleston, South Carolina, Barbara Jones brought a handful of protest
flyers to Rivers High School in the fall of 1969. Rivers was the first high
school to desegregate in South Carolina in 1963, when one African American
student, Millicent Brown, enrolled in the school.[1] Six years later the school
was majority Black and overseen by a White principal, Willis Russell. Jones
distributed a flyer among students in reaction to the student unrest. "We are
tired of 'White Dictatorship,'" the flyer began. "Let us organize. We want
equality at Rivers High School," the handout read, "Equality Now." The flyer
demanded the administration hire a Black principal, support a Black student
organization, and eradicate racism at Rivers. The handout went on to argue
that "we must unite ourselves and speak out for what we believe in."[2] Jones'
organizing dovetailed with and continued the high school organizing tradition. She worked with other students to draft the letter. They sought support
and guidance from older college-aged activists, in this case the SCLC, who
had representatives working directly with students in the school. Additionally, Jones called for a peaceful process to address their concerns, which included meeting with the principal. If the school's administrations were to
"refuse to hear your grievances," then students proposed to formally submit
their grievances to the county board of education.[3]

Jones's protest was indicative of a strand of high school protest that became common during the late 1960s and 1970s in newly desegregated public schools. She organized within a school for fairer and more equitable
educational experiences, she was connected to college-aged youth organizers, and she called for peaceful protest if necessary to achieve their goals—
all were familiar themes. But the context of demanding change within a
school that had already been desegregated served as a marked departure.
While Jones and her peers continued a tradition of high school activism into
the late 1960s and early 1970s, White administrators reacted by implementing new forms of control that utilized modified disciplinary instruments in

schools that were desegregating. After reading the flyer for himself, the principal searched Jones's locker, where he found a ream of handouts. Russell immediately called the police to help "prevent any possibility of riot or disorder," and they promptly suspended Jones for distributing the "inflammatory" flyer.[4] Charleston authorities conveyed a clear message that they would meet student resistance with swift and punitive action. Their reaction was part of a larger response to student unrest during the desegregation of southern high schools in the late 1960s and early 1970s. With resounding frequency, Black students, Black teachers, and formerly all-Black high schools themselves were subject to hostile, punitive policies that increasingly relied upon law enforcement to maintain "law and order" as schools began to desegregate.

Barbara Jones and her peers understood the consequences for organizing in South Carolina. She aptly predicted how she would be treated for speaking up, writing in the flyer that "anytime a black student gets fed up with this white man's school system and stand up for their just right—they are labeled "violent', thrown into jail, expelled from school, etc."[5] Jones called out a new system of discipline and punishment that sought to control and monitor her actions during the volatile years of desegregation. There was a new disciplinary form of power that was part of a wider state apparatus in which schools were an integral part. Classrooms, hallways, and playgrounds were new sites of incarceration and integral parts of a growing carceral state—regardless of age—in the concerted effort to resist and rollback the gains made during the Black freedom struggle.

The unrest at Rivers High School occurred amid a shift in public perception. National discourse by the early 1970s posited that juvenile delinquency was a problem of significant magnitude, particularly in desegregated schools.[6] As historians V. P. Franklin, Gael Graham, Dionne Danns, Dara Walker, Aaron Fountain, Mario Garcia, and others have documented, high school protest gripped the nation in major cities, including Boston, New York, Chicago, Philadelphia, Detroit, San Francisco, Los Angeles, and other locales in the late 1960s and early 1970s.[7] Desegregation in the South further exacerbated the national anxiety and southern high school activists indelibly shaped the rise in protests. The local paper in Charleston, South Carolina, *The News and Courier*, reflected this national anxiety in an editorial from 1972, the "Battle in the Schools." Editors drew attention to the "silent, constant mass of unrest and discontent" that undergirded public schools after "adjustment to changes in the student body, which have brought in a larger portion of blacks to join the whites." Editors noted a "terror among the young people" while postulating that "parents . . . are afraid for the safety of their children. Boys are beaten, girls subjected to indignities, and the social and moral tone of school life is deteriorating."[8] Like schools across the nation, public schools in Charleston were increasingly framed as violent spaces throughout the late 1960s and 1970s. Alton C. Crews, superintendent of the Charleston County School District, noted that "teachers, particularly those working in inner-city schools, have been harassed and physically abused" and went on to highlight the "ominous threat of renegade students and non-student troublemakers walking off the street into school buildings and disrupting the learning process." The local chapter of the American Federation of Teachers issued a statement that noted "there exists in Charleston County schools a climate of unprecedented violence, fear and intimidation."[9]

The activism of southern high school students like Barbara Jones in South Carolina illustrates how desegregated schools became the front lines of a wider struggle. As historian Vincent Willis demonstrated, Black youth carried an "uncompromising commitment to equal education after *Brown*" and high school students carried forth the resistance of previous decades. As a result, they transformed high schools into a contested desegregated space.[10] New battle lines were drawn in a concerted, coordinated attack on Black students, teachers, and the very essence of public schools.

After the desegregation of schools and the wave of student activism that transformed public education in the South, segregationists and recalcitrant Whites waged a tripartite assault on Black students, teachers, and schools to stymie the insurrection that developed across the nation of which Barbara Jones was a part. Black students both prompted and were surveilled by increasingly stringent legislation at local, state, and federal levels that targeted the bodies of Black youth in newly desegregated high schools. As Black high school activists shaped a national movement that included the desegregation of schools, legislative actions attempted to restrain and control the movement, mitigating its impact and shaping how desegregation unfolded across the nation, which grew to include close surveillance by law enforcement. Such policies informed an evolving carceral state in which schools were a critical site, dashing the integrationist or liberatory ideals boldly put forth by young activists of previous decades and those that supported them. The repressive state apparatus also terminated the gainful employment of nearly one-half of the Black teaching force in the South, denying access to the economic promises gestured after the milestone legislation in the Civil Rights Act of 1964. Finally, as Whites avoided desegregation at all costs, they closed Black schools, used public funding to construct racially segregated White private schools, and facilitated an ideology of "school choice" that struck a serious blow to the vitality of Black schools and the communities that they served. White resistance to the gains and demands made by Black high school activists decimated historically Black high schools and neighborhoods, necessitating further resistance and promulgating an assault on Black education that facilitated the crippling divestment in public education for all students.

Mapping the trajectory of southern high school activism elucidates how southern school districts and states maintained the historic criminalization of Black youth in newly desegregated schools. Southern schools—specifically schools under court mandates to desegregate—were concomitant sites of a national project that transcended regional boundaries and renegotiated hegemonic control after student activism transformed both schools and the front lines of the Black freedom struggle.[11] In addition to criminalizing young Black youth, White segregationists continued to attack Black schools, closing them down and "cleaning up" the neighborhoods they served through "urban renewal" projects. Black teachers also suffered as casualties in the larger assault on Black education, losing access to a profession that was a mainstay of the Black community. It was a tripartite attack on Black students, teachers, and schools that undermined the intentions of desegregation and the activists who sought to achieve the beloved community.

Criminalization of Black Students

Throughout the 1960s White school administrators threw the book at Black students who transgressed social and political mores by joining the freedom struggle. Brenda Travis, who was sixteen when she attempted to buy bus tickets from the Whites-only counter of the local Greyhound bus terminal in McComb, Mississippi during the summer of 1961, served a month-long prison sentence. The school board amplified the punishment by expelling those students who did not sign a statement opposing the civil rights movement, as the local courts leveled maximum fees on those arrested. Yet Brenda Travis fared the worst. She was charged as a minor, convicted as a delinquent, and ordered to attend Oakley Training School. She spent over six months in the reformatory school before moving to Alabama.[12] The students in Birmingham faced similar repercussions during the summer of 1963. Arrested, imprisoned in makeshift jail cells, and expelled from school,

Black youth in the Children's Crusade faced the full brunt of the law.[13] To be expelled by the local school board, subsequently uprooted, and essentially run out of town sent a powerful message to other young people who put themselves on the front lines of the movement.

The growing visibility of unrepentant high school student activists like Brenda Travis across the South intersected with the politics of the Cold War and McCarthyism to contribute to the delinquency scare of the postwar period. Anxiety over "juvenile delinquency" was institutionalized by the Senate Subcommittee on Juvenile Delinquency, established in 1953, which promulgated reports of rising youth crime and raised serious concern in political spheres. The blockbuster films *Blackboard Jungle* and *Rebel Without a Cause* released one year after the *Brown* decision in 1955, solidified emerging anxieties around "juvenile delinquency" and informed a national and collective understanding about education reform.[14] The ideology of juvenile unrest, rebellious adolescents, and youth lawlessness indelibly shaped policy as the nation connected juvenile delinquency to the heightened anxiety around desegregation, which ultimately facilitated the rise of a police state in public schools.

The issues of juvenile delinquency prompted the Kennedy administration to target youth transgressions at the federal level. President Kennedy signed into law the Juvenile Delinquency and Youth Offenses Act in 1961, seeking to research and disseminate information about the "problem" of criminal behavior among youth and to develop pilot programs to identify effective methods to address it. For federal legislators, juvenile delinquency diminished "the strength and vitality of the people of our Nation." It was a phenomenon that they traced to dropping out of school, youth unemployment, and "deprived family situations." Moving beyond the regular White House Conferences on Children and Youth that had been in place for decades, the Juvenile Delinquency Act was milestone legislation as the first federally supported initiative to tackle adolescent crime prevention.[15] While the Act fell short of placing law enforcement agents or police in schools, the legislation opened new pathways to achieve it.

With the rising tide of calls for integrated schools, legislative understandings of juvenile delinquency were racialized from their inception in the 1950s. Southern legislators who opposed desegregation used the issue of juvenile delinquency as a way to prevent it. A "riot" in Washington, D.C., one of the cities that was part of the *Brown* case, provided a national platform to articulate the elevated anxieties of lawlessness and desegregation. On Thanksgiving Day in 1962, a traditional fall football match in

Washington, D.C., resulted in what the nation decried as a "race riot." The game was between the all-White St. John's Catholic High School and Eastern High School, a predominantly Black public school in D.C. for the city championship game. It was a traditional fall classic that drew thousands of spectators. After the game, in which St. John's defeated Eastern by a score of 20 to 7, extensive fighting occurred, leaving forty people injured. The violence prompted great alarm, and the Archdiocese canceled sports playoffs that season.[16]

The "riot" also inspired a special congressional investigation. The biracial investigatory committee's report observed a "wave of lawlessness" and blamed the schools and a lack of discipline in the schools for the unrest after the game. To fan the rising flames of fear, the committee also reported a "stockpiling" of potential weapons including "umbrellas with sharp points, broken bottles, rocks, knives, and chains."[17]

Unrest in Washington, D.C., in 1962 also became a flashpoint for senators who opposed school desegregation. It presented an opportunity for segregationists to use the nation's capital to advocate for maintaining segregation by linking desegregated public schools with violence, vice, and lawlessness.[18] As one of the five cities in the *Brown* decision and at the heart of the nation's capital, the incident presented a new stage to voice opposition and to relay anxieties and fears of the prospects of desegregating public schools. As Southern Manifesto signatory Senator Spessard Holland of Florida noted, "The events at the District of Columbia stadium on Thanksgiving Day clearly demonstrate the futility of mass integration of the races without adequate preparation and adjustment"[19] For Senator Holland and other segregationists, integration would lead to a situation "so injurious as to cause a riot."[20] The report of the special commission argued that integration was to blame, too. It noted that schools prior to the *Brown* decision were "adequate and often exemplary." However, the report found that after desegregation and the "rapid growth in numbers of Negro pupils, many with low mental rating" led to a deterioration or "neutralization" of the once high standards of the D.C. public school system.[21]

The findings aggregated various elements of school discipline and law enforcement that established a blueprint of sorts for school disciplinary policy during desegregation. The special commission advocated for policy and public services in schools to surveil and discipline youth. The committee called for a race relations detail in the city police department so that they could stay connected with communities to purportedly diffuse racial tensions. They proposed the development of an advisory council in local precincts in addition to stricter student disciplinary codes. The committee also recommended streamlining disciplinary procedures and creating administrative positions for human relations.[22]

As congressional leaders contemplated how to control juvenile delinquency in relation to desegregation, southern states passed their own legislation seeking to tamp out any "disruption" on the school premises. In effect, state and local laws passed in Dixie expanded the boundaries of the Juvenile Act of 1961 by using law enforcement in schools to address what they saw as delinquency in their high schools.

Like federal juvenile delinquency policy, much of the southern legislation that focused on student discipline either anticipated or followed a massive campaign of high school student–led protest and resistance. Alabama passed legislation in 1963, for instance, that authorized local school boards to "prescribe rules and regulation with respect to behavior and discipline of pupils enrolled in the schools."[23] Legislators were "empowering local boards of education to take certain actions" and provided significant latitude to local office holders to determine what "problems" were "detrimental to the best interest and welfare of the pupils of such class as a whole." It also allowed school boards to categorically place or track students based on "social attitudes," "their hostility toward the school environment," and "morals."[24] Legislators passed the school discipline act in a special legislative session called during the summer of 1963 in the midst of the Children's Crusade, in which thousands of youth participated and over one thousand children were arrested for taking part in the boycotts and walkouts. At stake was the board's right to punish students for walking out and engaging in protest. The legislature authorized local school boards to "remove, isolate, separate, or group pupils" based on their discretion and reinstated their authority to do so after the Fifth Circuit Court of Appeals overturned the expulsion of over one thousand children who participated in the Children's Crusade.[25] This legislation presaged state policies that threatened to dock pay or even terminate the contracts of teachers whose students participated in walkouts.[26]

Mississippi legislators acted similarly, calling for an extraordinary legislative session during the summer of 1964 to pass a series of laws to punish not only college volunteers but any students or youth in preparation for and anticipation of the Freedom Summer campaign, the largest voter registration project of the freedom struggle. Legislators passed laws to punish young offenders under the age of twenty-one, reinforcing the notion that adolescents and children of the movement should suffer the same consequences as adults. The law provided that any child or minor under the age of twenty-one would not be tried or brought through the judicial system through the Youth Court, which was designed to protect the constructed category of youth. Rather, youth and children arrested or fined for any "breach of peace" or refusing to "comply with or obey a request, command, or order of a law enforcement officer," would be subjected to the same courts of law and judicial proceedings as any adult. Such legislation cast aside the distinctions crafted to protect youth and treated them as adults.[27]

In South Carolina, legislators substantively overhauled an existing law to address the issue of student protest and juvenile delinquency. Less than one month after the February 8, 1968, Orangeburg Massacre in South Carolina in which state law enforcement shot and killed three students and wounded twenty-eight others at the historically Black South Carolina State University in Orangeburg, South Carolina, state legislators revisited an existing code on student discipline. The law, known as the "disturbing schools" law, was on the books since 1919 and prohibited any person "willfully or unnecessarily . . . to interfere with or to disturb in any way or in any place the students or teachers of any school." Originally known as "An Act to Protect Schools and Colleges Attended by Women and Girls," the law was passed to prohibit the unwanted presence of men and "obnoxious behavior" on school grounds. After the Orangeburg Massacre, however, legislators fundamentally altered the language and scope of the bill, striking the gendered language around "women and girls," which was the very rationale of the original legislation. By cutting this language, local and state authorities were free to interpret and distribute justice as they saw fit for protest and student demonstrations in the school.[28] After 1968 local officials were free to call the police for any "disturbing" act, conducted by anyone regardless of age, race, or gender.

These extraordinary southern legislative acts advanced the line of federal legislation that increasingly adopted punitive measures to suppress any and all transgressions among youth. As southern states put forth legislation and enacted policies that criminalized Black youth in schools, congressional leaders employed and normalized racialized understandings of juvenile delinquency through policies aimed at curbing it. President Lyndon B. Johnson initiated the first phases of a larger "war on crime" in the 1960s, fueled in part by what social scientists saw as a debilitating "pathology" in Black families and communities and reported in the infamous Moynihan Report in 1965. This coincided with passage of the Law Enforcement Assistant Act of 1965 that channeled federal money into the law enforcement apparatus for the prevention and control of crime. Nicholas Katzenbach's Crime Commission Report of 1967 drew attention to low education rates and the problems associated with the "slum school." It pathologized criminality among Black youth and pointed toward larger issues of poverty and the failure of public education. Though considered progressive by many of the day, the report associated juvenile delinquency with race, thereby racializing crime while placing blame on the child and their families, finding that "the educational handicaps that seem most closely related to delinquency appear in the slum child."[29] Drawing on racially tinged language like the "slum child" and "slum schools," it focused attention on increasing resources for under-resourced schools and the communities they served. The recommendations also called for more support or "manpower" in the criminal justice system, falling short of critiquing the racist policies that underpinned the law enforcement system.[30] The racialization of Black youth also informed the Omnibus Crime Control and Safe Streets Act of 1968, which facilitated burgeoning support for law enforcement and widened further the pathways for surveillance and discipline of "slum schools," making special consideration for "thrill-bent juveniles and minors prone to criminal behavior."[31]

Legislators responded to and reinforced the fear at the local level brought upon by desegregation and what was viewed as an increasingly "militant" Black freedom struggle. For White legislators, unrest was everywhere. When Barbara Jones passed around flyers in her high school about making curricular changes and calling for greater student organization in Charleston, South Carolina—and school administrators called the police in response— she was agitating in a society that was already on edge about "violence" and political unrest in the schools. One could not turn a page in the local newspapers without reading stories of school violence—the very spaces that were in the process of fully desegregating. By 1970 public schools at all levels, from kindergarten through college, were facing full desegregation as opposed to the token segregation practiced since the *Brown* decision. Much like the football "riot" in the nation's capital in 1962, the local press in Charleston, South Carolina, reported about the violence that accompanied cherished local high school football games, lamenting that "violence has become an unfortunate part of Friday night contests." One article in 1972 covered the story of "a middle-aged white man, who had accompanied his daughter and a neighbor to a local game, was walking through a darkened parking area when he was attacked by several teen-age boys . . . it appeared he was picked at random. The man was slugged in the neck with some sort of weapon then held on the ground and kicked in the face."[32] In the same moment that schools desegregated, the local press linked violence with the same spaces, marring the reputation of already beleaguered institutions struggling to desegregate.

District officials across the South like those in South Carolina who raised alarm by implying teachers were under regular attack during the tumultuous process of desegregation prompted federal investigation. One congressional report cited that 11 percent of teachers had something stolen from them in any given month during the school year and, of that, six thousand teachers had something stolen by force, threats, or weapons. It was also reported that over five thousand teachers each month are physically attacked in public schools.[33] It was a larger fear that all teachers and administrators felt during desegregation. "I'm scared to death to go down there," one teacher in Los Angeles stated in 1976 in reference to going to a predominantly Black and Latinx school, "and if I were a woman I'd be even more afraid."[34]

By the late 1960s high school student dissent prompted urgent discourse on a national level among administrators, teachers, education scholars, and practitioners. As one article on the topic of student activism noted, high school activism "has become a near mania with the mass-media; it is a topic of discussion at the cocktail party, on the subway, and in the classroom."[35] Principals and administrators were on edge. Ongoing student unrest incited the National Association of Secondary Principals (NASSP) to investigate the pervasiveness, depth, and scope of student protest. The NASSP reported in March of 1969 that 59 percent of the high schools and 56 percent of the junior high schools experienced some form of student unrest, dissent, or protest.[36] *The New York Times* covered the report and extended coverage of the growing social issue to the rest of the nation. In the spring of 1969 one headline in *The New York Times* read "High School Unrest Rises, Alarming U.S. Educators," noting that "unrest has emerged in every region of the country, disrupting schools in suburbs and rural areas as well as cities." One report described high schoolers as "unhappy about everything from bans on miniskirts and long hair to racial discrimination and the draft."[37]

Sensationalized and frontpage coverage of protest failed to examine the premise and origins of student activism that unfolded in the high schools. Students in high school, like Barbara Jones in Charleston, South Carolina, continued the struggle of previous generations. Jones and her cohort used the same strategies of the movement such as walkouts, forming student associations, and demanding curricular reform as they brought an older political struggle to their schools. In one demonstration, Black students organized a walkout at North Charleston High School in February 1971 and then submitted a list of grievances, which included a request for Black history courses. Students in North Charleston followed the demands regularly made in the tradition, which included calls for curricular reform and more Black teachers and administrators. They also demanded an audience with the principal to air concerns. Students in nearby Garrett High School in North Charleston also walked out of school and boycotted classes to make similar demands of their administration for their voice to be heard and their grievances addressed.[38] In one of the surrounding suburbs, high school students on James Island walked out of school to boycott classes but also refused to vacate the premise.[39]

These students built upon the same principles of the civil rights movement and extended the tradition into the era of desegregation. Legislators, policymakers, school board members, and parents in South Carolina—and across the South—interpreted this as violent behavior, however, and branded and treated them as criminals.

High school student protestors—like those across the South—posed a serious challenge to an anxious public rattled by the growing accounts of violence in desegregated schools. After the series of protests in 1970 and 1971, White parents organized to influence policy in newly desegregated schools according to their own logic and interpretation of the unrest. This translated into controlling students through increased surveillance and disciplinary policy. A group of over 250 White parents gathered in response to the unrest in North Charleston. They wanted to "put teeth" into school rules that disciplined students. Parents were concerned about the unrest and questioned the traditional authority of school principals. "I don't think that the principals have enough backbone to stand up to the Negro population," one parent noted.[40] Others called out the "illegal" boycotts and walkouts connected to civil rights issues. For the hostile parents in attendance, such activism moved beyond "basic discipline." To them, "criminal offenses should be treated as such."[41] They petitioned the district and intimated a desire for the presence of law enforcement officers—who were literally in the same community meetings of Whites to show support—arguing it was "necessary to remove the disruptive elements from the premises."[42] Parents called for the police, pleading for them to "visit the schools daily same as they do the banks."[43] In Columbia, South Carolina, a group of concerned parents demanded that the school board extend its reliance on law enforcement, calling for police in every high school and deputized bus drivers.[44]

In short, parents escalated the call for police and openly invited them into the schools on the behalf of all students. The overwhelming White presence garnered the attention of local police and school board members ensured that law enforcement would be used to protect the sons and daughters of White parents.

Meetings with angry White parents and school board members were a space to vent other grievances about desegregation. One father in the same board meeting about student protests complained about Black History Week. The material presented at school, he insisted, "was not history."[45] Parents were influential in dictating other decisions, too. Their vocal opposition contributed to the removal of the principal at Garret High School in North Charleston at the end of the year, essentially holding him accountable for what they described as a "year culminating in riots, near riots and fighting between students."[46] Whites flexed their power and political weight in the changing school order—and school and police officials acquiesced.

The school board in response adopted more uniform "get tough" policies.[47] After the walkouts and the parents' organized outcry, the school district adopted new disciplinary codes that deemed any walkouts illegal and subjected activist students to immediate suspension and potential litigation. In Columbia, South Carolina, the school board adopted a uniform policy on discipline across the district in the summer of 1970 before desegregation began in earnest. Drawing on the "disturbing school" laws already in the books, the district-wide police outlined a list of infractions that would lead to suspension or expulsion.[48] The board also identified other breaches of conduct that were subject to suspension and expulsion, including action that "evidences disrespect for school authority" or constituted an "invasion of the rights of others," both of which were used by authorities to characterize recent school protests in Charleston. The board also granted school principals the right to notify law enforcement and swear out warrants if students refused to leave school grounds once ordered to do so.[49] M. C. Hursey, superintendent of Charleston County Schools, said of the proposed policy change, "If you want police, we will have them."[50] The board stood firm behind their decree of law and order in Charleston, noting that the policy adopted is "the rules we will operate under until someone takes us to court."[51]

Administrators and school boards sided with angry White parents. Principals and superintendents increasingly viewed student protest as a direct affront to their responsibility to provide an education to all students. It was also argued that students who chose to protest violated the rights of non-protesting students to receive an education. "We're here to educate all children, regardless of race or color," Ashley Hutchinson, the principal of North Charleston High School noted, "but we have to have peace and quiet to do it."[52] Making an argument for the rights of taxpayers in Charleston County, the district superintendent Gordon Garrett noted, "No individual or group of individuals can be allowed to disrupt the educational process and the rights and safety of all young people must be protected."[53] In referencing taxation, Garrett argued that school policy should conform to taxpayers' purpose, which drew upon an ideology of what historian Camille Walsh notes as "racial taxation." Taxpayers became the trope through which to advocate and defend the "rights" of taxpayers, namely White citizens because Black citizens were never viewed as legitimate taxpaying citizens, or that the burden of Black education consistently fell upon the state.[54] The rights of taxpayers was a defense of White supremacy in the era of desegregation.

This was the first time principals and the county school board in Charleston County, South Carolina, dealt with disciplinary problems on a wider scale that involved dozens of students, pushing administrators during the late 1960s far beyond individual acts of protest that marked the beginning of the decade. Board members and school administrators reacted swiftly and punitively, taking full advantage of the revised criminal statutes that empowered them to work in concert with law enforcement. Their reaction intersected with a growing affinity between law enforcement and school officials. School administrators' "get tough" policies in Charleston readily drew upon law enforcement officers who were already alerted to "violence incidents" that occurred in Black or formerly all-White, desegregated schools.[55] The local school board contacted the South Carolina Law Enforcement Division—the same unit that killed three protestors on the campus of South Carolina State in Orangeburg—to investigate the student walkout at a recently desegregated high school, Garrett High School where Black students walked out in protest after a meeting to discuss demands was canceled by the administrations in 1971. The students involved in the melee following the walk-out at Garrett High School were criminally charged with assault and battery of a high and aggravated nature.[56] After a student walkout at James Island High School in which thirty people were arrested (all but one were Black), police officers were stationed outside the school, with support from county and state police as well, and given orders to arrest anyone from the school grounds who refused to attend class.[57] After a series of fights, disturbances, and protests in the capital city of South Carolina, the Solicitor in the Fifth Judicial Circuit was in close correspondence with the district superintendent. In addition to recommending that the district share information about the "Disturbing Schools" laws to all parents, teachers, and staff, he encouraged the district to communicate in no uncertain terms that transgressions of the law "should be immediately reported to law enforcement and that appropriate criminal charges be made." All violations of the law, no matter how minor, would be referred to his office for prosecution. Additionally, the state would demand compensation for any damages caused to school property from parents.[58]

The racial intent of the new laws became unmistakable in the capital city of South Carolina when three Black students were expelled from Keenan High School in Columbia after a melee there on the first day of school in 1970, the same year in which full-scale desegregation unfolded across the city. The board initially suspended the students for five days and then later expelled them. Though the fight broke out between Black and White students, no White students were reprimanded.[59] The incident reflected the influence and power of White parents during the desegregation process in heavily policing public schools and prosecuting Black students. It also illuminates the legal process prompted by student unrest and the rush to codify disciplinary procedure, justifying the process underway in desegregated schools and conveying that the system was "fair" and "objective." Though the three students from Keenan were not granted a hearing and the district discipline policy placed the burden on parents to ask for a hearing, the district went to great lengths to ensure that students should be granted due process as they anticipated legal challenges.[60]

To the dismay of many White parents, stiffer penalties and police presence did little to quell student unrest. To the contrary, the presence of armed guards or the threat to call the police to settle in-school disputes provoked sustained protest. In March of 1972 over two hundred students assembled in the auditorium of Dreher High School in Columbia, South Carolina, after administrators suspended one Black student, but the White student in physical confrontation was not reprimanded. A teacher called the police, and when an officer showed up, some students left the auditorium, allegedly breaking windows and physically assaulting a student.[61] During that same month in the same city in Lower Richland High School, student unrest unfolded after administrators suspended one Black student and suspended another Black student with recommendation for expulsion when they reportedly made "an improper proposal to a white female student."[62] Physical confrontations ensued and official closed schools across the city and patrolled them with police.

Black parents and community organizers built upon the activism of students in schools and organized to defend their children in desegregated White schools. The Black Coalition for Justice in the Schools—a grassroots association of Black parents, activists, and community organizers in Columbia, including renowned South Carolina activist Modjeska Simkins—mobilized promptly in Columbia. They called for a boycott of city schools. In a damning press release, they held the school board and administrators accountable for the disturbances at school. "They control and run the schools," the release chastised. "They have used their power to benefit themselves, the well-to-do professional and the white businessmen they represent."[63] They outlined a series of demands, including the removal of all police and guns from school, dropping all charges against the students, returning students to school while the rights to due process were upheld, the resignation of principals at the high schools, and newly appointed board members based on their recommendations, among other demands.[64]

Tensions reached a boiling point at the local school board meeting in the spring of 1972. In anticipation of the Black Coalition, the school board responded by limiting time for speakers. It quickly descended into conflict. The board responded in ways unsatisfactory to the Coalition, reducing the police force to only 25 percent and promising only investigations into the conduct of principals, and denying their ability to drop charges.[65] Local prominent attorney H. Simmons Tate Jr., observed that the "meeting was orderly and consisted of considerable debate," largely between the board and Modjeska Simkins. Then James Redfern, II—a popular local organizer and Director of Operations of the Columbia-based Blacks United for Action—"took over the meeting." According to Tate's report, Redfern called in groups of Black parents and organizers to the meeting and "began haranguing" the board and agitating his supporters with "short punchy demands or statements," who were "shouting support in unison."[66] According to Tate, Redfern intimated he and the Coalition had "plenty of things" in their pockets and did not want to use them, noting that he did not want to "burn any buildings down."[67] Redfern and his supporters brought in an amplifier and drums and proceeded to sing, dance, and pray. The school board members and administrators retreated to a separate room in the building to negotiate. Doors were barricaded, and it was difficult to leave. In Tate's words, the board, administrators, and supporters "were held against our will with the threat of physical violence."[68] As an anxious Tate concluded his report, "it is difficult to describe in words the feeling of being helpless before a mob of people incensed and raised to a fever pitch by a very skillful agitator."[69] The board did not budge, and the meeting came to a tense though nonviolent conclusion at 7:00 A.M.

The "fact-finding" committee who investigated the myriad school incidents in Columbia made several recommendations. The suggestions focused on "racially mixed balances" in administration, coaching, and counseling at the school. They suggested "human relations" workshops for faculty, staff, administration, and students. They recommended a stronger curriculum, which included improvements from remedial literacy to vocational education, and they suggested integrating Black history and culture into the curriculum.[70] No suggestions were made about removing police, revising "disturbing schools" legislation, or enacting equitable, antiracist school discipline. "Order" was maintained, and the Black Coalition's demands were summarily dismissed.[71]

The growing affinity between law enforcement and school boards overseeing desegregated districts in South Carolina reflected a national movement to restore law and order.[72] Teachers and administrators sought more uniform policy across the district, which often relied on security provided through law enforcement.[73] Working with law enforcement and adopting uniform policies to discipline young people signified a paradigmatic shift of disciplinary responsibility away from the discretion of teachers, which previously worked under a prevailing *in loco parentis* approach, to that of elected school officials and law enforcement.[74] It marked a shift that shaped the essence of public education after 1970.

Though cast by the local press and as violent behavior, grievances and the voices of protestors were rarely, if ever, given a platform in the debate. Students were protesting the developing policies that disproportionately targeted them. Moreover, students often drew on the strategies and aims of previous generations to challenge the new disciplinary policies. Students who were part of the 1964 Freedom Summer project in Mississippi utilized boycotts and made concerted demands and calls upon public officials to improve education and protect their rights to protest. The resulting cases ultimately served as precedent in the monumental *Tinker v. Des Moines* (1969) decision.[75] Barbara Green and other students formed the Black Culture Club at Lower Richland High School in Columbia, South Carolina, in the early 1970s. They advocated for quality education for all students but were primed to protest issues of unjust disciplinary policies as well. In early February of 1973 students at Lower Richland High School—a site of student unrest since it desegregated—caught wind of the detainment of their Black classmate, Thomas Seymore. Students milled about, circulated news, and became incensed. Name-calling and minor altercations may have ensued, but nothing tantamount to a "riot" resulted, property was not damaged, and heated discussions occurred largely in the time between classes. However, administrators suspended several students and the board ultimately sought expulsion for behavior that "contributed to the substantial and material disruption of the function of the school."[76] The lawsuit filed on behalf of Green drew attention to the fact that there was no physical disruption and altercation, while also noting a larger pattern of harassment.[77] Though the courts sided with the district, it illustrates how student protest changed from earlier decades and grew to include protesting unfair treatment in desegregated schools.

Yet local White parents and school administrators perceived high school student activism as a violent disruption that hampered their children's right to acquire an education and their responsibility to provide it. The uniform "get tough" policies that shaped the area were negotiated and implemented by various White powerbrokers. It was a new path of resistance that drew upon the burgeoning legislative arsenal stockpiled at the local level. Increased surveillance and discipline were not a foregone conclusion: White powerbrokers intentionally negotiated and selected to proceed with concerted attacks on the Black student body. Policies at the local and state level—like those that unfolded across South Carolina—intersected with and shaped policies at the federal level that punitively targeted young people in high school.

Policies such as those in South Carolina formed the basis of the Juvenile Justice and Delinquency Prevention Act of 1974, milestone legislation that established what historian Elizabeth Hinton identified as "the modern American system of juvenile justice."[78] It federalized programs across the nation and those percolating from the South that stemmed from issues connected to desegregation. Beyond supporting the use of juvenile courts and prisons, it established a federal office designated specifically for policing youth and eradicating juvenile delinquency. The Act was extraordinary, citing that juveniles were arrested for all serious crimes in the country and based on the premise that "delinquency" could be prevented through training and effective programming. Such training and programming included support for local and state police and law enforcement as well as private agencies.[79] The law significantly increased funding for eradicating juvenile delinquency, from $14 to $600 million in block grants. Provisions of the recently amended Elementary and Secondary Education Act, first passed by LBJ in 1965, contained funding for salary and expenses related to the

Federal Law Enforcement Training Center, further solidifying the growing affinity between schools and the law. It also included public education programming in schools with the purpose of "encouraging respect for law and order . . . to improve public understanding of and cooperation with law enforcement agencies."[80] Laws policing juvenile delinquency dovetailed with police in schools and the national movement toward "law and order" shepherded through by President Nixon as a major campaign promise in 1968, stating that the nation was torn asunder by "unprecedented lawlessness" and "unprecedented racial violence," living in a nation where one cannot travel to cities in the country "without fear of a hostile demonstration."[81]

School violence—or what was pegged as violence—shaped the desegregation of schools and schools, turning them into sites that abetted the rise of mass incarceration and law and order of the 1970s.[82] Federal investment in racialized notions of juvenile delinquency paved the way for the national expansion of law enforcement in everyday social services, but particularly schools. The uptick in the police presence in our schools throughout the 1960s and early 1970s coincided with rising anxieties in urban centers that experienced civil rights and Black Power insurrection and sustained protest. In Los Angeles, a special "CRASH" unit—Community Resources Against Street Hoodlums—targeted youth around the enforcement of curfews to stem further unrest in the city. Drawing resources from the Law Enforcement Assistance Act, police created specialized units to target youth in schools. With the aerial support of a helicopter and state-of-the-art surveillance equipment, Los Angeles was flexing the strength and demonstrating the repressive prowess of new, federally supported school disciplinary logic. With police involved in Indianapolis city schools since 1948, the city created the Indianapolis Public School Police in 1970. Police in Flint, Michigan, worked formally in the schools since 1953. In Tucson, Arizona, the police department received federal support to rotate police across all junior high school campuses. The city of Baltimore also brought police into schools after the rebellions in 1967 that racked the area. Aided throughout the next decade by increasing financial support for law enforcement in schools, police in the city schools were renamed the Baltimore School Police Force in 1984.[83] In Boston in the 1970s city officials employed a special force of city police trained for antiwar protests to quell antibusing riots and marches sparked by court orders to desegregate schools. Eventually federal marshals were employed to keep the peace.[84] Four or five security guards were in every high school in Newark, New Jersey. Philadelphia officials hired at least two for each high school. In Chicago, nearly three hundred officers in plain clothes surveilled fifty-one high schools.[85] The National Urban League reported in 1971 that their survey of fifty-one major cities across the country, all but four did not employ their own security personnel or local police in the schools. They described some "panicked systems" in which nearly every school is staffed with security personnel or armed police.[86] Police, in short, were everywhere and becoming part of the daily operations of schools, planting themselves into the very culture of public education.

Court cases coming out of Mississippi and South Carolina increasingly pleaded for due process. South Carolina legislators passed the School Discipline Law in 1973, which further clarified the right of boards of trustees or school boards to suspend or expel students while also ensuring a standard of due process and notification of the rights of appeal and hearing.[87] But the phenomenon of unprecedented suspensions and expulsions in desegregated schools prompted judicial intervention, too. The courts in turn provided due process for all students in the *Gault* (1967) and *Winship* (1970) decisions, which applied a more uniform due process for students, including notice of the charges, the right to counsel, and a right to appeal, in addition to other enumerated rights of citizens in the judicial system. The case in *Goss v. Lopez* in 1975 cemented students' right to due process, entitling them to more rights akin to citizenship, such as a hearing before school suspension. Such steps further established students' rights to due process that protected them from discriminatory application of school policies.[88]

Court affirmations that students had a right to due process meant that the locus of student discipline would shift toward the courts and privileged bureaucratic, administrative procedure. On the surface it appeared that the courts had recognized students' constitutional rights. Yet the effect of these protections was to create a more centralized disciplinary policy. The resulting system was at once inherently racist and colorblind—it recognized an objective due process but ignored the systemic racism that undermined that objectivity and the process by which authorities removed students from school. By doing so, it also institutionalized these policies and practices, normalized them, and made them part of the "natural" landscape of education. But while due process was centralized, so were the policies that meted out "justice" during desegregation. The racial biases of the laws themselves never surfaced in court cases, leaving the issue of systemic racism and the carceral logic of new school disciplinary policies unchecked.[89] The "rights" won by students merely cemented for Black students and students of color a pathway to the courts and prison.

Increased surveillance buttressed by local, state, and federal policies that racialized juvenile delinquency laws, coupled with the growing affinity between public schools and law enforcement, led to staggering numbers of young people expelled from school or placed behind bars. Crime rates among adolescents grew to unprecedented levels. The movement sparked the ire of civil rights organizers. Civil rights advocate and lawyer Marian Wright Edelman in a comprehensive survey conducted through the Children's Defense Fund (CDF) in 1974 and 1975 surmised that "statistically a child is more likely to be suspended if he is black, poor, and in high school." At the high school level, Black students were suspended more than three times as often as White students. In their survey, over 50 percent of all students suspended were Black even though less than 40 percent of the districts were Black or Latinx.[90] The CDF reports found that one in thirteen students was suspended from high school. Fifteen states reported suspending over 30,000 students during the 1972–1973 school year. California alone suspended over 142,000 students, and these data did not include the highly policed schools in Los Angeles. One district in California suspended over 40 percent of its students. Districts in New Jersey reported suspending over one-third of its students. In Louisiana, nearly 20 percent of its districts suspended over 10 percent of its students.[91] The Southern Regional Council echoed their concerns, publishing a seminal study in 1973 titled "The Student Pushout," which reported similarly disastrous results on Black families and communities.[92] Historian Elizabeth Hinton postulated that youth crime reportedly increased by nearly 144 percent between 1960 and 1974, as compared to 17 percent of adults during the same time period. In the years prior to the passage of the Juvenile Justice and Delinquency Prevention Act in 1974, the arrest rate among youth rose to nearly 20 percent and in the year the act was signed into law, young people constituted nearly one-third of felony arrests across the nation. Black youth under the age of eighteen accounted for more than one-half of arrests for murder and violent crimes.[93]

The results of these policies were staggering in in-school suspensions and school expulsions alone. As legal scholar Derek Black noted, Black students were suspended or expelled at younger ages than White students and suffered from such disciplinary retaliation of at least twice the rate of their White peers. In high schools, Black students were expelled at three times the rate of White students.[94] After the process of desegregation began in the city of Milwaukee, Wisconsin, high school suspension rates increased from 30 to 45 percent and one junior high school had a suspension rate of

105 percent, meaning it was not uncommon for students to be suspended more than once. Of all junior and senior high schools in the city, Black students received 57 percent of the suspension rates though they made up less than one-third of the student population.[95] In Columbia, South Carolina, the Children's Defense Fund found that 22 percent of all students in secondary schools were suspended at least once during the 1972–1973 school year.[96] The school district reported in 1974 that two high schools—Columbia and Lower Richland High School—suspended over one-half of Black students enrolled for up to twenty days, losing a total of over twenty-five hundred days out of school. Administrators at Columbia High School suspended only 17 percent of its White students, who lost a total of 279 days. Of the seven high schools in the district, only two schools suspended (slightly) more White students, but Black students were still suspended for more days than White students.[97] Local education organizer Hayes Mizell found that by 1976, 77 percent of all suspensions in grades 6 through 12 were among Black students. With over thirty-two hundred suspensions among Black students compared to less than one thousand among White students, Black students in the capital of South Carolina were suspended at a rate of three times that of Whites.[98] Though most suspensions were categorized for truancy or tardiness, a significant portion–in some schools over one-half–suspensions were categorized as "disruptive" or "disobedient."[99] In Edgefield County in South Carolina, it was reported in 1975 that 342 Black students—approximately 10 percent of the entire district—were suspended at least once, losing a total of over one thousand school days. This was twice the number of White suspensions. More specifically, at Strom Thurmund High School, nearly 25 percent of Black students were suspended at least once, compared to only 9 percent of Whites—a statistic illustrating racial disparities befitting its namesake.[100] The numbers in South Carolina prompted the Office of Civil Rights to investigate, finding the Richland County School District of Columbia to be ineligible for funding from the Emergency School Aid Act of 1972. Though the ineligibility was later waived, the efforts of Hayes Mizell and the American Friends Service Committee to illuminate racial disparities led to serious federal oversight before policymakers distributed funding once again.[101]

The sheer number of juvenile crimes fueled the notion of Black pathology and a collective, largely White insistence on discipline and punishment. For policymakers, the numbers justified further action. Many eyes were on Los Angeles, where, as historian Judith Kafka notes, officials in the early 1970s reported 167 incidents of weapons on school campuses, over 200 assaults against school personnel, 745 assaults against students, and over 10,000 "criminal incidents" on school campuses.[102] In the first "Safe School Report" mandated by Congress and released in 1978, the findings confirmed the state of violence, finding that approximately 8 percent of the nation's schools had a serious problem with crime. On any given month, over 25 percent of the nation's schools were subject to vandalism. It also found that security devices and security personnel were effective in reducing crime and consequently called for more emphasis on personnel training and even greater appropriations.[103]

Not all violence was imaginary, and some schools became sites of tragedy in the wake of desegregation. Students at the historically Black Dudley High School in Greensboro, North Carolina, protested after a Black student, Claude Barnes, was not seated as student council president in spite of the fact that he secured hundreds of more write-in votes than his White opponent. Protests escalated across the city and spilled over to the campus of the HBCU North Carolina A&T—the epicenter of the sit-in movement nine years prior. The National Guard was called in and tension escalated, which culminated in the shooting death of A&T student, Willie Grimes.[104] In 1971 in Wilmington, North Carolina, high school students prompted a citywide uprising that resulted in two deaths, the burning of a local grocery, and ongoing exchanges of gunfire. After the dust had settled, ten were arrested, charged, and convicted of arson and intent to harm first responders and emergency personnel. The "Wilmington Ten" included eight Black high school students—Willie Vereen, Wayne Moore, Marvin Patrick, William Wright, Reginald Epps, Connie Tindall, James McKoy, and Jerry Jacobs. All were sentenced to at least twenty-nine years in prison.[105] That same year, Wesley Parks, a twenty-five-year-old White man of Drew, Mississippi, fired a single bullet into a small group of Black teenagers after high school commencement. The bullet struck and killed Jo Etha Collier, an eighteen-year-old student who had graduated that same evening with honors from Drew High School. The school was in the midst of controversy as it had recently been desegregated, though Mississippi officials framed the incident as one without apparent motivation and a random act of violence that they attributed to drunkenness.[106] Historian Walter Stern examined the town of Destrehan, Louisiana, as it sunk into chaos after Gary Tyler—aged sixteen at the time of the incident—was sentenced to death for killing a White thirteen-year-old student, Timothy Weber, in 1974.[107] The conviction was based on, at best, scant and suspect evidence and a coerced confession. It was also built upon a longer history of protest that included court challenges and nonviolent demonstrations, as well as resistance to disciplinary policies disproportionately applied to Black students after schools desegregated there.

With civil rights protest now branded as inherently violent, the shift in disciplinary logic criminalized in schools what is remembered as peaceful protests—marches, boycotts, or dissemination of literature, for instance. As Hayes Mizell, a community organizer who worked with the American Friends Service Committee in South Carolina, noted, "Most discipline problems are what I call perceived misbehavior [which is] something resulting from our value system, our orientation, and our authority." By the 1970s Mizell reasoned that school authorities who oversaw the implementation of wildly unpopular desegregation initiatives, "think others should be obedient to that authority."[108] It was a position held by the state. As Lieutenant Governor Earle E. Morris stated, "I feel that students must be encouraged . . . to realize a respect for the authority of the law."[109] All of this was done from the legislators' perspective to maintain the peace and keep order. "Restoration of peace in the public schools," the News and Courier proffered in an editorial in 1971 in the midst of desegregation, "will depend on the willingness of students to submit to school discipline and to demonstrate an ability to behave themselves."[110]

The principal at Dreher High School in Columbia, South Carolina, James A. Wilsford, captured much of the sentiment of White administrators when he pathologized the Black students and families he served. In his interpretation of unrest in the city he noted that Black students were unprepared for a "competitive, middle-class high school." Wilsford callously generalized the Black students he was charged to educate by using racist language and stereotypes including "apparent toughness, the swaggering, the 'jiving' around, the loud talk, the vulgarity, the sexual permissiveness." In addressing the situation, he noted that "Neither I nor my staff need be in ego struggles with children. Childish behavior does not intimidate us."[111] The fact-finding committee charged with examining the unrest in Columbia in the early 1970s assigned blame to desegregation or a move to a "unitary" system that was no longer segregated by race. The system did not foster "an atmosphere which is conducive to successful integration." Moreover, the committee noted, "there has been a lack of positive support for the unitary school system by officials and persons in leadership positions."[112]

Many teachers were complicit in the criminalization, too. As Judith Kafka found in Los Angeles, teachers sought more uniform policy across the district, which often relied on security provided through law enforcement.[113]

Additionally, the larger history and meaning of high school activism were lost upon many educators. "For the first time in history, high school students throughout the United States are protesting the situations in which they find themselves," Marc Libarle, a former teacher in the New York City public school system, falsely observed in 1970, "the current generation in the high schools has discovered that the situation they confront as students is inhuman, and that the status they hold is one of subjugation."[114] It was not the first time, and the unrest unfolding in much of the South was rooted in deeper forms of resistance. There was a cohort of Black teachers in southern high schools that inherited the history and training to address such students with care. Yet they, too, were under attack under the changing educational order.

The Attack on Black Teachers

Black teachers had long been a part of shaping the politics of historically Black high schools. A small cadre of teachers labored judiciously to elevate the consciousness and build the strategic skill set of future change agents through what historian Jarvis Givens identified as a "fugitive pedagogy."[115] As critical actors in the freedom struggle who transformed their classrooms and schools into sites of resistance, the small cohorts who joined the front lines—from the equalization campaigns of the 1940s through the NAACP purge of the 1950s—paid the professional and economic price. But all teachers, regardless of political affiliations, faced retribution. "A struggle centers here," NAACP lawyer Jack Greenberg noted of the Black professional teaching class in the *Journal of Negro Education* in 1951, "there will undoubtedly be innocent persons who will suffer."[116] Greenberg accurately predicted the storm that was about to befall Black teachers, but educators were more than innocent bystanders—complicit in movement building or otherwise. Teachers in historically Black high schools were an integral part of the Black southern economy. Placed alongside a small cadre of doctors, lawyers, and other professionals, Black teachers represented the bulk of educated African Americans in the South and, with the recent wave of litigation that legally equalized the salary of Black teachers, they occupied a significant and influential place in the South. Desegregation threatened to undermine the entire Black middle and professional class.

A deeper psychological fear and stress compounded the economic anxiety Black teachers faced. The massive dismissal of teachers did not transpire solely upon the pretext of working for "subversive" organizations such as the NAACP, which limited the number of teachers threatened to a finite number like Septima Clark or Gladys Noel Bates who put their careers on the line to advance the cause of salary equalization.

Court-ordered desegregation enforced by racist policymakers threatened tens of thousands of Black teachers across the South. Whites who were committed to maintaining segregation and charged with overseeing the transition to desegregated schools at the local level posed an ominous challenge to the entire Black teaching profession. The overarching threat was palpable across the South. John Potts, a veteran educator who served as President of the Palmetto State Teachers' Association, noted that his relationship to the civil rights movement was "more important to the members of the interviewing committee than my educational qualifications for the position," which to him sounded like an "insidious witch hunt."[117] Black teachers were easily and summarily dismissed during the desegregation process. As one report from 1970 on the displacement of Black teachers noted, some Black teachers were literally told in the middle of their class that their contracts were not renewed for the following year. As one educator recalled of the time, the politics of desegregation "just made [us] sick."[118] The larger impact of desegregation on a community of professional educators who came from and respected the southern Black communities they served was an insurmountable loss to not only the profession but the entire South. Tragically, White administrators and legislators ultimately affirmed Black educators' fears of wide-scale displacement in the wake of the *Brown* decision. According to Samuel B. Ethridge, the head of the National Education Association's Center for Human Rights—an organization founded after the merger of Black and White teacher associations—the effect of the *Brown* decision on Black teachers was "absolutely devastating."[119]

Black teachers were apprehensive about the prospects of desegregation. Their jobs were at stake, and the writing was on the wall that desegregation would present serious challenges. More than one year prior to the *Brown* decision in Topeka, Kansas, Darla Buchanan received notice that her services would be discontinued. As the superintendent, Wendell Godwin, wrote to Buchanan in March of 1953:

Due to the present uncertainty about enrollment next year in schools for negro children, it is not possible at this time to offer you employment for next year. If the Supreme Court should rule that segregation in the elementary grades is unconstitutional our Board will proceed on the assumption that the majority of people in Topeka will not want to employ negro teachers next year for White children. It is necessary for me to notify you now that your services will not be needed for next year. This is in compliance with the continuing contract law. If it turns out that segregation is not terminated, there will be nothing to prevent us from negotiating a contract with you at some later date this spring.[120]

Black teachers were pushed out, displaced, demoted, dismissed, and terminated in the wake of the *Brown* decision. In a system that struggled to see the value in integrated *student* populations, little protection and understanding was extended to Black teachers. Tragically, African American teachers were in the position to defend and support Black youth in the hostile environment of desegregated schools.

By the fall of 1964 every southern state had desegregated, permitting at least a handful of students to enter previously all-White schools. Teachers, already timid in openly supporting the civil rights movement, were faced with uncertainty. Prior to the *Brown* decision, approximately eighty-two thousand Black teachers were employed to teach over two million Black students.[121] Within the first decade after the *Brown* decision, over three thousand Black teachers lost their positions in the border states alone. It is estimated that over thirty-eight thousand teachers lost their jobs in the seventeen southern and border states during the decade following the decision. One survey concluded that almost forty thousand African American teachers were unemployed by 1972.[122] Though numbers have been difficult to ascertain, even a conservative estimate that thirty-five thousand teachers lost their position means that nearly one-half of the Black teaching profession was eliminated after *Brown*.

The number of those dismissed or displaced accelerated after the increased rate of desegregation after the *Green* (1968) and *Alexander* (1969) cases terminated gradual desegregation plans. In the South, which experienced court-mandated desegregation orders in ways the North did not, Black southern teachers bore the brunt of teacher displacement and dismissal.[123] In a report released in late 1970, it was found that one-third of the 10,500 teachers in Alabama were dismissed or demoted that year alone.[124] The National Education Association (NEA) found the state of Mississippi a "focal point of massive trouble" as one thousand teachers were unemployed in late August, just weeks before the start of the school year in 1970.[125] The national teacher association also found that Louisiana faced "desperately serious problems" as hundreds of Black teachers were displaced after full-scale desegregation.[126] In South Carolina, where tenure laws did not exist, teachers with decades of experience were not receiving contracts.[127] This was tantamount to professional annihilation in the wake of desegregation.

The role teachers played was a detrimental loss to Black students. Black students lost allies, advocates, and defenders in a brutal system that afforded no protection. Without their help, Black youth were susceptible to discipline and incarceration, but also misplacement in lower, remedial academic tracks as well as special education programs. Black teachers practiced what was later labeled as emancipatory or culturally relevant pedagogy that affirmed and facilitated the value of Black communities, history, and aspirations.[128] White teachers did not.

Black principals were targeted as well. As Vanessa Siddle Walker has examined with the illustrious careers of principal N. L. Dillard in Caswell County, North Carolina, principal Ulysses Byas of Gainesville, Georgia, and principal (and later state senator) Horace Tate in Georgia, Black principals held integral positions across the South.[129] Customarily bestowed the title of "professor" to denote the respect they inspired, Black principals were stalwart advocates for quality Black education. Trained through the decades of Jim Crow to successfully navigate the violent, paradoxical whims of White supremacy, Black professors secured funding and guaranteed the means, albeit limited, to secure an education for the communities they served. They were lynchpins of their communities. As Siddle Walker noted, "the principal also held the responsibility for being the visionary liaison between the community's desire for education and the school's desire to deliver it." Such work, she noted, required "not only an educational vision for the school but also an understanding of the necessity of political maneuvering."[130] Their ranks were decimated in the wake of *Brown*, however, delivering a devastating blow to communities they served. Some estimates suggest that over 90 percent of all Black principals lost their job after *Brown*. In North Carolina, over 200 Black principals led high schools, but only 3 remained in the leadership position by 1970. The number of elementary school principals plummeted from 620 to 170. The state of Kentucky employed 350 Black principals in 1954 yet by 1970 had retained only 34. In Alabama, the number of principals dropped from 250 to 40.[131] One estimate from the NEA places the number of Black administrators and principals who lost their position at over 2,200 by 1975.[132]

In addition to displacement and demotion, hiring practices or, rather, the refusal to hire Black teachers in proportion to the increasing number of

Black students in public schools as Whites fled, detrimentally impacted the Black teaching profession. Whites were hired over Black teachers at alarming rates. In the South, 65 percent of the national increase of White teachers across the nation between 1970 and 1976 occurred in the region. This amounted to six White teachers hired for every Black teacher hired during the same time.[133] One report released in 1970 by the Race Relations Information Center noted that in over one hundred districts in the South, 86 percent of all newly hired teachers were White.[134] The predicament of pushing out Black teachers through the hiring process is striking when compared to the fact that Whites were leaving the public school system. In other words, more Whites were employed in the district as over 5 percent of the White student population left for private schools or racially exclusive suburban schools.[135]

The economic toll was staggering. The NEA estimated that during the 1970–1971 school year alone, the seventeen southern and border states most impacted by desegregation, Black teachers (and the communities they served) experienced a loss of income over $240 million.[136] More numerous than doctors and lawyers, Black teachers constituted the bulwark of a professional middle class.

As daunting as the numbers of dismissals were, demotion or displacement was the more common route, according to a report released in 1970 by the Race Relations Information Center. Black principals were placed into district administrative positions or reassigned to work with new federal programs. Some high school principals were demoted to lead a middle or elementary school. Some principals were placed under White supervisors. Some found themselves back in the classroom, with leadership responsibilities stripped away. Black teachers were placed in classrooms and age groups outside their field of expertise. English teachers found themselves teaching science. Some veteran teachers with decades of experience were hired as "floaters," serving as aides to White teachers and without classrooms of their own. This, in turn, sometimes led to termination or voluntary resignation from the school system.[137] As one report sponsored by the U.S. Office of Education in South Carolina noted, Black teachers and administrators "have been displaced appallingly."[138]

Initially, the courts did not stand with teachers. A case filed the year of the *Brown* decision in Missouri denied teachers adequate protection from discriminatory school boards as they drafted and implemented plans to desegregate school districts. As part of the plans to desegregation in Mobley, Missouri, the school board dismissed fourteen qualified and experienced teachers in the school district. All 125 White teachers retained their positions. When the teachers and the NAACP filed a lawsuit, the court in *Brooks v. Mobley* (1959) did not find the district acted with racial discrimination when they did not renew their contracts.[139]

As civil rights organizations focused on the right to vote and the ongoing struggle to desegregate schools, Black teachers were left with the difficult burden of defending their profession by themselves. It was up to them to construct a legal defense of their right to teach in desegregated schools by building upon seminal court cases that addressed the hiring, dismissal, and transfer of educators during desegregation.[140]

Yet teachers continued to fight, and the courts eventually responded by providing some protection to teachers. J. Rupert Picott, the executive secretary of the Virginia State Teacher Association, with the support of the National Education Association, filed suit when teachers were dismissed in the aftermath of *Brown* in the state of Virginia. In *Mary Franklin v. the School Board of Giles County, Virginia* (1965) the courts upheld the due process rights of seven dismissed teachers.[141] In *Wall v. Stanly Board of Education* (1966), the court ordered local districts to hire teachers without regard to race and instead of best ability, which was largely determined by "ability, temperament, disposition and attitude."[142] In *Lee v. Macon* (1967), the courts decreed that state departments of education were to support and assist the desegregation of faculty. It was also noted that administrators were not to use race in hiring, assignment, or reassignment "except that race will be taken into account to for the purpose of correcting the effect of the past segregated assignment of teachers in the dual system." The cases also instructed school boards to take "affirmative steps" to achieve desegregation.[143] Additionally, pressure from southern teachers' associations, the National Education Association, and the NAACP pushed the Office of Education to revise its Guidelines for Desegregation of Schools to state that race should not be a determining factor in the hiring, firing, or demotion of teachers in 1967. Drawing its authority from the Civil Rights Act of 1964 and court decisions, the Office of Education pressured school districts to avoid the wholesale dismissal of Black teachers.[144] These were hollow victories, however, leaving the criteria for hiring and firing teachers up to the interpretation of local districts and school boards. It also supported a colorblind approach to hiring teachers in a racialized institution.

With minimal protection from the courts provided years after the unchecked purge, Black teachers were largely left on their own. Numbers were underreported as many educators did not press the issue in states that resisted desegregation or begrudgingly supported it. The Race Relations Information Center in Tennessee reported that statistics were virtually nonexistent in 1970, in part because districts did not keep track of race in hiring processes since 1954 or administrators did not see the displacement of Black teachers as an issue. The report they released in 1954 spoke to the hesitancy of Black teachers to report their displacement. Gathering such information or encouraging teachers who have been demoted, dismissed, or displaced, was likened to "pulling teeth." For every complaint, they felt there were scores of others behind them. Teachers who were demoted feared losing the positions they were able to maintain. Dismissed teachers feared placement on "black lists" and branding as "trouble maker[s]."[145] Hayes Mizell organized the Teachers Rights Center as part of his work in South Carolina. In efforts to monitor the status and expected backlash against Black teachers, Mizell experienced numerous difficulties that explain a much lower turnout. In addition to the fact Mizell was an "outsider," little information was obtained because, without the power of unionization, teachers often did know until the start of the school year their employment status. Teachers and administrators who received a contract early did not know where they would be assigned, so they could not always report demotion. Responses to questionnaires were meager.[146] Mizell also reported that several Black teachers did not want to contest unfair treatment, including fear of losing the lesser job they were granted or a sense that such legal resistance would be futile—and expensive.[147] As his report noted: "There is little or no recourse where support is needed, thus many of the black educators find it more convenient to accept firing, demotion, or token promotions rather than insisting on the protection of their rights."[148]

White policymakers often rested on the "objective" criterium included within teacher education tests and requirements to enter the profession. The National Teacher's Examination (NTE) is a case in point. Educational experts and testing officials created the NTE in the late 1930s, which initially sought to credential new teachers. But across the South, districts that were mandated to equalize salaries developed new pay scales based on "merit." The ostensibly scientific NTE was a means to do it and the effects of the exam were detrimental to the Black teaching profession.[149] In South Carolina, after legislators were mandated by the courts to equalize teacher salaries, they used scores from the newly employed NTE to determine their precise salary. While this new pay scale seemed racially neutral on the surface, the NTE was an entirely new obstacle for Black teachers. In the first year under the bill's control, 95 percent of White teachers scored well enough on the NTE to have grades in the A and B range, whereas only 43 percent of Black teachers received those grades, and therefore matching pay.[150] Due to the unequal provision of education, Black teachers did not have access to the same training programs for the NTE, such as those offered at the state's flagship and all-White University of South Carolina. In adopting race-neutral and "objective" criteria, southern districts placed Black teachers at a significant disadvantage due to different educational backgrounds and academic training that privileged White applicants.

At a moment of desegregation, racial unrest, and increased discipline, Black teachers lost a strong foothold in public schools, which left Black children in many cases defenseless in hostile schools. It affirmed the cautionary tone of preeminent sociologist Oliver C. Cox, who in 1951 warned that the "loss of the Negro faculty constitutes a cultural loss to the Negro community."[151] The school Black students attended offered a degree of protection. Though segregated, historically Black high schools had teachers who knew their families, friends many had known since childhood, and a safe space that protected children from the violent realities of Jim Crow. Black schools, while unequal in material and significant ways, were much safer in many respects than the desegregated schools students saw on TV. As legal scholar Irving Joyner recalled of her Black teachers during the era of segregation: "As a rule, teachers knew the students, their families and special circumstances or experiences that impacted their ability to become good students. As students progressed from grade-to-grade, teachers followed and encouraged their academic development. In a very real sense, each teacher, as a part of a teaching team, was invested in the students and regularly contributed to the learning process even after the student was no longer assigned to their classroom."[152] Cutting to the core of a pedagogical issue, Black teachers at the Training Coordination Center for Displaced Teachers held at the flagship HBCU South Carolina State University spoke for many when they maintained that White teachers had little capacity for—or interest in—teaching Black students.[153] Recollections of academic excellence, high expectations, a sense of community reflect what Vanessa Siddle Walker has termed "institutional care," in which teachers combined personal understanding and assiduousness in working with students and their families with support structures to succeed.[154] It served as a critical backdrop to Black high school education that was ripped away during the divestment during segregation.

Disinvesting in Black Education

The assault on Black education did not end with disciplining students and dismissing teachers. Historically Black high schools received the same treatment afforded Black students and teachers. Black high schools were downgraded as legitimate sites of quality education. In addition to closing schools, district officials "demoted" schools. Principal Dillard's beloved Caswell County Training School in North Carolina, for instance, was demoted to a middle school, though it was renamed in his honor to Dillard Middle School. In the city of Montgomery, Alabama, the county board of education converted McDavid Elementary into a vocational school as they closed the historically Black high school.[155] In Columbia, South Carolina, district officials closed the historically Black Booker T. Washington High School. The option to indefinitely close the public schools constituted the most extreme form of legal resistance, and one that southern governors and legislators employed with exacting discrimination after the *Brown* decision. In notable instances, southern governors and school boards shuttered their public schools in locales across the South—or passed the legislation to accommodate the closure of public schools and support the rise of private academies—to avoid desegregation orders.[156]

In one of the most nefarious instances of school closures, the local school board in Prince Edward County in consultation with the Virginia state legislature closed the public school system to avoid desegregation orders. The closure lasted for five years from 1959 to 1964—the longest school closure in the nation to avoid desegregation.[157] Prince Edward County was also home to the incipient student rebellion led by Barbara Johns in 1951, which prompted the NAACP to include the case in their litigation against school segregation. The move was not only an indictment against desegregation, but the student movement as well.

Measured as an assault on students, the decision to close schools in Prince Edward County achieved its intended effect, and the move inspired a catastrophic impact on young people. Shirl Nunnally Early was in second grade when they closed the schools in Prince Edward County. "I was embarrassed," she recalled, "I took it personally that I was out of school for four years, and I think it made me feel insecure. You're dumb. You know how kids think because you missed all this time from school."[158] Alejia "Mickie" Pride

Carrington was nine when the county closed their schools. In the next four years, Mickie attended school for a total of thirty days. She briefly attended school in the neighboring Lunenburg County, but the school could not accommodate all the students from Farmville.[159] Makeshift schools sufficed for some. Others studied at home. Melvin Nunnally studied on the family farm and grassroots summer programs. During the summer of 1965, the same year that Head Start originated, Nunnally attended "Operation Catch-Up" at High Rock Baptist Church, walking over two miles to attend the school.[160] Dorothy Holcomb traversed six miles round trip to attend school in the basement of a church in Prospect. Then her father claimed residence in Appomattox to attend school there.[161] James Ghee was about to enter ninth grade when the schools closed. He attended training centers in the basement of First Baptist Church run in coordination with the Virginia Teachers Association, the NAACP, and the American Friends Service Committee. The next year he enrolled in Luther P. Jackson High School in the neighboring Cumberland County. After the first month, Ghee and thirty of his classmates were informed that they were overcrowding the school and would have to return to Farmville.[162]

Southern school districts regularly closed historically Black high schools that organizers, educators, and civic leaders had carefully constructed, supported, and cultivated since Reconstruction. These school closures were less visible than shuttering an entire school system, but they were no less violent or detrimental to Black students and the communities they served.

In Alabama, school officials closed the state's flagship and historically Black high school, Booker T. Washington High School, in 1970. Following recommendations by the Office of Education, the city of Montgomery closed Booker T. Washington after a long and proud history. City officials cited dilapidated buildings, but the impending "integration order" was the determining catalyst. Residents were crestfallen. E. P. Walace, who entered Booker T. Washington in 1915 and his five children also graduated from the school, spoke for many alumni when he noted that "the whole spirit of Booker T. Washington will be lost . . . and the sentiment and tradition will die."[163] To add insult to injury, Booker T. Washington was part of an ongoing discussion of a large urban renewal project that included building an interstate through the Black section of town. In addition to razing residential homes, plans included rezoning the land where the school once proudly stood to build a service station.[164]

Civil rights attorney Fred Gray with the support of NAACP counsel Jack Greenberg filed objections to the plan in Montgomery. Calling for "pairing"

Black and White schools as opposed to closing Booker T. Washington and the elementary schools, their plans put forth an alternative to a one-way desegregation plan in which Black students went to White schools without reciprocity.[165] Yet the case and the principles behind it were summarily dismissed. As Black schools were seen as institutionally inferior—in this case Booker T. Washington "needed repair"—Black high schools, much like the teachers they employed, were the first on the chopping block.

Students often protested the closure of schools. Zeno Johnson, president of the student council at the school, wrote an impassioned letter to U.S. District Judge Frank M. Johnson about "the school that is so dear to our hearts." He asked for an injunction, pleading, "We have learned to love it dearly as an intricate part of our lives . . . In our academic work and in another activities, we have always felt that we should do our best at all times to prove that we were capable of keeping the banners of our school high and not trailing in the dust." Johnson recognized the role of the teachers and administrators at their school in Montgomery, noting that they provided "the type of education that will help us to prepare ourselves to help make our city, state and nation better places in which to live."[166] It was ignored. Johnson replied condescendingly, stating, "I feel certain that with the zeal and dedication you and other [BTW students] have demonstrated, you will make a valuable contribution to one of the other schools here in the Montgomery school system."[167] Lenise Brown, a former student at Booker T. Washington who enrolled at Robert E. Lee High School in 1970, cut through the paternalism to issue a stern rebuke: "If Judge Johnson believes that we can make such invaluable contributions, why can't we make it at the school of our choice?"[168]

As part of the court order to desegregate schools, two formerly all-White public high schools in Montgomery took in Black students. Since Booker T. Washington was closed and the city discontinued secondary grades at George Washington Carver High School (grades 10–12), the city invested funds to expand facilities of previously all-White schools during the summer of 1970 to meet the needs of desegregation.[169] The schools that received extra funding and remained open were Robert E. Lee High School and Jefferson Davis High School—two predominantly White schools named after enslavers and stalwart defenders of the Confederacy. The schools that closed—George Washington Carver and Booker T. Washington—were named after Black icons. Additionally, in a region where football dominates, Robert E. Lee stood to benefit with the transfer. During the first year of integration, the school embarked upon a record-setting winning streak after former BTW offensive backs Ralph Stokes and David Lewis and defensive backs George Pugh and Mike Washington joined the Lee team. Washington and Stokes later played for the University of Alabama—the first Black students from Montgomery to go to the University of Alabama and two of the first Black football players to suit up for the Crimson Tide.[170] A select number of individual students benefitted but the system, the majority of Black students, and the teachers who taught in it, did not.

Closing Black high schools and recruiting the best and brightest of Black students were only part of the larger systemic assault on Black education. Historically Black high schools were integral sites in reshaping the southern landscape after desegregation as well. Segregationists who attempted to preserve their traditions closed and reconfigured Black high schools as part of larger, more insidious plans to maintain segregation across southern cities through "urban renewal" projects.

Urban renewal projects in Columbia, South Carolina, illustrate how historically Black high schools figured prominently in the reshaping of urban spaces during and after desegregation. In the capital city of the Palmetto State, the Housing Authority and the University of South Carolina with support from the federal Urban Renewal Program—which invested twice the amount that the city spent on renewal projects—partnered in an extensive "urban renewal" project.[171] The Planning Department formally investigated and deemed parts of the city—which were predominantly Black—as "slums" in 1965. A. C. Flora, the director of the city's Planning Commission, claimed that residents of these areas were "subjected to a level of deprivation inconceivable to most Columbians." As such, White city planners saw themselves as humanitarians undertaking renewal projects for "humanitarian reasons."[172] In addition to this rationale, the timing was also suspect because the push for urban renewal occurred less than six months after the school desegregated. The stated objectives of the renewal project included goals to "eliminate deteriorating and slum conditions while providing a further expansion area" for the university.[173] The "blighted areas" contained the Wheeler Hill neighborhood, an all-Black section of the city. The university did not hide or sugarcoat how they saw the area. To the university Board of Trustees and the White architects of urban renewal, it was a "pocket of destitution and slum."[174]

Booker T. Washington High School had served the Wheeler Hill community since Reconstruction and was revered as the cultural centerpiece of the community. But the school and the community it served stood in the way of city planners, who saw the area as beneficial to the predominantly

White university and its growth. As it stood occupied by Black residents, however, it hindered "progress" and was a blight that had to be removed. As Douglass Fitzgerald, the vice president of operations at the university, was quoted in the student newspaper, *The Gamecock*, the Wheeler Hill area was "contagious to the university."[175] Fitzgerald also noted that his job was to "clean out the jungle behind those houses."[176] As one university student candidly wrote in the student newspaper, "expansion is for our own benefit, for our education."[177] University officials and students who invested in the idea of cultivating a "homogenous" campus saw the surrounding Black neighborhood as a contagion to be removed for the betterment of all.

The historically Black Booker T. Washington High School stood less than a half-mile from the center of the university's revered meeting space, the "Horseshoe." By 1962 university president Thomas Jones expressed direct interest in the school and even saw a need for it, given that university facilities encroached upon three sides of the school. Writing on behalf of the university, Jones contacted the superintendent of schools and forthrightly stated that he sought to "acquire it as soon as it can be made available" so that "this island be eliminated."[178] The school was handled as a "special situation." In justifying the destruction of Booker T. Washington, the University of South Carolina built upon the rhetoric of urban renewal and argued that their faculty could offer the best instruction "in a homogenous setting and an atmosphere as far removed as possible from distractions, intrusions and the discords of 'through traffic.'"[179] The Black high school, the university stated, was a "major area which is not part of the campus and which nevertheless generates traffic across and through campus."[180] They went on to note that "the obvious undesirability" of the situation necessitates the acquisition of the school and its absorption into campus because "progress" demanded it.[181]

The "progress" inherent to the urban renewal plans in Columbia led to widespread and abrasive displacement as the city removed Black residents. By the mid-1970s, the project entailed clearing of over 100 "slum acres," removing 371 families, 171 individuals and the demolition of more than 1,200 homes. Of 7 major clearing sites, only 1 was designated for public housing, which offered less than 100 units for displaced families.[182] Students who stayed or socialized on campus were physically displaced, too. Surrounded by campus, Black students at the high school found themselves overwhelmed by White university students. White students and faculty filed numerous complaints of "loud and boisterous" behavior from BTW students, which led to demands for greater surveillance and law enforcement presence.

There were complaints of parking. The Carolina Research Development Foundation also took note of dilapidated housing posing serious "risks" to the community.[183] Such complaints only reified the notion that the school should be shut down and students should be removed.[184]

A narrative of progress implied that such removal and destruction were inevitable or a foregone conclusion. Or, as university officials commented, "It was the obvious way to go."[185] But this was not the case. Such sentiment ignored alternatives proffered through concerted collaborations between local, state, and federal entities, and private organizations like the Carolina Research and Development Foundation to clear the space that was now contested.[186] Black community members organized to contest these public-private arrangements and fought back to enact a different vision and use of the space. Local actors in Columbia, for instance, proposed that the high school should be used as a Black cultural center, the first of its kind in the city.[187] Local organizers also supported "Project Unity," a cooperative body between the residents of Wheeler Hill and the university that sought to empower and educate the local community during the process of renewal. This included adult basic education courses, social events, and hiring local residents to help achieve the aims of the organization.[188] Yet the proposals stemming from the Black community were denied, precluding any collaborative and shared use of the space. The university, citing a lack of support from the federal government, even terminated Project Unity. Urban renewal was ultimately a top-down imitative that did not take seriously the ideas of impacted residents.[189]

The closure of historically Black high schools in Virginia, Alabama, and South Carolina was replicated across the South. The assault was systematic, and defenders of segregation post-*Brown* assaulted the entire *system* of public education. Since the 1950s southern legislators opted instead to amend their state constitutions and to pass new laws that protected segregated school systems. Once the *Brown* decision was reached, they worked overtime and met in extraordinary sessions beyond their required terms to identify legally defensible solutions. They established special commissions and held focused hearings to craft the means to circumvent segregation.[190]

In addition to closing Black schools, Whites utilized privatization to avoid desegregation while providing their children a way out of the public, increasingly desegregated system. The architects of segregation after *Brown* leveraged funding to establish all-White private schools with public money. South Carolina legislators passed laws denying funds to schools that had been "forced" to integrate by federal decree. Virginia legislators approved a state constitutional amendment to permit public funds to be used as tuition grants for White families attending private schools. Voters in Georgia ratified a state constitutional amendment that allowed the state legislature to provide "grants of state, county or municipal funds . . . for educational purposes, in discharge of all obligations of the state to provide an adequate education for its citizens." Mississippi legislators passed similar legislation to use public funds to defray the cost of attending private schools established to avoid desegregation.[191] Such publicly funded tuition grants would eventually become known as "vouchers"—an effective means of abdicating public and constitutional responsibility to provide an education.

With public funding, tax cuts for those who enrolled in private schools, and other modes of statewide support, segregationists across the South established a network of nonsectarian "segregation academies," private schools established immediately prior to and well after the *Brown* decision to avoid desegregation. These private schools enjoyed the support of Citizen's Councils, making explicit the connection between private schools and White supremacy across the embattled South. Legislators in South Carolina passed the Tuition Grants Bill in 1963, which allocated $250,000 to cover the tuition costs carried by families to enroll in schools founded solely to provide refuge from desegregated public schools. By 1967 the state operated forty-four private academies. Mississippi underwent a similar pattern of privatization and growth. By 1968 there were forty-three state-supported private academies and hundreds of other private schools outside the jurisdiction of the state.[192]

The number of private schools rose precipitously as the courts mandated full-scale desegregation plans that moved beyond token levels of integration. When the Supreme Court finally enforced full-scale desegregation of every grade level by 1969, Mississippi doubled the number of private schools it funded, operating at least 100 private schools that were part of an extant 250 private schools. Across the South, between 300 and 400 state-supported private schools were part of an informal private school system of over 1,500 private schools that served approximately 300,000 children. The Southern Regional Council, a regional organization to maintain interracial peace, cited an estimated 500,000 students who enrolled in schools after the *Green v. County School Board* (1968) and *Alexander v. Holmes County Board of Education* (1969) cases, reflecting a private school population that nearly doubled in less than two years. By 1975 departments of education across the former Confederacy reported over one million students in private schools.[193]

During the summer of 1970 the summer of widespread desegregation in Montgomery, Alabama, St. James—a private school built in 1954—constructed new facilities (on Country Club Drive) and was making plans for a high school. A spate of other schools opened that summer, including Hooper Academy, which started the summer prior to desegregation and served children across twelve grades and was planning to enroll up to three hundred students.[194] In Columbia, South Carolina, concerned citizens organized a segregationist academy, Hammond Academy—named after the notorious enslaver and pedophile James H. Hammond—in 1966 to avoid integration, raising high and proud the Confederate flag for their opening ceremonies.[195] In Mississippi, private school enrollment skyrocketed, especially in the private academies established by the Citizen's Councils. By 1976 public school enrollment among Whites in the capital city of Jackson dropped from 54 percent to 31 percent, or from over twenty-one thousand to less than nine thousand students.[196] Formed by Council School Foundation, private Citizen's Councils schools were explicitly segregationist, where student applications stated that "forced congregation of persons . . . is a moral wrong [and] disastrous." Moreover, the curriculum was "designed solely for the educational responses of white children."[197] By 1971 the Council School Foundation operated six schools serving approximately fifty-three hundred students.[198]

One of the most illustrative instances of privatization occurred in Prince Edward County, Virginia. Local districts had the support to privatize their schools. After the district closed its schools, residents formed the Prince Edward County Corporation in 1955 with the purpose to maintain a segregated or separate school system. They formed the organization days after the *Brown II* decision declared desegregation with "all deliberate speed."[199] The Prince Edward School Foundation operated from the premise that *any* form of segregated schooling—or no schooling at all— was better than attending desegregated school. In its first year of operation, the private segregated school was held in fifteen different buildings, from empty buildings to church basements. Approximately fifteen hundred students enrolled. Supplies were limited and books were scarce. Desks were made of folding chairs and desktops were falling apart. Tuition remained high despite state grants that appropriated funds to cover private school tuition and tax breaks to those who made donations.[200] Less affluent White families had to take out second mortgages on their farms and homes to afford tuition.[201]

Still, Prince Edward Academy produced results for its students, which demonstrated the privileges afforded to Whites. As public schools shut their doors, the private school was accredited each year since 1959 and it was reported that 74 students of the 101 students of the class of 1966 were in college. In 1967 fifty-one of seventy students were accepted into colleges and universities.[202] While extracurriculars were barred across the county, the Academy boasted a basketball team and field trips to nearby Charlottesville to study the Revolutionary War. They had an active PTA and a music program.[203] Cultivating an elitist image with headmasters, headmistresses, and lower and upper schools, the school presented a stark image to the violent, desegregated schools portrayed in the press. The school offered a collegiate preparatory curriculum while offering practical classes for students who have "limited educational aspirations."[204] Plans were also drawn to build a new campus in 1963 at the cost of $175,000.[205]

Representative Watkins M. Abbot of Virginia praised the schools for supporting the "private enterprise system and individual initiative." For Abbot, privatization was an answer to the "forces of welfare statism reaching down from Washington."[206] The *Farmville Herald* provided full support for the privatization of schools as well, stating that the NAACP forced the decision to close public schools. In a sentiment echoed throughout the community, many believed that the NAACP sought to prevent "any schooling at all in order to present a stronger case to the Federal courts on behalf of forcing the restoration of public education."[207] Others condemned Black families and passed the blame to them. "There will be no schooling," one local editorial lamented, "because there has been no initiative in the Negro community for establishing a substitute system." In fact, the writer opined, "the white people of Prince Edward deserve sympathy" for their determination to make the best of a bad situation."[208]

Though never the panacea envisioned by segregationists, segregation academies and the network of private schools that rose after 1954 redefined the role of private education. These schools did not so much function as religious institutions as their predecessors had since the founding of public education in the United States. As public education deteriorated in the wake of the school wars over access, private education became a southern ideal and investment in public education eroded. Observing the White flight and deterioration of public education during the time, John Sessions, a member of the Board of Education in Washington, D.C., noted prophetically in 1966: "The schools have deteriorated so badly that regardless of their race, people who can afford the cost are taking their kids out of public school." The chair of the board commented that it was "disturbing to think that our school system could become not just all-Negro, but that it could be made up almost totally of poor children."[209]

. . . . . .

Black teachers, elders, and civil rights organizers had long debated the extent to which high school youth should be on the front lines of a movement for justice and equity—or if they should be on the front lines at all. Yet White supremacists and policymakers never wavered. They had no doubt about where they stood: they always saw Black youth, regardless of age, as threats and, as such, cut them down. By the 1970s full-scale desegregation had been implemented through the letter of the law. In response to continuing activism by youth, White policymakers exacted new forms of discipline, punishment, and wholesale removal to reconstruct a system of education in their image. As the educational landscape changed into what we recognize today, White policymakers reinvented disciplinary means and codified a carceral logic to quell youth agency once again. But it was not enough to stifle dissent and protest. As in the past, student resistance and rebellion continued and was carried forth by another generation.

Epilogue

· ·

When Zyahna Bryant entered in Charlottesville High School in Virginia as a freshman in 2015, she enrolled in Advanced Placement courses like many college-bound students. She quickly noticed the lack of Black students in those college preparatory courses. Soon after, she founded a Black Student Union at the school. Bryant also served on the Charlottesville Youth Council, advocating around issues of access to Advanced Placement courses, equity in educational policy, and gun violence in schools. Bryant organized protests, marched, and spoke at city council and school board meetings. She earned the ire of right-wing extremists across the nation after Breitbart published a petition she spearheaded when she was fifteen years old. The petition called on the city of Charlottesville to remove the statue of Robert E. Lee from Lee Park in the city's historic district, in addition to renaming the park.[1]

At Charlottesville High School, Zyahna Bryant was at the vanguard of the most recent manifestation of the long historic trajectory of high school student activism. Bryant advocated for policies and issues that previous generations of activists had also fought for, such as a higher quality of education, access to the best courses, safety, and eradicating racist policy and commemoration where it was identified. There were other lessons learned, too. Forming a Black Student Union and leading efforts to remove a vaulted Robert E. Lee statue in his home state brought Bryant into the crosshairs of people who supported the Confederacy and claimed that Bryant was "trying to dismantle culture, education, and the very fabric of history."[2] It was after this incident that Bryant learned or experienced firsthand the truth that has underpinned high school student activism. "White supremacists have no boundaries for kids," Bryant reported in an interview. "They didn't care that I was a 10th-grader or 11th-grader in high school."[3]

Though *de jure* segregation was abolished, Bryant and her cohort of Black students and students of color did not have equal access to the best courses. They—and all youth—were subject to gun violence. They walked by the same Confederate memorials as their predecessors. They also faced the very same denial of youth and life that defined the experiences of youth activists who came before them. Like Claudette Colvin, Hezekiah Watkins,

Millicent Brown, and those who came of age sixty or more years ago, Zyahna Bryant also came of age learning about youth killed unjustly through state-sanctioned violence. As Claudette Colvin grieved over the loss of her peer Jeremiah Reeves and as the state forced youth to process the brutal murder of Emmett Till, so too did Bryant and today's youth come of age with the untimely death and murder of young people, including Trayvon Martin, Jordan Davis, Tamir Rice, Michael Brown, Rekia Boyd, Ma'Khia Bryant, and Adam Toledo. We also learned firsthand of the state's historic denial of protection of young people through the testimony of police officer Darren Wilson. He shot and killed eighteen-year-old Michael Brown and, though he just turned eighteen and graduated from high school less than three months prior to his murder, Wilson described him as someone with superhuman strength, likening him to the Hulk, falsely assigning violent aggression and a "demonic" disposition to someone who barely reached legal adulthood.[4]

One reality today is that Black children and youth have a statistically higher chance of losing their life at the hands of police and state-sanctioned violence. As a White law enforcement agent of the state, Wilson did not see the person in front of him as a youth or someone who should be afforded the protections typically ensured to young people. Connected with the ongoing terrorism of *all* Black families, which includes the names of those cut down by state-sanctioned violence like Eric Garner, George Floyd, and Breonna Taylor, slain youth have necessitated a national Black Lives Matter movement. One national study found that Black children were six times more likely to be killed by police. Another found that police killed 140 children between 2003 and 2018 and yet another report cited that over 100 children had been killed since 2015.[5]

Zyahna Bryant occupied a position that was in essence akin to those who came before her. Bryant was intimately familiar with this history. She expressed gratitude for her ancestors, "true giants," in her words, "Black women who have created much of the contemporary political theory that serves as the context and background for a lot of my work." Bryant was also cognizant that their voices were too often silenced and ignored by history. "Do not wait until we have passed or reached our breaking point to honor us or to give us our well-deserved flowers," Bryant wrote in *Teen Vogue*. "Honor us while we are well. Honor us as we are doing the work that others choose not to do. Honor us in the rooms where we are not present."[6] Their voices and lived experiences inspire a book that centers a narrative around Black high school youth. A recent historiographical shift to document the stories, voices, and recollections of high school youth activism in the past helps contextualize the more recent iteration of a dynamic youth movement—one that pundits and popular reporting often fail to take seriously.

Now elders in an intergenerational movement, many of the youth activists of previous generations stay engaged. The Black freedom struggle in and of itself could be an educative space, impacting the transitioning of young people into adulthood in myriad ways.[7] It was a diffuse activism spread through and across a wide spectrum. Malcolm Hooks, a youth veteran of the Birmingham Children's Crusade, worked various jobs and maintained a commitment to the principles of the movement. He recalled "the courage I had obtained during the movement gave me the strength to deal with various people at my job"—a useful skill while working in a managerial position that included supervising White workers.[8] Another veteran of the Birmingham crusade, Miriam Taylor McClendon, spoke of acquiring a new awareness that prepared her for adulthood and professional life. She remembered, "My years in the movement taught me to evaluate and to analyze. They sowed the seeds or laid the groundwork for everything that came after."[9]

Some youth activists remained committed in more direct ways. Reverend James Blake, the NAACP Youth Council leader who organized the first sit-in in Charleston, South Carolina, in 1960 and spoke of "a new kind of Black youth," continued a life of activism. He worked to desegregate other spaces in Charleston, completed theology school, pastored various African Methodist Episcopal churches in South Carolina, and directed the South Carolina Commission for Farmworkers.[10] After desegregating Rivers High School in Charleston, South Carolina, in 1963, Millicent Brown enlisted in the freedom struggle, joining the ranks of the Student Nonviolent Coordinating Committee. She studied at Howard University and earned a Ph.D. in history from Florida State University. Dr. Brown remains an advocate for civil rights and justice in the Lowcountry today, part of which includes directing the "Somebody Had To Do It" project, which documents the voice and stories of the "first children" to desegregate White schools.[11] After joining the student protests at R. R. Moton High School in Prince Edward County in 1951, Joy Cabarrus Speakes continues a life of civic engagement. She serves on the board of the Robert Russa Moton Museum, which occupies the same building she walked out from in 1951. She also speaks to the younger generation "to encourage young people to participate and that they can make a difference regardless of their age and that they should if they felt that something was unfair or wrong." For Speakes, "they [youth] should not just sit on the sideline, they should participate."[12]

Guided by principles of the civil rights movement, teachers and educators remained on the front lines, too, and continued to impact their profession.[13] The remaining educators in a decimated Black teaching profession stayed in the classroom and wrought institutional and curricular change. Many remain engaged by serving in desegregated schools and teaching White children, many of whom never encountered Black teachers. Lois Simms, a teacher in Charleston, South Carolina, taught lessons of enslavement and the civil rights movement to White students in a school that was desegregated as a result of that movement.[14] Some remained involved politically, elected to serve on school boards to determine local policy during the era of desegregation. After teaching and serving as an administrator, Herman Harris served sixteen years on the Montgomery Board of Education after a distinguished thirty-one years in the field of education. He was described as someone "unafraid to take a hard stance."[15] Black teachers who remained in the profession and in colleges of education advocated "multicultural education" in the 1990s, integrating the histories and cultures of Black communities and other communities of color sidelined by a mainstream White history. The curricular movement also inspired more recent attempts to enact a culturally relevant and sustaining pedagogy.[16]

Historically Black high schools remained as sites of resistance, discourse, and the discord that shaped public education after the *Brown* decision. Historically Black high schools like Burke High School in Charleston, South Carolina, and A. H. Parker High School in Birmingham, Alabama, remain pillars in the communities they serve. Memorialized with historic markers and remembered locally with long, proud traditions, historically Black high schools are strong symbols of the Black community.[17] While most institutions are remembered publicly with markers, local museums, or by local alumni associations, White school boards, voters, and legislators shuttered many historically Black high schools during desegregation—and many still, like Burke and A. H. Parker High Schools, remain under constant threat of closure. Others emerged with different governance structures or identities during prevailing shifts in educational policy after the *Brown* decision. For instance, after Booker T. Washington High School in Montgomery closed in 1970 around the politics of desegregation, it reopened as a magnet school with the support of a federal grant in 1996.[18] Magnet schools were designed as part of a larger national education policy movement to reinvigorate public education through voluntary desegregation, which included elements of competition and attracting White students to a Black school or neighborhood with a specialized curriculum. As such, Black high schools like Booker T. Washington are critical components in a larger, problematic history of privatization and "school choice" that unfolded after the *Brown* (1954) decision.[19]

The legacy of Black high school student activism shapes and contextualizes the contemporary youth movement, which intersects with a diverse array of issues, identities, and analyses. Young people have been on the front lines of a multitude of social movements that have traversed the five decades since the passing of the "classic" phase of the southern Black freedom struggle.[20] Young people "after the movement" in the 1990s participated in ways that were in direct connection to previous generations of activism. Youth in the Black Student Leadership Network, for instance, actively recruited youth leadership in concert with Children's Defense Fund and their Freedom School program, which had origins during Reconstruction but emerged as a popular education program for activists in the 1960s. Youth movements have also grown in nuanced ways that built upon yet transformed notions of high school and youth activism. Youth activists formed Southerners on New Ground in 1993 and organized intentionally for and across race, class, gender, and sexuality, intersecting with and elevating the pressing concerns of the LGTBQ community and their allies. Youth activists transformed what it meant to advocate for better education as well. Young people in the Algebra Project, a math-based curriculum reform movement founded by civil rights activists Bob Moses and Dave Dennis, participated in nonviolent protests, marches, and demonstrations aimed at raising money and resources for failing public schools. They disrupted the state of Maryland's plans to build a juvenile detention center, which the state designed to house minors charged as adults, by occupying the site in protest. They also attempted to make a citizen's arrest of the state school superintendent.[21]

Young people also formed a critical core of the water protectors that gathered with Standing Rock Sioux to protest the construction of the Dakota Access Pipeline that cut through Indigenous land, threatening their water supply. In 2016 youth pushed forward the Indigenous-led #NoDAPL movement that included a relay run nearly two thousand miles to deliver a petition, direct confrontation with construction crews, a private security force hired by the oil company, and two U.S. presidential administrations.[22] High school youth galvanized a nation after Nikolas Cruz killed fourteen of his peers and three staff members who worked at Marjory Stoneman Douglass High School. Over one million people marched in solidarity with the high school activists who made the demand to remove guns from our schools and demand common-sense gun reform legislation.[23] It was one of the largest coordinated mass protests led by and held in solidarity with young people in high school. At the same time, a global environment justice movement has captivated the attention of the world. Greta Thunberg, at the age of fifteen, began protesting outside the Swedish parliament demanding legislative action at the conclusion of a summer that was the hottest on record in her country.[24]

Young people, in particular high school youth, remain at the front of the struggle for full inclusion and justice. Some also remain the victims of supremacist violence and racist policy that includes the school-prison nexus and police in our schools. The historic and integral role of Black high school activism and the schools that supported them through U.S. history presages the contemporary moment. Recognizing this history avoids the whitewashing of current and future youth movements. It also reminds us that the ideals of youth remain unrealized. The future lies in investing in historically Black high schools and supporting without equivocation Zyahna Bryant and other youth who have taken the torch from previous generations.

Acknowledgments

This book was inspired by walking daily by the S. H. Kress Building, the site of the first sit-in in Charleston led by high school students, which was one block from my office at the College of Charleston in South Carolina, but it truly began while working for or with Dave Dennis, Millicent Brown, Kendall Deas, Pastor Thomas Dixon, Smurf, Evangelist Patricia Wright, Dan Ryan, Kim Bowlin, Daron Calhoun, Jesse Williams, Rev. Jeremy Rutledge, and other stalwart defenders and advocates for public education. Their insights, experience, and commitment to the fight is real and humbling. Their keen ability to push and push back still leave me in awe.

Michelle Purdy offered invaluable feedback, encouragement, and support early on in this book project. I am indebted to her generous commitment of time and the kind friendship she has shown since meeting at the History of Education Society conference in 2008.

Speaking with those on the front lines has been a true honor and a learning experience for which I am forever grateful and indebted. I am deeply indebted to Richard Bailey, Rose Bell, Millicent Brown, Minerva King, Bo Brown, Linda Chapman, Joe Delpit, Harvey Gantt, Herman Harris, Jacqueline Martin, Inevva May-Pitman, Beula Russel, Lois Simms, Hymethia Thompson, Hezekiah Watkins, and the many others who had the patience and took the time to share their histories and their profound understanding of this history through the years. Dave and Nancy Dennis, in particular, have been life savers and a support for me and my family for the past decade. My family and our daughters are forever grateful for their kindness, love, and patience.

Those who took the time to discuss the book imparted insights that still show me the way. A very special thank you to Chris Span, James Anderson, Yoon Pak, Derrick Alridge, Mario Perez, Stanley Thangaraj, Kevin Lam, Kevin Zayed, Mari Crabtree, Michael Hevel, Stefan Bradley, Robert Chase, Theo Moton, Kim Ranson, Mirelsie Velázquez, Sharon Lee, Kara Brown, Christian Anderson, Gloria Boutte, Christine Finnan, David Martinez, Jason Coy, Bobby Donaldson, Eddie Cole, Juan Carrillo, Walter Stern, Alex Hyres, Dara Walker, Adam Domby, Hilary Green, and Herbert Sosa for taking the time to impart your knowledge, friendship, and laughs throughout the years. I am grateful to have worked on the same campus with Phyllis Jestice, who has taken the time to read and mark up not one, but *two* of my book projects as an affiliated faculty member in her History Department at the College of Charleston.

Daron Calhoun, Curtis Franks, Patricia Lessane, and Georgette Mayo have offered me space, support, and access to sources at the Avery Research Center—a historic school in Charleston, South Carolina, that remains and will always remain one of the most meaningful spaces in my life.

Brandon Prioa at the University of North Carolina Press provided editorial support that was critical in shaping and completing this manuscript. His critiques and encouragement were instrumental.

As a rising scholar and talented research assistant, Chris Getowicz provided urgent support and a talented hand during a busy time of the semester. I am also deeply grateful for the assistance Cindy Jones, Candace Livingston, Joshua Burns, Detrice Roberts, and Katherine Blanton provided while finishing this book.

Finally, my wife Claire and our daughters, Edith and Nina—both of whom blessed us with their arrival into the world as I was researching and writing this book— have provided the inspiration to finish this project. I pray the time I had to spend away from you to finish this manuscript can help us better understand what we need to do to support your future.

Notes

Introduction

1. Claudette Colvin, quoted in "The Other Rosa Parks."

2. Claudette Colvin, quoted in "The Other Rosa Parks"; Hoose, *Claudette Colvin*; "Negro Guilty of Violation"; Garrow, *The Walking City*; Theoharis, *Rebellious Life*, 32–34; Kitchen, "Interview with Claudette Colvin"; Carson, "To Walk in Dignity," 14; Parks, *Rosa Parks*, 111–12; McGuire, *At the Dark End of the Street*, 84–92; see also Hale, "Future Foot Soldiers," 615–52.

3. As Julian Bond, former Student Nonviolent Coordinating Committee (SNCC) activist and chairman of the NAACP, stated in a study by the Southern Poverty Law Center on the status of civil rights education, students learn "sanitized versions" of Dr. King and Mrs. Parks, "but the stories of bravery and sacrifice in the movement for civil rights were absent from their memories and their high school curricula," quoted in "Teaching the Movement," 5. Parks did not work directly with Colvin before the arrest. See also Clayborne Carson, "To Walk in Dignity," 14; Parks, *Rosa Parks*, 111–12. For more on how Colvin illustrates the use and abuse of civil rights history, see Theoharis, *More Beautiful and Terrible History*, 204–5.

4. "NAACP Geared for Fight"; "School Board to Delay"; "Va. Pupils' Strike Ends"; "Desegregation Move"; Kluger, *Simple Justice*, 128, 175–81, 467–80. For a full account of the Prince Edward County School history, see Titus, *Brown's Battleground*; Waugh, "'Issue Is the Control,'" 76–94; Waugh, "From Forgotten to Remembered"; Bonastia, *Southern Stalemate*; Smith, *They Closed Their Schools*.

5. Minerva King, interview with the author, December 12, 2011; Harvey Gantt, interview with the author, November 28, 2011; see also Hale, "'Fight Was Instilled,'" 4–28.

6. Hymethia Washington Thompson, interview with the author, August 26, 2008; Hezekiah Watkins, interview with the author, August 26 and 27, 2008; Dr. Gene Young, interview with the author, August 7, 2008; W. R. Bo Brown, interview with the author, July 25, 2013; "Agitators Seek Troops"; "Racial Agitator Leads."

7. On conceptions of childhood and the intersection with the civil rights movement, see de Schweinitz, *If We Could Change*; Berghel, "What My Generation Makes," 422–40; Delvin, *Girl Stands at the Door*; Capshaw, *Civil Rights Childhood*; Hale, "Future Foot Soldiers," 615–52; Hale, *Freedom Schools*.

8. Favors, *Shelter in a Time*; Jackson, "Leaders in the Making."

9. On college student activism, see Biondi, *Black Revolution on Campus*; Turner, *Sitting In and Speaking Out*; Zinn, *SNCC*; Bradley, *Harlem vs. Columbia University*; Rogers, *Black Campus Movement*; Cohen and Snyder, *Rebellion in Black & White*;

Williamson, *Radicalizing the Ebony Tower*, 64–68; Baker, *Paradoxes of Desegregation*, 108–21. Recent scholarship has also begun to document the role of White southern college students. See Michel, *Struggle for a Better South*; Cole, *The Campus Color Line*.

10. Halberstam, *Children*, 4.

11. See Cohen and Snyder, *Rebellion in Black & White*.

12. "Tougaloo College application," General Education Board, Reel 39969, "Tougaloo College," MDAH; Vincent, *A Centennial History of Southern University*, 98; Folder "Cade, John B. (Dean) History of S. U. Rough Copies," Box John B. Cade, 1945–1966, Courtesy of John Brother Cade Papers, SU; Meriwether, *History of Higher Education*, 125; McMillan, "Negro Higher Education," 9–18.

13. Favors, *Shelter in a Time*, 5.

14. Givens, *Fugitive Pedagogy*, 7–11.

15. Favors, *Shelter in a Time*, 5–8.

16. V. P. Franklin, *Education of Black Philadelphia*; Chamberlain, "'And a Child Shall Lead the Way'"; Stewart, *First Class*; Pierson, *Laboratory of Learning*; Kridel, *Progressive Education*; Driskell, *Schooling Jim Crow*. On the history of Black high schools in Philadelphia, see Kitzmiller, *Roots of Educational Inequality*; Hyres, "Persistence and Resistance."

17. Du Bois, *Philadelphia Negro*, 182–86.

18. A. Morris, *Origins of the Civil Rights Movement*, 4; Du Bois, *Philadelphia Negro*, 182–86.

19. Charron, *Freedom's Teacher*, 3.

20. Krug, *Shaping of the American*; Krug, *Shaping of the American, Vol 2*; Reese, *Origins of the American*; Fenske, *History of American Public*; Angus and Mirel, *Failed Promise*; Labaree, *Making of an American*; Steele, *Making a Mass Institution*; G. S. Hall, "High School," 63–73.

21. Evers, "Annual Report, 1957," 84.

22. DeGroot, "Culture of Protest," 5.

23. V. S. Walker, *Their Highest Potential*, 212.

24. de Schweinitz, *If We Could Change the World*; Susan Berghel, Fieldston, and Renfro, *Growing Up America*; Berghel, "What My Generation Makes of America," 422–40; Bynum, *NAACP Youth*; Levine, *Freedom's Children*; Gelman, *Death Blow to Jim Crow*; Levinson, *We've Got a Job*; Hale, *Freedom Schools*; Halberstam, *The Children*; Chamberlain, "'And a Child'"; Kinchen, *Black Power*; King, "Emmett Till Generation," 155–68; Ides, "'Dare to Free Yourself,'" 295–319; V. P. Franklin, "Documenting the Contributions," 663–71; Theoharis, *More Beautiful and Terrible*, 142–48; Myers, "Local Action and Global," 282–93. On discussion of Black childhood and resistance in the nineteenth century see Webster, *Beyond the Boundaries*; see also Berghel, Fieldston, and Renfro, *Growing Up America*.

25. Libarle and Seligson, *High School Revolutionaries*, xviii.

26. S. M. Franklin, *After the Rebellion*; Hogan, *On the Freedom Side*.

27. Danns, "Chicago High School," 138–50; Danns, *Something Better*; D. Walker, "Black Power, Youth Politics"; D. Walker, "Black Power and the Detroit"; V. P. Franklin, *Young Crusaders*; Graham, *Young Activists*; Graham, "Flaunting the

Freak Flag," 522–43; Fountain Jr. "War in the Schools"; Rury and Hill, "An End of Innocence," 486–508; Willis, *Audacious Agitation*; Willis, "Let Me In;" Schumaker, *Troublemakers*; Fernandez, *Young Lords*; Garcia and Castro, *Blowout!*; Ruhl, "'Forward You Must Go'"; Burrow Jr., *Child Shall Lead Them.*

28. Mintz, *Huck's Raft*; Zelizer, *Pricing the Priceless Child*; Kett, *Rites of Passage*; Ariés, *Centuries of Childhood*; Fass, *End of American Childhood*; Heywood, *History of Childhood*; Fass and Grossberg, *Reinventing Childhood*; Lindenmeyer, "Right to Childhood"; Chudacoff, *How Old Are You?.*

29. Ritterhouse, *Growing Up Jim Crow*; Reynolds, *Maintaining Segregation.*

30. W. King, *Stolen Childhood*; W. King, *African American Childhoods.*

31. Agyepong, *Criminalization of Black Children*; G. K. Ward, "Birth of a Juvenile Court," 1–10; see also Lindenmeyer, "A Right to Childhood," 18–20; Streib, *Death Penalty for Juveniles*, 2–20; Beatty, Cahan, and Grant, *When Science Encounters*, 7; Zelizer, *Pricing the Priceless Child*, 29; "White House Conference," 5–6, 18.

32. Berghel, "'What My Generation Makes,'" 423–24; Ides, "'Dare to Free Yourself,'" 298–300; Bynum, *NAACP Youth, 1936–1965*; de Schweinitz, *If We Could Change*, 1–6, 11–24.

33. Ritterhouse, *Growing Up Jim Crow*, 60; Kett, *Rites of Passage*, 111; Mintz, *Huck's Raft*, 188–90; Zelizer, *Pricing the Priceless Child*, 28; Heywood, *A History of Childhood*, 28–29.

34. By the 1930s, nearly 55 percent of America's youth enrolled in, though they did not necessarily complete, high school. Federal statistics indicated that 4.3 million students enrolled in high school, representing a growth of 400 percent in just 30 years. From 1930 to 1932 high school enrollment grew by 17 percent. By 1930 three-quarters of fourteen- to seventeen-year-olds were high school students and by 1940, half of the country's seventeen-year-olds were high school graduates. The percentage of seventeen-year-olds who graduated from high school grew to 50.8 percent by 1940 as well, marking the first time that one-half of school age population finished high school. The graduate rate blossomed to 62.3 percent by 1956. By 1950 more than 80 percent of fourteen- to seventeen-year-olds enrolled in high school. *Statistical Abstract of the United States, 1930*, 108–15; *Statistical Abstract of the United States, 1940*, 112–13; de Schweinitz, *If We Could Change the World*, 29–35, 228. Mintz, *Huck's Raft*, 238–39; Kett, *Rites of Passage*, 245; Herbst, "High School and Youth in America," 168.

35. *Statistical Abstract of the United States, 1940*, 113–14; Anderson, *Education of Blacks in the South*, 188–93; Rury and Hill, *African American Struggle*, 9–12, 26–27.

36. Thomas Jesse Jones of the United States Bureau of Education published a report in 1916 that emphasized the private nature of secondary education, reporting that 11,000 students enrolled in private secondary schools compared to 8,700 in enrolled in public secondary schools. Two-thirds of all Blacks in secondary schools attended private schools, which was striking compared to the fact that only one-fourth of African Americans in border states attended private schools. Jones, "Negro Education," 15–16; Thompson, "Does Negro Education Need," 311–13.

37. Givens, *Fugitive Pedagogy*, 7–11.

38. The university awarded diplomas based on a 60 percent satisfactory completion rate, which gives some indication of what satisfactory completion meant for entrance exams before the turn of the century, Vincent, *A Centennial History of Southern University*, 23–25.

39. Meriwether, *History of Higher Education*, 125.

40. McDaniel, "Edwin Augustus Harleston," 12.

41. National Education Association, *Report of the Committee of Ten*.

42. *The Comet: A Medium of Student Expression* (February 1933; June 1936; January 1939; March, 1939), South Caroliniana Library, University of South Carolina.

43. Bailey, *Neither Carpetbaggers or Scalawags*, 128–29. The city of Montgomery was also supported by the Cleveland Union Aid Commission with the recruitment of teachers, to Edwin Beecher to J. W. Alvrod, July 1, 1867, Records of the Education Division of the Bureau of Refugees, Freedmen, and Abandoned Lands, 1865–1871, National Archives and Records Administration (NARA), M803, 1695200, Frames 187–206; Freedmen's Bureau papers, Monthly reports in Alabama, January 1866–June 1879, Frame 77, May 1867, Frame 101, February 1868, Frame 190.

44. Bailey, *Neither Carpetbaggers or Scalawags*, 128–29; Sway, "Swayne School," 209–10. (*The American Missionary* is also digitized through the Cornell University Library http://ebooks.library.cornell.edu/a/amis/amis.html.)

45. Bailey, *Neither Carpetbaggers nor Scalawags*, 128–29.

46. Bailey, "Elijah Cook," 89–90. He also helped establish Selma University.

47. Bailey, *Neither Carpetbaggers nor Scalawags*, 130, 278–79.

48. Board of Education of Montgomery County minutes, January 12, 1937.

49. Board of Education of Montgomery County Alabama, May 10, 1915; Board of Education Montgomery Alabama, August 13, 1915; Board of Education Montgomery Alabama, October 13, 1915; on the purchase of desks and blackboards, see Board of Education Montgomery Alabama, November 8, 1915, and December 13, 1915; "Contracts Given on Negro School"; Dr. Richard Bailey, conversation with the author, February 2, 2012; see also the Swayne College/Booker T. Washington Historical Marker (Alabama Historical Association, 2003); on name change, Board of Education Montgomery Alabama, March 13, 1916.

50. "Prospectus of the Charleston Industrial School," in Dart Family Papers, Box 1, Folder 5, "Prospectus of the Charleston Industrial School & Home for Girls and 7th Annual Prospectus for the Chas. Normal & Industrial School, 1895, 1901," Avery Research Center; on the Avery Normal Institute, see Drago, *Initiative, Paternalism, and Race Relations*.

51. "Prospectus of the Charleston Industrial School," in Dart Family Papers, Box 1, Folder 5, "Prospectus of the Charleston Industrial School & Home for Girls and 7th Annual Prospectus for the Chas. Normal & Industrial School, 1895, 1901," Avery Research Center.

52. The main building contained twelve classrooms, a chapel, a library and had a capacity of five hundred students. "Prospectus of the Charleston Industrial School," and "Fifth Annual Circular and Prospectus," and "Prospectus of the Charleston Industrial School & Home for Girls and 7th Annual Prospectus for the Chas. Normal

& Industrial School, 1895, 1901," in Dart Family Papers, Box 1, Folder 5, Avery Research Center.

53. "Prospectus of the Charleston Industrial School," in Dart Family Papers, Box 1, Folder 5, "Prospectus of the Charleston Industrial School & Home for Girls and 7th Annual Prospectus for the Chas. Normal & Industrial School, 1895, 1901," Avery Research Center.

54. "Seventh Annual Prospectus of the Charleston Normal Industrial Institute," in Dart Family Papers, Box 1, Folder 5, "Prospectus of the Charleston Industrial School & Home for Girls and 7th Annual Prospectus for the Chas. Normal & Industrial School, 1895, 1901," Avery Research Center; Reverend John Dart, Dart Family Papers, Box 1, Folder 6, "Colored and Industrial School Stationary," Avery Research Center.

55. "Prospectus of the Charleston Industrial School," in Dart Family Papers, Box 1, Folder 5, "Colored Industrial School Prospectus," Avery Research Center.

56. "Fifth Annual Circular and Prospectus," in Dart Family Papers, Box 1, Folder 5, "Prospectus of the Charleston Industrial School & Home for Girls and 7th Annual Prospectus for the Chas. Normal & Industrial School, 1895, 1901," Avery Research Center.

57. Dart recounts of the trial of the eight men indicted for the murder in *The Famous Trial of the Eight Men Indicted for the Lynching of Frazier R. Baker and His Baby*, 1899 (copy found in the John L. Dart Family Papers, Box 1, Folder 7, Booklet: The Famous Trial of Eight Men . . . John Lewis Dart, 1899–1908," Avery Research Center).

58. Dart, "Memorial" in *Famous Trial*, 64–68.

59. Dart, "Preface" in *Famous Trial*; "Prospectus of the Charleston Industrial School," in Dart Family Papers, Box 1, Folder 5, "Prospectus of the Charleston Industrial School & Home for Girls and 7th Annual Prospectus for the Chas. Normal & Industrial School, 1895, 1901," Avery Research Center.

60. "Commercial Democracy," in *Southern Reporter*, April 9, 1904, Vol. 4, No. 49, in John L. Dart Family Papers, Box 1, Folder 9, Avery Research Center.

61. "Commercial Democracy," in *Southern Reporter*, April 9, 1904, Vol. 4, No. 49, in John L. Dart Family Papers, Box 1, Folder 9, Avery Research Center.

62. "Editorial," in *Southern Reporter*, April 9, 1904, Vol. 4, No. 49 in John L. Dart Family Papers, Box 1, Folder 9, Avery Research Center.

63. Fairclough, *Class of Their Own*, 357; Dittmer, *Local People*, 75.

64. Moody, *Coming of Age*, 229.

65. Moody, *Coming of Age*, 135.

66. V. S. Walker, *Hello Professor*; V. S. Walker, *Lost Education of Horace Tate*; V. S. Walker, *Their Highest Potential*; V. W. Littlefield, "Teaching Survival and Combat," 17–34; Alridge, "Teachers in Movement"; Loder-Jackson, *Schoolhouse Activists*; Baker, *Paradoxes of Desegregation*; Cecelski, *Along Freedom Road*; Baker, "Pedagogies of Protest."

67. Charron, *Freedom's Teacher*, 3.

68. Littlefield, "'Teaching Survival and Combat,'" 26; Charron, *Freedom's Teacher*, 3–5; T. M. Morris, *Womanpower Unlimited*; on Black parent teacher associations, see Woyshner, *National PTA, Race*.

69. Gilmore, *Gender and Jim Crow*, 32.

70. Ransby, *Ella Baker*, 4–5.

71. Littlefield, "'Teaching Survival and Combat,'" 17.

72. Ramsey, *Reading, Writing, and Segregation*, 1–45; Baumgartner, *In Pursuit of Knowledge*; Walker, *Lost Education of Horace Tate*; Hale, "'We Are Not Merging,'" 463–81; Hale, "'Development of Power,'" 444–59; Gilmore, *Gender and Jim Crow*, 32–34.

73. Hale, "'Development of Power,'" 444–59; Murray, *History of the North Carolina*, 17–19; "Proposed Constitution for the Alabama State Teachers Association," in ASTA Box 13, Folder 31, "Zelia S. Evans" in ASTA collection, ASU; "The Alabama State Teachers Association Report of the Constitution Committee," ASTA Box 13, Folder 39, "ASTA Constitution," in ASTA collection, ASU; Perry, *History of the American*, 15–19; Fairclough, *Class of Their Own*, 311–14; on the history of laboratory school supported by Alabama State, see Pierson, *Laboratory of Learning*; Picott, *History of the Virginia Teachers*, 15–18; C. D. Thompson, *History of the Mississippi*, 1, 7; Potts, *History of the Palmetto*, 33–34. For a discussion on the workings of the Georgia Teachers and Education Association, see Walker, *Hello Professor*, 135–58.

74. "Constitution and By-Laws—The National Association of Teachers in Colored Schools," in *The Bulletin*, Vol. 7–9 (June–July 1929), in National Education Association Collection, Box #3044, File 10, "The Bulletin"; see Perillo, *Uncivil Rights*; D'Amico, "Claiming Profession." The NEA went through organizational battles of the 1895–1923 and identified as a professional association, distinct from a union. They sought to raise salaries and organize local branches into a federation within the NEA, a claim that at times advocated for a greater teacher voice, though it still largely focused on professionalization. Calls for higher salaries were couched in rhetoric around professionalization, not unionization. Urban, "Teacher Activism," 194–95; Perry, *History of the American Teachers Association*, 47–48. This is also reflected in White teacher organizations of New York and the quest for professional rights in the 1930s, particularly in the context of attempting to improve education. Though different in their relation to social issues, the Teachers Guild and the Teachers Union demanded a change in rights. See Perillo, *Uncivil Rights*, 31–37.

75. Fultz, "Charleston, 1919–1920," 633–49; Rabinowitz, "Half a Loaf," 565–94.

76. Thompson, "Editorial Comment," 539–42; Fairclough, *Class of Their Own*, 309–10, 345–49; Charron, *Freedom's Teacher*, 154–56; Potts, *History of the Palmetto*, 61–68; Baker, *Paradoxes of Desegregation*, 54–56; Simms, *Chalk and Chalkboard*, 8–10; Drago, *Initiative, Paternalism*, 240–42; Bolton, *Hardest Deal of All*, 45–60; Edward S. Bishop Sr., interview with Charles Bolton, February 27, 1991; "A. L. Johnson to Mr. A. J. Noel, January 14, 1948" and "A. L. Johnson to James A. Burns, February 23, 1948," Box 2, Gladys Noel Bates Papers, Mississippi Department of Archives and History (MDAH), Jackson, MS; Gladys Noel Bates, interview with Catherine Jannik, December 23, 1996, Vol. 689, The University of Southern Mississippi Center for Oral History and Cultural Heritage, Hattiesburg, MS (also available: http://www.lib.usm.edu/legacy/spcol/coh/cohbatesg.html); "Community in Which I Live" [1949], Box 3, Gladys Noel Bates Papers, MDAH.

77. Favors, *Shelter in a Time of Storm*, 5–9.

78. Baumgartner, *In Pursuit of Knowledge*, 5–10, 177–204.

79. Baldwin, "A Talk to Teachers," 42.

80. Jones, "Negro Education," 78–79; Anderson, "The Black Public High School," 186–237.

81. Baumgartner, "Searching for Sarah," 82.

82. Devlin, *Girl Stands at the Door*, xxix.

83. Odem, *Delinquent Daughters*; Chatelain, *South Side Girls*.

84. Hale, "Future Foot Soldiers or Budding Criminals?" 615–52.

85. Drago, *Initiative, Paternalism*, 231–35; Lau, *Democracy Rising*, 176–77; Chamberlain, "'And a Child Shall.'"

86. Fairclough, *Class of Their Own*, 309–10, 345–49; Charron, *Freedom's Teacher*, 154–56; Baker, *Paradoxes of Desegregation*, 54–56; Bolton, *Hardest Deal of All*, 45–60; Hale, "Development of Power," 444–59.

87. "NAACP Geared," 12; "School Board to Delay," 1; "Va. Pupils' Strike," 1–2; "Desegregation Move Started," B-4; Kluger, *Simple Justice*, 467–80. For a full account of the Prince Edward County school closure, see Bonastia, *Southern Stalemate*; Titus, *Brown's Battleground*; B. Smith, *They Closed Their Schools*; Tushnet, " Strategy of Delay," 105–37; K. M. Turner, "Both Victors and Victims," 1669–700; Hoose, *Claudette Colvin*, 25, 44–45 (quotation on 25); "Negro Guilty of Violation," 7-A; Theoharis, *Rebellious Life*, 31–33, 53–54; Levine, *Freedom's Children*, 22–25; Parks and Haskin, *Rosa Parks*, 111–12; Robinson, *Montgomery Bus Boycott*, 42–43; "Before Rosa Parks."

88. Harvey Gantt, interview with the author, November 28, 2011; Hale, "Fight Was Instilled in Us," 23; Lau, *Democracy Rising*, 216–17; Charles McDew, interview with Katherine Shannon, August 24, 1967, Civil Rights Documentation Project, Moorland Spingarn Research Center, Howard University (transcript in possession of author, courtesy of Joellen ElBashir); Charles McDew, interview with Katherine Shannon, August 24, 1967, Civil Rights Documentation Project, Moorland Spingarn Research Center, Howard University (transcript in possession of author, courtesy of Joellen ElBashir), 76; Dave Dennis, interview with the author, October 25, 2011 (quotation); Dittmer, *Local People*, 110; Huntly and McKerley, *Foot Soldiers for Democracy*.

89. Malcolm X quoted in Handler, "Malcolm X Terms"; Young, "Day We Went," *Friends* (February 9, 1964), Southern Christian Leadership Conference (SCLC) collection, Box 135, Folder 26, "Young—"Teens on the March in Birmingham—1964,'" King Center, Atlanta, GA; Branch, *Parting the Waters*, 180–87; Charles McDew, interview with Katherine Shannon, August 24, 1967, Civil Rights Documentation Project, Moorland Spingarn Research Center, Howard University (transcript in possession of author, courtesy of Joellen ElBashir), 76; Dave Dennis, interview with the author, October 25, 2011 (quotation); Dittmer, *Local People*, 110.

90. Delmont, "Thomas L. Bynum," 936; Baumgartner, "Searching for Sarah," 73–85; Steele and Hyres, "Reimagining the High School"; V. P. Franklin. "Documenting the Contributions," 663–71; J. D. Smith, "High School Newspapers," 843–62.

91. Bynum, *NAACP Youth*, 1–3.

92. Hale, *Freedom Schools*.

Chapter 1

1. R. Wright, *Black Boy*, 196.

2. R. Wright, *Black Boy*, 178–79; Fabre, *Unfinished Quest*, 46–47.

3. R. Wright, *Black Boy*, 182–87; Fabre, *Unfinished Quest*, 48–55; M. Walker, *Richard Wright*, 28–30, 48–50.

4. R. Wright, *Black Boy*, 192–97; Fabre, *Unfinished Quest*, 52–56; M. Walker, *Richard Wright*, 28–31.

5. R. Wright, *Black Boy*, 62–65.

6. R. Wright, *Black Boy*, 82–83; Fabre, *Unfinished Quest of Richard Wright*, 25–26; M. Walker, *Richard Wright*, 25. On violence faced by children and adolescents in the nineteenth and twentieth centuries, see W. King, *African American Childhoods*.

7. Ritterhouse, *Growing Up Jim Crow*, 3–6.

8. R. Wright, *Black Boy*, 83.

9. Reynolds, *Maintaining Segregation*, 2–10, 44–45.

10. Carrigan, *Making of a Lynching*, 1–7; Bernstein, *First Waco Horror*, 87–114; "Punished a Horror," 10; Du Bois, "The Waco Horror," 1–3; "Mob Lynches Negro Boy"; "Monday Nights Crime," *Nashville Banner*, December 16, 1924, and "$5,000 Reward for Arrest of Mob Offered," *Nashville Tennessean*, December 17, 1924, Papers of the NAACP, Part 07: The Anti-Lynching Campaign, 1912–1955, Series A: Anti-Lynching Investigative Files, 1912–1953, Folder 001527-017-1012.

11. R. Wright, *Black Boy*, 84.

12. Ritterhouse, *Growing Up Jim Crow*; de Schweinitz, *If We Could Change*; Reynolds, *Maintaining Segregation*; DuRocher, *Raising Racists*; Capshaw, *Civil Rights Childhood*.

13. Dr. Horace Huntley interview with Carrie Delores Hamilton Lock, October 18, 1995, Birmingham Civil Rights Institute, Oral History Project, Vol. 10; Huntley and McKerley, *Foot Soldiers for Democracy*, 200–207.

14. Hines, "Rape and the Inner Lives," 914–15.

15. See Geoff K. Ward, "Rewriting the Racial Contract," 127–232.

16. S. M. Franklin, *After the Rebellion*, 49–50.

17. R. Wright, *Black Boy*, 193–94.

18. R. Wright, *Black Boy*, 193, 195.

19. Wright does not allude to it, but Michel Fabre suggests a compromise was reached when Lanier relented to the Wright's talk after he removed incendiary passages of it, Fabre, *Unfinished Quest*, 54.

20. J. D. Anderson, *Education of Blacks*; H. A. Williams, *Self-Taught*; Span, *From Cotton Field*; Foner, *Reconstruction*, 96–99. Du Bois, *Black Reconstruction*, 638; Lynch, *Facts of Reconstruction*, 34.

21. Sewell and Dwight, *Mississippi Black History Makers*, 48–49; "Historical Research Project," in File 10708, "Source Material for Mississippi History, Hinds

County," Folder "Education, Negro," Mississippi Department of Archives and History.

22. "Historical Research Project," in File 10708, "Source Material for Mississippi History, Hinds County," Folder "Education, Negro"; Bolton, *Hardest Deal of All*, 36–37; Flucker and Savage, *African Americans in Jackson*, 24.

23. "Historical Research Project," in File 10708, "Source Material for Mississippi History, Hinds County," Folder "Education, Negro"; Bolton, *Hardest Deal of All*, 36–37; "Lanier High School Awarded $500,000 Grant," January 30, 2014, Jackson Public Schools, in Lanier High School Subject File, MDAH; *The Lanier High School* (Jackson, MS, 1951–1952), 4–5, in Lanier High School Subject File, MDAH; Flucker and Savage, *African Americans of Jackson*, 23.

24. V. S. Walker, *Lost Education*, 153.

25. Fass, "What Mother Needs," 86–124; Kett, *Rites of Passage*, 185–89, 211, 229–30; Zelizer, *Pricing the Priceless Child*, 34–36.

26. Drago, *Initiative, Paternalism, and Race*, 227–29; H. Kwon, "Unveiling History."

27. "Subject: Junior Division, February 24, 1925," in NAACP Papers, Part 19, Series A, Reel 1, Frame 42; College chapter list, in NAACP Papers, Part 19, Series A, Reel 1, Frames 36–37; "Chapters Already Established," in NAACP Papers, Part 19, Series A, Reel 1, Frame 2.

28. For a thorough and impressive examination of the legal context and social experiences of out-of-state study programs in which southern states subsidized the education of Black students who studied outside the south, see Jordan-Taylor, "'I'm Not Autherine Lucy'"; W. C. Hines, *South Carolina State University*, 195; Sanders, "Deferred Dreams and Exiled Citizens."

29. Counts, *New Social Order?*, 40, 43; Cremin, *Transformation of the School*, 224–34. For a broader history of Counts and the radical progressives, see Gutek, *Educational Theory of George S. Counts*; Gutek, *George S. Counts and American Civilization*.

30. R. Scott Baker provides outstanding analysis of activism embedded at Burke High School and the ideology around it, see Baker, "Pedagogies of Protest," 2777–803; on education of Black teachers during the 1930s see Fairclough, *Class of Their Own*, 339–40; V. S. Walker, *Their Highest Potential*, 26–27. Dr. Clinton Irving Young, who served as principal during the time the Kress sit-in, is emblematic of the well-educated Black administrators who led institutions during the last decade of segregation. He held degrees in education from the Teachers College and Columbia University and Wilberforce University in Ohio. The 1959 Bulldog (Burke High School Yearbook) in Lois A. Simms Papers, Box 2, Folder 23, "Burke High School Yearbook, 1959," Avery Research Center. Dr. Eugene Hunt completed graduate school courses at the University of Chicago and Northwestern University, "Vita Sheet, Eugene C. Hunt," in Eugene Hunt Collection, Box 1, Folder 1, "Vita," Avery Research Center; Dr. Dannetta K. Thornton Owens, Interview with the author, March 2, 2016; Beulah Russell, interview with the author, January 11, 2016.

31. Historian Adam Fairclough estimated that by 1928 over 23,000 educators, which was over one-half of all teachers in Black schools enrolled in courses during

summer sessions. Fairclough, *Class of Their Own*, 319–20; Ogren, "Out-of-Class Project," 22–23; Fultz, "Determination and Persistence," 4–34.

32. Du Bois, "Does the Negro," 328–35; Jelks, *Benjamin Elijah Hays*; Charron, *Freedom's Teacher*; Alridge, *Educational Thought*.

33. Givens, *Fugitive Pedagog*.

34. Dr. John Hope quoted in, *A Year Book on Negro Education in Alabama in 1930–1931*, p. 77 in ASTA Collection, Box 15, Folder 52, "Articles, News Clippings, Pamphlets, Certificates," Alabama State University archives.

35. Woodson, "Negro History Week," 57; Fairclough, *Class of Their Own*, 321; Givens, *Fugitive Pedagogy*.

36. C. J. Cunningham, "Education for a Changing Civilization," "Mankind at the Cross-roads," and "Meaning of a Liberal Education," in Charles J. Cunningham Papers, Box 1, Folder 3, "Class Papers/Notes 1933, n.d.," MDAH. This education was supplemented with East, *Mankind at the Crossroads*; Martin, *Meaning of a Liberal*; Kilpatrick, *Education for a Changing*.

37. C. J. Cunningham, "Meaning of Education," in Charles J. Cunningham Papers, Box 1, Folder 4, "Compositions, 1932–1933; n.d.," MDAH.

38. Hale, "'It Only Takes a Spark'"; Lois Simms, interview with the author, December 5, 2011; L. A. Simms, "A Comparative Study of Provisions for the Education of Negro and White Pupils in the Public Schools of South Carolina," in Lois A. Simms Papers, Box 1, Folder 12, "Biographical Records: Academic Work, Howard University," Avery Research Center; Simms, *Chalk and Chalkboard Career*, 26–27, 33. The Avery Normal Institute benefitted from the mission of the American Missionary Association, see Richardson, Jones, and Martin, *Education for Liberation*, 29–45; for a full history on the Avery Normal Institute, see Drago, *Initiative, Paternalism*.

39. *Mississippi Educational Journal: A Monthly Magazine for Teachers in Colored Schools*, Vol. xi, October 1934, No. 1; the national shift toward educators embracing Progressive pedagogy during the interwar period, see Cuban, "Rural and Urban Schools," 115–48.

40. W. A. Walter, "Why Limit the Study," 88–89; Fairclough, *Teaching Equality*, 43–44.

41. Eugene Hunt, "Burke High School Teaching Materials," in Eugene Hunt Collection, Box 3, Folder 2, Avery Research Center; Mrs. Lois Simms, interview with the author, December 5, 2011; see also Simms, *Chalk and Chalkboard Career*. The Avery Normal Institute benefited from the mission of the American Missionary Association, see Richardson, Jones, and Martin, *Education for Liberation*, 29–45; for a full history on the Avery Normal Institute, see Drago, *Initiative, Paternalism, and Race Relations*; L. A. Simms, "Assignments for English II and III," in Lois A. Simms Papers, Box 2, Folder 20, "Plan Books for English and History, 1956–1957 and 1959–1960," Avery Research Center; for a contextual description of John Dewey, Progressive Education, and the impact on black educators, including teachers at Avery and Burke, see Baker, "Pedagogies of Protest," 2785–88; teaching government and the electoral process was a common pedagogical practice, see V. S. Walker, *Lost Education*, 152–54.

42. Kridel, *Progressive Education*, 2–19.

43. de Schweinitz, *If We Could Change*; Bynum, *NAACP Youth*; see also Sullivan, *Lift Every Voice*, 60–72; Finch, *NAACP*; Janken, *White*.

44. Hale "Future Foot Soldiers?," 615–52.

45. de Schweinitz, *If We Could Change*, 7–10; Sullivan, *Lift Every Voice*, 145–47.

46. Juanita Jackson, "The NAACP Challenges Youth," Part 19, Series A, Reel 2, Frame 0005–6.

47. Robert Bagnall to Mr. C. H. Maxon, February 14, 1923, Part 19, Series A, Reel 1, Frame 31; Madison Jones, the Youth Director in 1942, claimed that youth organization occurred much earlier. 1922 report cited in "Statement to the Board of Directors Regarding the Youth Work of the Association," Part 19 Series C Reel 11, Frame 863; "Subject: Junior Division, February 24, 1925," in NAACP Papers, Part 19, Series A, Reel 1, Frame 42; College Chapter List, NAACP Papers, Part 19, Series A, Reel 1, Frames 36–37; "Chapters Already Established," NAACP Papers, Part 19, Series A, Reel 1, Frame 2; de Schweinitz, *If We Could Change*, 160–63; Bynum, *NAACP Youth*, 1–5.

48. "Assistant Director of Branches to Harry Burleigh, June 21, 1921," and "Maud Cuney Hare to Catherine Lealted," June 24, 1921, in NAACP Papers, Part 19, Series A, Reel 1, Frames 36–37; "Chairman to Pearl Flagg," October 20, 1919, "How to Form a Junior Division [1925]," Part 19, Series A, Reel 1, Frames 3–4.

49. "Subject: Junior Division, February 24, 1925," in NAACP Papers, Part 19, Series A, Reel 1, Frame 42; Robert Bengall, "To the Junior Divisions," August 5, 1926, in NAACP Papers, Part 19, Series A, Reel 1, Frame 44.

50. "Subject: Junior Division, February 24, 1925," in NAACP Papers, Part 19, Series A, Reel 1, Frame 42; College Chapter List, in NAACP Papers, Part 19, Series A, Reel 1, Frames 36–37; "Chapters Already Established," Part 19, Series A, Reel 1, Frame 2.

51. Constitution of the Youth Division of the NAACP, in NAACP Papers, Part 19, Series A, Reel 1, Frame 0016.

52. From this point forward, "Youth Councils" were largely ascribed to high school youth. "Resources in Negro Youth," in NAACP Papers, Part 19, Series C, Reel 9, pp. 7–8; Bynum, "We Must March Forward," 491.

53. NAACP Papers, Part 19, Series A, Frames 915–916; NAACP Papers, Part 19, Series A, Reel 2, Frame 19. To further strengthen the tie between education and the NAACP, the largest percentage of young people polled expressed a desire to enter the teaching profession more than any other occupation.

54. "Memorandum from Mr. White," in NAACP Papers, Part 19, Series A, Reel 1, Frame 50.

55. "General Sessions for Youth Section N.A.A.C.P. Conference" (1936), in NAACP Papers Part 19, Series A, Reel 2, Frames 0018–0019.

56. "General Sessions for Youth Section N.A.A.C.P. Conference" (1936), Part 19, Series A, Reel 2, Frames 0018–0019. For more information see Bynum, "'We Must March Forward'"; V. P. Franklin, "Documenting the Contributions," 664–65.

57. Bynum, "'We Must March Forward!,'" 488–89; Bynum, *NAACP Youth*, 3–4.

58. "Resources in Negro Youth," p. 8; in NAACP Papers, Part 19, Series C, Reel 9, Frames 782–801; Finch, *NAACP*, 76–77; de Schweinitz, *If We Could Change*, 163–65; Juanita Jackson quoted in, "'We Must March Forward,'" 490.

59. "For the Full Emancipation of the American Negro," in NAACP Papers, Part 19, Series A, Reel 1, Frame 66.

60. "Appendix I, Objectives of Youth Council," in NAACP Papers, Part 19, Series A, Reel 1, Frame 66.

61. Juanita Jackson "The NAACP Challenges Youth," Part 19, Series A, Reel 2, Frame 0002.

62. "General Sessions for Youth Section N.A.A.C.P. Conference" (1936), Part 19, Series A, Reel 2, Frame 0018.

63. "General Sessions for Youth Section N.A.A.C.P. Conference" (1936), Part 19, Series A, Reel 2, Frame 0224.

64. "General Sessions for Youth Section N.A.A.C.P. Conference" (1936), Part 19, Series A, Reel 2, Frames 0026–0027.

65. "Appendix II Suggestions for Program Activities," Part 19, Series A, Reel 1, Frame 73.

66. "Appendix II Suggestions for Program Activities," Part 19, Series A, Reel 1, Frame 73; Appendix I Suggestions for Program Activities, Part 19, Series A, Reel 1, Frame 70; "N.A.A.C.P. Youth March Forward! National Youth Program, September 1936–June 1937," in NAACP Papers, Part 19, Series 1, Reel 1, Frame 82–83; On the NAACP records on youth and antilynching demonstrations, see Part 19, Series A; see also Bynum, *NAACP Youth*, 6–9.

67. Appendix I Suggestions for Program Activities, Part 19, Series A, Reel 1, Frame 70.

68. Appendix I Suggestions for Program Activities, Part 19, Series A, Reel 1, Frame 70.

69. "National Youth Program, 1938–1939," in NAACP Papers, Series A, Reel 1, Frame 170; Bynum, *NAACP Youth and the Fight for Black Freedom*, 5–8.

70. "N.A.A.C.P. Youth March Forward! National Youth Program, September 1936–June 1937," in NAACP Papers, Part 19, Series 1, Reel 1, Frame 82–83.

71. "Program," Part 19, Series A, Frames 0923–0924; "General Sessions for Youth Section N.A.A.C.P. Conference" (1936), Part 19, Series A, Reel 2, Frame 0021; Juanita Jackson to youth delegates, June 16, 1934, Part 19, Series A, Reel 1, Frame 834.

72. Baltimore Youth Conference Discussion Questions, Part 19 Series A, Reel 1, 912.

73. "A Pledge for Youth," Part 19 Series A, Reel 1, 970.

74. Baltimore Youth Conference Summary, Part 19 Series A, Reel 1, 917–18.

75. Baltimore Youth Conference Summary, Part 19 Series A, Reel 1, 919.

76. "Resources in Negro Youth," p. 7, in NAACP Papers, Part 19, Series C, Reel 9, Frames 782–801.

77. "Resources in Negro Youth," p. 7, in NAACP Papers, Part 19, Series C, Reel 9, Frames 782–801; "Statement to the Board of Directors Regarding the Youth Work of the Association," Part 19 Series C Reel 11, Frame 863. In 1940 Madison Jones cites

53 Youth Councils and 14 college chapters, "Proposed Report of the Youth Director for the 1941 Annual Report," Part 19, Series C, Reel 11, Frame 814. The initial report of 300 Youth Councils inaccurate compared to the Youth Director reports of 1942, which cite 1940 as the peak of youth membership with 133 Youth Councils, "Statement to the Board of Directors Regarding the Youth Work of the Association," Part 19 Series C Reel 11, Frame 863. Discrepancies due to a lack of a definitive number of Youth Councils indicate that membership in the association was a regular issue. In the South, there were less than 400 NAACP members in 1916. In the 1940s the NAACP counted only 83 Youth Councils, 49 organization committees, and 23 college chapters. For a full history of the NAACP and its development of legal strategy, internal conflict, and the growing national prominence of the country's most notable civil rights organization, see Sullivan, *Lift Every Voice*, 60–72; Finch, *The NAACP*; Bynum, *NAACP Youth*.

78. "For the Full Emancipation of the American Negro," in NAACP Papers, Part 19, Series A, Reel 1, Frame 66.

79. "Handbook for Officers of Youth Councils," in NAACP Papers, Part 19, Series C, Reel 1, Frames 52–55.

80. de Schweinitz, *If We Could Change*, 11–24.

81. See, de Schweinitz, *If We Could Change*, 17.

82. de Schweinitz, *If We Could Change*, 19–21.

83. Meir Muller, et al. "Another 100 Years?"; de Schweinitz, *If We Could Change*, 16–18.

84. U.S. Department of Commerce, *Statistical Abstract of the United States, 1930*, 108–15; U.S. Department of Commerce, *Statistical Abstract of the United States, 1940*, 112–13; de Schweinitz, *If We Could Change*, 29–35, 228. The number of Black high school youth was significantly lower and, often, was not even provided for. In Mississippi, by 1940, still only 5 percent of children attended high school, see C. Thompson, *The History of the Mississippi*, 17; Graham, *Young Activists*; Anderson, "Black Public High School," 236–37; Krug, *Shaping of the American*, 301, 307–14; Mintz, *Huck's Raft*, 238–39.

85. de Schweinitz, "Holding on to the 'Chosen Generation,'" 297.

86. Walter White memorandum on Junior Branches, May 12, 1923, in NAACP Papers, Part 19, Series A, Reel 1, Frames 32–33.

87. Walther White memorandum on Junior Branches, May 12, 1923, in NAACP Papers, Part 19, Series A, Reel 1, Frames 32–33.

88. On the history of the National Negro Congress, see Gelman, *Death Blow*.

89. "Our National Secretary" E.E. Strong" in *Congress Vue v 1 no. 2 May 1943* in Edward E. Strong Papers, Box 2, Folder "Writings about Edward E. Strong," HU; Gelman, *Death Blow*, 13–17, 69–71; S. M. Franklin, *After the Rebellion*, 53–55; Haviland, *James and Esther Cooper Jackson*, 36–37; Kelley, *Hammer and Hoes*, 200–201.

90. Strong quoted in Gelman, *Death Blow*, 71.

91. "Cast Your Vote for Youth in 1940," in Edward E. Strong Papers, Box 3, Folder "Southern Negro Youth Congress All-Southern Negro Youth Conferences, New Orleans, 1940," HU.

92. New Orleans Conference Highlights and Delegates Backgrounds, in Edward E. Strong Papers, Box 3, Folder "Southern Negro Youth Congress All-Southern Negro Youth Conferences, New Orleans, 1940," HU.

93. "Minutes of the Executive Board of the Southern Negro Youth Congress, March 29–30, 1947," in SNYC Papers, Box 1, Folder Executive Board 1947, HU.

94. "SNYC Constitution," in SNYC Papers, Box 1, Folder "SNYC Constitution," HU; "Southern Negro Youth Congress, How We are Organized, Manual of Organization, 1947," in SNYC Papers, Box 1, Folder "SNYC Manual of Organization, 1947," HU.

95. Draft Constitution of SNYC Edward E. Strong Papers, Box 3, Folder "Southern Negro Youth Congress—Draft Constitution," HU; S. M. Franklin, *After the Rebellion*, 61–62.

96. "The Southern Negro Youth Congress," in Edward E. Strong Papers, Box 3, Folder "Southern Negro Youth Congress—Histories," HU.

97. Draft Constitution of SNYC, in Edward E. Strong Papers, Box 3, Folder "Southern Negro Youth Congress—Draft Constitution," HU.

98. "Southern Negro Youth Congress" (a history), in Edward E. Strong Papers, Box 3, Folder "Southern Negro Youth Congress—Histories," HU.

99. SNYC minutes, Birmingham, December 4, 1946, in SNYC Papers, Box 1, Folder Membership Committee 1946–1947.

100. SNYC, "Southern Negro Youth Congress College Program," and "S.N.Y.C. High School Program," in Manual of Organization, 1947, SNYC Papers, Box 1, Folder "SNYC Manual of Organization, 1947," HU.

101. "Souvenir Program of the 2nd All-Southern Negro Youth Congress," in SNYC Papers, Box 6, Folder "2nd conference 1938," HU; "Souvenir Bulletin of the Southern Negro Youth Conference," in SNYC Papers, Box 6, Folder "1st Conference 1937," HU; "Third All-Southern Negro Youth Congress," in SNYC Papers, Box 6, Folder "3rd Conference," HU.

102. "Aptheker Address," in SNYC Papers, Box 6, Folder "1939 SNYC 3rd Conference," HU.

103. "Edward Strong to Rev. James Robinson, June 20, 1940," in SNYC Papers, Box 9, Folder "NAACP," HU.

104. "NAACP Youth gin Annual Conference," *August Bulletin, 1939,* Vol. 1, #2, and "NAACP Students," in *Southern Negro Youth Congress Bulletin,* January 1943, in SNYC Papers, Box 8, Folder "Monthly Bulletin," HU.

105. "The Southern Negro Youth Congress" in Edward E. Strong Papers, Box 3, Folder "Southern Negro Youth Congress—Histories," HU.

106. "Edward Strong to Rev. James Robinson, June 20, 1940," in SNYC Papers, Box 9, Folder "NAACP," HU.

107. "Walter White to Edward E. Strong, December 14, 1939," and "Edward Strong to Walter White, February 1, 1940," in SNYC Papers, Box 9, Folder "NAACP," HU.

108. "The Southern Negro Youth Congress," in Edward E. Strong Papers, Box 3, Folder "Southern Negro Youth Congress—Histories," HU; Kelley, *Hammer and Hoes,* 202–8.

109. William F. Richardson, quoted in "Greetings from the National Chairman" in "Souvenir Program of the 2nd All-Southern Negro Youth Congress," in SNYC Papers, Box 6, Folder "2nd conference 1938," HU; Gelman, *Death Blow*, 64–71; Southern Negro Youth Congress, "How We Are Organized, Manual of Organization, 1947" in SNYC Papers, Box 1, Folder "SNYC Manual of Organization, 1947," HU; Florence Castile to Johnnie Moore, October 10, 1947, in SNYC Papers, Box 5, Folder "Tuskegee, AL," HU; Lewis, Hash, and Laeb, *Red Activists*; E. Jackson, *This Is My Husband*.

110. "The Southern Negro Youth Congress," in Edward E. Strong Papers, Box 3, Folder "Southern Negro Youth Congress—Histories," HU.

111. "The Southern Negro Youth Congress" in Edward E. Strong Papers, Box 3, Folder "Southern Negro Youth Congress—Histories," HU; S. M. Franklin, *After the Rebellion*, 66–67.

112. "SNYC Constitution" in SNYC Papers, Box 1, Folder "SNYC Constitution," HU; Southern Negro Youth Congress, "How We Are Organized, Manual of Organization, 1947," in SNYC papers, Box 1, Folder "SNYC Manual of Organization, 1947," HU.

113. Gelman, *Death Blow*, 2–15.

114. *SNYC August Bulletin, 1939*, Vol. 1, #2, in SNYC Papers, Box 8, Folder "Monthly Bulletin," HU.

115. "Spotlight on New Orleans," *August Bulletin, 1939*, Vol. 1, #2, in SNYC Papers, Box 8, Folder "Monthly Bulletin," HU; "Birmingham Report, July 1944," "Birmingham Report, June 1944," in SNYC Papers, Box 8, Folder "Monthly Summary of Race Relations," HU; "Labor Union's Aid Asked by Youth Group," *Chicago Defender* November 9, 1940, in Edward E. Strong Papers, Box 2, Folder "Writings about Edward E. Strong," HU; "Our National Secretary" E. E. Strong" in *Congress Vue v 1 no. 2 May 1943* in Edward E. Strong Papers, Box 2, Folder "Writings about Edward E. Strong," HU.

"Southern Negro Youth Congress" (a history), in Edward E. Strong Papers, Box 3, Folder "Southern Negro Youth Congress—Histories," HU; Gelman, *Death Blow*, 15–16, 83–84.

116. SNYC Papers, Box 6, Folder "3rd Conference 1939 Registration Forms," HU; Haviland, *James and Esther Cooper*, 38–39.

117. "Inez McAdams, 20, Application," "Florence J. Valentine, 20, Application," "Hazel P. Tucker, 24, Application," "Weaton, 25, Application" "Miriam L. Mateer [?], 19," "Frank J. Hutchings, Jr., 22," "Emmett Reed, 24, Application" in SNYC Papers, Box 2, Folder "3rd Leadership Training School 1946," HU.

118. "Fall Program," and "Spotlight on New Orleans," *August Bulletin, 1939*, Vol. 1, #2, in SNYC Papers, Box 8, Folder "Monthly Bulletin" HU; "What Is the Southern Negro Youth Congress?" in SNYC Papers, Box 8, Folder "What Is the SNYC?," HU.

119. Draft Constitution of SNYC, in Edward E. Strong Papers, Box 3, Folder "Southern Negro Youth Congress—Draft Constitution," HU.

120. Edward Strong, "Negro Youth and the Fight for Freedom and Opportunity" in *Official Proceedings, Second National Negro Congress, 1937*, in Edward E. Strong Papers, Box 1, Folder "Writings by Edward E. Strong—Negro Youth and the Fight for Freedom and Opportunity, Oct. 1937," HU.

121. Gelman, *Death Blow*, 116–20.

122. Bynum, *NAACP Youth and the Fight for Black Freedom*, 10–11, 20–21.

123. "What Is the Southern Negro Youth Congress?" SNYC Papers, Box 8, Folder "What Is the SNYC?," HU.

124. "How Much More Policy Tyranny in Jefferson County?" in Edward E. Strong Papers, Box 3, Folder "Southern Negro Youth Congress—Fliers, Notices," HU; Kelley, *Hammer and Hoes*, 216–17.

125. SNYC, "South Negro Youth Congress College Program," and "S.N.Y.C. High School Program," in "Manual of Organization, 1947," in SNYC Papers, Box 1, Folder "SNYC Manual of Organization, 1947," HU.

126. "Citizenship Campaign," *August Bulletin, 1939*, Vol. 1, #2, in SNYC Papers, Box 8, Folder "Monthly Bulletin," HU; Kelley, *Hammer and Hoes*, 212–14.

127. "Resolutions," Part 19, Series A, Reel 1, 969.

128. "N.A.A.C.P. Youth March Forward! National Youth Program, September 1936–June 1937," NAACP Papers, Part 19, Series 1, Reel 1, Frame 82–83.

129. Draft Constitution of SNYC, in Edward E. Strong Papers, Box 3, Folder "Southern Negro Youth Congress—Draft Constitution," HU.

130. "Southern Negro Youth Congress" (a history), in Edward E. Strong Papers, Box 3, Folder "Southern Negro Youth Congress—Histories," HU.

131. "The Southern Negro Youth Congress," in Edward E. Strong Papers, Box 3, Folder "Southern Negro Youth Congress—Histories," HU.

132. "Outline for Panel Discussion" December 2, 1944, in SNYC Papers, Box 6, Folder "6th Conference," HU.

133. "Textbook Survey for Youth Councils," Part 19, Series A, Reel 1, Frame 0169.

134. William Pickens to Branch Officers, February 17, 1938, in NAACP Papers, Part 19, Series A, Reel 1, Frame 0161; "Textbook Survey for Youth Councils," Part 19, Series A, Reel 1, Frame 0169; on William Pickens see Pickens, *Heir of Slaves*.

135. "Textbook Survey for Youth Councils," Part 19, Series A, Reel 1, Frame 0169.

136. William Pickens to Branch Officers, February 17, 1938, in NAACP Papers, Part 19, Series A, Reel 1, Frame 0161; "Textbook Survey for Youth Councils," Part 19, Series A, Reel 1, Frame 0169.

137. Bynum, *NAACP Youth and the Fight for Black Freedom*, 10–12. "Textbook Survey," in NAACP Papers, Part 19 Series 1, Reel 1.

138. Fairclough, *Class of Their Own*, 312.

139. Woodson, "Negro History Week," 57; Fairclough, *Class of Their Own*, 320–22.

140. Perry, *History of the American*, 199–201.

141. Mississippi Educational Advance, *Mississippi Educational Journal: A Monthly Magazine for Teachers in Colored Schools*, v. 18, p. 74–76, MDAH.

142. Walter, "Why Limit the Study," 88–89; Fairclough, *Teaching Equality*, 43–44.

143. "Third All-Southern Negro Youth Congress," in SNYC Papers, Box 6, Folder "3rd Conference," HU.

144. "Building Character."

145. Peguese, "Negro Achievement Week."

146. Quoted in Kelley, *Hammer and Hoe*, 202.

147. "Subject: Junior Division, February 24, 1925," in NAACP Papers, Part 19, Series A, Reel 1, Frame 42.

148. Appendix II Suggestions for Program Activities, Part 19, Series A, Reel 1, Frame 73.

149. "Constitution for Youth Councils," Part 19, Series B, Reel 10, Frame 428.

150. Juanita Jackson, "The NAACP Challenges Youth," Part 19, Series A, Reel 2, Frame 0002.

151. Juanita Jackson, "The NAACP Challenges Youth," Part 19, Series A, Reel 2, Frame 0005–6.

152. Juanita Jackson, "The NAACP Challenges Youth," Part 19, Series A, Reel 2, Frame 0005–6.

153. "Cast Your Vote for Youth in 1940," in Edward E. Strong Papers, Box 3, Folder "Southern Negro Youth Congress All-Southern Negro Youth Conferences, New Orleans, 1940," HU.

154. Draft Constitution of SNYC, in Edward E. Strong Papers, Box 3, Folder "Southern Negro Youth Congress—Draft Constitution," HU.

155. Edward Strong, "Negro Youth and the Fight for Freedom and Opportunity," in *Official Proceedings, Second National Negro Congress, 1937*, in Edward E. Strong Papers, Box 1, Folder "Writings by Edward E. Strong—Negro Youth and the Fight for Freedom and Opportunity, Oct. 1937," HU.

Chapter 2

1. "Leroy Aiken to Louis Burnham, December 9, 1946," in SNYC Papers, Box 5, Folder "Moncks Corner, SC," HU.

2. Burton, Burton, and Appleford, "Seeds in Unlikely Soil," 176–96; Baker, *Paradoxes of Desegregation*, 87–107.

3. Booker T. Washington High School, *Washingtonian*, 35, 40, 46.

4. "Leroy Aiken to Louis Burnham, December 9, 1946," in SNYC Papers, Box 5, Folder "Moncks Corner, SC," HU; "The Berkeley Wildcat," in SNYC Papers, Box 5, Folder "Moncks Corner, SC," HU; "Berkeley Council SNYC Educational Institute, Feb. 15–16, 1947," and "Summary of SNYC Institute Held in Berkeley County," in SNYC Papers, Box 5, Folder "Moncks Corner, SC," HU; Lau, *Democracy Rising*, 163–64; Gelman, *Death Blow*, 228–35; S. M. Franklin, *After the Rebellion*, 59–60.

5. U.S. Department of Commerce, *Statistical Abstract 1930*, 108–15; U.S. Department of Commerce, *Statistical Abstract 1940*, 112–13; de Schweinitz, *If We Could Change*, 29–35, 228; Mintz, *Huck's Raft*, 238–39; Kett, *Rites of Passage*, 245; Rury and Hill, *African American Struggle*, 2–5.

6. U.S. Department of Commerce, *Statistical Abstract, 1930*, 108–15; U.S. Department of Commerce, *Statistical Abstract, 1940*, 112–13; de Schweinitz, *If We Could Change*, 29–35, 228; C. Thompson, *The History of the Mississippi*, 17; Graham, *Young Activists*; Anderson, "Black Public High School," 236–37; Krug, *Shaping of the American*, 301, 307–14; Mintz, *Huck's Raft*, 238–39.

7. Baker, *Paradoxes of Desegregation*, 89; Pierce, *White and Negro Schools*, 104–5.

8. Sullivan, *Lift Every Voice*, 60–72; Finch, *NAACP*; Bynum, *NAACP Youth, 1936–1965*; Janken, *White*; Gergel, *Unexampled Courage*; Fass, "All Our Children," 171–214.

9. V. P. Franklin, "Documenting the Contributions," 665; Thuesen, *Greater Than Equal*, 159–99; Herman Taylor to Thurgood Marshall, October 28, 1946; Ruby Hurley to Curtis Todd, October 31, 1946; Ruby Hurley to Lillian McQueen, October 17, 1946; Herman Taylor to Curtis Todd, November 11, 1946, in Papers of the NAACP, Part 03: The Campaign for Educational Equality, Series B: Legal Department and Central Office Records, 1940–1950 (ProQuest—NAACP Papers).

10. Devlin, *Girl Stands*, 69–85; "Aim New Blow," 1; Rivera Jr., "Parents Sue School Board," 1.

11. Devlin, *Girl Stands*, 73–74.

12. Devlin, *Girl Stands*, 69–85; "Aim New Blow," 1.

13. Devlin, *Girl Stands*, 80–82; "Parents Picke.," 2; Carper, "Steps Taken," 1.

14. Devlin, "Girls on the Front Line," 69–105.

15. Branch, *King Years*; Griswold del Castillo, *World War II*; Kruse and Tuck, *Fog of War*; Welky, *Marching across the Color Line*; Sullivan, "In the Shadow of War"; Dittmer, "We Return Fighting," 1–18; Williams, *Medgar Evers*, 22–36; Hall, "Long Civil Rights Movement," 1234–35. Hall also cites Bayard Rustin as someone who puts forth a "classical" phase of the civil rights movement from *Brown* through the Voting Rights Act of 1965, which has since become entrenched in our understandings of the movement, see Rustin, *Down the Line*, 111–22.

16. The lawsuit *Wrighten v. Board of Trustees of University of South Carolina* (1947) prompted the state to build a "separate but equal" law school at South Carolina State, Hines, *South Carolina State University*, 190–95; Drago, *Initiative, Paternalism*, 231–35; Lau, *Democracy Rising*, 176–77; Felder, "The Law School at South Carolina," 34–38; see also Battle and Franks, "Avery."

17. On the history of the Avery Normal Institute, see Drago, *Initiative, Paternalism*; Battle and Franks, "Avery."

18. Chamberlain, "'And a Child Shall Lead,'" 47–56; "Mayor Leland Speed," 1.

19. Drago, *Initiative, Paternalism*, 231–35; Lau, *Democracy Rising*, 176–77; Chamberlain, "'And a Child Shall Lead.'"

20. Hale, "'Fight Was Instilled,'" 15–21; Baker, "Pedagogies of Protest," 2777–803.

21. Baker, "Pedagogies of Protest," 2777–803; Kridel, *Progressive Education*, 2–22.

22. See Tushnet, "Campaign in the 1940s," 82–104; Fairclough, *Teaching Equality*; Kluger, *Simple Justice*; Sullivan, "In the Shadow."

23. Thompson, "Editorial Comment," 539–42.

24. Fairclough, "Teachers Organize," 309–53.

25. A. L. Johnson to Mr. A. J. Noel, January 14, 1948, and A. L. Johnson to James A. Burns, February 23, 1948, in Gladys Noel Bates Papers, Box 2, "Scrapbook, 1948–1960," MDAH. Similarly, organized educators in South Carolina within the Palmetto Education Association adopted aggressive stances on equalizing salaries and resources. See Potts, *History of the Palmetto*, 61–68; Baker, *Paradoxes of Desegregation*, 54–56; Charron, *Freedom's Teacher*, 163; Simms, *Chalk and Chalkboard Career*, 8–10; Drago, *Initiative, Paternalism*, 240–42.

26. Gladys Noel Bates, interview with Catherine Jannik, December 23, 1996, The University of Southern Mississippi Center for Oral History and Cultural Heritage; Bolton, *Hardest Deal of All*, 45–60; Edward S. Bishop Sr., interview with Charles Bolton, February 27, 1991; "Community in Which I Live," in Gladys Noel Bates Papers, Box 3, "Speeches and Papers, 1948, 1968, 1991–1992"; Robert L. Carter to A. L. Johnson, April 19, 1949, in Gladys Noel Bates Papers, Box 2, "Scrapbook, 1948–1960," MDAH.

27. Hale, "We Are Not Merging"; Hale, "Future Foot Soldiers."

28. Fairclough, "Teachers Organize"; Fairclough, *Race & Democracy*, 99–105.

29. Gladys Noel Bates, interview with Catherine Jannik, December 23, 1996, The University of Southern Mississippi Center for Oral History and Cultural Heritage; Bolton, *Hardest Deal of All*, 45–60; Edward S. Bishop Sr., interview with Charles Bolton, February 27, 1991; "Community in Which I Live" (Gladys Noel Bates Papers, Box 3, "Speeches and Papers, 1948, 1968, 1991–1992").

30. "Address Delivered at the Black Women's Political Action Forum, February 1, 1991, Jackson, MS" in Gladys Noel Bates Papers, Box 3, "Speeches and Papers, 1948, 1968, 1991–1992"; Gladys Noel Bates, "The Gladys Noel Bates Teacher-Equalization Pay Suit, May 16, 1992," in Box 3, "Speeches and Papers, 1948, 1968, 1991–1992," MDAH.

31. "Address Delivered at the Black Women's Political Action Forum, 1 February 1991, Jackson, MS" in Gladys Noel Bates Papers, Box 3, "Speeches and Papers, 1948, 1968, 1991–1992"; Gladys Noel Bates, "The Gladys Noel Bates Teacher-Equalization Pay Suit, 16 May 1992," in Box 3, "Speeches and Papers, 1948, 1968, 1991–1992," MDAH; Robert L. Carter to A. L. Johnson, 19 April 1949, in Gladys Noel Bates Papers, Box 2, "Scrapbook, 1948–1960," MDAH; Bolton, *Hardest Deal of All*, 46–49.

32. Lewis, *In Their Own Interests*, 157–61; Wilkerson, "Negro School Movement," 17–29.

33. Alston v. School Board of City of Norfolk, 112 F.2d 992 (4th Cir. 1940).

34. Baker, *Paradoxes of Desegregation*, 89; "Application by Jackson Municipal Separate School District," Series 1645, State Building Commission General Files, Box 6593, Folder "Hinds Country "Lanier High School," MDAH; "Report of the Survey of the Montgomery County School System (Montgomery: State of Alabama Department of Education, 1948), p. 111, 115 in Box 10, Education, Administrative & Financial Services, School System Surveys Marengo Co to Montgomery County (1948), ADAH; Jas. A Hope, "Report of the State Superintendent of Education, 1934," 30–31, South Caroliniana.

35. "Jessie Cade to John Brother Cade, October 13, 1943," Courtesy of John Brother Cade Papers, Box John B. Cade, 1947–1952, Folder "Jessie Lola Cade (Miss), 1941–1945," Archives and Manuscripts Department, John B. Cade Library, Southern University and A&M College, Baton Rouge, LA.

36. Prince Edward County School Board minutes, August 3, 1944, and October 5, 1944, January 4, 1945, Prince Edward County School Board District, Farmville, VA.

37. Prince Edward County School Board minutes, August 3, 1944, Prince Edward County School Board District, Farmville, VA.

38. Prince Edward County School Board minutes, June 28, 1945, July 5, 1948, August 1, 1945, December 6, 1945, May 2, 1946, September 5, 1946, April 3, 1947, May 1, 1947, December 4, 1947, Prince Edward County School Board District, Farmville, VA.

39. Prince Edward County School Board minutes, October 14, 1948, Prince Edward County School Board District, Farmville, VA.

40. Prince Edward County School Board minutes, November 3, 1949, December 12, 1950 March 2, 1950, April 6, 1950, and June 1, 1950, February 6, 1951 Prince Edward County School Board District, Farmville, VA; "New Negro School, Improvement to Farmville High School, Prospect Elementary School, Top Fund Needs," *Farmville Herald,* February 7, 1950 and "Board Members, Architect Study Negro School Plans," *Farmville Herald,* August 11, 1950, in "Farmville Herald School Closings: 1950–1955" Longwood University; B. Smith, *They Closed Their Schools,* 3–26.

41. "Savannah Organizes Largest Youth Council," "Trip of Youth Director," "1942 Banner Year," *NAACP Youth News Letter* December, 1942, in Papers of the NAACP, Part 19, Youth File, Series C; Group II Series E, Youth File, Youth newsletters, 1942–1943 (ProQuest); "Goal. . . . . 15,000 members," *Youth News Letter* (February 1944), NAACP Youth Papers, NAACP Papers, Part 19: Youth File, Series C: 1940–1955, Youth News Letters, 1944–1945 (ProQuest).

42. Franklin D. Roosevelt to Miss Esterh V. Cooper, in "Proceedings Sixth All-Southern Negro Youth Conference," in SNYC Papers, Box 6, Folder "5th Conference 1942," HU.

43. "Youth Work Boomed in 1943," *NAACP Bulletin*, Vol. 3, No. 2 (February 1944), P, 1, in Modjeska Simkins Papers, Topical Papers, University of South Carolina Digital Collection (http://library.sc.edu/p/Collections/Digital/Browse/Simkinspapers).

44. "Handbook for Officers of Youth Councils," in NAACP Papers, Part 19, Series C, Reel 1, Frames 52–55.

45. "Handbook for Officers of Youth Councils," in NAACP Papers, Part 19, Series C, Reel 1, Frames 52–55.

46. de Schweinitz, *If We Could Change*, 176–80; de Schweinitz, "Holding On," 293–98.

47. NAACP Papers, Part 19, Series C, Reel 9, "Membership and Committee Rules"; "The Youth News Letter," in NAACP Papers, Part 19, Series C, Reel 27, Frames 4–6. The newsletter extended the focus on children *The Crisis* adopted years earlier, de Schweinitz, *If We Could Change*, 157–59.

48. "Your Protest Needed," *Youth News Letter* (February 1944), in NAACP Youth Papers, Papers of the NAACP, Part 19: Youth File, Series C: 1940–1955, Youth News Letters, 1944–1945 (ProQuest).

49. Youth Work Boomed in 1943," *NAACP Bulletin,* Vol. 3, No. 2 (February 1944), P, 1, in Modjeska Simkins Papers, Topical Papers, University of South Carolina Digital Collection (http://library.sc.edu/p/Collections/Digital/Browse/Simkinspapers).

50. Bynum, *NAACP Youth*, 25–30, quote on p. 30.

51. "New Orleans Conference Highlights and Delegates Backgrounds," in Edward E. Strong Papers, Box 3, Folder "Southern Negro Youth Congress All-Southern Negro Youth Conferences, New Orleans, 1940," HU; Gelman, *Death Blow*, 225–26.

52. Letter from the New York Youth Committee for Concerned Peace Efforts, April 27, 1939, in NAACP Papers Part 19, Series A, Reel 1, 0189–0190.

53. Bynum, *NAACP Youth*, 30–31.

54. "Negro Youth Hold Meeting in Birmingham," October 3, 1940, in Edward E. Strong Papers, Box 2, Folder "Writings about Edward E. Strong," HU.

55. "Conscription and Negro Youth," *S.N.Y.C. News*, October 1940, in Edward E. Strong Papers, Box 2, Folder "Writings about Edward E. Strong," HU.

56. "Edward Strong to Rev. James Robinson, June 20, 1940," in SNYC Papers, Box 9, Folder "NAACP," HU.

57. "The Poll Tax Bill Must Pass," *Southern Negro Youth Congress Bulletin*, January 1943, in SNYC Papers, Box 8, Folder "Monthly Bulletin" HU.

58. NAACP Papers, Part 19, Series C, Reel 9, Frame 823; Sullivan, *Lift Every Voice*, 256–60.

59. "Fifth All-Southern Negro Youth Congress Statement of Principles," SNYC Papers, Box 6, Folder "5th Conference 1942" HU; "SNYC Monthly Bulletin, October 1944, vol. 8, no. 9," SNYC Papers, Box 8, Folder "Monthly Bulletin" HU.

60. Southern Negro Youth Congress Memorandum, in SNYC papers, Box 1, Folder Executive Board 1945, HU.

61. "The Southern Negro Youth Congress presents Miss Esther V. Cooper"; "The Southern Negro Youth Congress presents Esther Cooper Jackson and James E. Jackson, Jr." in SNYC Papers, Box 2, Folder "Press Info—Lectures of Esther and James Jackson," HU; see also Haviland, *James and Esther Cooper Jackson*; Gelman, *Death Blow*, 225–26.

62. "Legislative Statement of SNYC, 1947," in SNYC Papers, Box 7, Folder "8th Conference," HU.

63. "Louis E. Burnham to [Friend], April 15, 1946," in SNYC Papers, Box 5, Folder "Birmingham, Al," HU. International connections such as those fostered by the SNYC led the organization to the difficulty terrain of civil rights organization in the Cold War, see Mary L. Dudziak, *Cold War Civil Rights*.

64. Bever, "It Took 10 Minutes"; Pan, "Undying Mystery," Waters, "Resurrecting,"; Streib, *Death Penalty*, 107–10; Banner, "When Killing a Juvenile."

65. "Forget Me Not: George J. Stinney," *Monthly Bulletin*, July 1944, Vol. 8, No. 7, in SNYC Papers, Box 8, Folder "Monthly Bulletin," HU.

66. "Forget Me Not: George J. Stinney," *Monthly Bulletin*, July 1944, Vol. 8, No. 7, in SNYC Papers, Box 8, Folder "Monthly Bulletin," HU.

67. See Dudziak, *Cold War Civil Rights*.

68. "Parker High School Graduates," 406; Talk On "New Bill of Rights," 6-1-44 in "Parker High School—Ed & Sch-Pub-Bhm" vertical file, Linn-Henley Research Library, Birmingham, Alabama.

69. "Citizenship Education Clinic Notice" and "State Teachers College chapter of Student Negro Youth Congress to All Student Organizations and Societies," [undated], in SNYC Papers, Box 5, Folder "Montgomery, Al State College," HU.

70. Sullivan, *Lift Every Voice*, 360–63; "Birmingham Report, July 1944," and "Birmingham Report, June 1944," in SNYC Papers, Box 8, Folder "Monthly Summary of Race Relations," HU; "Summer Activities Hit New Peak," *S.N.Y.C. News*,

October 1940, in Edward E. Strong Papers, Box 2, Folder "Writings about Edward E. Strong," HU.

71. Southern Negro Youth Congress, Executive Board Meeting, Masonic Temple Building, Birmingham Alabama, February 10, 11, 1945, in SNYC Papers, Box 1, Folder Executive Board 1945, HU.

72. "Manual of Organization, 1947," in SNYC Papers, Box 1, Folder "SNYC Manual of Organization, 1947," HU.

73. "Executive Board Meeting, President's Report on Perspective of Political Climate, 1947" in SNYC Papers, Box 1, Folder "Minutes Executive Board Meeting, 1947, HU.

74. "Know Your Government: A Manual of Citizenship Education," in Edward E. Strong Papers, Box 4, Folder "Southern Negro Youth Congress—Manuals," HU.

75. Resolutions of SNYC, SNYC Papers, Box 7, Folder "7th Conference—Resolutions," HU.

76. Training was held in Atlanta in 1944. Inez Adams, school schedule, Box 2, Folder "3rd Leadership Training"; "SNYC Third Leadership Training School August 5–August 18," "Dorothy Burnham to Mr. Edgar Holt, July 10, 1946," "Dorothy C. Burnham to Students of Atlanta Seminar, June 26, 1946," in SNYC Papers, Box 2, Folder "3rd Leadership Training School 1946," HU.

77. "Columbia Pact of Southern Youth," in SNYC Papers, Box 7, Folder "Columbia Pact of Southern Youth," HU; Lau, *Democracy Rising*, 156–62.

78. "Manual of Organization, 1947," in SNYC Papers, Box 1, Folder "SNYC Manual of Organization, 1947," HU.

79. "Manual of Organization, 1947," in SNYC Papers, Box 1, Folder "SNYC Manual of Organization, 1947," HU; "Southern Negro Youth Congress" (a history), in Edward E. Strong Papers, Box 3, Folder "Southern Negro Youth Congress—Histories," HU. This resolution closely followed of the "Durham Declaration" witted after the Conference on Race Relations, see "Durham Declaration," in *Southern Negro Youth Congress Bulletin*, January 1943, in SNYC Papers, Box 8, Folder "Monthly Bulletin" HU; Resolutions of SNYC, SNYC Papers, Box 7, Folder "7th Conference—Resolutions," HU.

80. "Operation Civil Rights," in NAACP Papers, Part 19, Series C, Reel 1, Frame 251; the interaction of young people with Washington, D.C., politics is also signified by the 1950 White House Conference on Children and Youth, the first year that conference organizers invited youth to participate, de Schweinitz, *If We Could Change*, 195–96.

81. Gelman, *Death Blow*, 218–19; Lau, *Democracy Rising*, 128–31; see also M. Brown, "Somebody Had To Do It."

82. Gelman, *Death Blow*, 228–29; Gergel, *Unexampled Courage*.

83. Louis Burnham to Annie Weston, April 20, 1946, in SNYC Papers, Box 1, Folder Membership Drive May 1946, HU.

84. "Southern Youth Legislature" call, in SNYC Papers, Box 7, Folder "The Call Coverage," HU.

85. SNYC press release, October 18, 1946, in SNYC Papers, Box 6, Folder "7th Conference," HU.

86. Gelman, *Death Blow*, 235–36.

87. John McCray, "Civil Liberties," in SNYC Papers, Box 6, Folder "1939 SNYC 3rd Conference" (though placed in this folder, this address was delivered at the 1946 conference in Columbia, SC).

88. "John H. McCray," in SNYC Papers, Box 7, Folder "7th Conference 1946 Speeches John H. McCray," HU.

89. Dittmer, *Local People*, 2–9.

90. "Address delivered by Paul Robeson," in SNYC Papers, Box 6, Folder "7th Conference," HU; Lau, *Democracy Rising*, 166–70.

91. "Excerpts of Speech by Congressman Adam Clayton Powell, Jr., October 18, 1946," in SNYC Papers, Box 6, Folder "7th Conference," HU.

92. W. E. B. Du Bois, "Behold the Land," in SNYC Papers, Box 6, Folder "7th Conference," HU.

93. W. E. B. Du Bois, "Behold the Land," in SNYC Papers, Box 6, Folder "7th Conference," HU.

94. "Columbia Pact of Southern Youth" in SNYC Papers, Box 7, Folder "Columbia Pact of Southern Youth," HU.

95. "Columbia Pact of Southern Youth" in SNYC Papers, Box 7, Folder "Columbia Pact of Southern Youth," HU.

96. "Columbia Pact of Southern Youth" in SNYC Papers, Box 7, Folder "Columbia Pact of Southern Youth," HU; Lau, *Democracy Rising*, 166–70.

97. "Columbia Pact of Southern Youth," in SNYC Papers, Box 7, Folder "Columbia Pact of Southern Youth," HU; Lau, *Democracy Rising*, 166–70.

98. "Columbia Pact of Southern Youth" in SNYC Papers, Box 7, Folder "Columbia Pact of Southern Youth," HU.

99. Resolutions of SNYC, in SNYC Papers, Box 7, Folder "7th Conference—Resolutions" HU; "Legislative Statement of SNYC, 1947," in SNYC Papers, Box 7, Folder "8th Conference" HU; Lau, *Democracy Rising*, 164–66.

100. "Leroy Aiken to Louis Burnham, December 9, 1946," in SNYC Papers, Box 5, Folder "Moncks Corner, SC," HU.

101. "Leroy Aiken to Louis Burnham, December 9, 1946," SNYC Papers, Box 5, Folder "Moncks Corner, SC," HU.

102. "The Berkeley Wildcat," and "Leroy Aiken to Louis Burnham, December 9, 1946," in SNYC Papers, Box 5, Folder "Moncks Corner, SC," HU; Lau, *Democracy Rising*, 163–64.

103. "The Berkeley Wildcat," in SNYC Papers, Box 5, Folder "Moncks Corner, SC," HU.

104. I. M. McCoy, "Inferiority," "The Berkeley Wildcat," in SNYC Papers, Box 5, Folder "Moncks Corner, SC," HU.

105. "S.N.Y.C. Institute Held in Berkeley County" and "Joys Chapter of the SNYC," "The Berkeley Wildcat," in SNYC Papers, Box 5, Folder "Moncks Corner, SC," HU.

106. Quote in "Berkeley Council SNYC Educational Institute, Feb. 15–16, 1947," and "Summary of SNYC Institute Held in Berkeley County," in SNYC Papers, Box 5, Folder "Moncks Corner, SC," HU; Lau, *Democracy Rising*, 163–64.

107. "Berkeley Council SNYC Educational Institute, Feb. 15–16, 1947," and "Summary of SNYC Institute Held in Berkeley County," in SNYC Papers, Box 5, Folder "Moncks Corner, SC," HU; "The Berkeley Wildcat," and "Leroy Aiken to Louis Burnham, December 9, 1946," in SNYC Papers, Box 5, Folder "Moncks Corner, SC," HU; Lau, *Democracy Rising*, 138–39, 164–66.

108. Lau, *Democracy Rising*; Gelman, *Death Blow*, 245–48.

109. Charron, *Freedom's Teacher*; Clark, Brown, and Brown, *Ready from Within*; Levine, "Birth of the Citizenship Schools," 388–414.

Chapter 3

1. Johns, "Barbara Johns"; Joy Speakes, interview with the author, June 30, 2017; see also, "Barbara Johns Leads Prince Edward."

2. Johns, "Barbara Johns"; Joy Speakes, interview with the author, June 30, 2017.

3. Johns, "Barbara Johns"; Joy Speakes, interview with the author, June 30, 2017; MacLean, *Democracy in Chains*, 13–15.

4. Titus, *Brown's Battleground*; Waugh, "'Issue Is the Control," 76–94; Waugh, "From Forgotten to Remembered"; Bonastia, *Southern Stalemate*; Smith, *They Closed Their Schools*; V. P. Franklin, *The Young Crusaders*, 32–34; Daugherity and Grogan, *Little Child Shall Lead Them*.

5. Viadero, "At the Crossroads," 82; Edwilda Allen Issac, interviewed by George Gilliam, Mason Mills (2001), of The Ground Beneath Our Feet Project, Virginia Center for Digital History, University of Virginia.

6. Joy Speakes, interview with the author, June 30, 2017.

7. Chapman, "Seeds Sown in Time," 1A, 9A; Reverend Williams and Joy Speakes, interview with the author, November 26, 2012, Farmville, VA.

8. Reverend Williams and Joy Speakes, interview with the author, November 26, 2012, Farmville, VA.

9. Joy Speakes, interview with the author, June 30, 2017; Chapman, "Seeds Sown in Time," 1A quote on 2A; Joy Speakes and Williams interview, 2012.

10. Joy Speakes, interview with the author, June 30, 2017; Reverend Williams and Joy Speakes, interview with the author, November 26, 2012, Farmville, VA; Smith, *They Closed Their Schools*, 3–26.

11. Joy Speakes, interview with the author, June 30, 2017.

12. Joy Speakes, interview with the author, June 30, 2017; Reverend Williams and Joy Speakes, interview with the author, November 26, 2012, Farmville, VA; Titus, *Brown's Battleground*, 1–6; B. Smith, "The Eyes of the World," 36–74; "High School Pupils Stage Strike"; K. M. Turner, "'Getting it Straight,'" 219–23; "Moton Students' Claims Unjustified"; "R. R. Moton Strike"; Viadero, "At the Crossroads," 81–82; Holley, "M. Boyd Jones," Theoharis, *More Beautiful and Terrible*, 142–44; Devlin, *Girl Stands*, 178–81.

13. "NAACP Geared"; "School Board to Delay"; "Va. Pupils' Strike Ends"; "Desegregation Move Started"; Kluger, *Simple Justice*, 128, 175–81, 467–80; see also Stokes, *Students on Strike*; Devlin, *Girl Stands*, 178–81.

14. "Attorneys Start Federal Suit"; Peeples, "Perspective on the Prince Edward," 15–19.

15. "NAACP Geared"; "School Board to Delay Reply"; "Va. Pupils' Strike Ends"; "Desegregation Move Started"; Kluger, *Simple Justice*, 128, 175–81, 467–80. For a full account of the Prince Edward County School history, see Bonastia, *Southern Stalemate*; Titus, *Brown's Battleground*; B. Smith, *They Closed Their Schools*.

16. Joy Speakes, interview with the author, June 30, 2017.

17. Branch, *Parting the Waters*, 7–9; Joy Speakes, interview with the author, June 30, 2017.

18. Joy Speakes, interview with the author, June 30, 2017.

19. Joy Speakes, interview with the author, June 30, 2017.

20. Joy Speakes, interview with the author, June 30, 2017.

21. Titus, *Brown's Battleground*, 1–7; B. Smith, "The Eyes of the World," 36–74; "High School Pupils Stage Strike," 1, 19. Like other segregated Black schools across the South, parents of students attending R. R. Moton High School demonstrated a long history of demanding a quality education through better facilities and resources. See K. M. Turner, "'Getting it Straight,'" 219–23; Reverend Williams and Joy Speakes, interview with the author, November 26, 2012, Farmville, VA; "Moton Students' Claims Unjustified," 1; "High School Pupils Stage Strike," 1, 19; "R. R. Moton Strike," 1.

22. "Petitions Charge Discrimination"; "Segregation Suit Attorney, Plaintiffs Meet Here Monday," December 25, 1963, in "Farmville Herald School Closings: 1950–1955," Longwood University.

23. Picott and Peeples, "A Study in Infamy," 393–94.

24. Tushnet, *NAACP's Legal Strategy*, 109–10; K. M. Turner, "Both Victors and Victims," 11669–700. The similar movement toward desegregation is also noted in the *Briggs v. Elliot* (1952) case that emerged from Clarendon County, SC, see Burton, Burton, and Appleford, "Seeds in Unlikely Soil,"176–200; Kluger, *Simple Justice*, 3–25.

25. Joy Speakes, interview with the author, June 30, 2017.

26. Prince Edward County School Board minutes, May 8, 1951, and June 12, 1951, Prince Edward County School Board District, Farmville, VA.

27. "AFRO Finds Charred Symbol"; Viadero, "At the Crossroads," 87; Speakes, interview with the author, June 30, 2017.

28. Viadero, "At the Crossroads," 82–83.

29. "Student Strike at R. R. Moton Enters 9th Day," *The Farmville Herald*, May 4, 1951.

30. Prince Edward County School Board minutes, June 29, 1951, Prince Edward County School Board District, Farmville, VA.

31. Viadero, "At the Crossroads," 82–83.

32. Robert L. Carter to A. L. Johnson, April 19, 1949, in Gladys Noel Bates Papers, Box 2, "Scrapbook, 1948–1960," MDAH; Potts, *History of the Palmetto*, 66–67; Fairclough, *Class of Their Own*, 345–49; Charron, *Freedom's Teacher*, 242–47; Gray, Reed, and Walton, *History of the Alabama State*, 151–54. Black college presi-

dents were often in a precarious role, too, and often harshly penalized civil rights activity, see J. Turner, *Sitting In and Speaking Out*, 23–24, 167–69; Williamson, J. (2004). "This Has Been Quite a Year," 554–76; "ASTA Reaction to the Supreme Court Decision of 1954," in Alabama State Teacher Association Records, Box 13, Folder 12, "ASTA History—ASTA Reaction to Supreme Court Decision of 1954," ASU; Cunningham, "Hell Is Popping Here," 35–62.

33. It is estimated that over 21,000 Black teachers lost their jobs between 1984 and 1989, for an introduction to the numbers of displaced and dismissed teachers in the wake of *Brown*, see J. Anderson, "'A Tale of Two Browns,'" 30–32; see also Fultz, "Displacement of Black Educators," 11–45.

34. S. P. Clark, *Echo in My Soul*, 116–18; R. W. Burnette to Charles T. Ferillo, February 21, 1979; Septima P. Clark to Carolyn L. Collins, November 6, 1985; and "Information—Mr. Burkey," Folder 33, "Chas. Co. Schools, 1950's dismissal," in Septima P. Clark Collection, Box 2, Avery Research Center, Charleston, SC; Charron, *Freedom's Teacher*, 242–47. Other educators who lost their jobs in South Carolina due to their work with the NAACP and equalization include J. T. W. Mims, principal of Bell Street High School and president of the Palmetto State Teachers Association from 1942–1944 and J. R. McCain, PSTA president between 1946 and 1948; Potts, *History of the Palmetto*, 66–67.

35. "Survey, Hinds County Public Schools, 1956," p. 54, in in Horace Ivy Collection, Series 1806, Box 5, MDAH.

36. Dobrasko, "Architectural Survey," 14; Baker, *Paradoxes of Desegregation*, 99–104.

37. "Survey, Hinds County Public Schools, 1956," p. 25, in Horace Ivy Collection, Series 1806, Box 5, MDAH.

38. "Survey, Hinds County Public Schools, 1956," p. 31–33, in Horace Ivy Collection, Series 1806, Box 5, MDAH.

39. Prince Edward County School Board minutes, December 14, 1951, and January 11, 1952, May 29, 1952, Prince Edward County School Board District, Farmville, VA; "Negro High School Sketches Arrive"; "School Board of County Advertises for Estimates on New Negro School," *Farmville Herald*, May 9, 1952, in "Farmville Herald School Closings: 1950–1955," Longwood University.

40. "ASTA Reaction to the Supreme Court Decision of 1954," in Alabama State Teacher Association Records, Box 13, Folder 12, "ASTA History—ASTA Reaction to Supreme Court Decision of 1954," ASU.

41. "Brinkley Elementary-Junior High School," and "Hill Junior-Senior High School," in Horace Ivy Collection, Series 1806, Box 21, "Description of Plants, Jackson Municipal Separate School District, 1956," MDAH.

42. "Lanier Junior-Senior High School," in Horace Ivy Collection, Series 1806, Box 21, "Description of Plants, Jackson Municipal Separate School District, 1956," MDAH. The city also upgraded the historic Robertson Elementary School and Rowan Elementary-Junior High School, effectively upgrading or replacing all existing Black schools in Jackson.

43. "History of McComb Schools," and "Educational McComb," in "McComb, Miss—Schools—History," subject file in McComb Public Library, McComb, Missis-

sippi. Schools in this era were part of the state's plan to equalize education to pre-emptively avoid desegregation. Bolton, *The Hardest Deal of All*, chapter two (33–61); "McComb Municipal Separate School District, 1958," in Horace Ivy Collection, Series 1806, Box 11, MDAH.

44. "City's Newest School, East Bay Negro Elementary, to Open Monday," *The News and Courier* (Charleston, SC), February 1, 1955.

45. Dobrasko, "Architectural Survey," 33.

46. "ASTA Reaction to the Supreme Court Decision of 1954," Alabama State Teacher Association records, Box 13, Folder 12, "ASTA History—ASTA Reaction to Supreme Court Decision of 1954," ASU.

47. "ASTA Reaction to the Supreme Court Decision of 1954," Alabama State Teacher Association records, Box 13, Folder 12, "ASTA History—ASTA Reaction to Supreme Court Decision of 1954," ASU; Gray, Reed, and Walton, *History of the Alabama State Teachers*, 123–33, 145–56.

48. Moran, "Education in South Carolina," 14–15.

49. "Youth and Finances Help," 18, South Caroliniana.

50. "Press Release—Youth Division, November 16, 1953," in NAACP Papers, Series 19, Part C, Reel 10. Such statements crystallized the prevailing thesis in the historiography that teachers were inactive Fairclough, *Class of Their Own*, 385–86. Dittmer, *Local People*, 75, noted in his analysis, "as a group black teachers in the 1950s refused to take a stand and the movement of the early 1960s passed them by."

51. Interview with Willie Shepperson by Rebekeh Bailey, Folder Civil Rights in Prince Edward County—Oral History Collection, "Interview 1998.1 Willie Shepperson."

52. As Marjorie Murphy notes, the NEA self-identified as a "professional" organization as opposed to a union, which educators typically associated with the American Federation of Teachers (AFT), see Murphy, *Blackboard Unions*, 203–6.

53. "Memorandum to Youth Councils and College Chapters From the New York City NAACP Youth Council," May 29, 1951, in NAACP Papers, Part 19, Series C, Reel 12, Frame 352.

54. "Statement to the Board of Directors Regarding the Youth Work of the Association," Part 19 Series C Reel 11, Frame 862.

55. "Statement to the Board of Directors Regarding the Youth Work of the Association," Part 19 Series C Reel 11, Frame 862.

56. For a complete history of Communism, the Cold War, and the civil rights movement, see Dudziak, *Cold War Civil Rights*; Bynum, *NAACP Youth and the Fight*, 62–69; "Memorandum to Youth Councils and College Chapters from the New York City NAACP Youth Council," May 29, 1951, in NAACP Papers, Part 19, Series C, Reel 12, Frame 352.

57. "Memorandum to Mr. Wright from Mr. Current," May 15, 1953, in NAACP Papers, Part 19, Series C, Reel 12, Frame 396.

58. "Herbert Wright to Irma Brownfield," April 30, 1952; "Irma Brownfield to Herbert Wright," April 26, 1952, in NAACP Papers, Part 19, Series C, Reel 12, Frame 356.

59. "Memorandum to Mr. Current from Herbert L. Wright," April 29, 1952, in NAACP Papers, Part 19, Series C, Reel 12, Frame 354.

60. "Suggested Changes for Youth Council and College Chapter Constitutions," in NAACP Papers, Part 19, Series C, Reel 12, Frame 400.

61. "Suggested Changes for Youth Council and College Chapter Constitutions," in NAACP Papers, Part 19, Series C, Reel 12, Frame 400; "Changes to College Chapter Constitution," in NAACP Papers, Part 19, Series C, Reel 12, Frames 402 and 410.

62. "Constitution for Youth Councils" (1954), in NAACP Papers, Part 19, Series C, Reel 12, Frames 427–38.

63. M. V. Williams, *Medgar Evers*, 73–83; Evers-Williams and Marable, *Autobiography of Medgar Evers*, 13–22. Payne, *I've Got the Light*, 47–56, 288–90; Dittmer, *Local People*, 166–69, see also J. Brown, *Medgar Evers*.

64. A. Morris, *Origins of the Civil Rights*, 17–25; Fairclough, *Race & Democracy*, 157–62; Sinclair, "Equal in All Places," 349–56. Dupuy Anderson, interview with Dawn Wallace, June 24, 1998 (LSU collection); Reginald R. Brown Sr., interview by Jeong Suk Pang, June 23, 1998 (LSU collection).

65. Rev. T. J. Jemison interview, June 15, 1995, T. Harry Williams Center for Oral History Collection, Louisiana State University; Martin Luther King Jr., "The Montgomery Story," in E. D. Nixon Collection, Box 2, Folder "NAACP 39th Anniversary (March 16, 1947), ASU.

66. Rev T. J. Jemison interview, June 15, 1995, T. Harry Williams Center for Oral History Collection, Louisiana State University, 15–16; Morris, *Origins of the Civil Rights Movement*, 18.

67. "Civil Rights Army Encamps"; "Berkeley Council SNYC Educational Institute, Feb. 15–16, 1947," and "Summary of SNYC Institute Held in Berkeley County," in SNYC Papers, Box 5, Folder "Moncks Corner, SC", HU; Lau, *Democracy Rising*, 163–64.

68. "History of McKinley High School," 3–6; "McKinley High School Alumni Association, Ribbon Cutting Ceremony" (Baton Rouge, 2006), subject file in Baton Rouge Reading Room, East Baton Rouge Parish Public Library, Baton Rouge, LA; Hendry and Edwards, *Old South Baton Rouge*, 61–62; Frazier, "History of Negro Education," 76–77. In his master's thesis, Frazier went so far as to ascertain a letter from T. H. Harris, then State Superintendent of Education, to confirm and validate that Baton Rouge High School was the first state approved high school to graduate a Black high school class, Frazier, "The History of Negro Education," 84–85.

69. By 1913 mayor of Baton Rouge Jules Roux and other city progressive sought to improve the city's sewer system and paved roads, among other city improvement projects. However, the large homeowners of Baton Rouge opposed the initiative. Roux approached Dr. Frazier and the committee who represented Black property owners in the city who, by law, could vote on proposals such as bonds that sought to increase the property tax. The mayor offered Frazier and the civic leaders a proposition to secure funding for a new high school if they could help secure the Black vote around a bonds issue for public improvement. The city council initially offered a sum of $7,000 but once the opposition courted the Black vote as well, they offered $25,000 for their support. Already in a position of civic leadership, Frazier was able to help deliver over 500 Black votes to secure passage of ten sepa-

rate bond propositions and, by extension, the $25,000 devoted to address the swelling Black student population. Frazier, "History of Negro Education," 71–80.

70. Frazier, "History of Negro Education," 86.

71. "History of McKinley High School," 5–6.

72. Huel Perkins, interview with Petra Munro Hendry and Dorian McCoy, May 11, 2006, McKinley High South Baton Rouge Oral History Project, LSU.

73. Joseph Delpit, interview with the author, October 7, 2015.

74. For a complete history of Old South Baton Rouge, see Hendry and Edwards, *Old South Baton Rouge.*

75. Freddie Pitcher, interview with Nita Clark and Courtney Grimes, June 25, 2002, McKinley High South Baton Rouge Oral History Project, LSU.

76. Joseph Delpit, interview with the author, October 7, 2015; Charles A. Ricard, interview with Petra Munro Hendry, July 15, 2005, Histories and Cultures of Old South Baton Rouge Project, LSU.

77. Joseph Delpit, interview with the author, October 7, 2015. Histories and Cultures of Old South Baton Rouge Project, LSU.

78. Charles A. Ricard, interview with Petra Munro Hendry, June 15, 2015, Histories and Cultures of Old South Baton Rouge Project, LSU.

79. Joseph Delpit, interview with the author, October 7, 2015.

80. Reverend Mary Moody, interviewed by Amy Horn, April 17, 2022, Histories and Cultures of Old South Baton Rouge Project, LSU.

81. Clayborne Carson, "To Walk in Dignity," 14; Rosa Parks, *Rosa Parks*, 111–12; "The Other Rosa Parks: Now 73, Claudette Colvin Was First to Refuse Giving Up Seat on Montgomery Bus," interview with Amy Goodman and Juan González, *Democracy Now!, National Public Radio* (March 29, 2013); Kitchen, "Interview with Claudette Colvin"; Colvin's case contributed to a blueprint for civil disobedience, but the relationship does not establish a causal or direct connection between the two events. Colvin is also unique because, unlike her peers in the Youth Council, she did not come from a professional background, Theoharis, *Rebellious Life*, 32–34; Robinson and Garrow (ed.), *Montgomery Bus Boycott*, 37–45; Jackson, *Becoming King*, 72–73; Gray, *Bus Ride to Justice*, 31–46; Burrow Jr., *Child Shall Lead Them*, 28–31.

82. Carson, "To Walk in Dignity," 13–15; Garrow, *Walking City*; Hoose, *Claudette Colvin*; On Dr. Gwen Patton, Rufus Lewis, Idessa Williams-Redden, see Dickson with Garner and Pyrlike, "They Just Knew I Would Protect It," 90–92. Kitchen, "'Awesome Story Revisited,'" 1, 2.

83. Bynum, *NAACP Youth and the Fight*, 93–94.

84. Alabama jurors sentenced Reeves to death in the ensuing trial. Though a successful appeal overturned the initial conviction, Alabama jurors convicted and sentenced Reeves to death for a second time. Lautier, "High Court Sets Aside"; "Execution of Wrongfully Convicted Black Teen Jeremiah Reeves Sparks Protest in Montgomery" Equal Justice Initiative. The state executed Reeves by the electric chair on March 28, 1958, at the age of twenty-two. Theoharis, *Rebellious Life*, 31–33; Levine, *Freedom's Children*, 22–25; Gray, Execution of Jeremiah Reeves; Younge, "She Would Not Be Moved."

85. M. L. King, "Statement Delivered at the Prayer Pilgrimage."

86. Gwen Patton, interview with the author, February 13, 2016; Patton, "Born Freedom Fighter," 572–76; "Gwen Patton, biographical notes," ASU archives.

87. Gwen Patton, interview with the author, February 13, 2016; Levine, *Freedom's Children*, 31, 41, 75–76.

88. Gwen Patton, interview with the author, February 13, 2016; Levine, *Freedom's Children*, 31, 41, 75–76.

89. Bailey, *Neither Carpetbaggers or Scalawags*, 128–29. The city of Montgomery was also supported by the Cleveland Union Aid Commission with the recruitment of teachers, to Edwin Beecher to J. W. Alvrod, July 1, 1867, Records of the Education Division of the Bureau of Refugees, Freedmen, and Abandoned Lands, 1865–1871, National Archives and Records Administration (NARA), M803, 1695200, Frames 187–206; Freedmen's Bureau Papers, Monthly reports in Alabama, January 1866–June 1879, Frame 77, May 1867, Frame 101, February 1868, Frame 190; Rev. O. W. Sway, "Swane School," in *The American Missionary* 35, no. 7 (July 1981), 209–10 (*The American Missionary* is also digitized through the Cornell University Library http://ebooks.library.cornell.edu/a/amis/amis.html.)

90. "January 12, 1937, Board of Education of Montgomery County minutes."

91. "Booker T. Washington School Dedication is Scheduled Today," *Montgomery Advertiser and Alabama Journal*, April 3, 1949; "Classes Open at $250,000 Negro School," *Montgomery Advertiser*, December 10, 1948, Folder 17, "Montgomery County Booker T. Washington," Montgomery County file, Alabama Department of Archives and History (ADAH).

92. Colvin quoted in Theoharis, *Rebellious Life*, 53; Burrow Jr., *Child Shall Lead Them*, 33–34.

93. Colvin did not meet Rosa Parks until the legal troubles that plagued the young Colvin. She pled not guilty to charges of violating segregation laws, disturbing the peace, and assaulting a police officer. The judge found Colvin guilty of assault and dropped the other two charges. Claudette Colvin quoted in Hoose, *Claudette Colvin*, 25, 44–45; "Negro Guilty of Violation of City Bus Segregation Law," *Montgomery Advertiser*, March 19, 1955.

94. "Education: The Freedom of Knowledge vs. Mankind," *The Parvenue*, March 1952, Avery Research Center; Hale, "Fight Was Instilled in Us," 18–19.

95. "History Department to Give Program About Negroes," "Significance of Negro History," *The Parvenue*, February 1956, Avery Research Center; "Negro History Course Proposal, 1958," Charleston County School District, Box 863; Pyatt, *Burke High School*, 113; Hale, "'Fight Was Instilled in Us,'" 18–19.

96. "Let's Discuss the Race Problem"; Pyatt, *Burke High School*, 97–118; Hale, "Fight Was Instilled in Us," 18–19.

97. Jacqueline Martin, interview with the author, October 7, 2015.

98. Millicent Brown, interview with the author, November 29, 2011, Orangeburg, SC.

99. Mrs. May-Pittman, interview with the author, July 26, 2013.

100. Mrs. May-Pittman, interview with the author, July 26, 2013, see also T. Morris, *Womanpower Unlimited*, 2–5, 66–72.

101. Mrs. May-Pittman, interview with the author, July 26, 2013; T. Morris, *Womanpower Unlimited*, 2–5, 66–72.

102. T. Morris, *Womanpower Unlimited*; see also Littlefield, "Teaching Survival," 26; Charron, *Freedom's Teacher*, 3–5; Robnett, "African-American Women," 1661–93.

103. T. Morris, *Womanpower Unlimited*, 37–38; Bo Brown, interview with the author, June 25, 2013; Bo Brown, conversation with the author, August 28, 2015.

104. Bo Brown, interview with the author, June 25, 2013; Bo Brown, conversation with the author, August 28, 2015.

105. Bolton, *Hardest Deal*, 45–60.

106. "Resolutions Adopted at ATA's 50th Convention," Palmetto State Teachers Association, *PSTA Journal*, October 1953, 15, South Caroliniana; "PEA Delegates at ATA Convention," Palmetto Education Association, *PEA Journal*, September 1954, 4, South Caroliniana.

Theodore R. Springer, "We Need the ATA Still," Palmetto Education Association, *PEA Journal*, September 1955, 8, South Caroliniana.

107. Dr. Howard Hale Long, "Some Questions and Problems Relating to the Segregation Cases," *The Bulletin: The Official Organ of the American Teachers Association*, Harper Council Trenholm Collection, Box 7/Container 45.

108. "For the Record: ATA and the NAACP," *The Bulletin: The Official Organ of the American Teachers Association*, Harper Council Trenholm Collection, Box 7/Container 45.

109. James McCain, "A Declaration of Purpose," Palmetto Education Association, *PEA Journal*, November 1955, 9–10; South Caroliniana Library.

110. "20,000 Attend NEA Convention in New York City," Palmetto Education Association, *PEA Journal*, September 1954, 3, South Caroliniana.

111. "Educators Express Views on Supreme Court's Decision," Palmetto Education Association, *PEA Journal*, November 1954, 8–9; "The Palmetto Education Association's Statement on Principles," *PEA Journal*, March 1955, 8, South Caroliniana; "The Palmetto Education Association's Statement of Principles," in Palmetto Education Association, *Organized for Action* 5, South Caroliniana.

112. "The Constitution of the Palmetto Education Association, 1957 Revision," in Palmetto Education Association, *Organized for Action* 5, South Caroliniana.

113. "Five Special ATA Projects," Palmetto Education Association, *PEA Journal*, September 1954, 6, South Caroliniana.

114. "Defend Academic Freedom," Palmetto Education Association, *PEA Journal*, January 1956, 3–4; "Teacher Discriminated Against in Fixing Salary May File Complaint," *Palmetto Education Association News*, May 1955, 2, South Caroliniana.

115. Carson, "To Walk in Dignity," 14; Parks, *Rosa Parks*, 111–12; "The Other Rosa Parks," interview with Amy Goodman and Juan González, *Democracy Now!*, National Public Radio, March 29, 2013; Kitchen, "Interview with Claudette Colvin"; Colvin's case contributed to a blueprint for civil disobedience, but the relationship does not establish a causal or direct connection between the two events. Colvin is also unique because, unlike her peers in the Youth Council, she did not come from a professional background; Theoharis, *Rebellious Life*, 32–34.

116. Parks, *Rosa Parks*, 111–12; Theoharis, *More Beautiful and Terrible History*, 204–5. Colvin's case established and contributed to a blueprint for civil disobedience. The relationship does not establish a causal connection between the two. For a thorough review of the operation of racial heteronormativity, see Ferguson, *Aberrations in Black* and Thangaraj, *Desi Hoop Dreams*; for a larger context on race and the politics of pregnancy in the postwar period, see Solinger, *Wake Up Little Susie*.

117. "Press Release—News Division," in NAACP Papers, Part 19, Series C, Reel 10, Frames 78–79.

118. "Federal Aid to Education," in NAACP Papers, Part 19, Series C, Reel 27, Frame 68; "1955 Program Guide for Youth Councils and College Chapters," in NAACP Papers, Part 19, Series C, Reel 10, Frame 339–48; "Press Release, April 17, 1952" NAACP Papers, Part 19, Series C, Reel 10, Frames 7–23.

119. "Integration March Set"; "Youth March for Integrated Schools—Washington, D.C." accessed on http://www.crmvet.org/tim/timhis58.htm.

120. "Youth March for Integrated Schools."

121. Young people also took note that the seventy-five student unions were outside the Communist bloc, "Youth March for Integrated Schools."

122. "Youth March for Integrated Schools."

123. Martin Luther King Jr., "Address at the Youth March for Integrated Schools," 8 April 1959, The Martin Luther King Jr. Papers Project, The Martin Luther King Jr. Research and Education Institute.

124. Martin Luther King Jr., "Address at the Youth March for Integrated Schools," 8 April 1959, The Martin Luther King Jr. Papers Project, The Martin Luther King Jr. Research and Education Institute.

125. Perillo, *Uncivil Rights*, 100–102; de Schweinitz, *If We Could Change*, 69; Guiner, "From Racial Liberalism," 92–118; K. Clark, *Prejudice and Your Child*.

126. Beal, *Warriors Don't Cry*; Bates, *Long Shadow of Little Rock*; Hampton, Fayer, and Flynn, "The Little Rock Crisis," 35–52; Devlin, "We Raised Our Hands," 219–62; see also M. Brown, "Somebody Had to Do It."

127. Loder-Jackson, *Schoolhouse Activists*, 56–58; Annie Marie Butler, interviewed by Dr. Horace Huntley, June 7, 1995, Birmingham Civil Rights Institute, Oral History Project, Vol. 7.

128. "Prince Edward Closes School Doors" [n.d.], *Farmville Herald;* "Tragedy in Prince Edward" [n.d.] *Farmville Herald,* "Action of Board 'Should Have Come As No Surprise,'" July 14, 1959, *Farmville Herald* in "Farmville Herald School Closings: 1950–1955," Longwood University, Prince Edward School Closing Collection; Bonastia, *Southern Stalemate*; Titus, *Brown's Battleground*.

129. NAACP Papers, "Youth Hit Economic Boycott," Part 19, Series C, Reel 27, Frame 276; Bynum, "'We Must March Forward,'" 488; de Schweinitz, *If We Could Change*, 166–70; Jonas, *Freedom's Sword*, 172–74; Morsell, "The National Association for the Advancement of Colored People," 99; Hughes, "Fight for Freedom," 182–88; Rogers, *Black Campus Movement*, 62; Bynum, "'We Must March Forward,'" 488; Oppenheimer, *Sit-In Movement of 1960*, 33–35; V. P. Franklin, *Young Crusades*, 58–59; see also Brooks, *Lucile H. Bluford*.

130. "Remarks of Roy Wilkins" [June 26, 1960], in "Annual Convention, 1960, Speeches," Papers of the NAACP, Part 01: Supplement, 1956–1960, Folder: 001411-012-0596; Hughes, "Fight for Freedom," 182–88.

Chapter 4

1. Rev. James Blake in "South Carolina Voices of the Civil Rights Movement," transcript, p. 198, Avery Research Center; Hale, "Fight Was Instilled in Us," 22–23.

2. Hale, "Fight Was Instilled in Us," 4; "24 Arrested Here in Demonstration," *News and Courier* (Charleston, S.C.), April 2, 1960; Baker, *Paradoxes of Desegregation*, chaps. 6, 7, and 8. For more on the larger story of desegregation in Charleston, see Burton, Burton, and Appleford, "Seeds in Unlikely Soil," 176–200; Cox Jr., "1963: The Year of Decision."

3. Joseph McNeil interview in Warren, *Who Speaks for the Negro*, 359–60; Chafe, *Civilities and Civil Rights*, 80–82, 121–24.

4. Minerva Brown King, interview with the author, December 12, 2011; Harvey B. Gantt, interview with the author, November 28, 2011; Hale, "Fight Was Instilled in Us," 22–23.

5. Joseph McNeil interview in Warren, *Who Speaks for the Negro*, 359–60; Chafe, *Civilities and Civil Rights*, 80–82, 121–24; A. Morris, *Origins of the Civil Rights Movement*, 197–99; A. Morris, "Black Southern Student," 749–52, 755–56; Bynum, *NAACP Youth Councils*; Collins, "Taking the Lead," 126–37.

6. "Biographical Sketch of I. D. Newman, c. 1980," in Isaiah DeQuincey Newman Papers, University of South Carolina, South Carolina Political Collections; Hale, "Fight Was Instilled in Us," 21; Lau, *Democracy Rising*, 183–84.

7. Hale, "Fight Was Instilled in Us," 21–22, 26; Minerva Brown King, interview with the author, December 12, 2011; Millicent Brown, interview with the author, November 29, 2011. See also *Millicent Brown v. Charleston County School District Number 20*, in J. Arthur Brown Papers, Box 2, Folder 2, Avery Research Center; Brown v. District No. 20, in Robert N. Rosen Legal Papers, 1941–1994, Box 16, Folder 9, Avery Research Center.

8. "Prospectus of the Charleston Industrial School," in Dart Family Papers, Box 1, Folder 5, "Prospectus of the Charleston Industrial School & Home for Girls and 7th Annual Prospectus for the Chas. Normal & Industrial School, 1895, 1901," Avery Research Center; Baker, "Pedagogies of Protest," 2777–803; Walker, *Their Highest Potential*.

9. Hale, "Fight Was Instilled in Us," 16–17; "Burke High School Teaching Materials," in Eugene C. Hunt Papers, Box 3, Folder 2, Avery Research Center.

10. Hale, "Fight Was Instilled in Us," 16–17; "Correspondence, 1940s–1950s," in Eugene C. Hunt Papers, Box 2, Folder 1, and "Vita Sheet, Eugene C. Hunt," in "Vita," Box 1, Folder 1, Avery Research Center.

11. Hale, "Fight Was Instilled in Us," 20; Rev. James Blake in "South Carolina Voices of the Civil Rights Movement," transcript, p. 218, Avery Research Center.

12. Hale, "Fight Was Instilled in Us," 20; Harvey B. Gantt, interview with the author, November 28, 2011.

13. Hale, "Fight Was Instilled in Us," 20; Harvey B. Gantt, interview with the author, November 28, 2011; Millicent Brown, interview with the author, November 29, 2011.

14. Simms, *Chalk and Chalkboard Career*, 78.

15. Hale, "Fight Was Instilled in Us," 21; The College of Charleston did not desegregate until 1967. See Morrison, *History of the College*; Chaddock and Matalene, *College of Charleston Voices*.

16. Chafe, *Civilities and Civil Rights*, 18–19, 122–23.

17. Harvey B. Gantt, interview with the author, November 28, 2011; Hale, "Fight Was Instilled in Us," 23.

18. Hale, "Fight Was Instilled in Us," 23; Minerva Brown King, interview with the author, December 12, 2011.

19. Hale, "Fight Was Instilled in Us," 23; Rev. James Blake in "South Carolina Voices of the Civil Rights Movement," transcript, p. 198, Avery Research Center; Rev. James Blake, interview with Thomas C. Dent, May 15, 1991, in Tom Dent Collection, Box 147, Item 14, Side 1, Amistad Research Center at Tulane University, New Orleans, Louisiana, accessed on November 23, 2021, at https://digitallibrary.tulane.edu/islandora/object/tulane%3A53916.

20. B. Ransby, *Ella Baker*, 239–72; Hogan, *Many Minds, One Heart*, 34–42; Carson, *In Struggle*, 19–26; Payne, *I've Got the Light of Freedom*, 95–102.

21. Lau, *Democracy Rising*, 216–18; Hogan, *Many Minds, One Heart*, 35–36.

22. Hale, *Freedom Schools*, 56; Charles McDew, interview with Katherine Shannon, August 24, 1967, Civil Rights Documentation Project, Moorland Spingarn Research Center, Howard University (transcript in possession of author, courtesy of Joellen ElBashir), 76; Dittmer, *Local People*, 110; Dave Dennis, interview with the author, October 25, 2011.

23. Watkins, *Pushing Forward*; Hale, *Freedom Schools*, 43; Lewis and D'Orso, *Walking with the Wind*, 150–75; Carson, *In Struggle*, 31–44; Stoper, *Student Nonviolent Coordinating Committee*, 7; Hogan, *Many Minds, One Heart*, 45–55; Arsenault, *Freedom Riders*.

24. Hale, *Freedom Schools*, 44; Watkins, interview with the author, August 26 and 27, 2008, and October 11, 2011.

25. Watkins, *Pushing Forward*; Hale, *Freedom Schools*, 44; Watkins, interview with the author, August 26 and 27, 2008, and October 11, 2011; Etheridge, *Breach of Peace*; Hogan, *Many Minds*, 51–55.

26. Watkins, interview with the author, August 26 and 27, 2008 and October 11, 2011; on Freedom Summer, see McAdam, *Freedom Summer*; and Watson, *Freedom Summer*.

27. Moody, *Coming of Age*, 132.

28. Moody, *Coming of Age*, 285–97; Salter Jr., *Jackson*, 7–8.

29. Moody, *Coming of Age*, 311–32.

30. Hale, *Freedom Schools*, 69–70; "History of McComb Schools," and "Educational McComb," in "McComb, Miss—Schools—History," subject file in McComb Public Library, McComb, Mississippi. Schools in this era were part of the state's

plan to equalize education to preemptively avoid desegregation. Bolton, *Hardest Deal of All*, 33–61.

31. Hale, *Freedom Schools*, 52–53; C. C. Bryant was also active in the area with Webb Owens and E. W. Steptoe, Dittmer, *Local People*, 101–2; Payne, *I've Got the Light*, 113–16.

32. Hale, *Freedom Schools*, 52–53; Brenda Travis quoted in "Making Amends"; Brenda Travis, interviewed by Alex F. et al., May 6 and 7, 2010, McComb Legacies Oral History Project.

33. Hale, *Freedom Schools*, 52–53; Branch, *Pillar of Fire*; Payne, *I've Got the Light*, 115–17.

34. Hale, *Freedom Schools*, 53; Brenda Travis, interviewed by Alex F. et al. May 6 and 7, 2010, McComb Legacies Oral History Project.

35. Hale, *Freedom Schools*, 53; Hogan, *Many Minds, One Heart*, 60–61; Dittmer, *Local People*, 107–115; Payne, *I've Got the Light*, 116–18.

36. Hale, *Freedom Schools*, 53; "Two Summit Negroes"; "Sit-in Youths Tried"; "Negro Trio Convicted"; Dittmer, *Local People*, 107–15; Payne, *I've Got the Light*, 118–28.

37. Hale, *Freedom Schools*, 54. See "Commodore Dewey Higgins: Dedication," Black History Gallery, Inc, McComb, MS; Hilda Casin, interview with the author, July 2, 2012.

38. Hale, *Freedom Schools*, 54; Brenda Travis, interviewed by Alex F. et al., May 6 and 7, 2010, McComb Legacies Oral History Project; Joe Lewis, interviewed by G. Taylor, S. Shuntell, M. Sabrena, C. Dominic, W. Vo'neicechsi, M. Alyssa, G. Hannah, I. Mai Li, R. Jacob, K. Wilson; with Deborah Dent-Samake, Vickie Malone, and Howard Levin, March 26, 2011; McComb, Mississippi, McComb Legacies Oral History Project; Dittmer, *Local People*, 107–15; Payne, *I've Got the Light*, 118–28; Curtis Muhammad, interview with Benjamin Hedin and Sam Pollard conducted for the *Blues House* documentary, June 18, 2014 (transcript and audio in possession of the author).

39. Hale, *Freedom Schools*, 54; Brenda Travis, interviewed by Alex F., et al., May 6 and 7, 2010, McComb Legacies Oral History Project. Brenda Travis, interviewed by Alex F., et al., May 6 and 7, 2010, McComb Legacies Oral History Project.

40. Jacqueline Martin, interview with the author, October 7, 2015.

41. Hale, *Freedom Schools*, 54; Eloise Carter quoted in "Making Amends."

42. Hale, *Freedom Schools*, 54; Zellner, *Wrong Side of Murder Creek*, 157. Zellner, the only White in the march from the Masonic Lodge, was savagely beaten, almost to the point of death.

43. Hale, *Freedom Schools*, 56; Zellner, *Wrong Side of Murder Creek*, 157.

44. Dave Dennis, interview with the author, October 25, 2011.

45. Hale, *Freedom Schools*, 56; Charles McDew, interview with Katherine Shannon, August 24, 1967, Civil Rights Documentation Project, Moorland Spingarn Research Center, Howard University (transcript in possession of author, courtesy of Joellen ElBashir), 76; Dittmer, *Local People*, 110; Dave Dennis, interview with the author, October 25, 2011.

46. Hale, *Freedom Schools*, 56; McDew, interview with Katherine Shannon, August 24, 1967, 100.

47. Hogan, *Many Minds, One Heart*, 63.

48. Branch, *Pillar of Fire*; Eskew, *But for Birmingham*; Gaillard, *Cradle of Freedom*, 125–37. On the larger history of protest in Birmingham by way of the labor movement and working class politics, see Kelley, *Hammer and Hoes*; Kelley, "'We Are Not What We Seem,'" 83–85; McKiven Jr., *Iron and Steel*; Krochmal, "Unmistakably Working-Class Vision," 923–60; Alabama Christian Movement for Human Rights, "People in Motion, Birmingham," Box 1, Folder 17, King Center.

49. Branch, *Parting the Waters*, 688–91; Levinson, *We've Got a Job*, 47–53; Walker, *Road to Damascus*.

50. Gaillard, *Cradle of Freedom*, 135–47; Burrow Jr., *Child Shall Lead Them*, 102–3.

51. Walker quotes in Eskew, *But for Birmingham*, 261; King and Carson, *Autobiography of Martin Luther King, Jr.*, 206–7.

52. Gaillard, *Cradle of Freedom*, 147–48; Eskew, *But for Birmingham*, 261; Loder-Jackson, *Schoolhouse Activists*, 64; Morris, "Black Southern Student Sit-in Movement"; McWhorter, *Carry Me Home*, 363.

53. Dr. Horace Huntley interview with Miriam McClendon, November 8, 1995, Birmingham Civil Rights Institute, Oral History Project, Vol. 11; Levinson, *We've Got a Job*, 59; Eskew, *But for Birmingham*, 262–63.

54. Branch, *Parting the Waters*, 751–53; Eskew, *But for Birmingham*, 261; Loder-Jackson, *Schoolhouse Activists*, 64.

55. Alabama Christian Movement for Human Rights, "People in Motion, Birmingham," Box 1, folder 17, King Center; McWhorter, *Carry Me Home*, 364.

56. Eskew, *But for Birmingham*, 261–62.

57. Branch, *Parting the Waters*, 750–55; Burrow, *Child Shall Lead Them*, 107–10.

58. Bevel quoted in Eskew, *But for Birmingham*, 263.

59. Parker, *"A Dream That Came True,"* 11–12; "Golden Educational Anniversary of Dr. Arthur Harold Parker, 1888–1939" and "Long Way From a Single Room" May 24, 1985, *Birmingham News* "Dr. A. H. Parker and 'A Dream That Came True'" in "Parker High School—Ed & Sch-Pub-Bhm" vertical file, Linn-Henley Research Library, Birmingham, Alabama; Loder-Jackson, *Schoolhouse Activists*, 23–27.

60. Eskew, *But for Birmingham*, 262; Branch, *Parting the Waters*, 752–55; McWhorter, *Carry Me Home*, 364; Lieutenant M. H. Mouse to Chief Jamie Moore, April 30, 1963, Alabama Christian Movement for Civil Rights, Theophilus Eugene Bull Connor Papers, 1959–1963, File 63, accessed at https://bplonline.contentdm.oclc.org/digital/collection/p16044coll1/id/29524/rec/10.

61. Dr. Horace Huntley interview with Danella James Bryant, June 23, 1995, Birmingham Civil Rights Institute, Oral History Project, Vol. 7.

62. Dr. Horace Huntley interview with Anne Thompson, January 31, 1997, Birmingham Civil Rights Institute, Oral History Project, Vol. 25.

63. Levinson, *We've Got a Job*; Burrow, *Child Shall Lead Them*, 121–22; Eskew, *But for Birmingham*, 263–65; McWhorter, *Carry Me Home*, 360–62.

64. Dr. Horace Huntley interview with Miriam McClendon, November 8, 1995, Birmingham Civil Rights Institute, Oral History Project, Vol. 11; Dr. Horace Huntley interview with Emily Thomas Ellis, July 12, 1995, Birmingham Civil Rights Institute, Oral History Project, Vol. 9.

65. Gwendolyn Sanders Gamble in Huntley and McKerley (eds.), *Foot Soldiers*, 144; Burrow, *A Child Shall Lead Them*, 115–17.

66. Dr. Horace Huntley interview with Willie Eatman, April 30, 1997, Birmingham Civil Rights Institute, Oral History Project, Vol. 26; Alabama Christian Movement for Human Rights, "People in Motion, Birmingham," Box 1, Folder 17, King Center.

67. Levinson, *We've Got a Job*, 82; Burrow, *Child Shall Lead Them*, 115–17.

68. James W. Stewart quoted in Huntley and McKerley, *Foot Soldiers*, 136.

69. Dr. Horace Huntley interview with Mary E. Streeter Perry, January 14, 1998, Birmingham Civil Rights Institute, Oral History Project, Vol. 31; Burrow, *Child Shall Lead Them*, 115–17.

70. Dr. Horace Huntley interview with Mrs. Margaret Askew, December 16, 1994, Birmingham Civil Rights Institute, Oral History Project, Vol. 1.

71. Dr. Horace Huntley interview with Anne Thompson, January 31, 1997, Birmingham Civil Rights Institute, Oral History Project, Vol. 25.

72. Dr. Horace Huntley interview with Miriam McClendon, November 8, 1995, Birmingham Civil Rights Institute, Oral History Project, Vol. 11; Dr. Horace Huntley interview with Della Stokes, February 21, 1996, Birmingham Civil Rights Institute, Oral History Project, Vol. 12.

73. Carl Grace quoted in Huntley and McKerley, *Foot Soldiers*, 164.

74. Betsy Butgereit and John Mangels, "Class of '63: Rights; '88: Me First," in "Parker High School—Ed & Sch-Pub-Bhm" vertical file, Linn-Henley Research Library, Birmingham, Alabama; Levinson, *We've Got a Job*, 111.

75. Dr. Horace Huntley interview with Willie Eatman, April 30, 1997, Birmingham Civil Rights Institute, Oral History Project, Vol. 26.

76. Dr. Horace Huntley interview with Willie Eatman, April 30, 1997, Birmingham Civil Rights Institute, Oral History Project, Vol. 26.

77. Levinson, *We've Got a Job*, 72.

78. Dr. Horace Huntley interview with Mrs. Margaret Askew, December 16, 1994, Birmingham Civil Rights Institute, Oral History Project, Vol. 1.

79. Dr. Horace Huntley interview with Edward Thompson, May 28, 1997, Birmingham Civil Rights Institute, Oral History Project, Vol. 28.

80. Annetta Streeter Gary quoted in Huntley and McKerley, *Foot Soldiers*, 120; Levinson, *We've Got a Job*, 72.

81. Dr. Dannetta K. Thornton Owens, interview with the author, March 2, 2016; Parker High School alumni, Gloria Washington Lewis Randall, Mary R. Hudson, Clifford L. Clark, Donna Melton, Edmonia L. Anderson, Gwendolyn May, William Yarbrough, James W. Whitaker, Claudia Cochran, Interview with the author, June 30, 2016; Detective R. A. Watkins to Chief Jamie Moore, May 3, 1963, Alabama Christian Movement for Civil Rights, Theophilus Eugene Bull Connor Papers, 1959–1963, 13.4, File 15–19, accessed at https://bplonline.contentdm.oclc.org/digital

/collection/p16044coll1/id/29570/rec/3; Carolyn Maull McKinstry quoted Huntley and McKerley, *Foot Soldiers*, 151; Eskew, *But for Birmingham*, 264; McWhorter, *Carry Me Home*, 366; Levinson, *We've Got a Job*, 72. R. C. Johnson was also the father of Alma Vivian Johnson Powell, the partner of General Colin Powell.

82. Annetta Streeter Gary quoted in Huntley and McKerley, *Foot Soldiers*, 120.

83. Carolym Maull McKinstry quoted in Huntley and McKerley, *Foot Soldiers*, 154.

84. Gwendolyn Sanders Gamble quoted in Loder-Jackson, *Schoolhouse Activists*, 66.

85. Annetta Streeter Gary quoted in Huntley and McKerley, *Foot Soldiers*, 120.

86. Loder-Jackson, *Schoolhouse Activists*, 66.

87. Woolfolk quoted in Levinson, *We've Got a Job*, 72–73.

88. James W. Stewart quoted in Huntley and McKerley, *Foot Soldiers*, 134; Loder-Jackson, *Schoolhouse Activists*, 66.

89. Dr. Horace Huntley interview with Deloris Givner Norman, July 8, 1996, Birmingham Civil Rights Institute, Oral History Project, Vol. 18.

90. Hailey, "Dogs and Hoses"; "Fire Hoses, Police Dogs," 2; "Hundreds of Hookey-Playing," 2; "Schools Lose by Absences."

91. Andrew Young, "The Day We Went to Jail in Birmingham," *Friends*, February 9, 1964, Southern Christian Leadership Conference (SCLC) collection, Box 135, Folder 26 "Young—'Teens on the March in Birmingham—1964,'" King Center, Atlanta, GA; Branch, *Parting the Waters*, 683; Hailey, "Dogs and Hoses," 1, 8; McWhorter, *Carry Me Home*, 367–68.

92. Branch, *Parting the Waters*, 758.

93. Hailey, "Dogs and Hoses," 8, Branch, *Parting the Waters*, 758.

94. Detective R. A. Watkins to Chief Jamie Moore, May 3, 1963, Alabama Christian Movement for Civil Rights, Theophilus Eugene Bull Connor Papers, 1959–1963, 13.4, File 15–19, accessed at https://bplonline.contentdm.oclc.org/digital/collection/p16044coll1/id/29574/rec/3; Bevel quoted in Eskew, *But for Birmingham*, 265–66, Branch, *Parting the Waters*, 758.

95. Martin Luther King Jr. "Speech at the 16th Street Baptist Church, May 3, 1963," Martin Luther King Jr. Papers Project, Stanford University (courtesy of David Garrow); Branch, *Parting the Waters*, 763.

96. King, quoted in Levinson, *We've Got a Job*, 115; King and Carson, *Autobiography of Martin Luther King, Jr.*, 211.

97. King and Carson, *Autobiography of Martin Luther King, Jr.*, 211.

98. Eskew, *But for Birmingham*, 268; Branch, *Parting the Waters*, 760–61; McWhorter, *Carry Me Home*, 371.

99. Hailey, "Dogs and Hoses," 1, 8; Burrow, *Child Shall Lead Them*, 125–26.

100. Diane McWhorter provides a critical view of Gadsden as a civil rights foot soldier, *Carry Me Home*, 366. Malcolm Gladwell throws shade on the romanticized version story and telling of this infamous photograph and statue in his *Revisionist History* podcast series, http://revisionisthistory.com/episodes/14-the-foot-soldier-of-birmingham.

101. Branch, *Parting the Waters*, 758–59; Levinson, *We've Got a Job*, 82.

102. Dr. Horace Huntley interview with Aldridge Willis, February 18, 1997, Birmingham Civil Rights Institute, Oral History Project, Vol. 26.

103. Annetta Streeter Gray in Huntley and McKerley, *Foot Soldiers*, 120.

104. Dr. Horace Huntley interview with Deborah Hill, May 12, 1997, Birmingham Civil Rights Institute, Oral History Project, Vol. 26; Dr. Horace Huntley interview with Ann Niles, January 7, 1999, Birmingham Civil Rights Institute, Oral History Project, Vol. 41.

105. Dr. Horace Huntley interview with Carolyn McKinstry, April 23, 1998, Birmingham Civil Rights Institute, Oral History Project, Vol. 35.

106. Hailey, "Dogs and Hoses," 1, 8; Branch, *Parting the Waters*, 756–57; Huntley and McKerley, *Foot Soldiers*, 128; "New Marching Groups Jailed," 2; Burrow, *Child Shall Lead Them*, 105–6.

107. Dr. Horace Huntley interview with Willie Eatman, April 30, 1997, Birmingham Civil Rights Institute, Oral History Project, Vol. 26; "New Marching Groups Jailed," 2.

108. Alabama Christian Movement for Human Rights, "People in Motion, Birmingham," Box 1, Folder 17, King Center; Dr. Horace Huntley interview with Annie Levison, July 5, 1995, Birmingham Civil Rights Institute, Oral History Project, Vol. 8; Levinson, *We've Got a Job*, 113; Levine, *Freedom's Children*, 81; "Hundreds of Hookey-Playing," 2.

109. Dr. Horace Huntley interview with Danella James Bryant, June 23, 1995, Birmingham Civil Rights Institute, Oral History Project, Vol. 7.

110. Annetta Streeter Gray in Huntley and McKerley, *Foot Soldiers*, 119.

111. Dr. Horace Huntley interview with Mary E. Streeter Perry, January 14, 1998, Birmingham Civil Rights Institute, Oral History Project, Vol. 31.

112. Dr. Horace Huntley interview with Floretta Scruggs Tyson, May 5, 1995, Birmingham Civil Rights Institute, Oral History Project, Vol. 5; Dr. Horace Huntley interview with Miriam McClendon, November 8, 1995, Birmingham Civil Rights Institute, Oral History Project, Vol. 11.

113. James W. Stewart in Huntley and McKerley, *Foot Soldiers*, 138–39; Levinson, *We've Got a Job*, 88.

114. Carl Grace quoted in Huntley and McKerley, *Foot Soldiers*, 167.

115. Levinson, *We've Got a Job*, 113; Levine, *Freedom's Children*, 83.

116. She only described the story years later. Dr. Horace Huntley interview with Miriam McClendon, November 8, 1995, Birmingham Civil Rights Institute, Oral History Project, Vol. 11.

117. "Fire Hoses, Police Dogs," 2.

118. Battle, "From Slavery to Jane Crow," 115–16; Battle, *Black Girlhood*; see also LeFlouria, *Chained in Silence*.

119. Gross, "African American Women"; Gross and Hicks, "Gendering the Carceral State"; 357–65; McGuire, "It Was Like All of Us," 906–31; Devlin, xxii–xxiii, n. 23; Huntley and McKerly, *Foot Soldiers*, xvi–xvii.

120. Dr. Horace Huntley interview with Eloise Staples, March 5, 1997, Birmingham Civil Rights Institute, Oral History Project, Vol. 26.

121. Dr. Horace Huntley interview with Willie Eatman, April 30, 1997, Birmingham Civil Rights Institute, Oral History Project, Vol. 26.

122. Walker quotes in Eskew, *But for Birmingham*, 261.

123. Young, *Easy Burden*, 149.

124. Reynolds, *Maintaining Segregation*, 156.

125. Carolyn Maull McKinstry in Huntley and McKerley, *Foot Soldiers for Democracy*, 155–56.

126. "Fire Hoses, Police Dogs," 2.

127. Boutwell quoted in Eskew, *But for Birmingham*, 266; Branch, *Parting the Waters*, 761–62; Levinson, *We've Got a Job*, 95.

128. Kennedy quoted in Eskew, *But for Birmingham*, 266; Branch, *Parting the Waters*, 762; Levinson, *We've Got a Job*, 95.

129. Malcolm X quoted in Handler, "Malcolm X"; Young, "The Day We Went to Jail in Birmingham," *Friends*, February 9, 1964, Southern Christian Leadership Conference (SCLC) collection, Box 135, Folder 26, "Young—"Teens on the March in Birmingham—1964,'" King Center, Atlanta, GA; Branch, *Parting the Waters*, 680–87.

130. Editorial from News of Lynchburg reprinted in the Congressional Record 109 Appendix, August 20, 1963, A5322.

131. Branch, *Parting the Waters,* 757–58.

132. King and Carson, *Autobiography of Martin Luther King, Jr.*, 206.

133. King and Carson, *Autobiography of Martin Luther King, Jr.*, 206.

134. Branch, *Parting the Waters*, 785–91; McWhorter, *Carry Me Home*, 389; Eskew, *But for Birmingham*, 293–95.

135. Rev. Fred Shuttlesworth quoted in Detective R. A. Watkins to Chief Jamie Moore, May 3, 1963, Alabama Christian Movement for Civil Rights, Theophilus Eugene Bull Connor Papers, 1959–1963, 13.4, File 15–19, accessed at https://bplonline.contentdm.oclc.org/digital/collection/p16044coll1/id/29570/rec/3; "Schools Lose by Absences," *Birmingham News*, May 8, 1963.

136. Eskew, *But for Birmingham*, 308–9; May 3 and 6, 1963, minutes, City of Birmingham Board of Education Minute Book, April 19, 1963–March 23, 1971, Linn-Henley Research Library, Birmingham, Alabama; Levinson, *We've Got a Job*, 135–36.

137. James W. Stewart, in Huntley and McKerley, *Foot Soldiers*, 140.

138. Dr. Horace Huntley interview with Ann Niles, January 7, 1999, Birmingham Civil Rights Institute, Oral History Project, Vol. 41.

139. May 3 and 6, 1963 minutes, City of Birmingham Board of Education Minute Book, April 19, 1963–March 23, 1971, Linn-Henley Research Library, Birmingham, Alabama.

140. Loder-Jackson, *Schoolhouse Activists*, 66–67.

141. Minutes, May 20 and May 21, 1963, of the Alabama Christian Movement for Human Rights and the Southern Christian Leadership Conference, Ruth Barefield-Pendleton Collection, Box 1, Civil Rights Institute, Birmingham.

142. Minutes, May 17 and 20, 1963, City of Birmingham Board of Education Minute Book, April 19, 1963–March 23, 1971, Linn-Henley Research Library, Birmingham, Alabama.

143. Minutes, May 20 and 21, 1963, of the Alabama Christian Movement for Human Rights and the Southern Christian Leadership Conference, Ruth Barefield-Pendleton Collection, Box 1, Civil Rights Institute, Birmingham.

144. Minutes, May 29, 1963, of the Alabama Christian Movement for Human Rights and the Southern Christian Leadership Conference, Ruth Barefield-Pendleton Collection, Box 1, Civil Rights Institute, Birmingham.

145. "Birmingham's Voter-Registration Drive [1963]," SCLC collection, Box 139, Folder "139:8 Alabama, Jul-Dec. 1963," King Center.

146. Branch, *Parting the Waters*, 825.

147. Relman Morin, "Summer of Crisis: Drive for Civil Rights Embroils Entire Nation." *Washington Sunday Star* reprinted in the Congressional Record 109 Appendix, August 20, 1963, 15411–412.

148. Fred Shuttlesworth, "Youth—Living for Today and Tomorrow," in Fred Shuttlesworth Collection, Box 4, Folder 43, "Shuttleworth Speech 'Youth Living for Today and Tomorrow,' Cincinnati, Ohio, 1964."

149. Branch, *Parting the Waters*, 818.

150. Hill, *Deacons for Defense*, 21–23.

151. Branch, *Parting the Waters*, 750, 766, 834; Stanton, *Freedom Walk*; "Eight Peace Marchers Jailed," *Birmingham News*, May 1, 1963, 2.

152. "The Citizens of Gadsden to President Kennedy" "William J. Douthard [undated]," and "Report on Gadsden Movement," in Southern Christian Leadership Conference Collection, Box 139, Folder "139:8 Alabama, Jul-Dec. 1963," Eric Rainey, Gadsden, Alabama, 1963 (http://www.crmvet.org/lets/lrainey.htm), *Freedomways*, 1st Quarter, Vol. 4, 1964; Gaillard, *Cradle of Freedom*, 158–62, 167; Branch, *Parting the Waters*, 834.

153. "Mr. Eddie James Sanders, Jr. (afadavit), in SCLC collection, Box 139, Folder "139:8 Alabama, Jul-Dec. 1963," King Center.

154. "Iam Sturdivant" and "Mrs Annie Pearl Avery," in Southern Christian Leadership Conference collection, Box 139, Folder "139:8 Alabama, Jul-Dec. 1963," MLK Center; quote on Lingo from Gaillard, *Cradle of Freedom*, 156.

155. "James Foster Smith," in Southern Christian Leadership Conference collection, Box 139, Folder "139:8 Alabama, Jul-Dec. 1963."

156. Levinson, *We've Got a Job*, 140–42; Eskew, *But for Birmingham*, 317.

157. Gaillard, *Cradle of Freedom*, 189–90.

158. Minutes, May 23, 1963, of the Alabama Christian Movement for Human Rights and the Southern Christian Leadership Conference, Ruth Barefield-Pendleton Collection, Box 1, Civil Rights Institute, B'ham.

159. Eskew, *But for Birmingham*, 318–19, n. 40.

160. "Yelling Whites Set off Melee," "Witness Sees Rage Erupt"; Gaillard, *Cradle of Freedom*, 190–91; Eskew, *But for Birmingham*, 318–19; McWhorter, *Carry Me Home*, 506–7; see "Barber of Birmingham."

161. "Yelling Whites Set off Melee"; "Witness sees rage Erupt"; Gaillard, *Cradle of Freedom*, 190–91; Eskew, *But for Birmingham*, 318–19; McWhorter, *Carry Me Home*, 506–7; "Board Closes Three Schools"; see "Barber of Birmingham."

162. Eskew, *But for Birmingham*, 318–19; Gaillard, *Cradle of Freedom*, 189–92; Levinson, *We've Got a Job*, 145; McWhorter, *Carry Me Home*, 481–83, 494–98, 502–7; "West End Mixing Protested."

163. Dr. Horace Huntley interview with Carrie Delores Hamilton Lock, October 18, 1995, Birmingham Civil Rights Institute, Oral History Project, Vol. 10; Dr. Horace Huntley interview with Florida Walker Hamilton, February 14, 1996, p. 4, Birmingham Civil Rights Institute, Oral History Project, Vol. 12; Huntley and McKerley, *Foot Soldiers for Democracy*, 204–7.

164. Huntley and McKerley, *Foot Soldiers*, 184–87.

165. Hale, *Freedom Schools*, 44–45; Favors, "Shelter in a Time of Storm," 205–6; Moody, *Coming of Age in Mississippi*, 297–99; Branch, *Parting the Waters*, 814–16.

166. Hale, *Freedom Schools*, 45; Watkins, interview with the author, August 26 and 27, 2008.

167. Hale, *Freedom Schools*, 45–46; Hymethia Washington Lofton Thompson, interview with the author, August 26, 2008.

168. Hale, *Freedom Schools*, 46; Charlie Brown, interview with the author, February 11, 2016; Hymethia Washington Lofton Thompson, interview with the author, August 26, 2008; Watkins, interview with the author, August 26 and 27, 2008; Dr. Gene Young, interview with the author, August 7, 2008; "Agitators Seek Troops"; "Racial Agitator Leads," 814–16.

169. "Historical Research Project" in File 10708, "Source Material for Mississippi History, Hinds County," Folder "Education, Negro"; Bolton, *Hardest Deal of All*, 36–37; "Lanier High School Awarded $500,000 Grant," January 30, 2014, Jackson Public Schools, Lanier High School (subject file) MDAH; *The Lanier High School* (Jackson, MS, 1951–1952), 4–5, Lanier High School Subject File, MDAH; Flucker and Savage, *African Americans of Jackson*, 23; Chamberlain, "'And a Child Shall Lead,'" 47.

170. Branch, *Parting the Waters*, 818.

171. Branch, *Parting the Waters*, 832–33.

172. Hale, *Freedom Schools*, 72–74; Quoted in "Executive and Central Committees, 1961–1967," in SNCC Papers, Subgroup A, Series II, Reel 3, File 326, University of Illinois at Urbana-Champaign Archives.

173. Branch, *Parting the Waters*, 864–69; Carson, *In Struggle*, 56–65; Franklin, *Young Crusaders*, 81–84.

174. Lyon, *Memories of the Southern*, 78–81; Branch, *Parting the Waters*, 864–69; Raiford, "Come Let Us Build," 1141; V. P. Franklin, *Young Crusaders*, 84–85.

175. Henrietta Fuller quoted in Lyon, *Memories of the Southern Civil Rights Movement*, 79.

176. Lyon, *Memories of the Southern*, 78–81; Raiford, "Come Let Us Build," 1141; *Congressional Record* (August/September 1963), 18040–41.

177. Hale, *Freedom Schools*, 154–64; Sturkey and Hale, *To Write in the Light*; Perlstein, "Teaching Freedom," 297–324; Adickes, *Legacy of a Freedom School*.

178. Hale, *Freedom Schools*, 154–64; Perlstein, "Teaching Freedom."

179. "Declaration of Independence," in the MFDP Papers, Box 14, Folder 4 "Freedom School: Background Data," The King Center Library and Archives.

180. "Declaration of Independence," in the MFDP Papers, Box 14, Folder 4 "Freedom School: Background Data," The King Center Library and Archives.

181. "Columbia Pact of Southern Youth" in SNYC Papers, Box 7, Folder "Columbia Pact of Southern Youth," HU.

182. Roscoe Jones, interview with the author, March 18, 2014.

183. Hale, *Freedom Schools*, 164; *Burnside v. Byars*, 363 F.2d n. 22681 (5th Cir. 1966); *Tinker v. Des Moines*, 393 U.S. 503; 89 S. Ct (1969); Staughton Lynd, interview with the author, August 28, 2006.

184. Hale, *Freedom Schools*, 164; "Issaquena M.S.U. Freedom Fighter, August 1965," MSU Folder, FIS; Rothschild, Case of Black and White, 110–15; Bolton, *Hardest Deal*, 143–45. Some of the leaders in the boycott movement did not return to school. The leaders of the Issaquena boycott took paying jobs with the Delta Ministry, a civil rights organization based in the Mississippi Delta. One of its leaders became the first to integrate the all-White IssaquenaSharkey public school. On this, see Rothschild, *Case of Black and White*, 115.

185. Schumaker, *Troublemakers*, 50.

186. Hale, *Freedom Schools*, 164; *Burnside v. Byars*, 363 F.2d n. 22681 (5th Cir. 1966); *Tinker v. Des Moines*, 393 U.S. 503; 89 S. Ct (1969); Staughton Lynd, interview with the author, August 28, 2006; Schumaker, "The Right to Free Speech: Students and the Black Freedom Struggle in Mississippi," in *Troublemakers*, 11–50.

187. Schumaker, *Troublemakers*, 47–50.

188. Anderson, "'A Tale of Two Browns,'" 30–32; see also Fultz, "Displacement of Black Educators," 11–45.

189. Jeffries, *Bloody Lowndes*, 1, 31, 149; Garrow, *Protest at Selma*, 63.

190. Herbers, "20 More Seized in Alabama," 1; Herbers, "Negroes Step Up Drive," 1; Fairclough, *To Redeem the Soul of America*, 231–33; Garrow, *Protest at Selma*, 88–90.

191. Adler, "Letter from Selma"; Norris, "Memory Marches On."

192. "Civil Rights Army," 1, 2; Deborah Webb, interview with the author, February 29, 2016; Herman Harris, interview with the author, February 25, 2016; Linda Chapman, Queen Barker, and Rose Bell, interview with February 26, 2016; "Whites Operate March Campsite"; Rankin, "St. Jude Opened Arms."

193. "Civil Rights Army," 1, 2.

194. Deborah Webb, interview with the author, February 29, 2016; Rankin, "St. Jude Opened Arms."

195. "K. T. Brown."

196. Herbers, "Negro Teachers Protest in Selma."

197. Fairclough, *To Redeem the Soul of America*, 232.

198. "A Biographical Sketch of Herman Harris," in Herman Harris Collection, Folder 4, "A Biographical Sketch of Herman Harris, Why Vote for Herman Harris," ASU Archives.

199. "A Biographical Sketch of Herman Harris," in Herman Harris Collection, Folder 4, "A Biographical Sketch of Herman Harris, Why Vote for Herman Harris," Alabama State University Archives.

200. "Assembly of Teachers Elects Two New Officials," March 8, 1967, and in Herman Harris Collection, Folder 11, "Newspaper Clippings 1965 & Various Dates" (Herman Harris), "A Biographical Sketch of Herman Harris," in Herman Harris Collection, Folder 4, "A Biographical Sketch of Herman Harris, Why Vote for Herman Harris," ASU.

201. "Teachers Pay Tied to Attendance," and "Real Problem, Bad Solution," *Alabama Journal* May 27, 1965, in Herman Harris Collection, Folder 11, "Newspaper Clippings 1965 & Various Dates," ASU; Loder-Jackson, *Schoolhouse Activists*, 66–67.

202. Herman Harris, "As Our Governor Said," *Montgomery Advertiser*, May 26, 1965, in Herman Harris Collection, Folder 11 "Newspaper Clippings 1965 & Various Dates," ASU.

203. Herman Harris, "As Our Governor Said"; "Your Schools, March 1970" in "Dual Association Merger—South Carolina," Box #0519, Folder 5, Gelman Library, George Washington State University.

204. "To Whom it May Concern," Folder 9, "Montgomery County Teachers Association," Richard Kennan to Herman Harris, July 13, 1965, Folder 10, "National Education Association"; Herman Harris to Robert Carter, June 2, 1965, Folder 7, "Correspondence from Herman Harris (1962–1965)"; Mr. and Mrs. Robert Crittenden to Herman Harris, May 26, 1965, telegram, Leonard Hall to Herman Harris, May 26, 1965, telegram, Henry Spears to Herman Harris, May 26, 1965, all in Herman Harris Collection, ASU.

205. Idessa Williams to Herman Harris, May 26, 1965, Folder 8, "Correspondence to Herman Harris (1964–2000)," Herman Harris Collection, ASU.

206. Mr. and Mrs. L. R. Williams to Herman Harris, June 1, 1965, Folder 8, "Correspondence to Herman Harris (1964–2000)," all in in Herman Harris Collection, ASU.

207. George W. Jones to Herman Harris, June 1, 1965, Folder 8, "Correspondence to Herman Harris (1964–2000)," all in Herman Harris Collection, ASU.

208. Graham, *Young Activists*, 51–81; Rury and Hill, "An End of Innocence," 486–508.

209. Walker, "Black Power"; Mirel, *Rise and Fall*, 332–34.

210. Bundy, "Revolutions Happen," 273–93; Tess Bundy, "Black Student Power in Boston," January 2018, *Black Perspectives and African American Intellectual History Society*, accessed at https://www.aaihs.org/black-student-power-in-boston/.

211. Fountain Jr., "Legacy of Berkeley High School's"; see also Fountain Jr. "Building a Student Movement"; Aaron G. Fountain Jr. "War in the Schools," 22–41.

212. Danns, "Chicago High School Students," 138–50; Danns, *Something Better*.

213. V. P. Franklin, "Black High School Student," 3–8; on student activism in Pennsylvania secondary activism, see Dwayne C. Wright, "Black Pride Day," 151–62.

214. Garcia and Castro, *Blowout!*; Dolores Delgado Bernal, "Grassroots Leadership Reconceptualized," 113–42; Munoz Jr., *Youth, Identity, Power*, 47–98.

215. Branch, *Parting the Waters*, 808–9, 834–36; Eskew, *But for Birmingham*, 312; Gaillard, *Cradle of Freedom*, 173–74; Loevy, *Civil Rights Act of 1964*, 38–42; Fairclough, *To Redeem the Soul*, 133–36.

216. King quoted in Gaillard, *Cradle of Freedom*, 174.

217. Branch, "March on Washington," in *Pillar of Fire*, 846–87; Gaillard, *Cradle of Freedom*, 179–84.

218. Levinson, *We've Got a Job*, 144–45; see also Stewart in *Foot Soldiers*, 132–41.

219. See Eskew, "Bombingham" in *But for Birmingham*, 53–84.

220. Minutes, May 23, 1963, of the Alabama Christian Movement for Human Rights and the Southern Christian Leadership Conference, Ruth Barefield-Pendleton Collection, Box 1, Civil Rights Institute, B'ham.

221. Wallace quoted in Gaillard, *Cradle of Freedom*, 191; Alabama Christian Movement for Human Rights, "People in Motion, Birmingham," Box 1, Folder 17, King Center.

222. Branch, *Parting the Waters*, 888–90; *Carry Me Home*, on Chamblis, 72–75, 520–21; Gaillard, *Cradle of Freedom*, 196–97; "Policy, FBI Sift Blast."

223. Branch, *Parting the Waters*, 890–92; McWhorter, *Carry Me Home*, 531; Gaillard, *Cradle of Freedom*, 198–200.

224. Dr. Horace Huntley interview with Deborah Sanders Avery, May 6, 1998, Birmingham Civil Rights Institute, Oral History Project, Vol. 35.

225. Dr. Horace Huntley interview with Eloise Staples, March 5, 1997, Birmingham Civil Rights Institute, Oral History Project, Vol. 26.

226. Dr. Horace Huntley interview with Denise Armstrong Wrushen, April 28, 1995, Birmingham Civil Rights Institute, Oral History Project, Vol. 42.

227. Dr. Horace Huntley interview with Carolyn McKinstry, April 23, 1998, Birmingham Civil Rights Institute, Oral History Project, Vol. 35.

228. Young, "The Day We Went to Jail in Birmingham," 4–5.

229. James W. Stewart in Huntley and McKerley, *Foot Soldiers*, 141.

Chapter 5

1. Hale, "Future Foot Soldiers," 645–48; M. E. Brown, "Civil Rights Activism"; Cox, "1963: The Year of Decision"; Lowe, "*Brown* on Trial," 33–55; Hale and Cooper, "Lowcountry, High Standards."

2. "To All Black Students at Rivers High School," in Folder "High School—Miscellaneous, 1967–69," Box 862, Charleston County School District Archives, Charleston, SC; Hale, "Future Foot Soldiers," 646–47.

3. "To All Black Students at Rivers High School," in Folder "High School—Miscellaneous, 1967–69" and "Suspension of Jones, Barbara, Mr. Willis I. Russell to Mr. Eugene C. Clark, November 14, 1969," Box 862, Charleston County School District Archives, Charleston, SC.

4. "Suspension of Jones, Barbara, Mr. Willis I. Russell to Mr. Eugene C. Clark, November 14, 1969," in Folder "High School—Miscellaneous, 1967–69," Box 862, Charleston County School District Archives, Charleston, SC; Hale, "Future Foot Soldiers," 647–48.

5. "To All Black Students at Rivers High School," in Folder "High School—Miscellaneous, 1967–69," Box 862, Charleston County School District Archives, Charleston, SC; Hale, "Future Foot Soldiers," 651.

6. Hale, "Future Foot Soldiers," 647–48; Graham, *Young Activists*, 5–6; Judith Kafka, *History of "Zero Tolerance,"* 56–58, 99–103; Judith Kafka, "'Sitting on a Tinderbox,'" 247–70; Hampel, *Last Little Citadel*, 103–22; Jordan, "Discourses of Difference," 90; "Brown v. Board of Education," 49; Schept, Wall, and Brisman, "Building, Staffing, and Insulating," 96–115; *National Association of Secondary School Principals [NASSP] Bulletin*, cited in Abrell and Hanna, "High School Student Unrest," 396; Libarle and Seligson, *High School Revolutionaries*, xiii; Bayers, "Social Issues and Protest Activity"; "In Public Schools," 8–10; Ravitch, *Troubled Crusade*, 146–49, 251; Perlstein, *Justice, Justice*, 117–19; Grant, *World We Created*, 2–3, 29–37; Hale, "Fight Was Instilled," 6–8; Mercer, "Detention of a Different Kind." On the desegregation and discipline of Black students in Charleston County, see Davis, "The Outliers."

7. V. P. Franklin, *Young Crusaders*; Danns, "Chicago High School," 138–50; Danns, *Something Better for Our Children*; Walker, "Black Power, Youth Politics"; Walker, "Black Power and the Detroit"; Graham, *Young Activists*; Graham, "Flaunting the Freak Flag," 522–43; Fountain Jr., "War in the Schools"; Rury and Hill, "End of Innocence," 486–508; Schumaker, *Troublemakers*; Fernandez, *Young Lords*; Garcia and Castro, *Blowout!*; Ruhl, "'Forward You Must Go.'"

8. "Battle in the Schools," 10-A (quotation); Kafka, *History of "Zero Tolerance,"* 14–16; Hale, "Future Foot Soldiers," 647–48.

9. Hale, "Future Foot Soldiers," 647–48; Gooding, "Teacher is Shot," 1-A; Isaac, "Burke Student Charged," 1-A, 4-A (quotation on 4-A).

10. Willis, *Audacious Agitation*.

11. Hinton, *From the War*; Kafka, *History of "Zero Tolerance"*; Balto, *Occupied Territory*; Suddler, *Presumed Criminal*; Camp, *Incarcerating the Crisis*; Suddler, *Presumed Criminal*.

12. Travis and Obee, *Mississippi's Exiled Daughter*, 45–57; Hale, *Freedom Schools*, 54–55; Travis, interview; "Striking Students Face"; "Girl Committed"; "19 of 119 Marchers"; "Reign of Terror"; "Fifteen Demonstrators"; Mississippi Sovereignty Commission Files, SCR ID # 2-36-1-43-1-1-1; Dittmer, *Local People*, 107–15; Payne, *I've Got the Light*, 118–28; Ward, *Black Child-Savers*, 205–6. The McComb school board, prompted by concerned local community members and activists conferred honorary degrees on Brenda Travis and other students who were expelled for their participation in the sit-in and formally recognized them forty-five years after the initial sit-in. See "Making Amends" on the criminalization of Black girls in schools, which is a direct consequence of this history and a continuation of the experiences like those of Brenda Travis, see M. W. Morris, *Pushout*.

13. Eskew, *But for Birmingham*, 308–9; May 3 and 6, 1963, minutes, City of Birmingham Board of Education Minute Book, April 19, 1963–March 23, 1971, Linn-Henley Research Library, Birmingham, Alabama; Levinson, *We've Got a Job*, 135–36.

14. Suddler, *Presumed Criminal*, 97–107; Kafka, "Disciplining Youth," 197–221; Kafka, *History of "Zero Tolerance,"* 59–63; Hartman, *Education and the Cold War*; Perlstein, "Imagined Authority," 407–25; Brooks, *Blackboard Jungle*; Balto, *Occupied Territory*, 164–66.

15. Public Law 87–274, "Juvenile Delinquency and Youth Offenses Act of 1961," Juvenile Delinquency and Youth Offenses Act of 1961, 42 U.S.C. § 2541 (1976); Wolf, "The Juvenile Delinquency Prevention Act"; Olson-Raymer, "Role of the Federal Government," 578–600; Hinton, *From the War*, 32–33.

16. *Congressional Record* (Senate) Vol. 109, Part 1 (January 9, 1963, to January 30, 1963), 823–44; Grant, "Archdiocese Drops Football," A1.

17. "Grid Riot," 1; *Congressional Record* (Senate) Vol. 109, Part 1 (January 9, 1963, to January 30, 1963), 824–25, 828–29.

18. Ward, "D.C. School Hearings," 82–110.

19. *Congressional Record* (Senate) Vol. 109, Part 1 (January 9, 1963 to January 30, 1963), 823–44.

20. Holland quoted in *Congressional Record* (Senate) (1963), 843.

21. Shane MacCarthey, letter to Superintendent Carl P. Hansen, *Congressional Record* (Senate) Vol. 109, Part 1 (January 9, 1963 to January 30, 1963), 1284.

22. "Grid Riot," 1; *Congressional Record* (Senate) Vol. 109, Part 1 (January 9, 1963, to January 30, 1963), 830.

23. Act No 460, Alabama Laws of the Legislature of Alabama, Vol. 2 (1963), p. 995.

24. Act No 460, Alabama Laws of the Legislature of Alabama, Vol. 2 (1963), p. 995.

25. Act No 460, Alabama Laws of the Legislature of Alabama, Vol. 2 (1963), p. 995; "Judge Tuttle Shows."

26. "Teachers Pay Tied to Attendance," and "Real Problem, Bad Solution," *Alabama Journal*, May 27, 1965, in Herman Harris Collection, Folder 11 "Newspaper clippings 1965 & various dates," ASU; Loder-Jackson, *Schoolhouse Activists*, 66–67.

27. Hale, *Freedom Schools*, 106–7; *Laws of the State of Mississippi: Appropriations, General Legislation and Resolutions* (Published by Authority, 1964), 487–88, 507–511, 543, MDAH; new laws permitted the names of such offenders to be published.

28. "No. 943, An Act to Amend Section 16-551" 2308, "South Carolina Statutes at Large, General and Permanent Laws—1968," in 1962 legislators racialized in 1962 to prohibit giving custody of White children to Black families, "Disturbing School Attended by Girls of Women, §16–551" *Code of Laws of South Carolina 1962*, v. 4 (Charlottesville: Michie Company, 1962). On the Orangeburg Massacre, see Sellers, *River of No Return*; Bass and Nelson, *Orangeburg Massacre*; Shuler, *Blood & Bone*.

29. Public Law 89-197, "Law Enforcement Assistance Act of 1965" Katzenbach, *Challenge of Crime*, 69–74 (quote on 69); Thompson, "Criminalizing Kids," 131–42.

30. Platt, "Saving and Controlling," 14–16; Katzenbach, *Challenge of Crime*, 12–15; Henning, "Challenge of Race and Crime," 1647.

31. Moynihan, *Negro Family*; Katzenbach, et al., *Challenge of Crime*; Public Law 90-351; 82 Stat. 197 Omnibus Crime Control and Safe Streets Act of 1968.

32. "Hoodlums vs. Fans."

33. Department of Health, Education, and Welfare, "Violent Schools," iii.

34. McCurdy, "Fear of Transfers," D1-3; quote in Kafka, *"History of 'Zero Tolerance,'"* 103.

35. Abrell and Hanna, "High School Student," 397; Graham, *Young Activists*, 167–94; Hendrick and Jones, *Student Dissent*, 3–48, 344–96.

36. Graham, *Young Activists*, 4–9; *National Association of Secondary School Principals [NASSP] Bulletin,* cited in Abrell and Hanna, "High School Student," 396; Libarle and Seligson, *High School Revolutionaries,* xiii; see also Graham, "Flaunting the Freak Flag," 522–43; Flacks, "Social and Cultural Meanings," 123–33.

37. Herbers, "High School Unrest Rises," 1; "Protests in High Schools," 18.

38. Stockton, "School District Trustees," 1-B; "Self-Policing Schools"; Hale, "Future Foot Soldiers," 649; Stockton, "Boycotting Pupils," 1-B; "Students Placed Under Bond."

39. Stockton, "James Island High School."

40. "Parents Meeting, North Charleston High School," February 19, 1971, in "Open and Executive Minutes, September 1960–November 1984," Box 1205, Charleston County School District Archives, Charleston, SC, CCSD archives.

41. "Parents Meeting, North Charleston High School," February 19, 1971, in "Open and Executive Minutes, September 1960–November 1984," Box 1205, Charleston County School District Archives, Charleston, SC, CCSD archives.

42. Stockton, "School District Trustees Order," 1-B; Stockton, "Boycotting Pupils," 1-B; Bigsbee, "North Charleston Pupils"; Hale, "Future Foot Soldiers," 649.

43. "Parents Meeting, North Charleston High School," February 19, 1971, in "Open and Executive Minutes, September 1960–November 1984," Box 1205, Charleston County School District Archives, Charleston, SC, CCSD archives.

44. "Concerned Parents Petition" [July 20, 1970] in Box 29, Folder "RCSD #1: Discipline: Gen: 1970–1972," M. Hayes Mizell Collection.

45. "Parents Meeting, North Charleston High School," February 19, 1971, in "Open and Executive Minutes, September 1960–November 1984," Box 1205, Charleston County School District Archives, Charleston, SC, CCSD archives.

46. Stockton, "School District Trustees Order," 1-B; in Cooper River School District Number Four, February 27, 1971, Minutes, in "Open and Executive Minutes, September 1960–November 1984," Box 1205, CCSD archives.

47. January 18, 1971, Minutes, Charleston County Board of Education, 1949–1972, CCSD archives; Stockton, "School District Trustees Order," 1-B; Stockton, "Boycotting Pupils," 1-B; Bigsbee, "North Charleston Pupils Suspended"; Hale, "Future Foot Soldiers," 649.

48. "In the matter of expulsion from Keenan High School" [November 24, 1970], p. 1 in Box 29, Folder "RCSD #1: Discipline: Gen: 1970–1972" in M. Hayes Mizell Collection; Folder "Racial Disturbance at Dreher High School and Lower Richland High School Investigation, 1972" in Box 29 M. Hayes Mizell Collection.

49. "Constituent School District Number Four of Charleston County Board Policy," February 19, 1971, in "Open and Executive Minutes, September 1960–November 1984," Box 1205, Charleston County School District Archives, Charleston, SC, CCSD archives; "Charleston County Board of Education Minutes, January 18, 1971," in Minutes, Chas. Co. Board of Education, 1949–1972 (reel), CCSD archives.

50. "Parents Meeting, North Charleston High School," February 19, 1971, in "Open and Executive Minutes, September 1960–November 1984," Box 1205, Charleston County School District Archives, Charleston, SC, CCSD archives.

51. "Parents Meeting, North Charleston High School," February 19, 1971, in "Open and Executive Minutes, September 1960–November 1984," Box 1205, Charleston County School District Archives, Charleston, SC, CCSD archives.

52. Stockton, "School District Trustees Order," 1-B; Stockton, "Boycotting Pupils," 1-B; Bigsbee, "North Charleston Pupils Suspended"; Hale, "Future Foot Soldiers," 649.

53. Stockton, "School District Trustees Order," 1-B; "Self-Policing Schools."

54. Walsh, *Racial Taxation*; Delmont, *Why Busing Failed*; Anderson, *Education of Blacks in the South*.

55. Bigsbee, "North Charleston Pupils Suspended."

56. Stockton, "Boycotting Pupils"; "Students Placed Under Bond."

57. Stockton, "James Island High School."

58. John W. Foard to Claud E. Kitchens, March 9, 1972, in Box 29, Folder "RCSD #1: Discipline: Gen: 1970–1972," M. Hayes Mizell Collection.

59. "In the matter of expulsion from Keenan High School" [November 24, 1970], p. 1 in Box 29, Folder "RCSD #1: Discipline: Gen: 1970–1972" in M. Hayes Mizell Collection.

60. "In the matter of expulsion from Keenan High School" [November 24, 1970], p. 1 in Box 29, Folder "RCSD #1: Discipline: Gen: 1970–1972" in M. Hayes Mizell Collection.

61. "Report of Richland County School District One Fact-Finding Committee," pp. 1–2 in Box 29, Folder "Racial Disturbance at Dreher High School and Lower Richland High School Investigation, 1972" in M. Hayes Mizell Collection.

62. "Report of Richland County School District One Fact-Finding Committee," pp. 2–3 in Box 29, Folder "Racial Disturbance at Dreher High School and Lower Richland High School Investigation, 1972" in M. Hayes Mizell Collection.

63. "Press Release, Black Coalition for Justice in the Schools," March 13, 1972 in Box 29, Folder "Racial Disturbance at Dreher High School and Lower Richland High School Investigation, 1972" in M. Hayes Mizell Collection; William C. Goodwin, "Group Votes to Boycott Until School Demands Met," *The State*, March 13, 1972, 1-B, 3-B in Box 7, M. Hayes Mizell Collection, https://digital.tcl.sc.edu/digital/collection/p17173coll25/id/1613.

64. "Press Release, Black Coalition for Justice in the Schools," March 13, 1972 in Box 29, Folder "Racial Disturbance at Dreher High School and Lower Richland High School Investigation, 1972" in M. Hayes Mizell Collection.

65. "Memorandum, Richland County School District, No. One," March 16, 1972, pp. 2–5 in Box 29, Folder "Racial Disturbance at Dreher High School and Lower Richland High School Investigation, 1972" in M. Hayes Mizell Collection.

66. "Memorandum, Richland County School District, No. One," March 16, 1972, pp. 5–6 in Box 29, Folder "Racial Disturbance at Dreher High School and Lower Richland High School Investigation, 1972" in M. Hayes Mizell Collection; Margaret N. O'Shea and Hugh E. Munn, "Coalition, District One Board Meet" [March 15, 1972], Box 7, M. Hayes Mizell Collection, https://digital.tcl.sc.edu/digital/collection/p17173coll25/id/1627.

67. Memorandum, Richland County School District, No. One," p. 7, March 16, 1972 in Box 29, Folder "Racial Disturbance at Dreher High School and Lower

Richland High School Investigation, 1972" in M. Hayes Mizell Collection; Marga-ret N. O'Shea and Hugh E. Munn, "Coalition, District One Board Meet" [March 15, 1972], Box 7, M. Hayes Mizell Collection, https://digital.tcl.sc.edu/digital/collection/p17173coll25/id/1627.

68. "Memorandum, Richland County School District, No. One," March 16, 1972, pp. 10–12 in Box 29, Folder "Racial Disturbance at Dreher High School and Lower Richland High School Investigation, 1972" in M. Hayes Mizell Collection.

69. "Memorandum, Richland County School District, No. One," March 16, 1972, p. 12 in Box 29, Folder "Racial Disturbance at Dreher High School and Lower Richland High School Investigation, 1972" in M. Hayes Mizell Collection; Margaret N. O'Shea and Hugh E. Munn, "Coalition, District One Board Meet" [March 15, 1972], Box 7, M. Hayes Mizell Collection, https://digital.tcl.sc.edu/digital/collection/p17173coll25/id/1627.

70. "Report of Richland County School District One Fact-Finding Committee," pp. 6–8, in Box 29, Folder "Racial Disturbance at Dreher High School and Lower Richland High School Investigation, 1972" in M. Hayes Mizell Collection.

71. "Position Paper, National Urban League" [July 21, 1971] in Box 15, Folder "ED: Discipline: NSRN: Position Paper, National Urban League," J. Hayes Mizell Collection, USC.

72. Kafka, *History of "Zero Tolerance,"* 92–94.

73. Kafka, *History of "Zero Tolerance,"* 103–9.

74. Kafka, *History of "Zero Tolerance,"* 6–9; Bybee and Gee, *Violence, Values and Justice*; Kaestle, *Pillars of the Republic.*

75. Hale, "Future Foot Soldiers," 32 n. 78; Hale, *Freedom Schools*, 161–66; Schu-maker, *Troublemakers*, 47–50; Graham, *Young Activists*, 4–6, 167–94; Hendrick and Jones, *Student Dissent*, 3–48, 344–96; Bayers, "Social Issues"; Grossberg, "Liberation and Caretaking."

76. Jimmy C. Bales to Coley Green, February 7, 1973, in Box 30, Folder RCSD #1: Discipline: Suspensions: Green vs. RCSD #1, 1973 in M. Hayes Mizell Collection.

77. *Barbara Green v. The Board of Commissioners of Richland County School District Number One* (Civil Action No. 73-240), February 26, 1973, and "Judge Simon's order in Lower Richland case (Green)" located in Box 30, Folder RCSD #1: Discipline: Suspensions: Green vs. RCSD #1, 1973 in M. Hayes Mizell Collection.

78. Hinton, *From the War on Poverty*, 220.

79. Juvenile Justice and Delinquency Prevention Act of 1974, Public Law 93-415; Hinton, *From the War on Poverty*, 220–22, 234–39.

80. Hinton, *From the War on Poverty*, 221, 234–39; "Education Amendments of 1974," Public Law 93-380-AUG. 21, 1974 (ESEA), accessed on October 7, 2020, at https://www.govinfo.gov/content/pkg/STATUTE-88/pdf/STATUTE-88-Pg484.pdf.

81. Richard Nixon quoted in "Transcript of Nixon's Acceptance," 47.

82. Stern, "Forgotten History of School Violence."

83. Hinton, *From the War on Poverty*, 92, 218–21, 234–39; Brown, "Understand-ing and Assessing," 592; Thompson, "Why Mass Incarceration Matters," 710–12;

Kafka, *History of "Zero Tolerance,"* 99–106; Noble, "Policing the Hallways"; Mulqueen, "School Resource Officers"; "Education Amendments of 1974"; French-Marcelin and Hinger and the ACLU "Bullies in Blue."

84. Tager, Rabrenovic, and Jones, *Boston Riots*, 198–200; 209–14; Bundy, "Revolutions Happen," 273–93; Hampel, *Last Little Citadel*, 103–22.

85. Graham, *Young Activists*, 185–86.

86. "Position Paper, National Urban League" [July 21, 1971] in Box 15, Folder "ED: Discipline: NSRN: Position Paper, National Urban League," J. Hayes Mizell Collection, USC.

87. Vaden, "Before the Corridor of Shame," 17, 49; South Carolina Code of Laws, Title 59-Education, Article 3.

88. Graham, *Young Activists*, 120–21; Grant, *World We Created*, 49–53; Black, *Ending Zero Tolerance*, 37–42.

89. Black, *Ending Zero Tolerance*, 36–38.

90. Children's Defense Fund, *Children Out of School*, 130.

91. Children's Defense Fund, *School Suspensions*, 10–12; Black, *Ending Zero Tolerance*, 35–36.

92. *Student Pushout*, 5 (second quote), 51, 75 (first quote).

93. Hinton, *From the War*, 223–24.

94. Black, *Ending Zero Tolerance*, 35–37; Levin and Hawley, *Courts, Social Science*, 383.

95. Larkin, "School Desegregation," 488–91; see also Children's Defense Fund, *Children out of School*.

96. Children's Defense Fund, *Children out of School*, 124–26.

97. "Richland County School District #1, Pupils Suspended for 1 to 20 Consecutive School Days, 1973–1974," in Box 30, Folder "RCSD #1: Discipline: Suspension: General, 1972–1976," M. Hayes Mizell Collection.

98. South Carolina Community Relations Program of the American Friends Service Committee, "A Report on Short-Term, Out-of-School Disciplinary Suspensions," p. 7 in Box 30, M. Hayes Mizell Collection.

99. "Richland County School District #1, Short-Term Suspensions, August 29–November 27, 1974," in Box 30, Folder "RCSD #1: Discipline: Suspension: General, 1972–1976," M. Hayes Mizell Collection.

100. Thomas C. McCain, Letter to Edgefield County Citizens [February 14, 1975] in Box 11, M. Hayes Mizell Collection, USC.

101. M. Hayes Mizell to William H. Thomas, January 27, 1975; William H. Thomas to M. Hayes Mizell, May 8, 1975; M. Hayes Mizell to Lamar Clements, July 12, 1977, Box 30, M. Hayes Mizell Collection, USC.

102. Kafka, *History of "Zero Tolerance,"* 103.

103. Department of Health, Education, and Welfare, "Violent Schools–Safe Schools" iii.

104. Chafe, *Civilities and Civil*, 185–92.

105. Their sentences were later overturned, for a full history, see Janken, *Wilmington Ten*.

106. Hale, *Freedom Schools,* 200; Mississippi Sovereignty Commission Files, SCR ID # 1-118-0-16-1-1-1; 8-20-2-82-1-1-1; 8-20-2-82-2-1-1; "Shooting Case Appeal Fails," *Times-Picayune* (4/24/1973); Orr-Klopfer, *Where Rebels Roost,* 561–90.

107. Stern, "Forgotten History."

108. Hayes Mizell, "Creative Strategies for Reducing Suspension and Dropouts" (May 2 and 3, 1979), Box 15, Folder "Discipline, Suspension Conferences, 1972–1981," J. Hayes Mizell Collection, USC.

109. "Morris Appeals to Students to Respect Law, Schools" *The State,* March 14, 1972, Box 7, M. Hayes Mizell Collection, https://digital.tcl.sc.edu/digital/collection/p17173coll25/id/1614.

110. "Self-Policing Schools," *The News and Courier,* February 24, 1971.

111. James A. Wilsford to Michael P. Kushner, February 20, 1973, p. 3, 11, Box 29, Folder "RCSD #1: Discipline: Gen: 1973–1974," J. Hayes Mizell Collection.

112. "Report of Richland County School District One Fact-Finding Committee," p. 4, Box 29, Folder "Racial Disturbance at Dreher High School and Lower Richland High School Investigation, 1972," M. Hayes Mizell Collection.

113. Kafka, *History of "Zero Tolerance,"* 103–9.

114. Libarle and Seligson, *High School Revolutionaries,* xiii.

115. See Givens, *Fugitive Pedagogy.*

116. Jack Greenberg, "Racial Integration," 586.

117. Potts, *A History of the Palmetto Education Association,* 67.

118. Hale, "'We Are Not Merging," 463–81; M. E. Brown, "Civil Rights Activism"; David S. Cecelski, *Along Freedom Road,* 8–9; Clark, *Echo in My Soul,* 118; Fultz, "Displacement of Black Educators," 1, 23; Potts, *History of the Palmetto,* 66–67.

119. Ethridge, "Impact," 217.

120. Tillman, "(Un)Intended consequences?" 281.

121. Madkins, "Black Teacher Shortage," 418–19; Hawkins, "Casualties," 26–31; Hudson and Holmes, "Missing Teachers," 388–93.

122. For an overview of the numbers of displaced and dismissed teachers in the wake of *Brown,* see Anderson, "'A Tale of Two Browns,'" 30–32; Tillman, "(Un)Intended consequences?," 280–303; Hudson and Holmes, "Missing Teachers," 388–93; Fultz, "Displacement of Black Educators," 28; Fairclough, "Costs of *Brown,*" 53–56; Milner and Howard, "Black Teachers, Black Students," 286; Milner and Howard also discuss the role of colorism in the displacement, dismissal, and demotion of Black teachers, 289–90; Smith and Smith, "For Black Educators," 7–12; on North Carolina, see Joyner, "Pimping Brown"; Parker, "Desegregating Teachers," 14–15; D'Amico, Pawlewicz, Earley, and McGeehan, "Where Are All the Black Teachers?" 27–30; Hale, "We Are Not Merging"; Hudson and Homes estimate that between 1984 and 1989, an additional 21,515 Black teacher candidates and teachers were eliminated from the profession due to new teaching certification and college of education admissions requirements, "Missing Teachers, Impaired Communities," 388–93; Fenwick, *Jim Crow's Pink Slip.*

123. Oakley, Stowell, and Logan, "Impact of Desegregation," 1576–98.

124. Hooker, "Displacement of Black Teachers," 18–19.

125. Hooker, "Displacement of Black Teachers," 28.

126. Hooker, "Displacement of Black Teachers," 26.

127. Hooker, "Displacement of Black Teachers," 32–34.

128. Milner and Howard, "Black Teachers, Black Students," 285–97; S. H. King, "Limited Presence of African-American Teachers," 116–20; Ladson-Billings, *The Dreamkeepers*; Ladson-Billings, "Toward a Theory," 465–91; Howard, "Powerful Pedagogy," 179–202; J. E. King, "Unfinished Business," 245–71.

129. Walker, *Their Highest Potential*; Walker, *Hello Professor*; Walker, *Lost Education*.

130. Walker, *Their Highest Potential*, 208.

131. Anderson, "'A Tale of Two Browns,'" 30–32; Tillman, "(Un)Intended Consequences?" 280–303; Hudson and Holmes, "Missing Teachers, Impaired Communities"; 388–93; Fultz, "Displacement," 28; Joyner, "Pimping Brown"; Parker, "Desegregating Teachers," 14–15; D'Amico et al., *"Where Are All the Black Teachers?"* 27–30.

132. Ethridge, "Impact of the 1954," 224.

133. Ethridge, "Impact of the 1954," 230.

134. Hooker, Race Relations Information Center "Displacement of Black Teachers," 6.

135. Thomas C. McCain, Letter to Edgefield County Citizens [February 14, 1975], Box 11, J. Hayes Mizell Collection, USC; Hooker, Race Relations Information Center "Displacement of Black Teachers," pp. 11–12.

136. Ethridge, "Impact of the 1954," 223–24.

137. Hooker, Race Relations Information Center "Displacement of Black Teachers," 1–6.

138. "Report: Training Coordination Center for Displaced Teachers" (1972), Box 11, J. Hayes Mizell Collection, USC.

139. Brooks v. School District of Mobley, Missouri, 267. F 2nd 733 (8th Cir. 1959); Ethridge, "Impact of the 1954," 219.

140. Hale, "'We are Not Merging.'"

141. *Franklin v. County School Board of Giles County*, 242 F. Supp. 371 (W.D. Va. 1965); Ethridge, "Impact of the 1954," 219; "Your Schools: Newsletter of the South Carolina Community Relations Program" (March 1970), Folder 5, "Dual Association Merger—South Carolina" Box #0519, NEA Papers; Hale, "We Are Not Merging," 467–69.

142. *Wall v. Stanly County Board of Education*, 259 F. Supp. 238 (M.D.N.C. 1966); "Your Schools: Newsletter of the South Carolina Community Relations Program" (March 1970), Folder 5, "Dual Association Merger—South Carolina," Box #0519, NEA Papers; Hale, "We Are Not Merging," 467–69.

143. *Lee v. Macon County Board of Education*, 267 F. Supp. 458 (M.D. Ala. 1967); Hale, "We Are Not Merging," 467–69; "Toward Merger—Faculty and Staff" in ASTA Collection, Folder 19, Box 12, "ASTA and AEA Merger," ASTA Collection.

144. Orfield, *Reconstruction of Southern Education*; Tillman, "Unintended Consequences of *Brown*," 286–88; Ethridge, "Impact of the 1954," 219–21.

145. Robert W. Hooker, Race Relations Information Center "Displacement of Black Teachers," 1–2; 16–18.

146. "What's Happening to Black Educators in S.C.?" (c. 1970), Box 11, J. Hayes Mizell Collection, USC.

147. "What's Happening to Black Educators in S.C.?" (c. 1970), Box 11, J. Hayes Mizell Collection, USC.

148. "Report: Training Coordination Center for Displaced Teachers" (1972), p. 2 in Box 11, J. Hayes Mizell Collection, USC.

149. Baker, "Testing Equality, 1936–1946," in *Paradoxes of Desegregation*, 44–62; Hooker, "Displacement of Black Teachers," 12–14.

150. Charron, *Freedom's Teacher*, 173; Baker, *Paradoxes of Desegregation*, 55–58.

151. Cox, "Vested Interests," 113.

152. Joyner, "Pimping Brown," 165.

153. "Report: Training Coordination Center for Displaced Teachers" (1972) in Box 11, J. Hayes Mizell Collection, USC.

154. Walker, *Their Highest Potential*, 201–5.

155. Walker, "Caswell County Training School," 166; "Vocational High School," 2.

156. Gordy, *Finding the Lost Year*; Muse, *Virginia's Massive Resistance*; Lewis, "Emergency Mothers," 72–103; Bonastia, *Southern Stalemate*; Titus, *Brown's Battleground*; B. Smith, *They Closed Their Schools*; Bolton, *Hardest Deal of All*; "Louisiana Legislature," 8; "Alabama"; "South Carolina"; J. W. White, "Managed Compliance," 54–58.

157. Titus, *Brown's Battleground*; Bonastia, *Southern Stalemate*; B. Smith, *They Closed Their Schools*; Gordy, *Finding the Lost Year*; Muse, *Virginia's Massive Resistance*; Lewis, "Emergency Mothers," 72–103.

158. Seto and Cox, "Outside the System," in possession of the author, courtesy of the Moton Museum.

159. Alejia "Mickie" Pride Carrington in Kessler, "The Healing Ground," *10 Stories 50 Years Later*, 27–28.

160. Melvin Nunnally in Morrissey and Crawford, "More Than You Might Think," *10 Stories 50 Years Later*, 27–28.

161. Dorothy Holcomb in Anderson and Trace in "A Legacy of Learning," 39–41.

162. Interview with James Ghee by Charles Edward Vaughn and James Lucaro, Folder "Civil Rights in Prince Edward County—Oral History Collection, Interview 1995.4 James Ghee"; see also, Joseph Blank, "The Lost Years," *Washington Post*, William Odum Collection, Folder 3, Longwood University; Barkan, "No Catching Up," *The Afro-American*, March 22, 1969, in William Odum Collection.

163. Glass, "Project Closing of School Brings Variety of Reaction," *Alabama Journal*, February 25, 1970, in Folder 17, "Montgomery County Booker T. Washington," Montgomery County File, Alabama Department of Archives and History (ADAH); Helms, "Negroes Ask City School," 17.

164. Bitter, "School Board Sends Money," 2; Massey, "In Two Years," 13; Massey, "Agency Has Tankful," 9.

165. Helms, "Negroes Ask City," 17; "Negroes Appeal Rejection," 12.

166. Helms, "Student Leader Hits," 23.

167. L. Brown, "Why?," 4.

168. L. Brown, "Why?," 4.

169. Butter, "7 Schools"; Butter, "Work Underway," 21.

170. Holliman, "Lee Keeps Streaking," 9; Canterbury, "Generals Roll On," 37; "Stokes, Washington Going," 51; Holliman, "Lee's Stokes"; Thomas, "Booker Transfers."

171. "Toward a Better East Point: Report No. 1" in Robert L. Sumwalt Papers, 1960–61, Box 2; "Resolution of the City Council of the City of Columbia" (June 15, 1961), in Robert L. Sumwalt Papers, 1960–61, Box 2; Betters, "United States Housing Act," 375–78.

172. "Columbia's Neighborhoods: An Analysis of Neighborhood Conditions" (Columbia, SC: City of Columbia Planning Department, January 1965), in Harold Brunton Papers, Box 28, Folder "Q. Land Acquisition."

173. Housing Authority of the City of Columbia S.C. and University of South Carolina, "Final Narrative Relocation Report," 1–3, 22–23; "HUD News" August 16, 1967; in Harold Brunton Papers, Box 29; Folder 4; "Federal Grant Set on USC Expansion," *The Columbia Record*, March 31, 1966.

174. "University Board of Trustees Resolution–Wheeler Hill Urban Renewal," February 20, 1968, in Harold Brunton Papers, Folder 15, Box 30.

175. "Wheeler Hill Died Unnecessarily," *The Gamecock*, September 9, 1976, in Harold Brunton Papers, Folder 15, Box 30.

176. Betsy White, "Mother Searches for Housing," *Columbia Reporter*, February 25, 1977, in Harold Brunton Papers, Folder 15, Box 30.

177. "Wheeler Hill Died Unnecessarily," *The Gamecock*, September 9, 1976, in Harold Brunton Papers, Folder 15, Box 30.

178. Thomas F. Jones to Dr. Guy L. Varn, November 20, 1962, in Thomas F. Jones Papers, 1962–1963, Box 2.

179. Ashley Halsey Jr. to Harold Brunton, "Rationale for Purchase of Booker T. Washington High School," May 13, 1964, in Harold Brunton Papers, Folder 4, Box 29; "Building Program—Long range plan" in Papers of Office of the Provost William H. Patterson 1969/1970, Box 1.

180. Ashley Halsey Jr. to Harold Brunton, "Rationale for Purchase of Booker T. Washington High School," May 13, 1964 in Harold Brunton Papers, Folder 4, Box 29.

181. Ashley Halsey Jr. to Harold Brunton, "Rationale for Purchase of Booker T. Washington High School," May 13, 1964 in Harold Brunton Papers, Folder 4, Box 29.

182. White, "Mother Searches for Housing" and Linda Owens, "Housing Authority Facing Continual Renewal Project," in Harold Brunton Papers, Folder 15, Box 30; Harold Brunton Jr. "A Plan for Campus Development," 13–17 in Box 1, Papers of Office of the Provost William H. Patterson 1969/1970; "Wheeler Hill Died Unnecessarily," *The Gamecock*, September 9, 1976, Harold Brunton Papers, Folder 15, Box 30.

183. James P. Cooper to Samuel Heyward, October 9, 1973, in Harold Brunton Papers, Folder 4, Box 29; H. Brunton to E. Taylor, September 24, 1969, in Harold Brunton Papers, Folder 15, Box 30; Joel B. Freid, "Demolition of certain vacant houses in the Wheeler Hill Community," (May 11, 1971), in Harold Brunton Papers, Folder 15, Box 30.

184. H. Brunton to E. Taylor, September 24, 1969, in Harold Brunton Papers, Folder 15, Box 30.

185. "Wheeler Hill Died Unnecessarily," *The Gamecock*, September 9, 1976, in Harold Brunton Papers, Folder 15, Box 30.

186. "Just a Dream"; "Landlord on the Hill," *Columbia Record*, August 30, 1976, in Harold Brunton Papers, Folder 15, Box 30.

187. Tim Beall to Richard Rempel, June 3, 1974, in Harold Brunton Papers, Folder 4, Box 29.

188. "Project Unity U.S.C. Wheller Hill" and Joel Freid "Memorandum" June 30, 1971, in Harold Brunton Papers, Folder 15, Box 30.

189. Donald Weatherbee to Thomas Jones, March 31, 1969, in Harold Brunton Papers, Folder 15, Box 30.

190. On the history of school choice and the role of southern segregationists, see Suitts, *Overturning Brown*.

191. "South Carolina"; J. W. White, "Managed Compliance," 54–58; "Byrnes Plans Study," 1, 2-A; "SC Leaders Adopt 'Wait-See' Attitude on Court Decision," 1; "SC Candidates Accent," 1, 7-A; "Virginia Lawmakers," 14; "Georgia"; Bolton, *Hardest Deal of All*, 105.

192. Suitts, Overturning Brown; Leeson, "Private Schools Continue," 22–25; McMillen, *Citizens' Council*, 297–304; Fuquay, "Civil Rights"; J. White, "Managed Compliance," 389–391.

193. Suitts, *Overturning Brown*; Leeson, "Private Schools Continue," 22–25; N. R. McMillen, *Citizens' Council*, 297–304; Fuquay, "Civil," 159–80; J. White, "Managed Compliance," 389–91; Terjen, "White Flight," 69; Nevin and Bills, *Schools That Fear Built*, 8–9.

194. "New Hooper Academy"; "St. James Completes."

195. "Hammond Academy File" in Dotsy Diane Lloyd Boineau Papers, in Bleser, *Secret and Sacred*; R. Brown, "Monster of All," 22.

196. Nevin and Bills, *Schools That Fear Built,* 3; Bolton, *Hardest Deal of All*, 108–9, 174–77; Ruby M. Thompson, "Nonpublic Schools 1967–68" and "Nonpublic Schools 1968–69" Division of Administration and Finance, State Department of Education, Jackson, MS, pp. 6–7 (Mississippi Department of Archives and History); Dreher, "How Integration Failed."

197. Nevin and Bills, *Schools that Fear Built*, 11–13.

198. Nevin and Bills, *Schools That Fear Built*, 11–13; McMillen, *Citizens' Councils*, 299–304; Jackson's Citizens' Council, "There Can Be No Compromise on the Matter of Segregation" (August 1964), Mississippi Department of Archives and History, https://jacksonfreepress.media.clients.ellingtoncms.com/news/documents/2017/11/15/Aspect_Bulletin_Aug._1964.pdf; Dreher, "How Integration Failed."

199. "Unhappy Situation," *Farmville Herald*, May 29, 1959; "Federal Domination," June 2, 1959; "Uncharted Seas," *Farmville Herald*, June 5, 1959, in "Farmville Herald School Closings: 1950–1955" Longwood University; Picott and Peeples, "Study in Infamy," 394.

200. Joseph P. Blank, "The Lost Years: What Happened to the Children When Prince Edward County, Virginia Closed its Public Schools," William Odum Collec-

tion, Box 1, Folder 3, "Odum Collection, Washington Post Article," Longwood archives; Broadwater, "We Were Just Going," 13, in possession of the author, courtesy of the Moton Museum.

201. Joseph P. Blank, "The Lost Years: What Happened to the Children When Prince Edward County, Virginia Closed its Public Schools," William Odum Collection, Box 1, Folder 3, "Odum Collection, Washington Post Article," Longwood archives; Nevin and Bills, *Schools That Fear Built*, 2–3.

202. "51 Seniors Plan Higher Education," "Fall Enrollment to Reach 1240," *The Reporter (Prince Edward School Foundation)* June 1967; Prince Edward County: A report to you [1960], Prince Edward School Closing Collection, Longwood University, Folder "Prince Edward County Schools."

203. *The Reporter (Prince Edward School Foundation)* December 1966, Prince Edward School Closing Collection, Longwood University, Folder "Prince Edward County Schools"; Prince Edward Academy reopens as Fuqua in the early 1990s, with a $10 million dollar investment. It was rebranded as a "rural model of excellence." Viadero, "At the Crossroads," 84–85.

204. Prince Edward County Foundation, "A Report to You," Prince Edward School Closing Collection, Longwood University, Folder "Prince Edward County Schools."

205. B. Blanton Hanbury to Patrons, July 1960, Prince Edward School Closing Collection, Longwood University, Folder "Prince Edward County Schools."

206. Real Revolutionaries, Remarks of Honorable Watkins M. Abbitt, *Congressional Record*, 90th Congress, Second Session.

207. "Prince Edward's Position," *Farmville Herald*, September 15, 1959, in "Farmville Herald School Closings: 1950–1955" Longwood University Collection; "A Job to Do," *Farmville Herald*, September 15, 1959, in "Farmville Herald School Closings: 1950–1955" Longwood University Collection; Picott and Peeples, "A Study in Infamy," 395; "Good News in Prince Edward," September 29, 1959, *Farmville Herald*; "Prince Edward's Consciousness," *Farmville Herald*, October 23, 1959, in "Farmville Herald School Closings: 1950–1955," Longwood University.

208. "The Wrong Answer in Prince Edward," *The Farmville Herald*, September 18, 1959, in "Farmville Herald School Closings: 1950–1955," Longwood University.

209. Leeson, "Private Schools Continue," 25.

Epilogue

1. Lewis, "Bryant Reflects on Black Student"; Shimshock, "Virginia Social Justice"; Vargas, "Girl Who Brought Down."

2. Shimshock, "Virginia Social Justice."

3. Bryant quoted in Vargas, "Girl Who Brought Down."

4. Calamur, "Ferguson Documents."

5. Equal Justice Initiative, "Black Children Are Six Times"; Kindy et al., "Police Shootings of Children"; Children's Defense Fund, "U.S. Gun Violence."

6. Bryant, "Charlottesville's Robert E. Lee"; Vargas, "Girl Who Brought."

7. Hale, *Freedom Schools*, 224–30.

8. Malcolm quoted in Huntley and McKerley, *Foot Soldiers*, 173.

9. McClendon in Huntley and McKerley, *Foot Soldiers*, 181.

10. James G. Blake interview with Thomas Dent, "South Carolina—Charleston: James G. Black Interview [Part I] (1991) accessed at https://digitallibrary.tulane .edu/islandora/object/tulane%3A53916; "Funeral Services Monday," 4.

11. M. Brown, "Somebody Had To Do It"; M. Brown, "Civil Rights Activism."

12. Joy Cabarrus Speakes, interview with the author, June 30, 2017; Joy Cabarrus Speakes, correspondence with the author, July 31, 2017; Hollingsworth, "Speakes Honored."

13. Alexander Hyres, "Dedication to the Highest of Callings"; Bryant, "School Desegregation, and the Black Freedom Struggle in Postwar Virginia, 1946–2004"; Hale, "It Only Takes a Spark": Lois Simms and Pedagogical Activism during the Black Freedom Struggle, in Alridge, Hale, and Loder-Jackson, *Schooling the Movement*.

14. Hale, "It Only Takes a Spark."

15. "Hundreds Celebrate"; "Harris Should Withdraw"; Lou Elliot and Michael Nutt, "Senate Rejects Harris as ASU Trustee," *Alabama Journal*, February 2–19, 1981, Herman Harris Collection, Folder "Herman Harris, A.S.T.A. President.

16. Banks, *Multicultural Education*; Banks and Banks, *Handbook of Research*; Paris and Alim, *Culturally Sustaining Pedagogies*; Ladson-Billings, "But That's Just Good Teaching," 159–65.

17. Hale, "History of Burke High School"; "Black History Month Special"; Birmingham City Schools, "Brief History."

18. Bailey, "BTW High School"; "Students Will Be Asked," 5.

19. For a larger history of school choice, see Hale, *Choice We Face*.

20. S. M. Franklin, *After the Rebellion*; Hogan, *On the Freedom Side*; V. P. Franklin, *Young Crusaders*.

21. Lisa Deer Brown and the McComb Young People's Project, conversations with the author, July 2, 2012; Farooq, "Baltimore Algebra Project"; Sullivan, "Algebra Project Mobilizes"; Moses and Cobb, *Radical Equations*; Payne, "Miss Baker's Grandchildren"; Hale, *Freedom Schools*, 220–23; Hogan, "Organizing at the Intersections," in *On the Freedom Side*, 35–64.

22. Nick Estes, *Our History*; Hogan, "Mní Wičoni-Water Is Alive: Indigenous Youth Water Protectors Rekindle Nonviolent Direct Action in Corporate America," in *On the Freedom Side*, 157–96.

23. V. P. Franklin, *Young Crusaders*, 225–36; Hassan, "Parkland Shooting Survivors"; Jamison, Heim, and Lang, "'Never again!'"

24. V. P. Franklin, *Young Crusaders*, 225–36; "Greta Thunberg."

Bibliography

Manuscript Collections

Atlanta, GA
  The King Center
    Mississippi Freedom Democratic Party (MFDP) Papers
    Southern Christian Leadership Conference (SCLC) Collection
Auburn, AL
  Alabama Historical Association
Baton Rouge, LA
  East Baton Rouge Public Library
    Baton Rouge Library Reading Room
  Louisiana State University
    Histories and Cultures of Old South Baton Rouge Project
    McKinley High South Baton Rouge Oral History Project
    T. Harry Williams Oral History Collection
  Southern University and A&M College
    John Brother Cade Papers
Birmingham, AL
  Birmingham Civil Rights Institute
    Oral History Project
    Ruth Barefield-Pendleton Collection
  Birmingham Public Library
    Theophilus Eugene Bull Connor Papers, 1959–1963
  Linn-Henley Research Library
    City of Birmingham Board of Education Minute Book
Charleston, SC
  College of Charleston Avery Research Center for African American
      History and Culture
    Arthur Brown Papers
    Charleston County School District Archives
    Dart Family Papers
    Eugene Hunt Collection
    Lois A. Simms Papers
    Robert N. Rosen Legal Papers
    Septima P. Clark Collection
Charlottesville, VA
  University of Virginia

Virginia Center for Digital History
The Ground Beneath Our Feet Project
College Park, MD
National Archives and Records Administration
Freedmen's Bureau Papers
Columbia, SC
University of South Carolina: South Caroliniana Library
Palmetto Education Association
Palmetto State Teachers Association
State Superintendent Reports
University of South Carolina
M. Hayes Mizell Collection
Modjeska Simkins Papers
South Carolina Political Collections
Isaiah DeQuincey Newman Papers
Farmville, VA
Longwood University
Civil Rights in Prince Edward County—Oral History Collection
Prince Edward School Closing Collection
William Odum Collection
Prince Edward County School Board District
Hattiesburg, MS
University of Southern Mississippi
Center for Oral History and Cultural Heritage
Jackson, MS
Mississippi Department of Archives and History
Charles J. Cunningham Papers
Division of Administration and Finance, State Department of Education
Gladys Noel Bates Papers
Horace Ivy Collection
Jackson Public Schools
Lanier High School Subject File
Mississippi Sovereignty Commission Files
State Building Commission General Files
Source Material for Mississippi History, Hinds County
Tougaloo College Civil Rights Collections
McComb, MS
Black History Gallery, Inc.
McComb Legacies Oral History Project
McComb Public Library
Montgomery, AL
Alabama State University Archives
Alabama State Teachers Association (ASTA) Records
Herman Harris Collection
Alabama Department of Archives and History

Education, Administrative & Financial Services, School System Surveys
      Marengo Co to Montgomery County Files
  Trenholm State Community College
  Harper Council Trenholm Collection
Stanford, CA
  Stanford University
    Martin Luther King Jr. Papers Project
    Martin Luther King Jr. Research and Education Institute
Urbana, IL
  University of Illinois at Urbana-Champaign Archives
    SNCC Papers
Washington, DC
  George Washington University
    Gelman Library
    George Washington University Libraries
      National Education Association (NEA) Collection
  Howard University
    Edward E. Strong Papers
    Southern Negro Youth Conference (SNYC) Papers
  Library of Congress
    Papers of the NAACP
      Anti-Lynching Investigation Files
      Part 01: Supplements, 1956–1960
      Part 03: The Campaign for Educational Equality
      Part 7: The Anti-Lynching Investigative Files, 1912–1953: Series A
      Part 19: Series A Papers
      Part 19: Series B Papers
      Part 19: Series C Papers
      Part 19: Series 1
      Series B: Legal Department and Central Office Records, 1940–1950
  Moorland Spingarn Research Center, Howard University
    Civil Rights Documentation Project
    Edward Strong Papers
  National Archives and Records Administration (NARA)
    The Freemen's Bureau
      Field Office Records for Alabama
      Records of the Education Division of the Bureau of Refugees, Freemen,
        and Abandoned Lands

Newspapers and Periodicals

Alabama Journal   *Commercial Appeal*
Alabama Tribune   *Enterprise-Journal*
Birmingham News   *Farmville Herald*
Charleston Evening Post   *Jackson Free Press*

PSTA Journal
South School News
Teen Vogue
The American Missionary
The Baltimore Sun
The Charleston City Paper
The Colored Alabamian
The Comet: A Medium of Student
    Expression
The Crimson White
The Crisis
The Gamecock
The Guardian
The Jackson Advocate
The Jackson-Clarion Ledger
The Los Angeles Times
The Memphis World
The Montgomery Advertiser

The Montgomery-Tuskegee Times
The Nashville Banner
The Nashville Tennessean
The Nation
The News and Courier (Charleston, SC)
The New York Times
The New Yorker
The Parent Teacher Journal
The Pittsburgh Courier
The Post and Courier (Charleston, SC)
The Richmond Afro-American
The Richmond Times Dispatch
The State
The Times and Democrat
The Washington Post
Times-Picayune
U.S. News and World Report
Washington Sunday Star

Oral Interviews and Personal Correspondence

Anderson, Edmonia L. June 30, 2016.
Bailey, Richard. February 2, 2012.
Barker, Queen. February 26, 2016.
Bell, Rose. February 26, 2016.
Brown, Charlie. February 11, 2016.
Brown, Millicent. November 29, 2011.
Brown, W. R. Bo. July 25, 2013 and August 28, 2015.
Casin, Hilda. July 2, 2012.
Chapman, Linda. February 26, 2016.
Clark, Clifford L. June 30, 2016.
Cochran, Claudia. June 30, 2016.
Delpit, Joseph. October 7, 2015.
Dennis, David. October 25, 2011.
Gantt, Harvey. November 28, 2011.
Harris, Herman. February 25, 2016.
Hudson, Mary R. June 30, 2016.
Jones, Roscoe. March 18, 2014.
King, Minerva Brown. December 12, 2011.
Lynd, Stoughton. August 28, 2006.
Martin, Jacqueline. October 7, 2015.

May, Gwendolyn. June 30, 2016.
May-Pittman, Ineva. July 26, 2013.
Melton, Donna. June 30, 2016.
Owens, Dannetta K Thorton. March 2, 2016.
Patton, Gwen. February 13, 2016.
Randall, Gloria Washington Lewis. June 30, 2016.
Russel, Beulah. January 11, 2016.
Simms, Lois. December 5, 2011.
Speakes, Joy. November, 26, 2012 and June 30, 2017.
Thompson, Hymethia Washington Lofton. August 26, 2008 and August 28, 2008.
Watkins, Hezekiah. August 26–27, 2008 and October 11, 2011.
Webb, Deborah. February 29, 2016.
Whitaker, James W. June 30, 2016.
Williams, Reverand. November 26, 2012.
Yarbrough, William. June 30, 2016.
Young, Dr. Gene. August 7, 2008.

Other Oral Histories and Interviews

Anderson, Dupuy. Interviewed by Dawn Wallace. June 24, 1998. T. Harry Williams Center for Oral History Collection, Louisiana State University Libraries.

Bates, Gladys Noel. Interviewed by Catherine Jannik. December 23, 1996. University of Southern Mississippi Center for Oral History and Cultural Heritage.

Bishop, Edward S. Interviewed by Charles Bolton. February 27, 1991. Tulane University Digital Library—Tom Dent Collection, Amistad Research Center.

Blake, James G. Interviewed by Thomas Dent. May 15, 1991.

Brown, Reginald R., Sr. Interviewed by Jeong Suk Pang. June 23, 1998. T. Harry Williams Center for Oral History Collection, Louisiana State University Libraries.

Butler, Annie Marie. Interviewed by Dr. Horace Huntley. June 7, 1995. Birmingham Civil Rights Institute, Oral History Project. Volume 7.

Ghee, James. Interviewed by Charles Edward Vaughn and James Lucaro. January 25 and April 22, 1995. Longwood University, Civil Rights in Prince Edward County, Oral History Collection.

Huntley, Dr. Horace. Interviewed by Willie Eatman, April 30, 1997, Birmingham Civil Rights Institute, Oral History Project, Volume 26.

———. Interviewed by Florida Walker Hamilton, February 14, 1996. Birmingham Civil Rights Institute, Oral History Project, Volume 12.

———. Interviewed by Carrie Hamilton Lock. October 18,1995. Birmingham Civil Rights Institute, Oral History Project, Volume 10.

———. Interviewed by Miriam McClendon. November 8, 1995. Birmingham Civil Rights Institute, Oral History Project, Volume 11.

———. Interviewed by Carolyn McKinstry. April 23, 1998. Birmingham Civil Rights Institute, Oral History Project, Volume 35.

———. Interviewed by Ann Niles, January 7, 1999, Birmingham Civil Rights Institute, Oral History Project, Volume 41.

———. Interviewed by Eloise Staples, March 5, 1997. Birmingham Civil Rights Institute, Oral History Project, Volume 26.

———. Interviewed by Floretta Scruggs Tyson. May 5, 1995. Birmingham Civil Rights Institute, Oral History Project, Volume 5.

———. Interviewed by Denise Armstrong Wrushen. April 28, 1995. Birmingham Civil Rights Institute, Oral History Project, Volume 42.

McDew, Charles. Interviewed by Katherine Shannon. August 24, 1967. Civil Rights Documentation Project, Moorland Spingarn Research Center, Howard University. Courtesy of Joellen El Bashir.

Muhammad, Curtis. Interviewed by Benjamin Hedin and Sam Pollard. June 18, 2014. *Two Trains Runnin'* (Avalon Films, 2016).

Shepperson, Willie. Interviewed by Rebekeh Bailey. 1998. Civil Rights in Prince Edward County—Oral History Collection.

Travis, Brenda. Interviewed by Alex F. et al. May 6 and 7, 2010. McComb Legacies Oral History Project.

Films

Brooks, Richard, dir. *Blackboard Jungle,* 1955. Metro-Goldwyn-Mayer (MGM).

Fryday, Robin and Gail Dolgin, dir. *Barber of Montgomery: Foot Soldier of the Civil Rights Movement.* 2011. The Video Project.

Internet Accessed Sources, Print Sources, Government Documents, and Unpublished Manuscripts

Act No 460, Alabama Laws of the Legislature of Alabama, Vol. 2 (1963), p. 995.

Alridge, Derrick. "Teachers in Movement." Accessed at https://teachersinthemovement.com.

"Barbara Johns Leads Prince Edward County Student Walkout." SNCC Digital Gateway. Accessed at https://snccdigital.org/events/barbara-johns-leads -prince-edward-county-student walkout/.

Bailey, Richard. "BTW High School Welcomes Back Graduates of All Ages." Alabama Black History, January 23, 2019. Accessed at https://alabama blackhistory.com/btw-high-school-welcomes back-graduates-of-all-ages/.

Battle, Mary, and Curtis Franks (co-curators). "Avery: The Spirit That Would Not Die, 1865–2015." College of Charleston, Avery Research Center: Lowcountry Digital History Initiative, May 2016. Accessed at http://ldhi.library.cofc.edu /exhibits/show/avery.

"Before Rosa Parks, A Teenager Defied Segregation On An Alabama Bus." National Public Radio, March 2, 2015. Accessed at https://www.npr.org/sections /codeswitch/2015/02/27/389563788/before-rosa-parks-a-teenager-defied -segregation-on-an-alabama-bus.

Bever, Lindsey. "It Took 10 Minutes To Convict 14-Year-Old George Stinney Jr. It took 70 Years after His Execution to Exonerate Him." *Washington Post,* December 18, 2014. Accessed on April 7, 2022, at https://www.washingtonpost .com/news/morning-mix/wp/2014/12/18/the-rush-job-conviction-of-14-year -old-george-stinney-exonerated-70-years-after-execution/.

Birmingham City Schools, "A Brief History of A. H. Parker High School." Accessed on November 13, 2021, at https://www.bhamcityschools.org/domain /1368.

"Black Children Are Six Times More Likely to Be Shot to Death by Police." Equal Justice Initiative, December 2, 2020. Accessed at https://eji.org/news/black -children-are-six-times-more-likely-to-be-shot-to-death-by-police/.

"Black History Month Special: A. H. Parker High School in Birmingham." WVTM13 (Birmingham, AL). Accessed at https://www.wvtm13.com/article /black-history-month-special-a-h-parker-high-school-in-birmingham/35461781.

Booker T. Washington High School (Columbia, SC). "Washingtonian, 1950." Accessed at https://localhistory.richlandlibrary.com/digital/collection /p16817coll18/id/273/rec/9.

"A Brief History of A.H. Parker High School." Birmingham City Schools. Accessed at https://www.bhamcityschools.org/domain/1368.

Brown, Millicent. "Somebody Had to Do It: First Children in School Desegregation. College of Charleston, Avery Research Center: Lowcountry Digital History Initiative, 2015. Accessed at http://ldhi.library.cofc.edu /exhibits/show/somebody_had_to_do_it.

Brown, Millicent E. "Civil Rights Activism in Charleston, South Carolina." Ph.D., diss., Florida State University, 1997.

Bryant, Zyahna. "Charlottesville's Robert E. Lee Monument Is Coming Down, Thanks to Me and Black Women Like Me" *Teen Vogue* July 10, 2021. Accessed at https://www.teenvogue.com/story/charlottesvilles-robert-e-lee-monument -coming-down-black-women-zyahna-bryant-op-ed.

Bundy, Tess. "Black Student Power in Boston." *Black Perspectives and African American Intellectual History Society.* January 9, 2018. Accessed at https:// www.aaihs.org/black-student-power-in-boston/.

Calamur, Krishnadev. "Ferguson Documents: Officer Darren Wilson's Testimony." National Public Radio News. November 25, 2014. Accessed at https://www.npr .org/sections/the two way/2014/11/25/366519644/ferguson-docs-officer-darren -wilsons-testimony.

Chamberlain, Daphne. "'And a Child Shall Lead The Way': Children's Participation in the Jackson, Mississippi, Black Freedom Struggle." Ph.D. diss., University of Mississippi, 2009.

Children's Defense Fund, "U.S. Gun Violence Epidemic is Killing More Children, More Often." Accessed on November 14, 2021, at https://www.childrensdefense .org/policy/resources/soac-2020-gun-violence/.

Congressional Record (Senate) Vol. 109, Part 1 (January 9, 1963, to January 30, 1963), 823–44.

———. "Grid Riot." In. *Congressional Record* (Senate) Vol. 109, Part 1 (January 9, 1963, to January 30, 1963), 830.

Cox, Maxie Myron, Jr. "1963: The Year of Decision: Desegregation in South Carolina." Ph.D. diss., University of South Carolina, 1996.

D'Amico, Diana. "Claiming Profession: The Dynamic Struggle for Teacher Professionalism in the Twentieth Century." Ph.D. diss., New York University, 2011.

Davis, Larissa. "The Outliers: Avoiding School Integration in Charleston County Constituent Districts, 1968–1981." B.A. thesis, Amherst College, 2013.

Department of Health, Education, and Welfare, "Violent Schools–Safe Schools: The Safe School Study Report to Congress." Vol. 1. Washington, DC, 1978, iii.

"Disturbing School Attended by Girls of Women, §16–551" *Code of Laws of South Carolina 1962*, v. 4. Charlottesville: Michie Company, 1962.

Dobrasko, Rebekah. "Architectural Survey of Charleston County's School Equalization Program, 1951–1955," University of South Carolina Public History Program. April 2005. Accessed at http://nationalregister.sc.gov/SurveyReports /EqualizationSchoolsCharleston.pdf.

Dreher, Arielle. "How Integration Failed in Jackson's Public Schools from 1969 to 2017." *Jackson Free Press*, November 15, 2017. Accessed at https://www .jacksonfreepress.com/news/2017/nov/15/how-integration-failed-jacksons -public-schools-196/.

"Education Amendments of 1974," Public Law 93-380-AUG. 21, 1974 (ESEA). Accessed at https://www.govinfo.gov/content/pkg/STATUTE-88/pdf /STATUTE-88-Pg484.pdf.

Equal Justice Initiative, "Black Children Are Six Times More Likely to Be Shot to Death by Police." December 2, 2020. Accessed on November 14, 2021, at https://eji.org/news/black-children-are-six-times-more-likely-to-be-shot-to -death-by-police/.

Favors, Jelani Manu-Gowon. "Shelter in a Time of Storm: Black Colleges and the Rise of Student Activism in Jackson, Mississippi." Ph.D. diss., Ohio State University, 2006.

Fountain, Aaron G, Jr. "The Legacy of Berkeley High School's Black Student Union." Black Perspectives and African American Intellectual History Society. August 14, 2018. Accessed at https://www.aaihs.org/the-legacy-of-berkeley -high-schools-black-student-union-2/.

Frazier, James Monroe. "The History of Negro Education in the Parish of East Baton Rouge, Louisiana." M.A. thesis, University of Iowa, 1937.

French-Marcelin Megan and Sarah Hinger and the ACLU. "Bullies in Blue: The Origins and Consequences of School Policing." American Civil Liberties Union, April 2017. Accessed at https://www.aclu.org/sites/default/files/field _document/aclu_bullies_in_blue_4_11_17_final.pdf.

Gladwell, Malcolm. "The Foot Soldier of Birmingham." *Revisionist History*, podcast audio, Season 2. Accessed at http://revisionisthistory.com/episodes/14 -the-foot-soldier-of-birmingham.

Gray, Jeremy. "The Execution of Jeremiah Reeves: Alabama Teen's Death Sentence Helped Drive Civil Rights Movement." February 4, 2015. Accessed at https:// www.al.com/news/index.ssf/2015/02/the_execution_of_jeremiah_reev.html.

"Greta Thunberg Is the 'Time' Person of the Year for 2019," National Public Radio News. December 11, 2019. Accessed at https://www.npr.org/2019/12/11 /787026271/greta-thunberg-is-time-magazines-person-of-the-year-for-2019.

Hale, Jon. "A History of Burke High School in Charleston, South Carolina since 1894." Lowcountry Digital Humanities Initiative. Accessed at https://ldhi .library.cofc.edu/exhibits/show/history_burke_high_school.

Hollingsworth, Emily. "Speakes Honored." *The Farmville Herald*, August 23, 2018. Accessed November 12, 2021, at https://www.farmvilleherald.com/2018/08 /speakes-honored/.

Hooker, Robert W. "Displacement of Black Teachers in the Eleven Southern States. Special Report." Race Relations Information Center. December 1970. Washington, D.C.: Office of Education, 1970.

Hyres, Alex. "Persistence and Resistance: African American High School Teachers and Students During the Long Civil Rights Movement in Charlottesville, Virginia, 1926–1974." Ph.D. diss., University of Virginia, 2018.

Jackson's Citizens' Council, "There Can Be No Compromise on the Matter of Segregation." Mississippi Department of Archives and History. August 1964. Accessed at https://jacksonfreepress.media.clients.ellingtoncms.com/news /documents/2017/11/15/Aspect_Bulletin_Aug._1964.pdf.

Jackson, Ramon M. "Leaders in the Making: Higher Education, Student Activism, and the Black Freedom Struggle in South Carolina, 1925–1975." Ph.D. diss., University of South Carolina, 2019.

Jamison, Joe, Lori Aratani Heim, and Marissa Lang. "'Never Again!' Students Demand Action against Gun Violence in Nation's Capital." *Washington Post*, March 24, 2018. Accessed at https://www.washingtonpost.com/local/march -for-our-lives-huge-crowds-gather-for-rally-against-gun-violence-in-nations -capital/2018/03/24/4121b100-2f7d-11e8-b0b0-f706877db618_story.html.

Jordan-Taylor, Donna. "'I'm Not Autherine Lucy': The Circular Migration of Southern Black Professionals Who Completed Graduate School in the North during Jim Crow, 1945–1970." Ph.D. diss., University of Washington, 2011.

Kindy, Kimberly, Julie Tate, Jennifer Jenkins, Ted Mellnik. "Police Shootings of Children Spark New Outcry, Calls for Training to Deal with Adolescents in Crisis." *Washington Post*, May 12, 2021. Accessed on November 14, 2021, at https://www.washingtonpost.com/nation/2021/05/12/children-police -shootings/.

King, Martin Luther, Jr. "Statement Delivered at the Prayer Pilgrimage Protesting the Electrocution of Jeremiah Reeves." April 6, 1958, The Martin Luther King Jr. Papers Project, The Martin Luther King Jr. Research and Education Institute. Accessed at https://kinginstitute.stanford.edu/kingpapers /documents/statement-delivered-prayer-pilgrimage-protesting-electrocution -jeremiah-reeves.

Kitchen, Sebastian. "Interview with Claudette Colvin." The Montgomery Bus Boycott. *Montgomery Advertiser*. Accessed November 12, 2021, at http://www .montgomeryboycott.com/claudette-colvin/.

Laws of the State of Mississippi: Appropriations, General Legislation and Resolutions. Jackson, MS: Published by Authority, 1964.

Lewis, Billy Jean. "Bryant Reflects on Black Student Union, Looks Toward Future." *Charlottesville Tomorrow*. July 22, 2019. Accessed at https://www .cvilletomorrow.org/articles/bryant-reflect-on-black-student-union-looks -toward-future.

M. Hayes Mizell Papers. Accessed at https://digital.library.sc.edu/collections/m -hayes-mizell-papers/.

Mercer, Louis. "Detention of a Different Kind: Chicago's Schools, Police, and the Origins of the School to Prison Pipeline." Ph.D. diss., University of Chicago, 2018.

Moynihan, Patrick. *The Negro Family: The Case for National Action*. Washington, D.C.: United States Department of Labor, 1965.

No. 943, An Act to Amend Section 16-551, 2308. *South Carolina Statutes at Large, General and Permanent Laws—1968*. Columbia, SC: 1968.

Noble, Kenneth. "Policing the Hallways: The Origins of School-Police Partnerships in Twentieth Century American Urban Public Schools." Ph.D. diss., University of Florida, 2017.

"The Other Rosa Parks." Interview by Amy Goodman and Juan González. Democracy Now!, National Public Radio. March 29, 2013. Accessed at https:// www.democracynow.org/2013/3/29/the_other_rosa_parks_now_73.

Peeples, Edward H. "A Perspective on the Prince Edward County School Issue." M.A. thesis, University of Pennsylvania, 1963.

Public Law 87–274, "Juvenile Delinquency and Youth Offenses Act of 1961," Juvenile Delinquency and Youth Offenses Act of 1961, 42 U.S.C. § 2541, 1976.

Public Law 89-197; 79 Stat. 828. Law Enforcement Assistance Act of 1965.

Public Law 90-351; 82 Stat. 197 Omnibus Crime Control and Safe Streets Act of 1968.

Rainey, Eric. "Gadsden, AL, 1963—Eric Rainey—SNCC Field Secretary." *Freedomways*, 1st Quarter, 1964. Accessed at https://www.crmvet.org/lets /lrainey.htm.

Rankin, Duane. "St. Jude Opened Arms, Empowered Weary Marchers." *Montgomery Advertiser*. March 1, 2015. Accessed at https://www.mont gomeryadvertiser.com/story/news/local/selma50/2015/03/01/st-jude-opened -arms-empowered-weary-marchers/24214139/.

Rhodes College Crossroads To Freedom Collection. Accessed at http://dlynx .rhodes.edu:8080/jspui/handle/10267/33718.

Ruhl, Melissa. "'Forward You Must Go': Chemawa Indian Boarding School and Student Activism in the 1960s and 1970s." M.A. thesis, University of Oregon, 2011.

Shimshock, Robert. "Virginia Social Justice Warriors Want to Tear Down Robert E. Lee Statue." *Breitbart*. March 31, 2016. Accessed at https://www .breitbart.com/politics/2016/03/31/virginia-social-justice-warriors-want-to -tear-down-robert-e-lee-statue/.

South Carolina Code of Laws, Title 59—Education, Article 3: Discipline. Accessed at https://www.scstatehouse.gov/code/t59c063.php (or) https://www .scstatehouse.gov/CommitteeInfo/SchoolSafetyTaskForce/Title%2059,%20 Chapter2063,%20Article%203.pdf.

Steele, Kyle, and Alex Hyres. "Reimagining the High School Experience: The Uses and Limitations of Student-Generated Documents." Manuscript under review, used with permission.

Stern, Walter C. "The Forgotten History of School Violence: Desegregation and the Making of Mass Incarceration in the United States," 2020, unpublished manuscript.

"Teaching the Movement: The State of Civil Rights Education in the United States 2011." Montgomery: Southern Poverty Law Center, 2011. Accessed at https:// www.splcenter.org/sites/default/files/d6_legacy_files/downloads/publication /TeachingtheMovement.pdf.

Theophilus Eugene Bull Connor Papers, 1959–1963. Accessed at https://bplonline .contentdm.oclc.org/digital/collection/p16044coll1/id/29570/rec/3.

"U.S. Gun Violence Epidemic is Killing More Children, More Often." Children's Defense Fund. Accessed at https://www.childrensdefense.org/policy/resources /soac-2020-gun-violence/.

Vaden, Luci. "Before the Corridor of Shame: The African American Fight for Equal Education after Jim Crow." Ph.D. diss., University of South Carolina, 2014.

Vargas, Theresa, "The Girl Who Brought Down a Statue." *Washington Post*, July 17, 2021. Accessed November 3, 2021, at https://www.washingtonpost.com/local

/zyahna-bryant-charlottesville-lee-statue/2021/07/17/9073933e-e688-11eb
-b722-89ea0dde7771_story.html.

Vincent, Charles. *"A Centennial History of Southern University* and A & M College,
1880–1980." Baton Rouge, Southern University, 1981.

Walker, Dara. "Black Power and the Detroit High School Organizing Tradition."
Black Perspectives and African American Intellectual History Society.
January 11, 2018. Accessed at https://www.aaihs.org/black-power-and-the
-detroit-high-school-organizing-tradition/.

———. "Black Power, Youth Politics, and Education in Detroit, 1966–1973." Ph.D.
diss., Rutgers University, 2018.

Waugh, Dwana. "From Forgotten to Remembered: The Long Process of School
Desegregation in Chapel Hill, NC and Prince Edward County Virginia." Ph.D.
diss., University of North Carolina, 2012.

White, John W. "Managed Compliance: White Resistance and Desegregation in
South Carolina, 1950–1970." Ph.D. diss., University of Florida, 2006.

Wolf, Jean G. *The Juvenile Delinquency Prevention Act: A Legislative
History, Report.* Washington D.C.: Education and Public Welfare Division,
May 13, 1974.

"Youth March for Integrated Schools, Presidential Delegation Statement."
October 25, 1958. Accessed at http://www.crmvet.org/docs/5810_youth
_statement.pdf.

Published Sources

"19 of 119 Marchers Will Be Tried Today." *Enterprise-Journal*, October 4, 1961.

"24 Arrested Here in Demonstration." *News and Courier*, April 2, 1960

"A Job to Do," *Farmville Herald*, September 15, 1959.

Abrell, Ronald L., and Charles C. Hanna. "High School Student Unrest
Reconsidered." *The High School Journal* 54, no. 6 (March 1971).

Adickes, Sandra. *Legacy of a Freedom School.* New York: Palgrave Macmillan,
2005.

Adler, Renata. "Letter from Selma, On the Trail to Montgomery." *The New Yorker*,
April 2, 1965.

"AFRO Finds Charred Symbol at School." *The Richmond Afro-American*, May 8,
1951.

"Agitators Seek Troops, Mayor Thompson Says." *Jackson-Clarion Ledger*, May 31,
1963.

Agyepong, Tera Eva. *The Criminalization of Black Children: Race, Gender, and
Delinquency in Chicago's Juvenile Justice System, 1899–1945.* Chapel Hill:
University of North Carolina Press, 2018.

"Aim New Blow at D. C. School Bias: Parents Petition Board to Abandon
Segregated Policy." *Pittsburgh Courier*, April 26, 1947, 1.

"Alabama." *Southern School News*, August 1955.

Alridge, Derrick P. *The Educational Thought of W. E. B. Du Bois: An Intellectual
History.* New York: Teachers College Press, 2008.

Alridge, Derrick, Jon Hale, and Tondra Loder-Jackson, eds. *Schooling the Movement: The Activism of Southern Black Educators from Reconstruction through the Civil Rights Era*. Columbia: University of South Carolina Press, forthcoming.

Anderson, Alexa, and Kelsey Trace. "A Legacy of Learning," *10 Stories 50 Years Later*. Farmville: Longwood University, 2014, 39–41

Anderson, James D. "The Black Public High School." In *Education of Blacks in the South*. Chapel Hill: The University of North Carolina Press, 1988.

——. "'A Tale of Two Browns': Constitutional Equality and Unequal Education." *Yearbook of the National Society for the Study of Education* 105, no. 2 (2006): 30–32.

Anderson, Robert E., ed. *The South and Her Children: School Desegregation 1970–1971. A Report*. Atlanta: Southern Regional Council, 1971.

Angus, David L., and Jeffrey E. Mirel. *The Failed Promise of the American High School*. New York: Teachers College Press, 1999.

Ariés, Phillipe. *Centuries of Childhood*. New York: Vintage Books, 1962.

Arsenault, Raymond. *Freedom Riders: 1961 and the Struggle for Racial Justice*. Oxford: Oxford University Press, 2006.

"Attorneys Start Federal Suit to End School Segregation; 20 Year Progress Reviewed." *The Farmville Herald*, May 25, 1951.

Bailey, Richard. "Elijah Cook." In *They Too Call Alabama Home: African American Profiles 1800–1999*. Montgomery: Pyramid Publishing, 1999.

——. *Neither Carpetbaggers nor Scalawags: Black Officeholders During the Reconstruction of Alabama, 1867–1878*. Montgomery: R. Bailey Publishers, 1991.

Baker, R. Scott. *Paradoxes of Desegregation: African American Struggles for Educational Equity in Charleston, South Carolina, 1926–1972*. Columbia: University of South Carolina Press, 2006.

——. "Pedagogies of Protest: African American Teachers and the History of the Civil Rights Movement, 1940–1963." *Teachers College Record* 113 (December 1, 2011): 2777–803.

——. "Testing Equality: The National Teacher Examination and the NAACP's Legal Campaign to Equalize Teachers' Salaries in the South, 1936–63." *History of Education Quarterly* 35, no. 1 (Spring, 1995).

Baldwin, Baldwin. "A Talk to Teachers." *Saturday Review*, December 21, 1963.

Balto, Simon. *Occupied Territory: Policing Black Chicago from Red Summer to Black Power*. Chapel Hill: The University of North Carolina Press, 2020.

Banks, James, ed. *Multicultural Education, Transformative Knowledge and Action: Historical and Contemporary Perspectives*. New York: Teachers College Press, 1996.

Banks, James, and Cherry Banks, eds. *Handbook of Research on Multicultural Education*. New York: Macmillan, 1995.

Banner, Stuart. "When Killing a Juvenile Was Routine." *The New York Times*, March 5, 2005, 4.

Bass, Jack, and Jack Nelson. *The Orangeburg Massacre*. Macon, GA: Mercer University Press, 1970.

Bates, Daisy. *The Long Shadow of Little Rock: A Memoir.* Fayetteville: University of Arkansas Press, 2007.

Battle, Nishaun T. *Black Girlhood, Punishment, and Resistance: Reimagining Justice for Black Girls in Virginia.* New York: Routledge, 2020.

———. "From Slavery to Jane Crow to Say Her Name: An Intersectional Examination of Black Women and Punishment." *Meridians* 15, no. 1 (January 1, 2016): 109–36.

"Battle in the Schools." *The News and Courier,* February 11, 1972, 10-A.

Baumgartner, Kabria. *In Pursuit of Knowledge: Black Women and Educational Activism in Antebellum America.* New York: New York University Press, 2019.

———. "Searching for Sarah: Black Girlhood, Education, and the Archive." *History of Education Quarterly* 60 (2020): 73–85.

Bayers, Alan E. "Social Issues and Protest Activity: Recent Student Trends." Washington D.C.: American Council on Education, Office of Research, February 1970.

Beal, Melba. *Warriors Don't Cry: A Searing Memoir of the Battle to Integrate Little Rock's Central High.* New York: Pocket Books, 1994.

Beatty, Barbara, Emily D. Cahan, and Julia Grant, eds. *When Science Encounters the Child: Education, Parenting, and Child Welfare in 20th Century America.* New York: Teachers College Press, 2006.

Berghel, Susan Eckelmann. "'What My Generation Makes of America': American Youth Citizenship, Civil Rights Allies, and 1960s Black Freedom Struggle." *The Journal of the History of Childhood and Youth* 10 (Fall 2017): 422–40.

Berghel, Susan Eckelmann, Sara Fieldston, and Paul M. Renfro. *Growing Up America: Youth and Politics Since 1945.* Athens: University of Georgia Press, 2019.

Bernal, Dolores Delgado. "Grassroots Leadership Reconceptualized: Chicana Oral Histories and the 1968 East Los Angeles School Blowouts." *Frontiers: A Journal of Women Studies* 19, no. 2 (1998): 113–42.

Bernstein, Patricia. *The First Waco Horror: The Lynching of Jesse Washington and the Rise of the NAACP.* College State: Texas A&M University Press, 2005.

Betters, Paul V. "The United States Housing Act 1949." *Annals of Public and Cooperative Economics* 20, no. 3 (September 1949): 365–78.

Bigsbee, Fred. "North Charleston Pupils Suspended." *Charleston Evening Post,* March 4, 1971.

Biondi, Martha. *The Black Revolution on Campus.* Berkeley: University of California Press, 2012.

Bitter, John. "School Board Sends Money Matters To Committees." *The Montgomery Advertiser,* April 20, 1970, 2.

Black, Derek. *Ending Zero Tolerance: The Crisis of Absolute School Discipline.* New York: New York University Press, 2016.

Blaine, Kisha. *Set the World on Fire: Black Nationalist Women and the Global Struggle for Freedom.* Philadelphia: University of Pennsylvania Press, 2018.

———. *Until I am Free: Fannie Lou Hamer's Enduring Message to America.* Boston: Beacon Press, 2021.

Bleser, Carol, ed. *Secret and Sacred: The Diaries of James Henry Hammond, A Southern Slaveowner.* Columbia: University of South Carolina Press, 1997.

"Board Closes Three Schools, 'Hopes' to Reopen Them Monday: Shores' Home Blasted; 1 Dead, 21 Hurt in Riot." *Birmingham News*, September 55, 1963.

Bolton, Charles. *The Hardest Deal of All: The Battle over School Integration in Mississippi, 1870–1980.* Jackson: University Press of Mississippi, 2005.

Bonastia, Christopher. *Southern Stalemate: Five Years without Public Education in Prince Edward County, Virginia.* Chicago: University of Chicago Press, 2012.

Bradley, Stefan M. *Harlem vs. Columbia University: Black Student Power in the Late 1960s.* Urbana: University of Illinois Press, 2009.

Branch, Taylor. *The King Years: Historic Moments in the Civil Rights Movement.* New York: Simon & Schuster, 2013.

———. *Parting the Waters: American in the King Years 1954–1963.* New York: Simon & Schuster, 1988.

———. *Pillar of Fire: America in the King Years, 1963–65.* New York: Simon & Schuster, 1998.

Broadwater, Jess. "We Were Just Going to School." In *10 Stories 50 Years Later*, Farmville: Longwood University, 2014, 13.

Brooks, Sheila Dean. *Lucile H. Bluford and the Kansas City Call: Activist Voice for Social Justice.* Lanham, MD: Lexington Books, 2018.

Brown, Ben. "Understanding and Assessing School Police Officers: A Conceptual and Methodological Comment." *Journal of Criminal Justice* 34 (2006): 591–604.

Brown, Jennie. *Medgar Evers.* Los Angeles: Melrose Square Publishing, 1994.

Brown, Lenise. *The Montgomery Advertiser*, October 20, 1970, 4.

Brown, Roselle. "Monster of All He Surveyed." *The New York Times*, January 29, 1989, 22.

"Building Character." *The Comet: A Medium of Student Expression*, February 1933. South Caroliniana Library, University of South Carolina.

Bundy, Tess. "'Revolutions Happen through Young People!' The Black Student Movement in the Boston Public Schools, 1968–1971." *Journal of Urban History* 42 (2017): 273–93.

Burrow, Rufus, Jr. *A Child Shall Lead Them: Martin Luther King Jr., Young People, and the Movement.* Minneapolis: Fortress Press, 2014.

Burton, Orville Vernon, Beatrice Burton, and Simon Appleford. "Seeds in Unlikely Soil: The *Briggs v. Elliot* School Segregation Case." In *Toward the Meeting of the Waters: Currents in the Civil Rights Movement of South Carolina during the Twentieth Century*, edited by Winfred B. Moore Jr. and Orville Vernon Burton. Columbia: University of South Carolina Press, 2008, 176–200.

Burton, Orville Vernon, and Winfred B. Moore, eds. *Towards the Meeting of the Waters: Currents in the Civil Rights Movement of South Carolina during the Twentieth Century.* Columbia: University of South Carolina Press, 2008.

Butter, John. "7 Schools, 1,300 Diplomas: That's It Till Next Year." *Montgomery Advertiser*, June 3, 1970.

——. "Work Underway on New Classrooms at Schools in City." *Montgomery Advertiser*, June 21, 1970, 21.

Bybee, Rodger W., and E. Gordon Gee. *Violence, Values, and Justice in the Schools.* Boston: Allyn and Bacon, 1982.

Bynum, Thomas L. *NAACP Youth and the Fight for Black Freedom, 1936–1965.* Knoxville: University of Tennessee Press, 2013.

——. "'We Must March Forward!': Juanita Jackson and the Origins of the NAACP Youth Movement." *The Journal of African American History* 94, no. 4 (October 1, 2009): 487–508.

"Byrnes Plans Study Before Commenting on Court Ruling" *The State*, May 18, 1954, 1, 2-A.

Camp, Jordan T. *Incarcerating the Crisis: Freedom Struggles and the Rise of the Neoliberal State.* Oakland: University of California Press, 2016.

Canterbury, Larry. "Generals Roll On." *Alabama Journal*, October 29, 1970, 37.

Capshaw, Katharine. *Civil Rights Childhood: Picturing Liberation in African American Photobooks.* Minneapolis: University of Minnesota Press, 2014.

Carper, Elsie. "Steps Taken for Peace in School Strike: Approval Is Given Plan for Fulltime Junior High Courses at Browne Annexes: Officials Take Steps to End School Strike." *Washington Post*, January 7, 1948, 1.

Carrigan, William. *The Making of a Lynching Culture: Violence and Vigilantism in Central Texas, 1836–1916.* Urbana: University of Illinois Press, 2004.

Carson, Clayborne. *In Struggle: SNCC and the Black Awakening of the 1960s.* Cambridge, MA: Harvard University Press, 1995.

——. "To Walk in Dignity: The Montgomery Bus Boycott." *OAH Magazine of History* 19 (January 2005): 13–15.

Cecelski, David S. *Along Freedom Road: Hyde County, North Carolina and the Fate of Black Schools in the South.* Chapel Hill: University of North Carolina Press, 1994.

Chaddock, Katherine E., and Carolyn B. Matalene, eds. *College of Charleston Voices: Campus and Community through the Centuries.* Charleston, SC: History Press, 2006.

Chafe, William H. *Civilities and Civil Rights: Greensboro, North Carolina, and the Black Struggle for Freedom.* Oxford: Oxford University Press, 1981.

Chapman, Rob. "Seeds Sown in Time: Local Minister Lives History." *The Farmville Herald*, April 24, 2014, 1A, 9A.

Charron, Katherine Mellen. *Freedom's Teacher: The Life of Septima Clark.* Chapel Hill: University of North Carolina Press, 2009.

Chatelain, Marcia. *South Side Girls: Growing Up in the Great Migration.* Durham, NC: Duke University Press, 2015.

Children's Defense Fund. *School Suspensions: Are They Helping Children: A Report.* Washington, D.C.: Washington Research Project, 1975.

Children's Defense Fund (Marylee Allen, Cindy Brown, Ann Rosewater). *Children Out of School in America.* Washington, D.C.: Washington Research Project, Inc., 1974.

Chudacoff, Howard P. *How Old Are You? Age Consciousness in American Culture.* Princeton: Princeton University Press, 1989.

"City's Newest School, East Bay Negro Elementary, to Open Monday." *The News and Courier* (Charleston, SC), February 1, 1955.

"Civil Rights Army Encamps on Montgomery Outskirts." *Montgomery Advertiser,* March 25, 1965, 1, 2.

Clark, Kenneth. *Prejudice and Your Child.* Boston: Beacon Press, 1963.

Clark, Septima P. *Echo in My Soul.* New York: E. P. Dutton, 1962.

Clark, Septima, Poinsette Brown, and Cynthia Stokes Brown. *Ready from Within: Septima Clark and the Civil Rights Movement.* Navarro, CA: Wild Tree Press, 1986.

Cohen, Robert, and David J. Snyder, eds., *Rebellion in Black & White: Southern Student Activism in the 1960s.* Baltimore: Johns Hopkins University Press, 2013.

Cole, Eddie R. *The Campus Color Line: College Presidents and the Struggle for Black Freedom.* Princeton: Princeton University Press, 2020.

Collins, James. "Taking the Lead: Dorothy Williams, NAACP Youth Councils, and Civil Rights Protests in Pittsburgh, 1961–1964." *Journal of African American History* 88, no. 2 (Spring 2003), The History of Black Student Activism.

"Contracts Given on Negro School." *The Colored Alabamian,* September 18, 1915.

Counts, George S. *Dare the School Build a New Social Order?* New York: John Day Company, 1932.

Cox, Oliver C. "Vested Interests Involved in the Integration of Schools for Negroes." *Journal of Negro Education* 20, no. 1 (1951).

Crawford, Emily. "More Than You Might Think," *10 Stories 50 Years Later.* Farmville: Longwood University, 2014, 27–28.

Cremins, Lawrence A. *The Transformation of the School: Progressivism in American Education, 1876–1957.* New York: Vintage Books, 1964.

Cuban, Larry. *How Teachers Taught: Constancy and Change in American Classrooms 1890–1990,* 2nd ed. New York: Teachers College Press, 1993.

Cunningham, Candace. "'Hell Is Popping Here in South Carolina': Orangeburg County Black Teachers and Their Community in the Immediate Post-Brown Era." *History of Education Quarterly* 61 (2021): 35–62.

D'Amico, Diana, Robert J. Pawlewicz, Penelope M. Earley, and Adam P. McGeehan. "Where Are All the Black Teachers? Discrimination in the Teacher Labor Market." *Harvard Educational Review* 87, no. 1 (Spring 2017).

Danns, Dionne. "Chicago High School Students' Movement for Quality Public Education, 1966–1971." *Journal of African American History* 88 (2003): 138–50.

———. *Something Better for Our Children: Black Organizing in Chicago Public Schools, 1963–1971.* New York, 2003.

Daugherity, Brian J., and Brian Grogan. *A Little Child Shall Lead Them: A Documentary Account of the Struggle for School Desegregation in Prince Edward County, Virginia.* Charlottesville: University of Virginia Press, 2019.

DeGroot, Gerard J. "The Culture of Protest: An Introductory Essay." In *Student Protest: The Sixties and After,* edited by Gerard J. DeGroot. London: Addison Wesley Longman, 1998, 5.

———. *Student Protest: The Sixties and After*. London: Longman, 1998.

Delmont, Mathew F. "Thomas L. Bynum. NAACP Youth and the Fight for Black Freedom, 1936–1965." *The American Historical Review* 119 (2014): 936.

———. *Why Busing Failed: Race, Media, and the National Resistance to School Desegregation*. Oakland: University of California Press, 2016.

de Schweinitz, Rebecca. "Holding on to the 'Chosen Generation': The Mormon Battle for Youth in the Late 1960s and Early 1970s." In Patrick D. Mason and John G. Turner. *Out of Obscurity: Mormonism Since 1945*. Oxford: Oxford University Press, 2016, 297.

———. *If We Could Change the World: Young People and America's Long Struggle for Racial Equality*. Chapel Hill: University of North Carolina Press, 2009.

"Desegregation Move Started with Letter." *Richmond Times Dispatch*, April 2, 1967.

Devlin, Rachel. *A Girl Stands at the Door: The Generation of Young Women Who Desegregated America's Schools*. New York: Basic Books, 2018.

———. "Girls on the Front Line: Grassroots Challenges in the Late 1940s." In *A Girl Stands at the Door: The Generation of Young Women Who Desegregated America's Schools*. New York: Basic Books, 2018, 69–105.

Dickson, Foster, Kevin Garner, and Kali Pyrlik, eds. *Taking the Time: Young Writers and Old Stories with Writings*. Montgomery, AL: Booker T. Washington Magnet High School, 2005.

———. "They Just Knew I Would Protect It, Preserve It, and Share It," In *Taking the Time: Young Writers and Old Stories*. Montgomery, AL: Booker T. Washington Magnet High School, 2005. 90–92.

Dittmer, John. *Local People: The Struggle for Civil Rights in Mississippi*. Urbana: University of Illinois Press, 1994.

———. "We Return Fighting." In *Local People: The Struggle for Civil Rights in Mississippi*. Urbana: University of Illinois Press, 1994.

Drago, Edmund L. *Initiative, Paternalism, and Race Relations: Charleston's Avery Normal Institute*. Athens, GA, 1990.

Driskell, Jay Winston. *Schooling Jim Crow: The Fight for Atlanta's Booker T. Washington High School and the Roots of Black Protest Politics*. Charlottesville: University of Virginia Press, 2014.

Du Bois, W. E. B. *Black Reconstruction in America, 1860–1880*. New York: Free Press, 1998.

———. "Does the Negro Need Separate Schools?" *Journal of Negro Education* 4, no. 3 (July 1935): 328–35.

———. *The Philadelphia Negro: A Social Study and History of Pennsylvania's Black American Population; Their Education, Environment and Work*. Pantianos Classics, 1899.

———. "The Waco Horror." *The Crisis* 2, no. 3 (1916): 1–3.

Dudziak, Mary L. *Cold War Civil Rights: Race and the Image of American Democracy*. Princeton, NJ: Princeton University Press, 2000.

DuRocher, Kristina. *Raising Racists: The Socialization of White Children in the Jim Crow South*. Lexington: University Press of Kentucky, 2011.

East, Edward M. *Mankind at the Crossroads*. New York: Scribner, 1928.

"Eight Peace Marchers Jailed." *Birmingham News*, May 1, 1963, 2.

Eskew, Glenn T. *But for Birmingham: The Local and National Movements in the Civil Rights Struggle*. Chapel Hill: University of North Carolina Press, 1997.

Estes, Nick. *Our History Is the Future: Standing Rock Versus the Dakota Access Pipeline, and the Long Tradition of Indigenous Resistance*. New York: Verso Press, 2019.

Etheridge, Eric. *Breach of Peace: Portraits of the 1961 Freedom Riders*. New York: Athens & Company, 2008.

Ethridge, Samuel B. "Impact of the 1954 Brown vs. Topeka Board of Education Decision on Black Educators." *Negro Educational Review* 30 (October 1979).

Evers, Medgar. "Annual Report, 1957, Mississippi State Office, N.A.A.C.P." In Myrlie Evers-Williams and Manning Marable, eds., *The Autobiography of Medgar Evers: A Hero's Life and Legacy Revealed through His Writings, Letters, and Speeches*. New York: Basic Civitas, 2005, 84.

Evers-Williams, Myrlie and Manning Marable, eds. *The Autobiography of Medgar Evers: A Hero's Life and Legacy Revealed through His Writings, Letters, and Speeches*. New York: Basic Civitas, 2005.

Fabre, Michel. *The Unfinished Quest of Richard Wright*. New York: William Morrow & Company, 1973.

Fairclough, Adam. *A Class of Their Own: Black Teachers in the Segregated South*. Cambridge, MA: Belknap Press of Harvard University Press, 2007.

——. "The Costs of *Brown*: Black Teachers and School Integration." *Journal of American History* 91 (June 2004): 53–56.

——. *Race & Democracy: The Civil Rights Struggle in Louisiana, 1915–1972*. Athens: University of Georgia Press, 1995.

——. "Teachers Organize." In *A Class of Their Own: Black Teachers in the Segregated South*. Cambridge: Harvard University Press, 2007, 309–53.

——. *Teaching Equality: Black Schools in the Age of Jim Crow*. Athens: University of Georgia Press, 2001.

——. *To Redeem the Soul of America: The Southern Christian Leadership Conference & Martin Luther King, Jr.* Athens: University of Georgia Press, 1987.

Farooq, Umar, "Baltimore Algebra Project Stops Juvenile Detention Center." *The Nation*, January 24, 2012.

Fass, Paula. "All Our Children: Race, Rebellion, and Social Change." In *The End of American Childhood*. Princeton: Princeton University Press, 2016, 171–214.

——. *The End of American Childhood: A History of Parenting from Life on the Frontier to the Managed Child*. Princeton: Princeton University Press, 2016.

——. "What Mother Needs to Know: The New Science of Childhood, 1890–1920." *The End of American Childhood: A History of Parenting from Life on the Frontier to the Managed Child*. Princeton: Princeton University Press, 2016, 86–124.

Fass, Paula, and Michael Grossberg, eds. *Reinventing Childhood after World War II*. Philadelphia: University of Pennsylvania Press, 2012.

Favors, Jelani M. *Shelter in a Time of Storm: How Black Colleges Fostered Generations of Leadership and Activism*. Chapel Hill: University of North Carolina Press, 2019.

"Federal Grant Set on USC Expansion." *The Columbia Record*, March 31, 1966.

"Federal Domination," *Farmville Herald*, June 2, 1959.

Felder, James L. *Civil Rights in South Carolina: From Peaceful Protests to Groundbreaking Rulings*. Charleston, SC: The History Press, 2012.

———. "The Law School at South Carolina: *Wrighten v. USC Board of Trustees*." In *Civil Rights in South Carolina: From Peaceful Protests to Groundbreaking Rulings*. Charleston, SC: History Press, 2012, 34–38.

Fenske, Neil R. *A History of American Public High Schools, 1890–1990: Through the Eyes of Principals*. Lewiston, NY: Edwin Mellen Press, 1997.

Fenwick, Leslie. *Jim Crow's Pink Slip: Public Policy and the Near-Decimation of Black Educational Leadership*, forthcoming.

Ferguson, Roderick. *Aberrations in Black: Toward a Queer of Color Critique*. Minneapolis: University of Minnesota Press, 2004.

Fernandez, Johanna. *The Young Lords: A Radical History*. Chapel Hill: University of North Carolina Press, 2020.

"Fifteen Demonstrators Are Fined, Draw Sentences." *Enterprise-Journal*, October 31, 1961.

Finch, Minnie. *The NAACP: Its Fight for Justice*. Metuchen, NJ: Scarecrow Press, 1981.

"Fire Hoses, Police Dogs Used to Halt Downtown Negro Demonstrations." *Birmingham News*, May 3, 1963, 2.

Flacks, Richard. "Social and Cultural Meanings of Student Revolt." In *Student Activism and Protest*, edited by Edward E. Sampson and Harold A. Korn. San Francisco: Jossey-Bass, 1970, 123–33.

Flucker, Turry, and Phoenix Savage. *African Americans of Jackson*. Charleston, SC: Arcadia Publishing, 2008.

Foner, Eric. *Reconstruction: America's Unfinished Revolution, 1863–1877*. New York: Harper & Row, 1988.

Ford, Nick Aaron. *Seeking a Newer World*. Great Neck, NY: Todd & Honeywell, 1983.

Foster, M., ed. *Readings on Equal Education: Qualitative Investigations into Schools and Schooling*. New York: AMS, 1991.

Fountain, Aaron G, Jr. "Building a Student Movement in Naptown: The Corn Cob Curtain Controversy, Free Speech, and 1960s and 1970s High School Activism in Indianapolis." *Indiana Magazine of History* 114, no. 3 (2018): 202–37.

———. "The War in the Schools: San Francisco Bay Area High Schools and the Anti-Vietnam War Movement, 1965–1973." *California History* 92, no. 2 (Summer 2015): 22–41.

Franklin, Sekou M. *After the Rebellion: Black Youth, Social Movement Activism, and The Post Civil Rights Generation*. New York: New York University Press, 2014.

Franklin, V. P. "Black High School Student Activism in the 1960's: An Urban Phenomenon?" *Journal of Research in Education* 10 (Fall 2000): 3–8.

———. "Documenting the Contributions of Children and Teenagers to the Civil Rights Movement." *Journal of African American History* 100 (2015): 663–71.

———. *The Young Crusaders: The Untold Story of the Children and Teenagers Who Galvanized the Civil Rights Movement.* Boston: Beacon Press, 2021.

Fultz, Michael. "Charleston, 1919–1920: The Final Battle in the Emergence of the South's Urban African American Teaching Corps." *Journal of Urban History* 27 (2001): 633–49.

———. "Determination and Persistence: Building the African American Teacher Corps through Summer and Intermittent Teaching, 1860s–1890s." *History of Education Quarterly* 61, no. 1 (2021): 4–34.

———. "The Displacement of Black Educators Post-Brown: An Overview and Analysis." *History of Education Quarterly* 44 (2006): 11–45.

"Funeral Services Monday for the Rev. Dr. James G. Blake." *The Times and Democrat*, December 19, 1999, 4.

Fuquay, Michael W. "Civil Rights and the Private School Movement in Mississippi, 1964–1971." *History of Education Quarterly* 42, no. 2 (Summer 2002): 159–80.

Gaillard, Frye. *Cradle of Freedom: Alabama and the Movement That Changed America.* Tuscaloosa: University of Alabama Press, 2004.

Garcia, Mario, and Sal Castro, eds. *Blowout! Sal Castro and the Chicano Struggle for Educational Justice.* Chapel Hill: University of North Carolina Press, 2009.

Garrow, David J. *Protest at Selma: Martin Luther King, Jr. and the Voting Rights Act of 1965.* New Haven: Yale University Press, 1978.

———. *The Walking City: The Montgomery Bus Boycott, 1955–1956.* Brooklyn, NY: Carlson Publishers, 1989.

Gelman, Erik S. *Death Blow to Jim Crow: The National Negro Congress and the Rise of Militant Civil Rights.* Chapel Hill: University of North Carolina Press, 2012.

"Georgia." *Southern School News*, September 3, 1954.

"Georgia." *Southern School News*, November 4, 1954.

Gergel, Richard. *Unexampled Courage: The Blinding of Sgt. Isaac Woodard and the Awakening of President Harry S. Truman and Judge J. Waties Waring.* New York: Sarah Crichton Books, 2019.

Gilmore, Glenda Elizabeth. *Gender and Jim Crow: Women and the Politics of White Supremacy in North Carolina, 1896–1920.* 2nd ed. Chapel Hill: University of North Carolina Press, 1996.

"Girl Committed as Delinquent." *Commercial Appeal*, October 10, 1961.

Givens, Jarvis R. *Fugitive Pedagogy: Carter G. Woodson and the Art of Black Teaching.* Cambridge: Harvard University Press, 2021, 7–11.

"Good News in Prince Edward." *Farmville Herald*, September 29, 1959.

Gooding, Dan. "Teacher Is Shot at Burke High School." *Charleston Evening Post*, November 21, 1973, 1-A.

Gordy, Sondra. *Finding the Lost Year: What Happened When Little Rock Closed Its Public Schools?* Fayetteville: University of Arkansas Press, 2009.

Graham, Gael. "Flaunting the Freak Flag: *Karr v. Schmidt* and the Great Hair Debate in American High Schools, 1965–1975." *Journal of American History* 91 (2004): 522–43.

——. *Young Activists: American High School Students in the Age of Protest.* DeKalb: Northern Illinois University Press, 2006.

Grant, Gerald. "Archdiocese Drops Football, Basketball Playoffs: D.C. Catholic High Schools Suspend Participation in City-Wide Playoffs Meeting Called 8 Negroes Injured." *Washington Post,* November 24, 1962, A1.

——. *The World We Created at Hamilton High.* Cambridge: Harvard University Press, 1988.

Gray, Fred D. *Bus Ride to Justice.* Montgomery, AL: New South Books, 2013.

Gray, Jerome A., Joe L. Reed, and Norman W. Walton. *History of the Alabama State Teachers Association.* Washington, D.C.: National Education Association, 1987.

Greenberg, Jack. "Racial Integration of Teachers—A Growing Problem." *Journal of Negro Education* 20, no. 4 (Autumn 1951).

"Grid Riot Blamed On Lack Of D.C. Schools Discipline." *The Baltimore Sun,* January 9, 1963, 1.

Griswold del Castillo, Richard. *World War II and Mexican American Civil Rights.* Austin: University of Texas Press, 2008.

Gross, Kali Nicole. "African American Women, Mass Incarceration, and the Politics of Protection." *Journal of American History* 102, no. 1 (June 1, 2015): 25–33.

Gross, Kali Nicole, and Cheryl D. Hicks. "Gendering the Carceral State: African American Women, History, and the Criminal Justice System." *Journal of African American History* 100, no. 3 (Summer 2015): 357–65.

Grossberg, Michael. "Liberation and Caretaking: Fighting over Children's Rights in Postwar America." In *Reinventing Childhood after WWII,* edited by Paula Fass and Michael Grossberg. Philadelphia: University of Pennsylvania Press, 2012.

Guiner, Lani. "From Racial Liberalism to Radical Literacy: *Brown v. Board of Education* and the Interest Divergence Dilemma." *Journal of American History* 9, no. 1 (2004): 92–118.

Gutek, Gerald L. *The Educational Theory of George S. Counts.* Columbus: Ohio State University Press, 1971.

——. *George S. Counts and American Civilization: The Educator as Social Theorist.* Macon, GA: Mercer University Press, 1984.

Hailey, Foster. "Dogs and Hoses Repulse Negroes at Birmingham." *The New York Times,* May 4, 1963, 8.

Halberstam, David. *The Children.* New York: Fawcett Books, 1999.

Hale, Jon N. *The Choice We Face: How Segregation, Race, and Power Have Shaped America's Most Controversial Education Reform Movement.* Boston: Beacon Press, 2021.

——. "'The Development of Power Is the Main Business of the School': The Agency of Southern Black Teacher Associations from Jim Crow through Desegregation." *Journal of Negro Education* 87 (Fall 2018): 444–59.

——. "'The Fight Was Instilled in Us': High School Student Activism and the Civil Rights Movement in Charleston, South Carolina." *South Carolina Historical Magazine* 114 (January 2013): 4–28.

————. *The Freedom Schools: Student Activists in the Mississippi Civil Rights Movement*. New York: Columbia University Press, 2016.

————. "Future Foot Soldiers or Budding Criminals?: The Dynamics of High School Student Activism in the Southern Black Freedom Struggle." *Journal of Southern History* 84 (August 2018): 615–52.

————. "'It Only Takes a Spark to Get a Fire Going': Lois Simms and Pedagogical Activism during the Black Freedom Struggle." In *Schooling the Movement: The Activism of Southern Black Educators from Reconstruction through the Civil Rights Era*, edited by Derrick Alridge, Jon Hale, and Tondra Loder-Jackson. Columbia: University of South Carolina Press, forthcoming.

————. "'We Are Not Merging on an Equal Basis': The Desegregation of Southern Teacher Associations and the Right to Work, 1945–1977." *Labor History*, 60 (2019): 463–81.

Hale, Jon N. and Clerc Cooper. "Lowcountry, High Demands: The Struggle for Quality Education in Charleston, South Carolina." In *Deferred Dreams, Defiant Struggles: Critical Perspectives on Blackness, Belonging and Civil Rights*, eds. Violet Showers Johnson, Gundolf Graml, and Patricia Williams Lessane. Liverpool, UK: Liverpool University Press, 2018, 154–174.

Hall, G. Stanley. "The High School as the People's College versus the Fitting School," *The Pedagogical Seminary* 9 (1902): 63–73.

Hall, Jacquelyn Dowd. "The Long Civil Rights Movement and the Political Uses of the Past." *Journal of American History* 91, no. 4 (March 2005).

Hampel, Robert L. *The Last Little Citadel: American High Schools Since 1940*. Boston: Houghton Mifflin Harcourt, 1986.

Hampton, Henry, Steve Fayer, and Sarah Flynn. *Voices of Freedom: An Oral History of the Civil Rights Movement from the 1950s through the 1980s*. New York: Bantam Books, 1991.

Handler, M. S. "Malcolm X Terms Dr. King's Tactics Futile." *The New York Times*, May 11, 1963, p. 9.

"Harris Should Withdraw His Name." *The Montgomery-Tuskegee Times*, March 5–March 11, 1960.

Hartman, Andrew. *Education and the Cold War: The Battle for the American School*. New York: Palgrave MacMillan, 2008.

Hassan, Adeel. "Parkland Shooting Survivors Release Ambitious Gun Control Plan." *The New York Times*, August 21, 2019.

Haviland, Sara Rzeszutek. *James and Esther Cooper Jackson: Love and Courage in the Black Freedom Movement*. Lexington: University Press of Kentucky, 2015.

Hawkins, D. B. "Casualties: Losses among Black Educators Were High after Brown." *Black Issues in Higher Education* 10 (1994): 26–31.

Helms, Judith. "Negroes Ask City School Busing, Pairing; Also Object to Closing 3 Schools." *Alabama Journal*, April 20, 1970, 17.

————. "Student Leader Hits Booker T Closing Plan." *Alabama Journal*, March 11, 1970, 23.

Hendrick, Irving G. and Reginald L. Jones, eds. *Student Dissent in the Schools*. Boston: Houghton Mifflin Company, 1970.

Hendry, Petra Munro, and Jay D. Edwards. *Old South Baton Rouge*. Lafayette, LA: University of Louisiana Press, 2009.

Henning, Kristen. "The Challenge of Race and Crime in a Free Society: The Racial Divide in Fifty Years of Juvenile Justice Reform." *George Washington Law Review* 86, no. 6 (2018).

Herbers, John. "20 More Seized in Alabama Drive: Dr. King Reads Bible in Jail as Selma Negroes Press Protests Over Voting." *The New York Times*, February 3, 1965, 1.

——. "High School Unrest Rises, Alarming U.S. Educators." *The New York Times*, May 9, 1969, 1.

——. "Negroes Step Up Drive in Alabama; 1,000 More Seized: Students Arrested in Selma and Marion." *The New York Times*, February 1, 1965, 1.

Herbst, Jurgen. "High School and Youth in America." *Journal of Contemporary History* 2, no. 3 (July 1967): 165–82.

Heywood, Colin. *The History of Childhood*. Cambridge, UK: Polity Press, 2001.

"High School Pupils Stage Strike for New School Building." *Richmond Afro-American*, May 5, 1951.

Hill, Lance E. *Deacons for Defense Armed Resistance and the Civil Rights Movement*. Chapel Hill: University of North Carolina Press, 2004.

Hines, Darlene Clark. "Rape and the Inner Lives of Black Women in the Middle West." *Signs* 14, no. 4 (July 1, 1989): 912–20.

Hines, William C. *South Carolina State University: A Black Land-Grant College in Jim Crow America*. Columbia; University of South Carolina Press, 2018.

Hinton, Elizabeth Kai. *From the War on Poverty to the War on Crime: The Making of Mass Incarceration in America*. Cambridge: Harvard University Press, 2016.

Hogan, Wesley C. *Many Minds, One Heart: SNCC's Dream for a New America*. Chapel Hill: University of North Carolina Press, 2007.

——. *On the Freedom Side: How Five Decades of Youth Activists Have Remixed American History*. Chapel Hill: University of North Carolina Press, 2019.

Holley, Joe. "M. Boyd Jones; Leader of Va. School That Played a Role in Desegregation." *Washington Post*, January 25, 2008.

Holliman, Ray. "Lee Keeps Streaking." *Alabama Journal*, October 21, 1970, 9.

——. "Lee's Stokes, Washington, Bama-Bound." *Alabama Journal*, December 9, 1970.

Holsaert, Faith S., Martha Prescod Norman Noonan, Judy Richardson, Betty Garman Robinson, Jean Smith Young, and Dorothy M. Zellner, eds. *Hands on the Freedom Plow: Personal Accounts by Women in SNCC*. Urbana: University of Illinois Press, 2010.

"Hoodlums vs. Fans." *The News and Courier*, September 8, 1972.

Hoose, Philip. *Claudette Colvin: Twice Toward Justice*. New York: Farrar Straus Giroux, 2009.

Howard, Tyrone. "Powerful Pedagogy for African American Students: A Case of Four Teachers." *Urban Education* 36, no. 2 (March 2001): 179–202.

Hudson, Midred J., and Barbara J. Holmes. "Missing Teachers, Impaired Communities: The Unanticipated Consequences of *Brown v. Board of Education* on the African American Teaching Force at the Precollegiate Level." *Journal of Negro Education* 63 (1994): 388–93.

Hughes, Langston. "Fight for Freedom." In *The Collected Works of Langston Hughes*, Vol. 10, "Fight for Freedom and Other Writings on Civil Rights." Columbia: University of Missouri Press, 2001, 182–88.

Hughes, Langston, Arnold Rampersad, Dolan Hubbard, and Leslie Catherine Sanders. *The Collected Works of Langston Hughes*. Columbia: University of Missouri Press, 2001.

"Hundreds Celebrate Longtime City Educator at Church Service." *The Montgomery Advertiser*, October 26, 2004.

"Hundreds of Hookey-Playing Demonstrators Arrested Here along with Negro Comedian." *Birmingham News*, May 6, 1963, 2.

Huntley, Horace, and John W. McKerley. *Foot Soldiers for Democracy: The Men, Women, and Children of the Birmingham Civil Rights Movement*. Urbana: University of Illinois Press, 2009.

Ides, Matthew. "'Dare to Free Yourself': The Red Tide, Feminism, and High School Activism in the Early 1970s," *Journal of the History of Childhood and Youth* 7 (Spring 2014): 295–319.

"Integration March Set: Demonstration in Capital Is Scheduled for April 18," *The New York Times*, April 4, 1959, p. 19.

"In Public Schools: A Crime Invasion." *U.S. News & World Report*, January 26, 1970, 8–10.

Isaac, Bobby. "Burke Student Charged with Shooting Teacher." *The News and Courier*, November 22, 1973, 1-A, 4-A.

Jackson, Esther Cooper. *This Is My Husband: Fighter for His People, Political Refugee*. Brooklyn: National Committee to Defend Negro Leadership, 1953.

Jackson, Troy. *Becoming King: Martin Luther King Jr. and the Making of a National Leader*. Lexington: University Press of Kentucky, 2008.

Janken, Kenneth Robert. *The Wilmington Ten: Violence, Injustice, and the Rise of Black Politics in the 1970s*. Chapel Hill: University of North Carolina Press, 2015.

———. *White: The Biography of Walter White, Mr. NAACP*. New York: New Press, 2003.

Jeffries, Hasan Kwame. *Bloody Lowndes: Civil Rights and Black Power in Alabama's Black Belt*. New York: New York University Press, 2009.

Jelks, Randal Maurice. *Benjamin Elijah Mays, Schoolmaster of the Movement: A Biography*. Chapel Hill: University of North Carolina Press, 2012.

Johns, Barbara. "Barbara Johns: 'And We Lived Happily Ever After.'" *The Farmville Herald*, April 24, 2014, 1A–2A.

Jonas, Gilbert. *Freedom's Sword: The NAACP and the Struggle Against Racism in America, 1909–1969*. New York: Routledge, 2005.

Jones, Thomas Jesse. "Negro Education: A Study of the Private and Higher Schools for Colored People in the United States." *Bulletin*, v. 39. Washington, D.C.: Department of the Interior, Bureau of Education, 1916.

Jordan, Kathy-Anne. "Discourses of Difference and the Overrepresentation of Black Students in Special Education." *Journal of African American History*, 90 (Winter, 2005): 128–49.

Joyner, Irving. "Pimping Brown v. Board of Education: The Destruction of African-American Schools and the Mis-Education of African-American Students." *North Carolina Central Law Review* 35 (2013): 160–202.

"Judge Tuttle Shows Humanitarian Qualities of Law in Birmingham School Board Ruling." *Alabama Tribune*, May 31, 1963.

"Just a Dream." *The Columbia Record*, August 30, 1976.

"K. T. Brown" and "Herman L. Harris." *Biographies of Participants in the Hands Uplifted for Freedom and Justice Permanent Exhibit*. Montgomery: Troy University, 5, 10–11. (Copy in possession of author, courtesy of Dr. Gwen Patton).

Kaestle, Carl F, and Eric Foner. *Pillars of the Republic: Common Schools and American Society, 1780–1860*. New York: Hill and Wang, 1983.

Kafka, Judith. "Disciplining Youth, Disciplining Women: Motherhood, Delinquency, and Race in Postwar American Schooling." *Educational Studies* 44 (2008): 197–221.

——. "'Sitting on a Tinderbox': Racial Conflict, Teacher Discretion, and the Centralization of Disciplinary Authority." *American Journal of Education* 114, no. 3 (May 2008): 247–70.

——. *The History of "Zero Tolerance" in American Public Schooling*. London: Palgrave Macmillan, 2011.

Katz, Michael B. and Mike Rose, eds. *Public Education under Siege*. Philadelphia: University of Pennsylvania Press, 2013.

Katzenbach, Nicholas et al. *The Challenge of Crime in a Free Society: A Report by the President's Commission on Law Enforcement and Administration of Justice*. Washington, D.C., 1967.

Kelley, Robin D. G. *Hammer and Hoes: Alabama Communists during the Great Depression*. Chapel Hill: University of North Carolina Press, 1990.

——. "'We Are Not What We Seem': Rethinking Black Working-Class Opposition in the Jim Crow South." *Journal of American History* 80, no. 1 (1993).

Kessler, Sarah. "The Healing Ground," *10 Stories 50 Years Later*. Farmville: Longwood University, 2014, 27–28.

Kett, Joseph F. *Rites of Passage: Adolescence in America, 1790 to the Present*. New York: Basic Books, 1977.

Kilpatrick, William H. *Education for a Changing Civilization*. New York: Macmillan, 1927.

Kinchen, Shirletta J. *Black Power in the Bluff City: African American Youth and Student Activism in Memphis*. Knoxville: University of Tennessee Press, 2016.

King, J. E. "Unfinished Business: Black Student Alienation and Black Teacher's Emancipatory Pedagogy." In *Readings on Equal Education: Qualitative Investigations into Schools and Schooling*, edited by M. Foster. New York: AMS, 1991, 245–71.

King, Martin Luther, Jr., and Clayborne Carson. *The Autobiography of Martin Luther King, Jr.* New York: Intellectual Properties Management in association with Warner Books, 1998.

King, Sabrina Hope. "The Limited Presence of African-American Teachers." *Review of Educational Research* 63 no. 2 (Summer 1993): 116–20.

King, Wilma. *African American Childhoods: Historical Perspectives from Slavery to Civil Rights*. New York: Palgrave, 2005.

———. "Emmett Till Generation: African American Schoolchildren and the Modern Civil Rights Movement in the South, 1954–1964." In *African American Childhoods: Historical Perspectives from Slavery to Civil Rights*. New York: Palgrave, 2005, 155–68.

———. *Stolen Childhood: Slave Youth in Nineteenth-Century America*. Bloomington: Indiana University Press, 1995.

Kitchen, Sebastian. "Awesome Story Revisited: Colvin Helped Light Flame of Civil Rights." *The Montgomery Advertiser*, February 4, 2005, 1, 2.

Kitzmiller, Erika. *The Roots of Educational Inequality*. Philadelphia: University of Pennsylvania, forthcoming.

Kluger, Richard. *Simple Justice: The History of* Brown v. Board of Education *and Black America's Struggle for Equality*. New York: Vintage Books, 1975, 2004.

Kridel, Craig. *Progressive Education in Black High Schools: The Secondary School Study, 1940–1946*. Columbia: Museum of Education, University of South Carolina, 2015.

Krochmal, Max. "An Unmistakably Working-Class Vision: Birmingham's Foot Soldiers and Their Civil Rights Movement." *Journal of Southern History* 76, no. 4 (November 2010): 923–60.

Krug, Edward A. *The Shaping of the American High School*. Madison: University of Wisconsin Press, 1969.

———. *The Shaping of the American High School: Volume 2, 1920–1941*. Madison: University of Wisconsin Press, 1972.

Kruse, Kevin, and Stephen Tuck. *Fog of War: The Second World War and the Civil Rights Movement*. New York: Oxford University Press, 2012.

Kwon, H. "Unveiling History: African American Art Education at Booker T. Washington High School during the Civil Rights Era in the Segregated South." *Studies in Art Education*, forthcoming.

Labaree, David. *The Making of an American High School: The Credentials Market and the Central High School of Philadelphia, 1838–1939*. New Haven: Yale University Press, 1988.

Ladson-Billings, Gloria. "But That's Just Good Teaching! The Case for Culturally Relevant Teaching." *Theory into Practice* 34, no. 3. (Summer 1995): 159–65.

———. *The Dreamkeepers: Successful Teachers of African American Students*. San Francisco: Jossey Bass, 1994.

———. "Toward a Theory of Culturally Relevant Pedagogy." *American Educational Research Journal* 32 (1995): 465–91.

Larkin, Joe. "School Desegregation and Student Suspension: A Look at One School System." *Education and Urban Society* 11 (August 1979): 485–95.

Lassiter, Michael D., and Andrew B. Lewis. *The Moderates' Dilemma: Massive Resistance to School Desegregation in Virginia*. Charlottesville: University Press of Virginia, 1998.

Lau, Peter. *Democracy Rising: South Carolina and the Fight for Black Equality Since 1865*. Lexington: University of Kentucky Press, 2006.

Lautier, Lewis. "High Court Sets Aside Jeremiah Reeves Conviction." *Memphis World*, December 10, 1954.

Leeson, Jim. "Private Schools Continue to Increase in the South." *Southern Education Report*, November 1966, 22–25.

LeFlouria, Talitha. *Chained in Silence: Black Women and Convict Labor in the New South*. Chapel Hill: University of North Carolina Press, 2015.

"Let's Discuss the Race Problem Intelligently." *The Parvenue*, June 1953, Avery Research Center.

Levin, Betsy and Willis D. Hawley, eds. *The Courts, Social Science and School Desegregation*. New Brunswick, NJ: Transaction Books, 1975.

Levine, David P. "The Birth of the Citizenship Schools: Entwining the Struggles for Literacy and Freedom." *History of Education Quarterly* 44 (2004): 388–414.

Levine, Ellen. *Freedom's Children: Young Civil Rights Activists Tell Their Own Stories*. New York: Putnam, 1993.

Levinson, Cynthia. *We've Got a Job: The 1963 Birmingham Children's March*. Atlanta: Peachtree Publishers, 2012.

Lewis, Andrew B. "Emergency Mothers: Basement Schools and the Preservation of Public Education in Charlottesville." In *The Moderates' Dilemma: Massive Resistance to School Desegregation in Virginia*, edited by Matthew D. Lassiter. Charlottesville: University Press of Virginia, 1998, 72–103.

Lewis, David, Michael Hash, and Daniel Laeb, eds. *Red Activists and Black Freedom: James and Esther Jackson and the Long Civil Rights Revolution*. New York: Routledge, 2010.

Lewis, Earl. *In Their Own Interests: Race, Class, and Power in Twentieth-Century Norfolk, Virginia*. Berkeley: University of California Press, 1993.

Lewis, John, and Michael D'Orso. *Walking with the Wind: A Memoir of the Movement*. New York: Simon & Schuster, 1998.

Libarle, Mark, and Tom Seligson, eds. *The High School Revolutionaries*. New York: Random House, 1970.

Lindenmeyer, Kriste. *"A Right to Childhood": The U.S. Children's Bureau and Child Welfare, 1912–46*. Urbana: University of Illinois Press, 1997.

Littlefield, Valinda W. "Teaching Survival and Combat Strategies During the Jim Crow Era: Ruby Middleton Forsythe and Fannie Phelps Adams." *South Carolina Women: Their Lives and Times*. Atanta: University of Georgia Press, 2012.

Loder-Jackson, Tondra L. *Schoolhouse Activists: African American Educators and the Long Birmingham Civil Rights Movement*. Albany: State University of New York Press, 2015.

Loevy, Robert D, ed. *The Civil Rights Act of 1964: The Passage of the Law That Ended Racial Segregation*. Albany: State University of New York Press, 1997.

"Louisiana Legislature Busy with Bills to Maintain Segregation." *South School News*, July 1956, 8.

Lovell, Kera. "Girls Are Equal Too: Education, Body Politics, and the Making of Teenage Feminism." *Gender Issues* 33, no. 2 (June 2016): 71–95.

Lowe, Stephen. "*Brown* on Trial: School Desegregation in Charleston, South Carolina, 1960–1964." *Avery Review* (Spring 2000): 33–55.

Lynch, John Roy. *The Facts of Reconstruction*. New York: Neale Publishing, 1913.

Lyon, Danny. *Memories of the Southern Civil Rights Movement*. Chapel Hill: Published for the Center for Documentary Studies, Duke University, by the University of North Carolina Press, 1992.

MacLean, Nancy. *Democracy in Chains: The Deep History of the Radical Right's Stealth Plan for America*. New York: Penguin Books, 2017.

Madkins, Tia C. "The Black Teacher Shortage: A Literature Review of Historical and Contemporary Trends." *Journal of Negro Education* 80, no. 3 (Summer 2011).

"Making Amends, Standing up for Equality, Honoring Heroes," *Enterprise-Journal*, June 23, 2006.

Martin, Everett Dean. *The Meaning of a Liberal Education*. New York: W. W. Norton, 1926.

Massey, Raymond. "Agency Has Tankful of Protests When Property Rezoning Is Asked." *Alabama Journal*, September 30, 1969, 9.

———. "In Two Years Black Housing Opportunities Have Improved." *Alabama Journal*, January 16, 1970.

"Mayor Leland Speed Says Best Relations Between White and Negro Citizens Will Be Maintained in Jackson." *Jackson Advocate*, November 30, 1946, 1.

McAdam, Doug. *Freedom Summer*. New York: Oxford University Press, 1988.

McCurdy, Jack. "Fear of Transfers to Inner City Haunts Teachers." *Los Angeles Times*, June 7, 1976, D1–3.

McDaniel, M. Akua. "Edwin Augustus Harleston: Envisioning the Talented Tenth." In *Edwin Augustus Harleston: Artist and Activist in a Changing Era*. Charleston: Avery Research Center, 2006, 12.

McGuire, Danielle L. *At the Dark End of the Street: Black Women, Race, and Resistance—A New History of the Civil Rights Movement from Rosa Parks to the Rise of Black Power*. New York: Alfred A. Knopf, 2010.

———. "'It Was Like All of us Had Been Raped': Sexual Violence, Community Mobilization, and the African American Freedom Struggle." *Journal of American History* 91, no. 3 (2004): 906–31.

McKiven, Henry M, Jr. *Iron and Steel: Class, Race, and Community in Birmingham, Alabama, 1875–1920*. Chapel Hill: University of North Carolina Press, 1995.

McMillan, Lewis K. "Negro Higher Education as I Have Known It." *Journal of Negro Education* 8 (January 1939): 9–18.

McMillen, Neil R. *The Citizens' Council: Organized Resistance to the Second Reconstruction, 1954–64*. Urbana: University of Illinois Press, 1971.

McWhorter, Diane. *Carry Me Home: Birmingham, Alabama, the Climactic Battle of the Civil Rights Revolution*. New York: Simon & Schuster, 2001.

Meriwether, Colyer. *History of Higher Education in South Carolina, with a Sketch of the Free School System*. Washington: Government Printing Office, 1889.

Michel, Gregg L. *Struggle for a Better South: The Southern Student Organizing Committee, 1964–1969*. New York: Palgrave MacMillan, 2004.

Milner, Richard H., and Tyrone C. Howard. "Black Teachers, Black Students, Black Communities, and Brown: Perspectives and Insights from Experts." *Journal of Negro Education* 73 (2004): 285–97.

Mintz, Steven. *Huck's Raft: A History of American Childhood.* Cambridge: Harvard University Press, 2004.

"Mississippi." *Southern School News,* January 6, 1955.

Mirel, Jeffrey. *The Rise and Fall of an Urban School System, Detroit, 1907–1981.* Ann Arbor: University of Michigan Press, 1993.

"Mob Lynches Negro Boy Who Shot Grocer. Body of Masked Men Take Him From Hospital. Samuel Smith, 15, Left Hanging Near Home of Ike Eastwood, Whom He Wounded Friday Night." *Nashville Tennessean,* December 16, 1924.

Moody, Anne. *Coming of Age in Mississippi: The Classic Autobiography of Growing Up Poor and Black in the Rural South.* New York: Bantam Bell, 1968; 1976.

Moore, Winfred B., Jr., and Orville Vernon Burton, eds. *Toward the Meeting of the Waters: Currents in the Civil Rights Movement of South Carolina during the Twentieth Century.* Columbia: University of South Carolina Press, 2008.

Moran, Robert. "Education in South Carolina: An Attempt at Equalization." Palmetto State Teachers Association, *PSTA Journal* (October, 1952): 14–15, South Caroliniana.

Morris, Aldon. "Black Southern Student Sit-in Movement: An Analysis of Internal Organization." *American Sociological Review* 46, no. 6 (December 1981).

———. *The Origins of the Civil Rights Movement: Black Communities Organizing for Change.* New York: The Free Press, 1984.

Morris, Monique W. *Pushout: The Criminalization of Black Girls in Schools.* New York: New Press, 2016.

Morris, Tiyi M. *Womanpower Unlimited and the Black Freedom Struggle in Mississippi.* Athens: University of Georgia Press, 2015.

Morrison, Nan. *A History of the College of Charleston, 1936–2008.* Columbia: University of South Carolina Press.

Morsell, John A. "The National Association for the Advancement of Colored People and Its Strategy." *Annals of the American Academy of Political and Social Science* 357 (1965): 97–101.

Moses, Robert P., and Charles E. Cobb. *Radical Equations: Civil Rights from Mississippi to the Algebra Project.* Boston: Beacon Press, 2001.

"Moton Students' Claims Unjustified, Board Feels Now." *The Farmville Herald,* April 27, 1951.

Muller, Meir, Eliza Braden, K. Kamania Wynter-Hoyte, Susi Long, and Gloria Boutte, G. "Another 100 Years?: Du Bois' Brownies' Book Goals, Just as Vital Today in the Education of Young Children and Their Teachers." *Journal of Negro Education.*

Mulqueen, Connie. "School Resource Officers More than Security Guards." *American School & University* 71 (July 1999).

Munoz, Carlos, Jr. *Youth, Identity, Power: The Chicano Movement.* New York: Verso, 1989.

Murphy, Marjorie. *Blackboard Unions: the AFT and the NEA, 1900–1980.* Ithaca, NY: Cornell University Press, 1990.

Murray, Percy. *History of the North Carolina Teachers Association.* Washington, D.C.: NEA, 1984.

Muse, Benjamin. *Virginia's Massive Resistance*. Bloomington: Indiana University Press, 1961.

Myers, Tamara. "Local Action and Global Imagining: Youth, International Development, and the Walkathon Phenomenon in Sixties' and Seventies' Canada." *Diplomatic History* 38 (2014): 282–93l.

"NAACP Geared for Public School Fight." *The Richmond Afro-American*, April 28, 1951.

National Education Association of the United States, Committee of Ten on Secondary School Studies. *Report of the Committee of Ten on Secondary School Studies: With the Reports of the Conferences Arranged by the Committee*. New York: Published for the National Educational Association by the American Book Co, 1894.

"Negro Guilty of Violation of City Bus Segregation Law." *Montgomery Advertiser*, March 19, 1955.

"Negro High School Sketches Arrive." *Farmville Herald*, October 16, 1951.

"Negro Trio Convicted in Sit-Ins." *Enterprise-Journal*, August 31, 1961.

"Negroes Admitted to Nine Schools." *Birmingham News*, September 10, 1963.

"Negroes Appeal Rejection of School Busing, Pairing." *Montgomery Advertiser*, April 12, 1970, 12.

"New Hooper Academy to Begin Classes Sept. 14." *Montgomery Advertiser*, August 16, 1970.

"New Marching Groups Jailed." *Birmingham News*, May 2, 1963, 2.

Nevin, David, and Robert E. Bills. *The Schools That Fear Built: Segregationist Academies in the South*. Washington: Acropolis Books, 1976.

"Nine Adults Arrested." *Birmingham News*, September 10, 1963.

Norris, Alana. "Memory Marches On: Selma to Recognize 50th Anniversary of March." *The Crimson White*, March 5, 2015.

Oakley, Deirdre, Jacob Stowell, and John R. Logan. "The Impact of Desegregation on Black Teachers in the Metropolis, 1970–2000." *Ethnic & Racial Studies* 32 (2009): 1576–98.

Odem, Mary E. *Delinquent Daughters: Protecting and Policing Adolescent Female Sexuality in the United States, 1885–1920*. Chapel Hill: University of North Carolina Press, 1995.

Ogline, Jill. *Brown's Battleground: Students, Segregationists, and the Struggle for Justice in Prince Edward County Virginia*. Chapel Hill: University of North Carolina Press, 2011.

Ogren, Christine A. "Out-of-Class Project: American Teachers' Summertime Activities, 1880s–1930s." *History of Education Quarterly* 56, no. 1 (2016): 22–23.

Olson-Raymer, Gayle. "The Role of the Federal Government in Juvenile Delinquency Prevention: Historical and Contemporary Perspectives." *Journal of Criminal Law and Criminology* 74, no. 2 (Summer 1983): 578–600.

"1,000 Skep Classes." *Birmingham News*, September 10, 1963.

Oppenheimer, Martin. *The Sit-In Movement of 1960*. Brooklyn, NY: Carlson Publishing, 1989, 33–35.

Orfield, Gary. *The Reconstruction of Southern Education: The Schools and the 1964 Civil Rights Act.* New York: Wiley, 1969.

Orr-Klopfer, Susan. *Where Rebels Roost: Mississippi Civil Rights Revisited.* M. Susan Klopfer, 2005.

Pan, Deanna, and Jennifer Berry Hawes. "An Undying Mystery: George Stinney." *Post and Courier*, March 25–29, 2018.

"Parents Picket in Protest of Three School Transfers." *Afro-American*, December 13, 1947, 2.

Paris, Django, and H. Samy Alim, eds. *Culturally Sustaining Pedagogies: Teaching and Learning for Justice in a Changing World.* New York: Teachers College Press, 2017.

Parker, A. H. *"A Dream That Came True": Autobiography of Arthur Harold Parker.* Birmingham, AL: Industrial High School, 1932–33.

Parker, Wendy. "Desegregating Teachers." *Washington University Law Review* 86 (2008): 1–52.

Parks, Rosa and James Haskins. *Rosa Parks: My Story.* New York: Dial Books, 1992.

Patton, Gwen. "Born Freedom Fighter." In *Hands on the Freedom Plow: Personal Accounts by Women in SNCC*, edited by Faith S. Holsaert, Martha Prescod Norman Noonan, Judy Richardson, Betty Garman Robinson, Jean Smith Young, and Dorothy M. Zellner. Urbana: University of Illinois Press, 2010, 572–76.

Payne, Charles M. *I've Got the Light of Freedom: The Organizing Tradition and the Mississippi Freedom Struggle.* Berkeley: University of California Press, 1995.

———. "Miss Baker's Grandchildren: An Interview with the Baltimore Algebra Project." In *Quality Education as a Constitutional Right: Creating a Grassroots Movement to Transform Public Schools*, edited by Theresa Perry et al. Boston: Beacon Press, 2010.

Peguese, Robbie. "Negro Achievement Week at Booker T. Washington." *The Comet: A Medium of Student Expression*, South Caroliniana Library, University of South Carolina, March 1939.

Perlstein, Daniel. "Imagined Authority: Blackboard Jungle and the Project of Educational Liberalism." *Paedagogica Historica* (2000): 407–25.

———. *Justice, Justice: School Politics and the Eclipse of Liberalism.* New York: Peter Lang, 2004.

———. "Teaching Freedom: SNCC and the Creation of the Mississippi Freedom Schools." *History of Education Quarterly* 30 (1990): 297–324.

Perrillo, Jonna. *Uncivil Rights: Teachers, Unions, and Race in the Battle for School Equity.* Chicago: University of Chicago Press, 2012.

Perry, Thelma D. *History of the American Teachers Association.* Washington, D.C.: National Education Association, 1975.

Perry, Theresa, et al., eds. *Quality Education as a Constitutional Right: Creating a Grassroots Movement to Transform Public Schools.* Boston: Beacon Press, 2010.

"Petitions Charge Discrimination in School Operation." *Farmville Herald*, April 7, 1960.

Pickens, William. *The Heir of Slaves: An Autobiography.* Boston: The Pilgrim Press, 1911.

Picott, J. Rupert. *History of the Virginia Teachers Association*. Washington, D.C.: National Education Association, 1975.

Picott, J. Rupert, and Edward H. Peeples. "A Study in Infamy: Prince Edward County Virginia." *Phi Delta Kappan* 45, no. 8 (1964): 393–94.

Pierce, Truman Mitchell. *White and Negro Schools in the South: An Analysis of Bi-Racial Education*. Englewood Cliffs, NJ: Prentice-Hall, 1955.

Pierson, Sharon Gay. *Laboratory of Learning: HBCU Laboratory Schools and Alabama State College Lab High in the Era of Jim Crow*. New York: Peter Lang, 2014.

Platt, Anthony. "Saving and Controlling Delinquent Youth: A Critique." *Issues in Criminology* 5, no. 1 (Winter 1970): 14–16.

"Policy, FBI Sift Blast Clues, Judge Decries 'Mockery of Law' in City." *Birmingham News*, September 16, 1963.

Potts, John F. *A History of the Palmetto Education Association*. Washington, D.C.: National Education Association, 1978.

Potts-Campbell, Leila. *Edwin Augustus Harleston: Artist and Activist in a Changing Era*. Charleston: Avery Research Center, 2006.

"Prince Edward's Position." *Farmville Herald*, September 1, 1959.

"Protests in High Schools." *The New York Times*, March 3, 1969, 18.

"Punished a Horror Horribly." *The New York Times*, May 17, 1916, 10.

Pyatt, Sherman E. *Burke High School, 1894–2006 (The Campus History Series)*. Chicago: Arcadia Publishing, 2007.

Rabinowitz, Howard N. "Half a Loaf: The Shift from White to Black Teachers in the Negro Schools of the Urban South, 1865–1890." *Journal of Southern History* 40 (1974): 565–94.

"Racial Agitator Leads as Children Go to Jail." *The Clarion-Ledger*, June 1, 1963.

Raiford, Leigh. "'Come Let Us Build a New World Together': SNCC and Photography of the Civil Rights Movement." *American Quarterly* 59, no. 4 (December 1, 2007): 1129–57.

Ramsey, Sonya. *Reading, Writing, and Segregation: A Century of Black Women Teachers in Nashville*. Urbana: University of Illinois Press, 2008.

Ransby, Barbara. *Ella Baker and the Black Freedom Movement a Radical Democratic Vision*. Chapel Hill: University of North Carolina Press, 2003.

Rankin, Duane. "St. Jude Opened Arms, Empowered Weary Marchers." *Montgomery Advertiser*, March 1, 2015.

Ravitch, Diane. *The Troubled Crusade: American Education, 1945–1980*. New York: Basic Books, 1983.

Reese, William. *The Origins of the American High School*. New Haven: Yale University Press, 1995.

"Reign of Terror Draws Denial." *Enterprise-Journal*, October 5, 1961.

Reynolds, Leann G. *Maintaining Segregation: Children and Racial Instruction in the South 1920–1955*. Baton Rouge: Louisiana State University Press, 2017.

Richardson, Joe Martin, and Maxine Deloris Jones. *Education for Liberation: The American Missionary Association and African Americans, 1890 to the Civil Rights Movement*. Tuscaloosa: University of Alabama Press, 2009.

Ritterhouse, Jennifer. *Growing Up Jim Crow: How Black and White Southern Children Learned Race*. Chapel Hill: University of North Carolina Press, 2006.

Rivera, A. M., Jr. "Parents Sue School Board, Charge Inferior Facilities: Students in Strike Last Fall." *The Pittsburgh Courier*, July 12, 1947, 1.

Robinson, Jo Ann Gibson, and David J. Garrow. *The Montgomery Bus Boycott and the Women Who Started It: The Memoir of Jo Ann Gibson Robinson*. Knoxville: University of Tennessee Press, 1987.

Robnett, Belinda. "African-American Women in the Civil Rights Movement, 1954–1965: Gender, Leadership, and Micromobilization." *American Journal of Sociology* 101, no. 6 (May 1996): 1661–93.

Rogers, Ibram. *The Black Campus Movement: Black Students and the Racial Reconstitution of Higher Education, 1965–1972*. New York: Palgrave Macmillan, 2012.

Rothschild, Mary A. *A Case of Black and White: Northern Volunteers and the Southern Freedom Summers, 1964–65*. Westport, CT: Greenwood Press, 1982.

"R. R. Moton Strike Enters 2nd Week." *The Farmville Herald*, May 1, 1951.

Rury, John L., and Shirley A. Hill. *The African American Struggle for Secondary Schooling, 1940–1980: Closing the Graduation Gap*. New York: Teachers College Press, 2012.

——. "An End of Innocence: African-American High School Protest in the 1960s and 1970s." *History of Education* 42 (2013): 486–508.

Rustin, Bayard. *Down the Line: The Collected Writings of Bayard Rustin*. Chicago: Quadrangle Books, 1971.

Salter, John R, Jr. *Jackson, Mississippi: An American Chronicle of Struggle and Schism*, 2nd ed. Lincoln: University of Nebraska Press, 2011.

Sampson, Edward E., and Harold Allen Korn. *Student Activism and Protest*. San Francisco: Jossey-Bass, 1970.

Sanders, Crystal. *Deferred Dreams and Exiled Citizens: Black Graduate Education in the Age of Jim Crow*, forthcoming.

"SC Candidates Accent Separate School Issue." *The State*, May 19, 1954, 1, 7-A.

"SC Leaders Adopt 'Wait-See' Attitude on Court Decision," *The State*, May 18, 1954, 1.

Schept, Judah, Tyler Wall, and Avi Brisman. "Building, Staffing, and Insulating: An Architecture of Criminological Complicity in the School-to-Prison Pipeline." *Social Justice* 41, no. 4 (2014): 96–115.

"School Board to Delay Reply to Petition." *The Farmville Herald*, May 11, 1951.

"Schools Lose by Absences." *Birmingham News*, May 8, 1963.

Schumaker, Kathryn. *Troublemakers: Students' Rights and Racial Justice in the Long 1960s*. New York: New York University Press, 2019.

"Self-Policing Schools." *The News and Courier*, February 24, 1971.

Sellers, Cleveland. *The River of No Return: The Autobiography of a Black Militant and the Life and Death of SNCC*. Jackson: University of Mississippi Press, 1990.

Seto, Dawn, and Lindsay Cox. "Outside the System." In *10 Stories 50 Years Later*. Farmville: Longwood University, 2014, 13.

Sewell, George A., and Margaret L. Dwight. *Mississippi Black History Makers*. Jackson: University Press of Mississippi, 1984.

Shuler, Jack. *Blood & Bone: Truth and Reconciliation in a Southern Town.* Columbia: University of South Carolina Press, 2012.

Simms, Lois Averetta. *A Chalk and Chalkboard Career in Carolina.* New York: Vantage Press, 1995.

Sinclair, Reginald Brown. "Equal in All Places: The Civil Rights Struggle in Baton Rouge, 1953–1963." *Louisiana History: The Journal of the Louisiana Historical Association*, 39, no. 3 (Summer 1998): 349–56.

"Sit-in Youths Tried, Given Maximum Fine." *Enterprise-Journal*, August 31 1961.

Smith, Bob. "The Eyes of the World are Upon Us." In *They Closed Their Schools: Prince Edward County, Virginia, 1951–1964.* Farmville, VA: Martha E. Forrester Council of Women, 1996, 36–74.

———. *They Closed Their Schools: Prince Edward County, VA, 1951–1964.* Farmville, VA: Martha E. Forrester Council of Women, 1996.

Smith, Jeffrey D. "High School Newspapers and the Public Forum Doctrine: Hazelwood School District v. Kuhlmeier." *Virginia Law Review* 74 (1988): 843–62.

Smith, John W., and B. M. Smith. "For Black Educators: Integration Brings the Axe." *Urban Review* 6 (1973): 7–12.

Solinger, Rickie. *Wake Up Little Susie: Single Pregnancy and Race Before Roe v. Wade.* New York: Routledge, 1992.

"South Carolina." *Southern School News*, April 7, 1955.

"South Carolina." *Southern School News*, May 4, 1955.

Span, Christopher M. *From Cotton Field to Schoolhouse: African American Education in Mississippi, 1862–1875.* Chapel Hill: University of North Carolina Press, 2009.

Spruill, Marjorie Julian, Valinda W. Littlefield, and Joan Marie Johnson. *South Carolina Women: Their Lives and Times.* Athens: University of Georgia Press, 2009.

"St. James Completes New Facilities." *Montgomery Advertiser*, August 16, 1970.

Stanton, Mary. *Freedom Walk: Mississippi or Bust.* Jackson: University Press of Mississippi, 2003.

Steele, Kyle. *Making a Mass Institution: Indianapolis and the American High School.* New Brunswick, NJ: Rutgers University Press, 2020.

Steele, Kyle, and Alex Hyres. "Reimagining the High School Experience: The Uses and Limitations of Student-Generated Documents." Manuscript under review, used with permission.

Stern, Walter C. "The Forgotten History of School Violence: Desegregation and the Making of Mass Incarceration in the United States." Unpublished manuscript.

Stewart, Alison. *First Class: The Legacy of Dunbar, America's First Black Public High School.* Chicago: Lawrence Hill Books, 2013.

Stockton, Robert P. "Boycotting Pupils to be Suspended." *The News and Courier*, March 4, 1971, 1-B.

———. "James Island High School Opens Under Police Guard." *The News and Courier*, March 21, 1972.

——. "School District Trustees Order 'Get Tough' Policy." *The News and Courier*, February 20, 1971, 1-B.

"Stokes, Washington Going to Alabama." *The Montgomery Advertiser*, December 10, 1970, 51.

Stokes, John A. *Students on Strike: Jim Crow, Civil Rights, Brown and Me.* Washington, D.C.: National Geographic, 2008.

Stoper, Emily. *The Student Nonviolent Coordinating Committee: The Growth of Radicalism in a Civil Rights Organization.* Brooklyn, NY: Carlson, 1989.

Streib, Victor L. *Death Penalty for Juveniles.* Bloomington: Indiana University Press, 1987.

"Striking Students Face Ouster for School Year." *Enterprise-Journal*, October 15, 1961.

The Student Pushout; Victim of Continued Resistance to Desegregation. Southern Regional Council and the Robert F. Kennedy Memorial, 1973.

"Students Placed Under Bond on Assault Charge." *The News and Courier*, March 4, 1971.

"Students Will Be Asked for Comments on Courses at Proposed Trade School." *The Montgomery Advertiser*, March 2, 1971, 5.

Sturkey, William, and Jon N. Hale, eds. *To Write in the Light of Freedom: The Newspapers of the 1964 Mississippi Freedom Schools.* Jackson: University Press of Mississippi, 2015.

Suddler, Carl. *Presumed Criminal: Black Youth and the Justice System in Postwar New York.* New York: New York University Press, 2019.

Suitts, Steve. *Overturning Brown: The Segregationist Legacy of the Modern School Choice Movement.* Montgomery, AL: New South Books, 2020.

Sullivan, Erin. "Algebra Project Mobilizes Students to Protest in Honor of National Day of Action to Defend Education." *The Nation*, March 4, 2010.

Sullivan, Patricia. "In the Shadow of War: Battlefields for Freedom." In *Lift Every Voice: The NAACP and the Making of the Civil Rights Movement.* New York: New Press, 2009.

——. *Lift Every Voice: The NAACP and the Making of the Civil Rights Movement.* New York: The New Press, 2009.

Sway, O. W. "Swane School." *The American Missionary* 35 (July 1981): 209–10.

Tager, Jack, Gordana Rabrenovic, and Ruth Owen Jones. *Boston Riots Three Centuries of Social Violence.* Boston: Northeastern University Press, 2019.

Terjen, Kitty. "White Flight: The Segregation Academy Movement." In Robert E. Anderson, *The South and Her Children: School Desegregation 1970–1971.* Atlanta: Southern Regional Council, 1971, 69.

Thangaraj, Stanley. *Desi Hoop Dreams: Pickup Basketball and the Making of Asian American Masculinity.* New York: New York University Press, 2015.

"The Wrong Answer in Prince Edward," *The Farmville Herald*, September 18, 1959.

Theoharis, Jeanne. *A More Beautiful and Terrible History: The Uses and Misuses of Civil Rights History.* Boston: Beacon Press, 2018.

——. *The Rebellious Life of Rosa Parks.* Boston: Beacon Press, 2013.

Thomas, Roy. "Booker Transfers Add Steam to the Lee Title Hopes." *The Montgomery Advertiser*, February 7, 1971.

Thompson, Charles H. "Editorial Comment: Discrimination in Negro Teachers' Salaries in Maryland." *Journal of Negro Education* 5 (1936): 539–42.

———. "Editorial Note: Does Negro Education Need Re-Organization and Re-Direction?" *Journal of Negro Education* 5, no. 3, (July 1936): 311–13.

Thompson, Cleopatra D. *The History of the Mississippi Teachers Association.* Washington, D.C.: NEA Teachers Rights, 1973.

Thompson, Heather Ann. "Criminalizing Kids: The Overlooked Reason for Failing Schools." In *Public Education Under Siege*, edited by Michael B. Katz and Mike Rose. Philadelphia: University of Pennsylvania Press, 2013, 131–42.

———. "Why Mass Incarceration Matters." *Journal of American History* 97, no. 3 (2010): 703–34.

Thuesen, Sarah Caroline. *Greater Than Equal: African American Struggles for Schools and Citizenship in North Carolina, 1919–1965.* Chapel Hill, NC, 2012.

Tillman, Linda C. "(Un)Intended Consequences? The Impact of the *Brown v. Board of Education* Decision on the Employment Status of Black Educators." *Education and Urban Society* 36 (2004).

Titus, Jill Ogline. *Brown's Battleground: Students, Segregationists, and the Struggle for Justice in Prince Edward County Virginia.* Chapel Hill: University of North Carolina Press, 2011.

"Transcript of Nixon's Acceptance Address and Excerpts From Agnew's Speech." *The New York Times,* August 24, 1972, 47.

Travis, Brenda Travis, and John Obee. *Mississippi's Exiled Daughter: How My Civil Rights Baptism Under Fire Shaped My Life.* Montgomery: New South Books, 2018.

Turner, Jeffrey A. *Sitting In and Speaking Out: Student Movement in the American South, 1960–1970.* Athens: University of Georgia Press, 2010.

Turner, Kara Miles. "Both Victors and Victims: Prince Edward County, Virginia, the NAACP, and 'Brown.'" *Virginia Law Review* 90 (October 2004).

———. "'Getting it Straight': Southern Black School Patrons and the Struggle for Equal Education in the Pre- and Post-Civil Rights Eras." *Journal of Negro Education* 72, no. 2 (Spring 2003): 219–23.

Tushnet, Mark V. "The Campaign in the 1940s: Contingencies, Adaptations, and the Problem of Staff." In *The NAACP's Legal Strategy against Segregated Education, 1925–1950.* Chapel Hill: University of North Carolina Press, 1987, 82–104.

———. *The NAACP's Legal Strategy against Segregated Education.* Chapel Hill: University of North Carolina Press, 2004.

———. "The Strategy of Delay and the Direct Attack on Segregation." In *The NAACP's Legal Strategy against Segregated Education.* Chapel Hill, NC, 2004, 105–37.

"Two Summit Negroes Jailed after Sit-Ins." *Enterprise-Journal,* August 21, 1961.

"Uncharted Seas," *Farmville Herald,* June 5, 1959.

"Unhappy Situation." *Farmville Herald,* May 29, 1959.

United States Department of Commerce. *Statistical Abstract of the United States,
1930*. Washington, D.C.: Government Printing Office, 1930, 108–15.

United States Department of Commerce, *Statistical Abstract of the United States,
1940*. Washington, D.C.: Government Printing Office, 1941, 112–13.

Urban, Wayne J. "Teacher Activism." In *American Teachers: Histories of a
Profession at Work*, edited by Donald Warren. New York: Macmillan
Publishing, 1989, 194–95.

"Va. Pupils' Strike Ends; JC Schools' Fight Set." *Richmond Afro-American*, May 12,
1951.

Viadero, Debra. "At the Crossroads." In *Lessons of a Century: A Nation's Schools
Come of Age*. Bethesda, MD: Editorial Projects in Education, 2000.

"Virginia Lawmakers Overwhelmingly Approve Interposition." *Southern School
News*, March 1956, 14.

"Vocational High School Will Start Here in Fall." *The Montgomery Advertiser*,
March 26, 1971, 2.

Walker, Margaret. *Richard Wright: Daemonic Genius: A Portrait of the Man,
A Critical Look at His Work*. New York: Amistad, 1988.

Walker, Vanessa Siddle. "Caswell County Training School, 1933–1969:
Relationships between Community and School." *Harvard Educational Review*
63, no. 2, Summer 1993.

———. *Hello Professor: A Black Principal and Professional Leadership in the
Segregated South*. Chapel Hill: University of North Carolina Press, 2009.

———. *The Lost Education of Horace Tate: Uncovering the Hidden Heroes Who
Fought for Justice in Schools*. New York: The New Press, 2018.

———. *Their Highest Potential: An African American School Community in the
Segregated South*. Chapel Hill: University of North Carolina Press, 1996.

Walker, Wyatt Tee. *Road to Damascus: A Journey of Faith*. New York: M. L. King
Fellows Press, 1985.

Walsh, Camille. *Racial Taxation: Schools, Segregation, and Taxpayer Citizenship,
1869–1973*. Chapel Hill: University of North Carolina Press, 2018.

Walter, W. A. "Why Limit the Study of the Negro." *Mississippi Educational Journal:
A Monthly Magazine for Teachers in Colored Schools*, 18, 88–89, Mississippi
Department of Archives and History.

Ward, Geoff K. "Birth of a Juvenile Court." In *The Black Child-Savers: Racial
Democracy and Juvenile Justice*. Chicago: University of Chicago Press, 2012,
1–10.

———. *The Black Child-Savers: Racial Democracy and Juvenile Justice*. Chicago:
University of Chicago Press, 2012.

———. "Rewriting the Racial Contract: The Black Child-Saving Movement." In *The
Black Child-Savers: Racial Democracy and Juvenile Justice*. Chicago: University
of Chicago Press, 2012, 127–232.

Ward, Jason Morgan. "The D.C. School Hearings of 1956 and the National Vision
of Massive Resistance." *Journal of Civil and Human Rights* 1, no. 1 (2015): 82–110.

Warren, Donald, ed. *American Teachers: Histories of a Profession at Work*. New
York: Macmillan, 1989.

Warren, Robert Penn. *Who Speaks for the Negro?* New York: Random House, 1965.

Waters, Dustin. "Resurrecting the Case of George Stinney." *Charleston City Paper,* August 31, 2016.

Watkins, Hezekiah. *Pushing Forward: The Story of Mississippi's Youngest Freedom Rider.* Spring, TX: Dogeared Press, 2019.

Watson, Bruce. *Freedom Summer: The Savage Season That Made Mississippi Burn and Made America a Democracy.* New York: Viking, 2010.

Waugh, Dwana. "'The Issue Is the Control of Public Schools': The Politics of Desegregation in Prince Edward County, Virginia." *Southern Cultures* 18 (Summer 2012): 76–94.

Webster, Crystal. *Beyond the Boundaries of Childhood: Northern African American Children's Political and Cultural Resistance.* Chapel Hill: University of North Carolina, 2021.

Welky, David. *Marching across the Color Line: A Philip Randolph and Civil Rights in the World War II Era.* New York: Oxford University Press, 2013.

"West End Mixing Protested; Kennedy Grabs State Guard." *Birmingham News.* September 10, 1963, 1, 5.

White, Betsy. "Mother Searches for Housing." *Columbia Reporter,* February 25, 1977.

"White House Conference on Child Health and Protection." *Parent Teacher Journal,* December-January 1930–1931, 5–6, 18.

Wilkerson, Doxey A. "The Negro School Movement in Virginia: From 'Equalization' to 'Integration,'" *Journal of Negro Education* 29 (Winter 1960): 17–29.

Williams, Heather A. *Self-Taught: African American Education in Slavery and Freedom.* Chapel Hill: University of North Carolina Press, 2005.

Williams, Michael Vinson. *Medgar Evers: Mississippi Martyr.* Fayetteville: University of Arkansas Press, 2011.

Williamson, Joy Ann. *Radicalizing the Ebony Tower: Black Colleges and the Black Freedom Struggle in Mississippi.* New York: Teachers College Press, 2008.

——. "This Has Been Quite a Year for Heads Falling": Institutional Autonomy in the Civil Rights Era. *History of Education Quarterly* 44 (2004): 554–76.

Willis, Vincent. *Audacious Agitation: The Uncompromising Commitment of Black Youth to Equal Education after Brown.* Athens: University of Georgia Press, 2011.

——. "Let Me In, I Have the Right to Be Here: Black Youth Struggle for Equal Education and Full Citizenship After the *Brown* Decision, 1954–1969." *Citizenship Teaching and Learning* 9, no. 1 (December 2013): 53–70.

"Witness Sees Rage Erupt at Ramsay." *Birmingham News,* September 4, 1963, 4.

Woodson, Carter G. "Negro History Week." *Mississippi Educational Journal: A Monthly Magazine for Teachers in Colored Schools* 18 (1934/35).

Woyshner, Christine. *The National PTA, Race, and Civic Engagement, 1897–1970.* Columbus: Ohio State University Press, 2009.

Wright, Dwayne C. "Black Pride Day, 1968: High School Student Activism in York, Pennsylvania." *Journal of African American History* 88, no. 2 (Spring 2003): 151–62.

Wright, Richard. *Black Boy*. 6th ed. New York: Harper & Row, 1966.

"Yelling Whites Set off Melee at Graymont." *Birmingham News*, September 4, 1963, 1.

Young, Andrew. *An Easy Burden: The Civil Rights Movement and the Transformation of America*. New York: HarperCollins, 1996.

———. "The Day We Went To Jail in Birmingham." *Friends* (9 February 1964): 3–11.

Younge, Gary. "She Would Not Be Moved." *The Guardian*, December 15, 2000.

"Youth and Finances Help Break Down Barriers," Palmetto State Teachers Association, *PSTA Journal* (January, 1952): 18, South Caroliniana.

Zelizer, Viviana A. *Pricing the Priceless Child: The Changing Social Value of Children*. Princeton: Princeton University Press, 1985.

Zellner, Bob. *The Wrong Side of Murder Creek: A White Southerner in the Freedom Movement*. Montgomery: New South Books, 2008.

Zinn, Howard. *SNCC: The New Abolitionists*. Boston: Beacon Press, 1965.

Index

United Mine Workers, 85
United Nations, 83
United Negro College Fund, 119
United States National Student
    Association, 123
Urban League, 119, 120
urban renewal projects, 206–7

Vereen, Willie, 193
veterans, Black, 26, 68, 70, 71, 72, 73,
    88, 89, 90. *See also* 1940s; Second
    World War
Vietnam War, 8
violence, White: bombings, 168–71;
    against protestors, 136; at protests,
    137; targets of, 171 (*See also*
    bombings)
violence against African Americans:
    Baker family, 16–17; against Black
    youth, 60; in schools, 193; targeting
    African Americans, 32. *See also* police
    violence
Virginia: Charlottesville High School,
    213–14. *See also* Farmville, Virginia;
    R. R. Moton High School; Prince
    Edward County, Virginia
Virginia State Teacher Association,
    200
Virginia Teachers Association, 204
vocational education, 13, 15, 18, 77
voter registration, 2, 124, 165, 178; in
    Birmingham, 153–54; focus on,
    85–86; in Mississippi, 161–62; during
    1940s, 86; SNYC's, 61; SNYC's focus
    on, 67; violence and, 156
voting rights, 61, 87, 148; focus on, 85;
    poll tax, 82; SNYC's focus on, 56.
    See also disenfranchisement, Black
Voting Rights Act, 2, 164

Wagner Bill, 57
Walker, Dara, 8, 173
Walker, Vanessa Siddle, 6, 20, 37–38,
    40, 198, 202
Walker, Wyatt Tee, 138, 144, 149

walkouts, student, 2, 167–68; at
    Burgland, 136; criminalization of,
    182; educators held responsible for,
    153; in Mississippi, 158–59; NAACP
    and, 99, 100; youth autonomy and,
    107. *See also* boycotts; R. R. Moton
    High School
Wallace, George, 157, 169
Wall v. Stanly Board of Education, 200
Walsh, Camille, 184
Walters, W. A., 42, 64
Ward, Geoff, 9
Ware, Virgil, 169
Washington, Booker T., 13, 15, 116
Washington, D.C.: March on Washing-
    ton, 168; unrest in, 177
Washington, Jesse, 32
Booker T. Washington High School
    (Atlanta), 5
Booker T. Washington High School
    (Columbia, South Carolina), 13, 38,
    64–65, 68, 206–7
Booker T. Washington High School
    (Montgomery, Alabama), 4, 5, 13, 18,
    115–16, 204–6, 216
water protectors, 217
Watkins, Hezekiah, 30, 132–34, 158, 213
Watkins, Hollis, 135, 136
Watson, Douglas, 164
Watson, John, 99
Webb, Deborah, 164
Weber, Timothy, 193
welfare funds, 75, 76
Wesley, Cynthia, 169
West End High School, 157–58
White, Paul Dudley "Tall Paul", 140
White, Walter, 46, 49, 54, 57, 63, 98
White flight, 211–12
White organizations, 48
White supremacy: Black high schools
    and, 39; education policy and, 18;
    Southern institutions and, 6; violence
    and, 171 (*See also* bombings)
whole-child approach to education,
    38–39, 40

9 781469 671390